Cinematic Canines

Cinematic Canines

Dogs and Their Work in the Fiction Film

EDITED BY
ADRIENNE L. McLEAN

Rutgers University Press

New Brunswick, New Jersey, and London

Library of Congress Cataloging-in-Publication Data
Cinematic canines : dogs and their work in the fiction film / edited by Adrienne L. McLean.
pages cm
Includes bibliographical references and index.
ISBN 978–0–8135–6356–5 (hardcover : alk. paper) — ISBN 978–0–8135–6355–8 (pbk. : alk.
paper) — ISBN 978–0–8135–6357–2 (e-book)
 1. Dogs in motion pictures. I. McLean, Adrienne L., editor of compilation.
PN1995.9.A5C555 2014
791.43'662—dc23   2013027193

A British Cataloging-in-Publication record for this book is available from the British Library.

Visit our website: http://rutgerspress.rutgers.edu

Manufactured in the United States of America

For Larry and my parents,
and
all of the dogs who are in this book
and those who sat by us while it was written

Contents

Acknowledgments

This project began as a panel that Joanna Rapf organized for the Society for Cinema and Media Studies conference in 2009. Rutgers University Press immediately expressed interest in a volume on the topic, and Joanna turned the editing duties over to me, one of the panelists. In no small measure this book rests on her prescience and enthusiasm, for which I am extremely grateful. I also extend heartfelt thanks to the contributors for their excellent work, especially those who paid attention to deadlines; you had to wait longer than should have been necessary to see the volume in print, but I appreciate your diligence and, especially, your grace and consideration. I am very thankful for the assistance of superlative archivists Barbara Hall and Val Almendarez and all the staff members of the Academy of Motion Picture Arts and Sciences library in Beverly Hills, and the extraordinarily generous Ned Comstock of the Cinematic Arts Library at the University of Southern California, as well as Jonathon Auxier and Sandra Aguilar, curators of the Warner Bros. Archives housed at USC—your research expertise was invaluable, and help was always cheerfully offered. Among other colleagues and friends to whom I owe thanks are Cosmas Demetriou, for providing resources on digital imaging; Monica Evans, of the University of Texas at Dallas, for information on dogs and computer gaming; also at UTD, Dean Dennis Kratz, for the Special Faculty Development Award, part of which went toward the preparation of this volume, and Michael Wilson, Deborah Stott, and Erin A. Smith, who are always a source of advice and support; and Pierson Blaetz and Shannon Fry (and of course Isadora), whose hospitality enabled my dogs and me to travel and work (and play!) in Los Angeles. I also could not have managed without all of my many dog friends and teachers, and their wonderful animals, for helping my academic and personal worlds to collide so fruitfully. And finally, a giant thank you to the staff at Rutgers University Press, especially Marilyn Campbell, Lisa Boyajian, Joe Abbott for his superb copyediting, and, as always, Leslie Mitchner, who continues to influence and support my work in all sorts of psychological and emotional, as well as material, ways.

Cinematic Canines

Rin Tin Tin in a Warner Bros. publicity shot in the 1920s. *Movie Star News*.

Introduction

• •

Wonder Dogs

ADRIENNE L. McLEAN

Even with the close harmony between
a dog and his owner, by which he obeys
any and all commands instantly, and even
reflects his master's moods, he must be
tricked into exhibiting the emotions which
surprise picture fans by their intensity and
make them sure the dog has been tortured.
—Catherine Brody, *Saturday Evening
    Post*, 1925

An extraordinary performance! Benji, the
dog, was acting! He wasn't doing tricks, like
a circus dog or a show dog. He was playing
a part, like an actor. And a good actor too.
A good actor convinces you with his whole
body that he really is scared or confused
or happy. A good actor makes you forget
that he is really a person playing a part. He
becomes the character he's playing.
—Rita Golden Gelman, *Benji at Work*, 1980

Could Uggie the dog win an Oscar?
—*Telegraph*, January 6, 2012

For a few weeks before and after the turn to 2012, two cinematic canines were the focus of a considerable amount of media attention. One was the then nine-year-old Jack Russell terrier Uggie, whose work in *The Artist*, a film that would soon be awarded an Oscar for Best Picture of 2011, was generally regarded as a highlight, if not the main attraction, of the black-and-white silent feature whose story concerned the triumphs and travails of a star couple in Hollywood in the 1920s. The other dog was the German Shepherd Rin Tin Tin, who had been one of Hollywood's most famous "wonder dogs" during the era in which *The Artist* was set (Rinty died in 1932). While Uggie and his scene-stealing abilities had always been part of the promotional and publicity campaigns for *The Artist*, where he was often linked to earlier terrier film stars such as Asta of MGM's "Thin Man" series of the 1930s and 1940s, the issue that dominated the coverage in early 2012 was whether Uggie should have been nominated—as were the other (human) stars of the film—for an Oscar (Jean Dujardin would win for best achievement by an actor in a leading role). Uggie had already won the "Palm Dog" award at the Cannes Film Festival for the "best canine performance in a film screened at the festival," and stories reported that his fans had launched a "Consider Uggie" Facebook campaign urging the Academy to "recognize his talents"; Uggie also had his own Twitter account, where similar exhortations could be made on his behalf (see Marc Lee, "Could Uggie the Dog Win an Oscar?" *Telegraph*, January 6, 2012; Alisa Manzelli, "*The Artist*'s Uggie: Underdog of the Oscars?" *Global Animal*, February 24, 2012).

The role Rin Tin Tin played in the Uggie stories is neatly condensed in a *Hollywood Reporter* headline of November 11, 2011: "How Rin Tin Tin Ruined Any Oscar Shot for 'The Artist's' [*sic*] Jack Russell." According to the article (by Greg Kilday), in 1929 (the first year that the Academy of Motion Picture Arts and Sciences gave out awards) Rin Tin Tin "received the most votes for best actor. But members of the Academy, anxious to establish the awards were serious and important, decided that giving an Oscar to a dog did not serve that end." Worse, according to a Reuters news story (January 24, 2012), as a result of Rin Tin Tin's win "the Academy drafted rules that specifically exclude animals being nominated for Oscars." Critic Xan Brooks, writing for the *Guardian*, called the incident "one of the darkest scandals in Academy history: the tale of a cherished Hollywood star, robbed of his rightful best actor Oscar by a craven Hollywood establishment"; but, Brooks continued, "justice may be at hand as the American author Susan Orlean calls on the Academy to come clean, admit its mistake and award a posthumous Oscar to Rin Tin Tin" ("Award Posthumous Oscar to Dog Star Rin Tin Tin, Says Biographer," January 4, 2012).

And, in fact, the source of all of the "Rin Tin Tin was robbed" stories was Susan Orlean, who had just published a book about the dog star in which she makes the same claim (Orlean 2011, 88–89; there is, however, no call therein for a posthumous Oscar). As the hyperbolic tone of Xan Brooks's comments is perhaps meant to imply, little of Orlean's version of Academy history is actually true: despite her claim that they "did not keep the ballots from those first Oscars," the original vote tallies do still exist and Rin Tin Tin's name is not among them; and there is not now nor ever has there been a "rule" prohibiting animals from being nominated.[1] But the issue of accuracy is less interesting than the apparent willingness of members of the press and public to believe that a dog, no less than a human actor, *could* win an Oscar—that some dogs might perform well enough to deserve Hollywood's top acting accolade.

In "Can Hollywood's Top Dogs Really Act?" (Brian Wheeler, *BBC News Magazine*, January 10, 2012), Orlean reiterates her claims about Rin Tin Tin but points out that very few dogs have, or have ever had, sufficient "'charisma' and 'presence' to be considered actors in their own right" or performed "in a way that is dazzling and that really does make you think they understand something beyond their specific training." The majority of the dogs we watch on the screen, then, are *not* acting but are "merely well-trained and are in roles that simply require them to go through a series of actions." (Just as there are "plenty of human actors who don't do a whole lot more than follow directions," most dogs are merely doing "tricks.") But Orlean is not alone in her claim that dogs can "act." The Reuters piece quotes one of Uggie's trainers, Sarah Clifford, describing a "take where Uggie actually reached out and tried to pull the gun out of [Jean Dujardin's] hand with his mouth [in the scene where Dujardin's character is trying to commit suicide]. He put his mouth on Jean's hand and started pulling his hand. We were so stunned. He wasn't told to do that. . . . That dog was responding to the actor in an emotional sense. I think that's a form of acting that was amazing to see." Clifford also said that in her ten years in the animal business she had "never experienced the kind of media attention Uggie was getting" from *The Artist*. Moreover, as a consequence of the coverage attending to the interest in Uggie, and the coincident publicity campaign for Orlean's book (another had also been published about Rin Tin Tin the year before; see Elwood 2010), previous movie dogs were recalled to memory as well—not only Asta, to whom Uggie was so frequently compared, but Lassie, Toto, Old Yeller, Benji, Beethoven—along with a few assorted horses, chimps, and bears.[2]

Many of these animals had been given awards for their film performances, just as Uggie won not only the Palm Dog (a takeoff on the Cannes Film Festival's Palme d'Or) but the "Pawscar" for "Best Scene Stealer" of the American Humane Association (an organization that, as will be discussed later, tries to oversee the treatment of animals on movie sets); Animal Planet's "People's Choice Award"; and the "Golden Collar Award" for "Best Dog in a Theatrical Film," given by a commercial dog-products website, Dog News Daily (it also gives awards to dogs on television and in direct-to-DVD films). Uggie would probably also have won the PATSY (Picture Animal Top Star of the Year) had the award not ended in 1986 owing to lack of funding (Lassie and Benji won it many times, before retiring as the only two members of the "PATSY Hall of

Fame"; there is some sign that the American Humane Association is now reviving the name).[3]

The larger question of whether Uggie or Rin Tin Tin deserved, or could ever deserve, an Oscar, however, can also be asked of these awards: for regardless of whether the dogs are walking the red carpet or appearing onstage to "receive" an award, they are on a leash, and at the other end of that leash is a human. For publicity purposes a co-star may walk the dog to the dais, but the award really honors the work of owners and/or trainers and means nothing, as such, to the animal. In a blog post for *Vanity Fair* Julie Miller also raises this issue: "Establishing a category for animal 'acting' at the Oscars . . . would require the Academy to accept that these furry, four-legged, camera-friendly creatures are consciously portraying characters on-screen. But are animal 'actors' capable of understanding complex emotion, let alone purposefully exhibiting it? Or are they just capable of doing tricks on command so that they get a treat when the director yells 'cut'?" ("Do Animals Deserve Academy Awards?" "The Hollywood Blog," vanityfair.com, January 6, 2012). The questions Miller poses turn out to be rhetorical, unfortunately, and instead of answering them, she resorts to a list (as most of the other stories cited do as well) of "the finest animal performances of all time."

Certainly it is true, as the epigraphs at the head of this introduction suggest, that the expressiveness of dogs in film, whether called "charisma," "presence," "scene-stealing," "acting," or simply "performance," is often assumed to be the result of "trickery," either by the dog at the behest of its trainer or by the formal techniques of film itself. Dogs can be trained, by shaping their behaviors with rewards of play or treats or, unfortunately, punishment or the threat of it, to do lots of things: to nod, wave, tilt their heads, bow, lick their lips, growl, bark, cover their eyes, pick up or fetch any number of objects, limp, run in certain directions, stop, back up, sit, lie down, roll over, crawl, tug, play dead, and combinations of all of these—the range of trainable dog actions is astonishing—in response to voice or hand signals. And a film can be edited to make a dog's expression appear to be "soulful" or "yearning" in a close-up when he or she is actually reacting to a plate of offscreen food. Training anecdotes abound in publicity material about what the trade called "flea features" from the 1920s on: trainers would use one dog's antipathy for another to stage a fight for a film and then rebuke the same animal for going after the other; the "shame" the dog felt was useful for making the dog "the picture of abject misery" (Catherine Brody, "Dog Stars and Horse Heroes," *Saturday Evening Post*, February 14, 1925). After the transition to sound, numerous stories arose about how trainers used mirrors on the set to get the animals to respond to hand signals without looking offscreen toward their trainers (see the essay by Fuller-Seeley and Groskopf in this volume).[4]

Too often for our tastes the animal-training methods used in Hollywood, at least, were appalling in their cruelty. Ann Elwood cites a 1933 article in *Popular*

Uggie on the red carpet at the Golden Globes in 2012. Collection of the author.

Science Monthly that listed practices that the studios were now forbidding (the implication being that such practices had been employed before): "overwork and lack of food and water; wiring (using a wire to cause certain performances); use of drugs, liquid smoke, and electric shocks; trussing, spiking, doping, and setting on fire; use of knotted wire, spiked bits, running wire, trip ropes, and pitfalls. Certainly wires were used to control dogs" (Elwood 2010, 159). It is likely, she believes, that Rin Tin Tin's trainer, Lee Duncan, also used "compulsion" methods to coerce certain tricks from his wonder dog; as perusal of training manuals of the era indicates, many people did.[5]

By the time the first animal welfare acts were passed in the early nineteenth century (see Beers 2006), science had at least granted that dogs have the capacity to feel pain and pleasure; previously, they had been thought to be nothing but "machines" that could not act but only merely *re*act, to stimuli such as food or punishment.[6] Only in the last few decades has research established that animals also feel emotion (see, for example, Coren 1994, 59–75; Coren 2002, 143–149; Horowitz 2009a; Homans 2012, 39–42, 112–113; Morell 2013). This research, however, only supports what many observant dog owners already know, that dogs are indeed capable of emotions like contentment, joy, fear, and even love. In fact, since dogs "have all of the same brain structures that produce emotions in humans" and "undergo the same chemical changes that humans do during emotional states" (Coren 2012, 50), dogs probably experience the emotions that at least a young child does, apparently maturing at a developmental stage equivalent to that of a human of between two and three years of age.[7] Fortunately for dogs whose owners like to dress them in silly costumes—and for what cinematic canines often have to endure during production—"a dog will not have the more complex social emotions, like guilt, pride, and shame" (52).

Does the ability to feel an emotion such as fear or love, though, mean that a dog can express something that it does not actually have a context or stimulus to feel, as would be required for the work of acting? It is human trainers who show animals, however smart or "biddable," *how* to perform; and it is humans who take the credit even as they extol the unusual abilities and intelligence of their particular charges. In Hollywood, for example, it was the "East Kennels," run by "Mr. and Mrs. Henry East," that dominated in the 1920s and early 1930s; the trainers of Skippy, who played Asta, the Easts claimed that "dogs in moving pictures are not trained to do tricks. They learn how to act naturally on cues" (see J. B. Griswold, "A Dog's Life in Hollywood," *American Magazine*, August 1938). Carl Spitz's Hollywood Kennels, whence came Toto (Terry) and Buck, the Saint Bernard in *The Call of the Wild* (1935), were also well known in the 1930s; Spitz's 1938 book *Training Your Dog*, which contains a chapter called "Career Dogs in the Movies," is likely to be somewhat harrowing to the trainer of today (if even a tiny puppy "becomes obstinate, you may have to use a little leather strap or whip" [127]). Rudd Weatherwax, whose Studio Dog Training Center trained all of the collies who played Lassie, garnered the most popular attention in the 1940s and 1950s; if his writings are to be believed, he was an early proponent of reward-based training ("Here is all you need—besides patience. A collar on your dog, a leash or piece of rope about ten feet long, and a pocket full of tasty tidbits to serve as a reward for learning his lessons well" [Weatherwax and Rothwell 1950, 65]). The book *Benji at Work* (Gelman 1980) is primarily a record of the training that Benji (who in his first film, in 1974, was played by a mixed-breed shelter dog named Higgins, and in subsequent films by a sequence of mixed-breed dogs named Benji) underwent at the hands of his owner, Frank Inn, to learn the commands that would enable Benji to "act" afraid or happy, chase a criminal down the street, and so on. Inn began his career helping to train Skippy at the Easts' kennels and then worked with Weatherwax in the training of Pal (the first Lassie) before forming his own independent training business. These days, there are several organizations based in or around Los Angeles that train and rent dogs for use in commercial films all over the world, among them Animal Savvy, Birds and Animals Unlimited, Hollywood Animals, Paws for Effect, and Worldwide Movie Animals.[8]

But again, most human actors are "trained" and perform "tricks," too, and have to "follow directions," as Orlean put it; they are told where to stand, what to say, and where to look, and some unquestionably fail to make us "forget" that they are really "a person playing a part." However, human actors are able to transmit information to their audience through spoken language, while dogs

Benji in a posed still from *Oh! Heavenly Dog* (Joe Camp, Twentieth Century–Fox, 1980). Benji's films remain among the most popular dog films of all time, and trainer Frank Inn's rescue of most of his movie dogs from a Burbank animal shelter helped bring attention to the value both of mixed-breed dogs and of rescue itself. *Movie Star News.*

are not; this obviously deprives dogs of a primary means of film communication and expression—although silent cinema, in which Rin Tin Tin and even Uggie were most successful, could not employ human speech as such either. In contrast to our all-too-human ability, even propensity, to dissimulate and to invent "identities," we believe that dogs can only be dogs, cats can only be cats, and so on up and down the food chain. Without language, animals probably cannot imagine and certainly cannot articulate alternatives to their experiential "present," and therefore they cannot enact the postures and gestures of someone not themselves.

The contours of these basic assumptions, however, have become considerably more fluid than they were in Rin Tin Tin's and Lassie's and even Benji's heydays.

As Cary Wolfe (2003a) writes, "A veritable explosion of work in areas such as cognitive ethology [the science of animal observation; see Horowitz in this volume] and field ecology has called into question our ability to use the old saws of anthropocentrism (language, tool use, the inheritance of cultural behaviors, and so on) to separate ourselves once and for all from animals [and has] more or less permanently eroded the tidy divisions between human and nonhuman" (xi). And the past couple of decades have also witnessed a veritable explosion of popular publications devoted to synthesizing and promulgating the research of which Wolfe speaks. Stanley Coren has written extensively on dogs and their language use—the ways they communicate both with other dogs and with humans—in books such as *The Intelligence of Dogs: Canine Consciousness and Capabilities* (1994) and *How to Speak Dog: Mastering the Art of Dog-Human Communication* (2000), as have Alexandra Horowitz in her best-selling *Inside of a Dog: What Dogs See, Smell, and Know* (2009a) and Brian Hare and Vanessa Woods in *The Genius of Dogs: How Dogs Are Smarter Than You Think* (2013). Dogs are able to communicate quite easily, not only with each other but with us, through forms of language-like behaviors involving posture, physical expression (tail and ear levels and movements, gazing and eyelid position, piloerection ["raised hackles"]), and vocalization. Dogs are even able to role-play and do so regularly in their interactions with other dogs and, of course, with their human "packs." Mature dogs willingly act like puppies in a play session; female dogs are happy to hump other dogs, cats, human legs, or pillows; dogs who are dominant in most canine social settings can feign submissiveness in order to get other dogs and animals to interact with them; dogs pretend that a fluffy toy is fierce prey that they must vanquish; and on and on.

Moreover, even as we believe that most of the "desirable" behaviors that our dogs exhibit are the result of our assiduous training (by whatever method), or possibly just our anthropomorphic treatment of them as furry humans, dogs are and always have been able to train *us* to take care of them and to help them achieve their own goals. Just like human actors, they can "make" us feel about them in certain ways, through their own agency as dogs. Dogs know how to beg us to feed them, even when they are not hungry, or how to get us off the phone or to go for a walk. It used to be taken as a sign of dogs' inferior intelligence that they continually come to us to solve problems like retrieving a ball from under the couch; now, we understand that dogs are doing the smartest thing of all, using us and our longer and more nimble appendages (and opposable thumbs) as their tools (see Horowitz 2009a, 175–181).

And yet: despite their intelligence and our growing understanding of "canine consciousness" and "dog-human communication," most of us still balk at the notion that a dog, or any animal, can play a fictional role in a feature film and actually comprehend it as a form of "make-believe." Not only is the range of emotions they can feel limited; so are their cognitive abilities. Dogs may have the consciousness to be able to compare what they are feeling now (the sun on their bodies in a bright room, one of Coren's examples) with what they *could* be feeling (leaving that sunny spot to retrieve a chew or a blanket that would make the experience even better [see Coren 1994, 75]), but we have, to date, little evidence that they are neurologically or emotionally or, most important, linguistically equipped to ponder and express what it would be like to be a cat, a bird, a robot, or a human. No matter how intelligent our dogs are, it is still a stretch for us to believe that they could reason or imagine their way into assuming another's identity, much less an abstract *narrative* identity such as "I am a fierce wolf-dog who has been wrongly accused of killing sheep and am trying to clear my name" or "I am the canine sidekick of a silent film star."

Thus we have circled back to the question of why there were so many stories devoted to whether or not Uggie, Rin Tin Tin, Lassie, Benji, et al. were actually "acting" in their films. And why dogs, and not other animals, are the stars of so many popular movies, ubiquitous in roles large and small, starting with *Rescued by Rover* in 1905 and moving through the waxing and waning of the "flea feature" in the silent and sound eras and on into the digitally driven present. The hyperbolic kudos cited above for Benji's "extraordinary" acting notwithstanding, it seems clear that a dog "acts" only in the sense that a baby or very small child does, without a true understanding of the meaning of the role he or she is playing. In his essay "Animal Actors" (2006) Murray Pomerance claims that what any animal "does in front of the camera, ultimately, is behave rather than perform. It is through editing, shot selection, and narrative technique that the animal behavior is transformed into a screen performance" (81). What, then, is behind the apparently earnest desire of so many to want Uggie or Rin Tin Tin to be "considered" Oscarworthy (why, for that matter, is Rin Tin Tin, or Asta, or Lassie, so famous still)? And why, in the end, do we care and think so much about dogs that, in addition to the critics and scholars already cited, everyone in this volume has been driven to study and to write about them rather than about apes, horses, or cats?

Marking the Territory

In March 2009 the humanities journal *PMLA* published a special issue on animals, and its first column was headed "Why Animals Now?" Perhaps not surprisingly, several of the journal's articles concerned dogs, in literature, art, and biography. The question that *Cinematic Canines* raises is "Why dogs in film now?" In a broad sense the volume shows that the representation of dogs in narrative cinema has not only contributed to their steadily growing popularity across the past century but also created powerful assumptions about what dogs "are" and, concomitantly, what sorts of relationships we "should" have with them. The mass-mediated ubiquity of dogs—as Susan McHugh puts it in her book *Dog* (2004), "dogs are everywhere in early cinema" and appear widely in film and digital texts today (108)—is therefore one impetus behind the essays that follow, which are all original to this volume. Another major influence is, of course, the growth of animal studies as an academic field.

It is hard not to notice the incredible increase in the social presence of dogs in the past few years (and the passion with which the rights of those dogs are fought for or, conversely, contested) and the accompanying spread of the phenomenon of the "dog person" or the "dog lover" whether as an effect of personal psychology, commercial blandishment, guilt about the destruction of animal species and habitats more widely, the urbanized atomization of modern existence, or the rising number of baby-boomer "empty nesters." Although chroniclers do not always agree about the reasons for it, the growth in dog culture in the United States over the past decade alone (Europe is not far behind) is, as is now continually being pointed out, nothing short of staggering.[9]

Michael Schaffer's *One Nation Under Dog* (2009) is one of several recent books that takes aim at the phenomenon. "What happened?" he asks, agog at his own figures: "Roughly 60 percent of U.S. households own pets. That translates into 68.5 million households, up 12 percent in only six years, more than twice the rate of human population growth" (14). Schaffer's book, which is subtitled *Adventures in the New World of Prozac-Popping Puppies, Dog-Park Politics, and Organic Pet Food*, investigates not only the sheer increase in the number of dogs and dog owners but the changes in our attitudes toward pets generally: "In 2001, 83 percent of American pet owners referred to themselves as their animal's 'mommy' or 'daddy.' The number had been 55 percent as recently as 1995. In 2007, an authoritative survey of pet ownership by the American Veterinary Medical Association (AVMA) reported that half of American pet owners considered their pet a member of the family" (18).

John Homans attacked the "question of the dog" again in 2012 in *What's a Dog For? The Surprising History, Science, Philosophy, and Politics of Man's Best Friend*. "Something has been happening with dogs in the last couple of decades," Homans writes; "New York, along with just about every other city in the Western world, is overrun with them. There were some 77 million dogs in the United States in 2010, compared with about 53 million in 1996. Pet food and products were a $38 billion industry in 2010" (6). Moreover, "there are, worldwide, some 300 million dogs (as compared to 7 billion people, 1.3 billion cows, and 1.3 billion sheep). Evolutionarily speaking, that's success" (10). But as Schaffer had already pointed out, "It's not like the animals have changed much. As any nostalgic pet-owning memoir will illustrate, the party in the relationship that changes is inevitably the human. Historians tell us that we've always been suckers for that doggie in the window. But exactly how that love manifests itself . . . has evolved dramatically. Compared to our subsistence-farming ancestors, we're all kings now. So compared to their ancestors, our [dogs] live like princes" (8). Homans concurs, noting that "dogs aren't good for much of anything that can be readily measured, in terms of their economic contribution. A very small percentage of them do useful work, and an even smaller percentage currently serve as food, an intermittent fact of canine existence ever since they first entered the human story. . . . As never before, the fact that the dog's history over the millennia has been shaped by its relationship with humans is precisely what makes it interesting to scientists—in part because its social nature can mirror our own predilections" (10–11).

Dogs, then, are unique in the animal kingdom because they are so substantially, in their myriad forms, "man-made" (breeds like Chihuahuas and Great Danes do not exist in nature); because their relationship to humans today is primarily as a custom-engineered domestic pet or companion animal; and because they have been created not only to want to please humans but also to work at their behest. Domestic cats, on the other hand, while about equally popular as pets, when they work for us at all usually do so independently; they do not live in packs, and they are therefore not anxious to please their "leaders." Cats can be trained, but there are few feline actors in film—with the possible exception of the preternaturally gifted Siamese Pyewacket in *Bell, Book and Candle* (1958), trained at the studios of Carl Spitz—who appear to demonstrate the virtuosic human-centered skill sets and actions of a Rin Tin Tin, a Lassie, or an Uggie.

Stanley Coren, in *The Intelligence of Dogs*, writes extensively about Rin Tin Tin and Lassie "as portrayed on the screen." Lassie's multiplatform impact on wide assumptions about what dogs were and could do (nine feature films beginning in the 1940s, a radio show that ran for almost six years, a television show for eighteen years, in addition to a Lassie cartoon series and countless books and even comics) was particularly great. Lassie, Coren states, made us believe "that this dog (thus, by extrapolation, all dogs) could think, plan, sympathize, feel pain, have emotions of sorrow and joy, remember complex facts, and even plan acts of retribution. Hadn't we actually seen Lassie do it?" (10; see also Wolf in this volume). The usefulness of dogs these days as predominantly *only* a companion to humans, then, is at once a reason for their increased physical presence and a motivating force behind our desire to be entertained by them in mass media such as film and television (and, now, computer games; see the afterword to this volume).[10]

The emergence of the new, or at least newly named, field of animal studies took place initially as the "humans" in the humanities evaluated and acknowledged their status as products and constructions of discourse, no longer the sole sources of meaning but constituents of it, uttering language but also uttered by it; and concomitantly, as I have already pointed out, the "tidy divisions" once separating animal from human—language, tool use, and so on—were collapsing as well, thus generating the rubric of "posthumanities" as a constituent field of investigation in what had once been an easily demarcated intellectual and philosophical domain run by and in the service of "mankind." However, while posthumanist debates in the academy about dogs often take place under the rubric of animal studies, clearly animal studies itself as a field, with respect to dogs, also draws its force and relevance from the fact that dogs are now perceived to

A posed still of Roddy McDowall being comforted by Lassie (Pal) in *Lassie Come Home* (Fred M. Wilcox, MGM, 1943). Collection of the author.

be more important and significant as elements of human culture than arguably they ever were before. In fact, according to Cary Wolfe, "the pressing relevance of the question of the animal has been generated in contemporary culture more outside the humanities than within. . . . Indeed, the humanities are, in my view, now struggling to catch up with a radical revaluation of the status of nonhuman animals that has taken place in society at large" (Wolfe 2003a, x–xi; for an overview of the field of animal studies see DeMello 2010; see also Wolfe 2003b; McHugh 2011).

"Posthumanist" Donna Haraway's two books on dogs and their interspecies relationships with humans, *The Companion Species Manifesto: Dogs, People, and Significant Otherness* (2003) and *When Species Meet* (2008), also concern the central but sometimes contentious debates at the heart of notions about what the dog "means" in contemporary life and commercial representation. For Haraway, "contrary to lots of dangerous and unethical projection in the Western world that makes domestic canines into furry children, dogs are not about oneself. Indeed, that is the beauty of dogs. They are not a projection, nor the realization of an intention, nor the telos of anything. They are dogs;

i.e., a species in obligatory, constitutive, historical, protean relationship with human beings" (12). Haraway does not deal with film as such, but her point that dogs are always already in a relationship with humans that is nevertheless contingent, and that ideally we should respect dogs' differences from what we perceive to be human (as Alexandra Horowitz puts it in her essay in this volume, "We fail to see the animal's behavior on its own terms, because we have defined the terms"), underscores some of the problems of the film dog. For "dangerous and unethical projection" aside, dogs in narrative cinema are always meant to be—indeed are constructed formally to be—about ourselves. Although they can, and do, communicate in registers of their own as well, they are hired, are called to the set as it were, precisely to signify as "projections" and "realizations of an intention"—of trainers, writers, directors, and studios, as well as of audiences and critics. While we need to understand what cinematic canines are "saying" and doing *as dogs*, the fact remains that, in commercial cinema, they are characters in our stories, not theirs.

And while "many scientists," James Homans claims, "still believe that even asking how a dog might be like a human being involves anthropomorphism—the cardinal sin in animal studies" (12), James Serpell argues in his essay "People in Disguise: Anthropomorphism and the Human-Pet Relationship" (2005) that anthropomorphism will never go away because it is something humans come by naturally, and for good reason. Pet owners "possess fewer physiological risk factors . . . for cardiovascular disease than nonowners, and they also exhibit improved survival and longevity following heart attacks. . . . Significantly, pet owners who report being very attached to their pets tend to benefit more from pet ownership than those who are less attached, and dog owners tend to do better than cat owners, perhaps because the attachment for dogs, on average, is stronger" (125). Moreover, even if our "more humane" posthumanist moment is still substantially about us, and our health, it is certainly possible to hope that the relationship is also one that works practically to the dog's advantage. In the spring of 2010 *Time* magazine reported that China and India were considering banning the eating of dogs and cats, in the interests of being read as "civilized" nations (China followed through on dogs in 2011).[11] While this does not mean that all dogs and cats would automatically be "better off," Haraway does claim that, "Generally speaking, one does not eat one's companion animals [nor get eaten by them]"; but she also notes that "one has a hard time shaking colonialist, ethnocentric, ahistorical attitudes toward those who do [eat or get eaten]" (Haraway 2008, 14).

All of the contributors to this book have, like Haraway, "gone to the dogs," and ultimately the answer to the question "Why dogs in film now?" is to be found in the essays that follow, which are engaged in helping us to think about and to understand the work of canines in commercial films around the world. At the same time, that we *want* to know about, indeed are fascinated by, film dogs is due to the vital presence of the animals themselves. As Jonathan Burt states in his book *Animals in Film* (2002), "the fact that the animal image can so readily point beyond its significance on screen to questions about its general treatment or fate in terms of welfare, suggests that the boundaries of film art . . . cannot easily delimit the meaning of the animal within its fictions" (11). Film narratives construct what dogs mean in the stories we want to tell; the reality of the dog onscreen as an other, an agent, a worker, a victim, a friend, a prop, a symbol of national identity or of oppression, of the human as well as the non- or even inhuman—all important variables that the essays in this anthology address—has, over the past century, helped us to understand and perhaps alter our relationships to the dogs we purchase, find, possess, love, train, use, abuse, and admire.

This volume, then, is something of a hybrid or crossbreed (doggy metaphors and puns can be hard to avoid) that employs the interpretive strategies and scholarly tools of film and media studies, animal studies, gender studies, and cultural studies. The scholarship on the representation of animals is quite extensive already, and dogs are included in some of this work (see Garber 1996; Baker 2001; Burt 2002; Rothfels 2002; McHugh 2004; Porter 2010; Malloy 2011; Pick 2011; Gross and Vallely 2012; see also Lippit 2000; Elwood 2010; Skabelund 2011, 134-197). But this collection is the first serious study devoted only to dogs in narrative cinema; moreover, although a couple of cartoon canines appear here and there for comparison purposes (and the afterword considers the implications of digitizing dogs in whole or in part for the film, home video, and video game markets), the essays are overwhelmingly about "real" dogs rather than versions created through cel or digital animation, no matter how closely observed those animals might be.

Shooting the Dog

We focus on dogs in live-action narrative films because, first, we are interested in the canine as well as human labors that result in representation itself and in the work that representations of dogs perform on us as spectators, whose relationships with animals are so potently shaped by the uses to which animals are put in reality-based narrative media such as film. "This time, the magic is real" was, after all, the tagline for *101 Dalmatians* (1996), Disney's live-action remake of its animated 1961 feature—and it was real Dalmatians that were bought and, in many cases, subsequently abandoned by owners unprepared for the breed's needs and activity level (see Malloy 2011, 10–11; see also the afterword of this volume). As Katherine Grier points out in her book *Pets in America* (2006), "Movie and television 'star' animals . . . became part of the collective life of the imagination created by mass media in the twentieth century. In a society that promoted pet keeping and practiced it widely, petless children could dream of owning an animal as smart as Lassie or as funny as Petey in the *Little Rascals* movies. It was a benign and presexual form of celebrity worship" (293).[12]

We do not deny that animated dogs might be "worshipped" and also affect our notions about the offscreen variety—the animated Dalmatians in the 1961 Disney feature also led to an increase in the purchase of Dalmatian puppies, and after Disney's *Lady and the Tramp* was released in Japan in 1955, the cocker spaniel surpassed the [Japanese] spitz as the most popular breed in the country (Skabelund 2011, 178)—but they are not of the same order of existence as the biological entities who can be recognized in the "having-been-there" that marks our interest in human actors as well and on whose fleshly bodies the motion picture image depends. The dogs who appear, by design or by accident, in documentary films also deserve attention. But we are choosing to limit our study to dogs playing characters in fiction films (even when those films are based on "true stories") because the narratives themselves are ways that we work out what dogs—whether "purebred" or "mongrel"—mean, what makes a dog "good" or "bad," a threat or a helpmeet, a source of national pride or of shame and disdain (for more on the "civilizing" of dogs through "pure breeding" in the nineteenth and twentieth centuries see Derr 2004; McHugh 2004; Grier 2006; Skabelund 2011; see also Garber 1996; Armbruster 2002; Elwood 2010; Superle 2012).[13]

As a corollary, then, the second reason for our chosen focus on the "real" is that in commercial cinema dogs are virtually never "shot" by accident, no matter how incidental they sometimes appear to be. In the opening few moments of Rouben Mamoulian's early sound film *Applause* (1929), there is a distant terrier peeing on the trash-filled street set; another that, in a visual pun, violently rips and shakes a broadsheet featuring the image of burlesque performer Kitty Darling (Helen Morgan), the woman whose decline and similarly violent discard the film will trace; and still another clutched by a little girl rushing to view the parade of the burlesque troupe itself. Dogs do not usually wander into the fictional film frame (as they did in early films or conceivably could still do in documentaries) but are purposefully present, their actions mediating between the spontaneous and the crafted, the accidental and the posed.[14] To understand the work that these dogs do on and off the screen, of many different kinds and according to many different narrative and formal strategies, requires an archaeological as well as ethological approach. We examine the traces of evidence in film texts—bodies and their contexts and actions, stances, and sometimes vocalizations—as well as promotional and publicity materials in order to comprehend the immediate situations of the dogs we are watching so intently and how those dogs inform our expectations and assumptions about, and ethical responsibilities toward, those with whom we interact on a daily basis in our own lives.

Technically, though, just like human actors, dogs are no more and no less than components of mise-en-scène. As such, they can be analyzed through their facial expressiveness (light-colored dogs that had humanlike whites to their eyes were preferred in Hollywood—otherwise "the eye is beady," said *Photoplay* in March 1935), their movements, and the way they are staged; their makeup and

A dog tears violently at a poster of the burlesque performer Kitty Darling (Helen Morgan) in *Applause* (Rouben Mamoulian, Paramount Pictures, 1929), presaging Kitty's career trajectory and loss of value across the rest of the film. Digital frame enlargement.

hairdressing (more common with film dogs than one might think, especially when more than one dog is playing the same role); costuming (rarer, but significant when it is present); the lighting that defines them in space; their relation to and interaction with setting and props, as well as other actors, human or animal; how they are framed by the camera, whether it is mobile or stationary, and what sort of lens is used to shoot them. They also are manipulated by editing, which can create movement out of physical stasis and suggest cause and effect through the juxtaposition of shots. Special effects, too, such as stop-motion photography, can be used to insert a stunt double (most dog stars had several stunt doubles) or even replace a live dog with a stuffed animal (such as the one that is thrown off a highway overpass in the 2004 comedy *Anchorman: The Legend of Ron Burgundy*).

At the same time, dogs in film can still be considered as historically contingent dogs rather than modified or disguised humans—this despite the frequency with which commercial films insist that dogs *are* nothing but furry humans, as has been the case since MGM's early "Dogville" shorts ("All Barkie!") like *The Dogway Melody* (1930) or *The Two Barks Brothers* (1931), in which costumed "talking" dogs lampoon popular feature films. And literal anthropomorphism remains true of many mainstream commercial vehicles such as the *Doctor Dolittle* (1998, 2001), *Beverly Hills Chihuahua* (2008, 2011, 2012), and

A still from a publicity "tour" of the two male "stars" (one of whom played a female) of MGM's "Dogville Barkies" (1929–1931). Collection of the author.

Cats and Dogs (2001, 2010) franchises, to name but a few, in addition to a large number of straight-to-DVD films including a reframed *Dr. Dolittle* series featuring the doctor's "daughter" (2006, 2008, 2009) and the ongoing entries in Disney's "Buddies" series. A spinoff of *Air Bud* (1997) and its sequels—most of which also were made for the home video market—in which a golden retriever plays various sports in league with a usually socially deprived or shy adolescent boy (there are often villains involved), the "Buddies" films "star" an endless sequence of puppies (narratively the offspring of the original Bud) playing five juvenile talking-dog characters (see the afterword).

Although in their relationship to the film industry and its modes of production dogs do resemble child actors—in the sense that, like children, dogs have little authority to control the uses to which they are put—the fact that dogs are legally nothing but property, commodities with "rights" that, beyond loose rubrics like "humane treatment," accrue mainly to their owners, makes them qualitatively different (see Beers 2006; Schaffer 2009; Homans 2012). A child performer may not be having a good time on a set and may, no less than a dog, be exploited by the work he or she is made to do. But we surely believe that children are protected from real harm and that at some point will be able to understand, to know, and possibly to resent but ideally to transcend and to forgive any unpleasant treatment or even trauma (the title of child star Jackie Cooper's autobiography is *Please Don't Shoot My Dog*, a reference to the way that a director got him to cry for a scene by threatening to kill the boy's beloved pet).

I have always had an ambivalent relationship, therefore, not only with most representations of dogs in film, credited or otherwise, but with books that have focused on them as well, which primarily catalogue or list and are usually lavishly illustrated with delightful pictures—books like *Hollywood Dogs* (Suarès 1993), *Movie Mutts: Hollywood Goes to the Dogs* (Silverman, "with Coco the Dog," 2001), and *Hollywood's Top Dogs: The Dog Hero in Film* (Painter 2008). This sort of material seems predicated on the unexamined notion that because we all adore dogs, we will adore any movie in which they appear. There are also any number of "movie lists" available on the Internet—see, for example, "A Huge List of Dog Movies" ("This list is so long, the biggest problem you'll have is deciding which one you want to watch first, enjoy!" [caninest.com/dog-movies/]).

Cinematic Canines, in contrast, is sometimes quite somber in tone, and not just because it is meant to be "scholarly." Often what we witness or extrapolate from the material investigated here is a sense of what Anat Pick (2011) calls the "martyrdom" of ordinary animals in films. Pick argues that "ordinariness and martyrdom are a startling combination," which she concludes "characterizes— and quite uniquely so—the current predicament of animals" in culture (184–185). Certainly I feel toward many of the dogs discussed here what Pick calls the "strangely fused experience" of watching the donkey in Robert Bresson's film *Au hasard Balthazar* (1966), in which the donkey is "a 'character,' but also—and more intensely—the real animal in excess of the fictional diegesis. One worries," Pick writes, "about the actual tail . . . set on fire, the pulling, kicking and shoving, all of which make Balthazar cinema's own beast of burden. Balthazar turns cinema itself—its cost on living bodies—into a creaturely medium" (192).

I worry about film dogs, with very few exceptions, in the same way—because it *is* so easy to be drawn to "super dogs," in Susan McHugh's words, like Lassie, who is "physically strong and beautiful, emotionally available and tactful" and who "tutors the people she encounters; in addition to saving their lives and reconciling their differences, she teaches them especially to understand and appreciate the charms of pastoral life and noble sentiments" (she also never performs the scatological bodily functions or sexual behaviors the management of which are so much a part of pet-keeping today) (McHugh 2004, 109). It is easier still to succumb to the seductive pleasures of a charming modern family comedy set in a chaotic but utopian universe in which dogs understand people, whether adult or child, transparently and perfectly, are funny and cute and cuddly even when they are lumbering and slobbery, and who seem wiser than the flawed humans whose lives they help to restore to order or harmony (see Garber 1996; Superle 2012).[15]

Despite the manifold pleasures and popularity of many dog films, then, ultimately the fundamental innocence and social and juridical, if not physical, powerlessness of the cinematic canine produces a "rupturing effect," in Jonathan Burt's words, that "unavoidably points beyond itself to wider issues"—as we hope this collection itself will, too. Are the sick, dying, destroyed or destroying dogs in films like *Forbidden Games* (1952), *Old Yeller* (1957), *To Kill a Mockingbird* (1962), *Amores perros* (2000), and *The Dancer Upstairs* (2002), or the horror films *Cujo* (1983) and *Man's Best Friend* (1993), "really" suffering or not? It is not always easy to tell. In 1940, classical Hollywood's Production Code was amended to "prevent all cruelty to animals in the production of motion pictures" ("cruelty" is not defined), and offscreen treatment was nominally regulated by the American Humane Association as well. But not until 1980 did the Film and Television Unit of the AHA, based principally in the Western Regional Office in Los Angeles, agree to oversee commercial film production in the United States and, when possible, through affiliated humane societies overseas (see Beers 2006; Pomerance 2006).

Therefore, when Rin Tin Tin grovels on the screen, I fear that he has been punished in real life for something he was tricked into doing. When I see Lassie lying limp and bedraggled in a puddle in the driving "rain," I know that there is no treat tasty enough to make that experience pleasant for a collie. The almost six-minute-long musical number "My Dog Loves Your Dog" in *George White's Scandals* (1934) is "cute," but the finale, in which multitudes of obviously uncomfortable and probably disposable dogs are literally dragged around on leashes, is not. I *do* love the musical number in which Eleanor Powell dances with "Buttons," a spotted terrier mix whom she trained, in *Lady Be Good* (1941) because the dog, like Powell, is clearly having a wonderful time—but what became of him later? (He reportedly was the pet of a prop man; see McLean 2009.) I adore the antics of the two spritely spotted terriers who play Flike (or Flaik) in Vittorio De Sica's Italian neorealist masterpiece *Umberto D* (1952) but am anguished by the scenes at the city pound where pet dogs, many loved by owners who simply lack the funds to pay for the required municipal license, are handled roughly by ligatures around their necks and loaded into what appears to be a real gas chamber. Even when I am howling with laughter at the over-the-top but closely observed behaviors of members of the professional dog-show "fancy" in the mockumentary *Best in Show* (2000), I am driven to worry about the status of the "line-bred" dogs that kennel clubs celebrate and that "star" in the film, whose health and soundness have been too often sacrificed to spurious notions of "breed purity."

Moreover, no matter how strenuously the American Humane Association website (americanhumanefilmtv.org) labors to assure me that "no animals were harmed" in the making of this or that film, even they admit that they cannot monitor all of them: "Due to limited resources, American Humane did not monitor some of the dog and puppy action" on entries in the "Buddies" franchise, for example (the website also lists several films that employ "illegitimate end credits" because they were not monitored at all). The AHA may claim that "no puppy mills were used" for the 1996 version of *101 Dalmatians*, but the fact remains that "two hundred thirty Dalmatian puppies and twenty adult Dalmatians were used in the filming"—a large number of dogs, much less of a demanding working breed such as the Dalmatian. And in the end, the rating the AHA gave the film was only "acceptable" (their highest is "outstanding").[16] As Susan McHugh points out, "circular fads" for certain breeds of dogs "follow the releases and re-makes of popular dog films that mis-represent them as low-maintenance family pets. Commercial successes and domestic pet tragedies alike stem from the intense marketing campaigns now centred on the release of such films, which bombard fast food restaurants, children's television programming and toy store shelves with promotional images of the celebrity breed dog" (McHugh 2004, 111; see also Malloy 2011, 10–11).

Regardless of which particular dog film-worker is the topic of discussion, then, it may be that dogs, like all animals, provoke a "crisis of representation" because the representation of animals in commercial cinema not only affects real-world situations but cannot be understood, properly, *as* representation. A fictional motion picture involving a dog—whether an early Edison trick film like *The Dog Factory* (1904) or a Pathé short like *The Policemen's Little Run* (1907); or a Roscoe Arbuckle comedy, a Lassie epic, or one of Benji's many films in the 1970s and 1980s; or *Good-Bye, My Lady* (1956), *The Adventures of Milo and Otis* (1986), *Homeward Bound* (1993), *Turner & Hooch* (1989), *Marley & Me* (2008), *Hachi: A Dog's Tale* (2009), and on and on—is always "documentary" in some sense, and the slippage between representational contexts, between dogs as fact and as fiction, can have profound consequences. To wit: *Amores perros*, a critically well-regarded film, employs canines as the narrative signifier of pain and loss, as well as love, and as the symbol of the difficulty of human relationships. But the dogs have a hard time of it—there are gruesome scenes of dogfights and other destroyed animals—and it seems to have been a shock to director Alejandro González Iñárritu that audiences responded so forcefully to the canine carnage in the film, to the extent that a disclaimer was added, unusually, to the opening credits in addition to those at the end, that "no animals were actually harmed during its production."[17] According to film critic Andrew Sarris, journalists were provided with program notes that also attempted to render the film's representation firmly fictional: "To find out more about the humanitarian way the dogs of *Amores Perros* were treated during the making of this film please ask your local press contact for our five-minute video THE DOGS OF AMORES PERROS, featuring interviews with the cast, crew and veterinarians of this amazing motion picture" (*New York Observer*, April 1, 2001).

Jonathan Burt reports that, to Iñárritu, "the humane message of the film is dependent on such imagery being shown. In these instances the violence perpetrated on animal and human bodies should not necessarily be seen differently. Iñárritu found the controversy misguided both because the fights were carefully faked and because of the hypocrisy involved in the critique" (Burt 2002, 162).

But again, Burt points out, the problem is the "split within the animal image—the artificial image that never can quite be read as artificial—[and that] ruptures all readings of it" (163). For Burt, therefore, and for me and the other contributors to this volume as well, the "unavoidable state of being drawn behind the animal's film image is the basis of the conflict over the control of animal imagery" (12)—especially the imagery of domestic animals like dogs, with whom we may have extensive familiarity in our day-to-day lives.[18]

Organization

The essays in this volume are arranged according to categories that the motion picture industry has traditionally used for all of its actors: stars and featured players; character and supporting actors; and stock, bits, and extras. These should not be taken as confining designations but merely as a useful if arbitrary rubric for helping us to understand how dogs are constituted and understood as performers and performances (there are chronological filmographies appended to each essay as well). The first section therefore is devoted to some of the best-known dogs in cinema's history (Strongheart, Rin Tin Tin, Asta, and Lassie) but also includes dogs who, once famous, have since been all but forgotten (Jean the Vitagraph Dog, Luke the Biograph Dog, and "Keystone Teddy"). Joanna Rapf's essay on Luke, comic actor Roscoe "Fatty" Arbuckle's American Staffordshire terrier, who was both the Arbuckle family pet and his co-star, focuses on Luke's film work, as well as that of the (then) better known Teddy. She traces the shifting contexts in which the canine performer in the early silent era worked, as the "knockabout" or slapstick comedy genre gave way to a gentler and more sentimentalized view of family life and pets. Complicating Luke's life, on and off the screen, was the fate of Arbuckle himself, whose career as one of the most popular comedians of the silent era was largely ended as a result of a scandal in the early 1920s.

Kathryn Fuller-Seeley and Jeremy Groskopf's essay considers Strongheart, the first German Shepherd star, and Rin Tin Tin, Strongheart's contemporary and rival, in light of the discourses of performance and acting that constructed all stars of the silent era. "Dog heroes" were ubiquitous in the 1920s, with Strongheart and Rin Tin Tin only the most popular of the wave of German Shepherds that came to the United States at the conclusion of World War I (Rin Tin Tin also lived the longest, and made the most films). According to Ann Elwood (2010),

> Of the fourteen dogs that had leading roles in movies in the 1920s, twelve were German shepherds. In addition to Strongheart and Rin-Tin-Tin, the other German shepherds were Peter the Great, Thunder, Lightning, Wolfheart, Ranger, Fang, Dynamite, Klondike, Champion, and Braveheart. (The other two dog stars were Bullet, a pit-bull or pit-bull mix, and Rex, a collie.) Of the forty-two

dogs whose names appeared on cast lists in the 1920s, at least twenty-six . . . were German shepherds. With the exception of Teddy and Duke, both Great Danes [Teddy was a Great Dane mix], the other dogs on cast lists tended to be small terriers or mongrels. (74)

The essay, like Rapf's, explores the ways that dogs were uniquely highlighted by silent film. Rin Tin Tin was sometimes called "the dog who saved Hollywood" and "the mortgage-lifter"; his popularity reportedly rescued Warner Bros. from bankruptcy in the 1920s, although the dog, and his owner/trainer, Lee Duncan, were dumped by the studio in 1929. The essay also considers the "multimedia" stardom—not only in films but books, advertising, dog food endorsements—of both dogs, as well as their fates and legacies in subsequent decades through the uses of their offspring and their links to the fashion for the "purebred" nobility of the German Shepherd.

Sara Ross and James Castonguay focus on crossword-puzzle favorite Asta, played initially by a wire-haired fox terrier named Skippy, who starred primarily in screwball comedies in the 1930s and 1940s. Their essay explores the way that Asta's star narrative was created to resemble those of human actors, including the fantasy life of "privilege" that Skippy/Asta was supposed to have led. But while Skippy's owners, the Easts, may have been paid hundreds of dollars a week, the dog himself was a "laborer, commodity, and manipulable image." Despite the dog's fame—Skippy was soon simply renamed Asta—not much attention was paid to the canine substrate who supported the character. When Skippy/Asta died in 1944, little notice was taken of it (in contrast to the deaths of Strongheart and Rin Tin Tin), because the character lived on in a succession of new dogs who were simply made up to look like the original. (In fact, Internet searches show that virtually any seller of "vintage" terrier items— from photos and figurines to stuffed toys—attempts, still, to link his or her merchandise to Asta.)

The rough collie Lassie remains perhaps the most famous dog ever to have lived, and Kelly Wolf's essay uses press materials to explore how Lassie (who was played first by a male dog named Pal) was mythologized and created as the exemplar of the "ideal dog": loyal, strong, smart, and protective. Lassie, as character and as dog, lived "in perfect harmony and understanding with the humans lucky enough to own her." Her star image also promoted wartime idealism and American heroism, and the essay explores the intersection of "breed purity" with the dog's appeal in human terms that linked her to anxieties about racial purity and gender as well. Lassie, despite her perfection, was part of a system of publicity and promotion that involved the distribution of dogs, claimed to be direct descendants of Lassie "herself," as "prizes" in audience giveaways. Mark Derr has described some of the problems associated with "line breeding," in which dogs in the same family are bred again and again to one another, to maintain purity in relation to a single dog; in the 1940s and early 1950s, "Lassie's heyday," the collie was considered "among the most brilliant of dogs. Now it is recognized as dull, having been bred for a long narrow snout and beautiful coat but not brains and good health" (Derr 1997, 175–176).

The book's second section considers dogs who rarely are named in their films' credits but whose labor, like that of human character or supporting actors, is crucial to the films' narrative meaning as well as audience appeal. Aaron Skabelund discusses how dogs were deployed symbolically and practically by the United States and Japan during World War II (the major European countries in the conflict—Britain, France, Germany, and the Soviet Union—made fewer films during the war and virtually none about military dogs). According to one analyst he cites, "the Allied and Axis militaries employed more than 250,000 canines for a variety of tasks including as messengers, sentries, draft animals, trackers, and patrol auxiliaries." Skabelund focuses on how, in contrast to conflicts since, military dogs in World War II came from civilian populations, and this itself was deployed by popular film as a way to "mobilize people, and especially children, for war." As pets dogs were part of the home front; on the battlefield dogs were figuratively and literally "part of the family" engaged in the war effort. The essay analyzes the way that movies about military canines, part of a "distinctive though small subgenre in both countries," shaped and reflected wartime mobilization and subsequent memories of the war.

In contrast to the United States and even Japan, some countries, such as Australia and South Africa, have made many fewer films that feature dogs, but there is a notable presence of canine characters in their prose fiction. As Jane O'Sullivan's essay explores, when dogs do occur as actors in Australian cinema, they are virtually always, like their literary counterparts, used to position wildness against domesticity. O'Sullivan notes that the films share a rural or remote setting (often the "outback"), and "define their canine characters as either 'good dogs' or 'bad dogs' in terms of the manner in which they negotiate the tricky balance between their species' history of wildness as carnivorous predators, and their cultural history of domestication—into trained working dogs and human companions, or 'pets.'" Australia's "national dog," the dingo, becomes a liminal figure in many of these films, as both good and bad dog (only one canine is given screen credit in the several films O'Sullivan discusses). In the end the dogs in Australian cinema are all "loaded dogs" who bear the burden "of signifying a human story and cultural mythology. Yet these dogs are also, and in the first place, living their own lives and 'telling' their own tales."

Giuliana Lund shows that dogs in South African cinema have a bifurcated existence in that country as well, demarcated along the lines of indigenous (cur) and imported (the European "purebred" bull terrier breeds) and whose fate, in film and literature as well as in life, is intimately interconnected to the native and "settler" identities of the apartheid and post-apartheid nation as a whole. Lund explores the "pattern of abuse [that] has become a significant focus of post-apartheid South African cinema, which increasingly features canines as a vehicle for social commentary to address the nation's persistent struggle with violence and the prospects for reconciliation and rehabilitation." Dogs exemplify both oppressed and oppressor in South African cinema, agents of the maintenance of apartheid as well as native "kaffir" victims of the cruelty and disdain of white "overlords." Lund traces a complicated narrative of a country in which dogs have been, and sometimes still are, representative of an ideology in which native people matter less than imported and "civilized" dogs.

The final essay in this section moves literally to the "end of the world," to films that take place in the Antarctic, the only continent with no permanent human population. In early 2006 the Disney feature *Eight Below* offered an Antarctic animal adventure in which Siberian huskies rather than penguins took center stage. A remake of the 1983 Japanese film, *Nankyoku Monogatari* [*Antarctica*], which is based on an incident that took place in 1958 (and that is also mentioned in the Skabelund essay), *Eight Below* tells the story of a group of dogs abandoned over winter at an Antarctic station. The action was updated to 1993, by which point a ban on introduced species had seen the removal of most of the dogs from the Antarctic continent. Leane and Narraway consider the Disney film in relation to both the Japanese original and a very different film centered on a dog in the Antarctic context, John Carpenter's iconic *The Thing* (1982), and examine the relationship all three features construct among humans, dogs, and the Antarctic environment, especially native Antarctic species. Considering both narrative and the semiotics of the moving image, the authors focus on the degree to which the dogs in these films are anthropomorphized and how this affects the way in which they are positioned in relation to the nature/culture boundary each film constructs.

The last section of the book comprises two essays on dogs that, while largely unnamed, nevertheless are a significant, if at times anomalous or briefly seen, component of the films in which they appear. Certainly in the films of Alfred Hitchcock dogs are minor "bits" in terms of the amount of screen time they occupy. Nevertheless, as Murray Pomerance shows, Hitchcock was himself a man who was "never without a dog." And as a director famously in control of the production and form of the films to which he attached his name and figure in so many ways, dogs are never, and could never be, incidental to his films. If we "look at the considerable and changing presence and action of dogs in Hitchcock's work," Pomerance writes, we find "an unheralded group of 'performances' that lend depth and intrinsic meaning to the Hitchcockian moment." Taking off from Charles Barr's observation that the Hitchcockian dog is a "kind of moral touchstone" (Barr 1999, 189), Pomerance traces the ways, beginning with Hitchcock's British sound features and ending with his final classical studio work, in which dogs have served as a carefully constructed and deceptively appealing relay for spectators into the often dark themes and concerns of the director's films.

Alexandra Horowitz's work on ethology, the science of animal observation, comes to the fore in the final essay of the section (and the book proper).

Horowitz closely observes a range of dog behavior across films in which the dogs are "minor" elements of a film's mise-en-scène or in which they have a brief scene or two and then disappear (Toto/Terry, arguably a featured, though uncredited, player in *The Wizard of Oz*, is the only exception to this). These dogs seem to be placed as a trope of "random realism," but their unusually expressive screen presences frequently overwhelm their apparent accidental status as prop or element of setting. Because of the anomalous behavior that they exhibit as dogs in the contexts in which their films place them, Horowitz shows that they virtually always are acting in ways that do not support the narrative project at hand. Dogs that are supposed to be closely engaged with a film character are not; dogs that are supposed to be wandering strays are instead obviously responding to training cues; dogs that are supposed to be vicious are in fact playing, or trying to play, with the human actors they are meant to be "attacking." Through ethology, even the "dog at the side of the shot" can help us to learn about and to understand canine behavior, as well as the often strange ways that humans have misunderstood the actions of the dogs we watch on the screen and with whom we live.

In the book's afterword I consider recent films featuring digitally manipulated dogs that function both as biological dogs and as "people in disguise." These digitized dogs (along with other animals) are now everywhere (the urtext is probably *Babe* [1995] and its sequel, *Babe: Pig in the City* [1998]; *Babe* is also discussed in Jane O'Sullivan's essay). Many of these films are not theatrically released but made for the home DVD market, where the profits they can earn are enormous and which makes them as disconcerting in their implications as any of the shorts in MGM's "Dogville Barkies" series of the early 1930s. The dogs in these features (the aforementioned *Beverly Hills Chihuahua*, *Doctor Dolittle*, and *Cats and Dogs* franchises, *Karate Dog* [2007], *Underdog* [2007], the numerous "Buddies" vehicles, *Marmaduke* [2010], and many others) often speak, with digitally animated lips and the voices of humans; they are endowed with emotion, foresight, personal awareness, and psychological complexity; and through the use of CGI they drive, dance the mambo, type, pop beer tops, do karate, play musical instruments (etc.). But, just as in the MGM shorts, or the case of Lassie or any of the other dogs discussed throughout this book, the actors, the "substrate," remain real dogs—often puppies, hundreds of which are used for a few weeks or even days and then replaced by a new pack. The fact that we think of these digital dogs as almost literally human is disturbing but also significant to questions of the dog's conflicted status today—certainly "agents," but also interchangeable raw material for all the stories Hollywood thinks people want to hear and see.

Although this book is not, nor is it meant to be, an encyclopedia or even a full history of dogs in film, taken together the essays create a reasonably comprehensive overview of the work of dogs and their images in narrative cinema, especially Hollywood cinema.[19] The label "wonder dog" was regularly applied, without irony, from the 1910s through the 1950s to any dog whose name became better known than, or was elided with, the often heroic fictional roles it played (see also Rex the Wonder Horse, who starred in serials in the 1920s and 1930s). Teddy, Luke, Strongheart and Rin Tin Tin (and all those other German Shepherds in the 1920s), Lassie, Benji, and many others—all were called "wonder dogs," and for good reason. But in addition to analyzing canine representation in film, this book suggests that almost any dog that endured the rigors of life on a movie set—not to mention auditions, hair and makeup, and whatever happened to it when the "job" was over—was a wonder dog as well. No less than the dog-human relationship generally, the stories and contexts that this book traces, to borrow the eloquent words of Donna Haraway, "are full of waste, cruelty, indifference, ignorance, and loss, as well as of joy, invention, labor, intelligence, and play" (Haraway 2003, 12).

Notes

1   The Reuters article quotes Orlean as follows: "The reporting that I did, indicated that Rin Tin Tin got most votes for best actor. But as much as he was admired and beloved, the Academy was trying to establish itself as a serious new awards program and they thought 'We can't give awards to animals. This will cause all sorts of embarrassment for us.' So the rules were then drafted so that no non-human could receive an Oscar." But numerous documents in the Academy Archive at the Academy of Motion Picture Arts and Sciences (where Orlean did research, according to her book and the publicity about it) show the opposite of what she claims: far from winning the most votes, Rin Tin Tin's name as Best Actor was used to *disparage* the newly established Academy Awards. Producer Jack Warner penciled in Rin Tin Tin, as well as other joke names, on his "Official Nomination Paper" for "Academy Awards of Merit" and was chastised by the organization's president for not taking the awards seriously as a result (Warner also wrote in "Nanette—Rinty's Frau" for Best Actress). Darryl Zanuck, who worked for Warner Bros. at the time, also wrote a letter to the Academy in which he named his boss, Jack L. Warner, the best producer, himself the best associate producer, the best director "any Warner Brothers Director" (to be "selected by drawing straws"), the best writer "any writer under contract to Warner Brothers," and finally, for "most popular player—Rin-Tin-Tin," a Warner Bros. "star." Again, a joke. Moreover, the first Oscars were not given in 1927, as Orlean claims in her book (88), but in 1929, and Rin Tin Tin's career was itself on something of a downward slide by 1928 (Warner Bros. broke its contract with the dog and his owner/handler, Lee Duncan, the following year).

2   Uggie also published his own book, *Uggie: My Story* ("as barked to Wendy Holden"), in 2012 and was famous enough to appear in an uncredited cameo as "America's Favorite Dog" in the satirical political comedy *The Campaign* (2012), where he was punched in the "face" by the bumbling congressional hopeful played by Will Ferrell.

3   The PATSY was created in 1939 by the Hollywood office of the American Humane Association but apparently not awarded until 1951, when the first one went to Francis the Talking Mule. See Beck and Clark 2002, 235–242; en.wikipedia.org/wiki/PATSY_Award. From 1958 both variants, film and television, were handed out until the awards were discontinued; there are concrete paw prints of some of the winners in the courtyard of the Burbank Animal Shelter, where several of them, including the original Benji (Higgins), came from. The Palm Dog was begun in 2001 and is given

for the best performance by a canine, or group of canines, live or animated. The Pawscars include several categories that seem to be created as the situation arises ("Best Inspirational 'Tail'" being given for the 2011 film *Dolphin Tale*, for example) and were started in 2011 as an "unofficial, animal-centric spin on the Oscars"; Animal Planet partners with the American Humane Association for its "People's Choice Award," which was begun in 2012. See americanhumane.org/animals/programs/no-animals-were-harmed/pawscar-awards.html.

4 As Tom Hanks said of his work with the giant Dogue de Bordeaux in *Turner & Hooch* (1989), "You know, when you make a movie with a dog, you have to work with the dog for weeks prior to shooting it. Otherwise, he won't take his eye off the trainer. So, I would go off and play with I think actually three dogs that portrayed [Hooch]. It was a part too big for one dog." See npr.org/2012/10/13/162821265/actor-tom-hanks-plays-not-my-job.

5 See Elwood 2010, 131–162, for a description of popular training methods of the early part of the twentieth century. For the evolution of training methods in Hollywood it is useful to compare Spitz 1938 with Weatherwax and Rothwell 1950; Spitz's methods are largely compulsion-based (unwanted behavior is punished, force is used to elicit a desired behavior), while Weatherwax appears to have employed rewards (the unwanted behavior is ignored, the desired behavior is rewarded with a treat or toy). In 1985 Karen Pryor published *Don't Shoot the Dog! The New Art of Teaching and Training*, which condensed the research of behaviorist B. F. Skinner, among others, on "operant conditioning" into an easy-to-read manual that any pet owner could follow. Pryor explained how desired behaviors could be shaped quickly and easily through positive reinforcement rather than force, and the book, which became a best seller and has been reprinted in several new editions since, helped transform the training of dogs and other animals (and humans as well) such that reward-based rather than punitive methods are arguably now dominant among professional trainers, including those working in the film industry. So-called clicker training, in which a behavior is "clicked" and marked and then rewarded, is popularly linked to Pryor's influence; see "Karen Pryor Clicker Training" at clickertraining.com, as well as the website for the Karen Pryor Academy for Animal Training and Behavior, karenpryoracademy.com. See also Horowitz in this volume.

6 Stanley Coren (2012) lays the assumption that "animals like dogs are . . . filled with the biological equivalent of gears and pulleys," and are therefore machines that don't think but "can be programmed to do certain things," at the feet of René Descartes in the sixteenth century. Nicolas de Malebranche later extended Descartes's ideas, and Coren quotes Malebranche's famous dictum that animals "eat without pleasure, cry without pain, act without knowing it: they desire nothing, fear nothing, know nothing" (49).

7 For more on research into dogs and their hormonal/chemical similarities to and differences from humans—for example, the actions in both dogs and humans of oxytocin, commonly called the "love hormone" because it "increases trust and attachment," but which also can play a role in "ethnocentrism," or the exclusion, even dislike, of outsiders (Homans 2012, 27)—see Horowitz 2009a; Coren 2012; Homans 2012; Hare and Woods 2013; Morell 2013.

8 Sometimes film dogs are owned by trainers who work at these organizations; others are clients managed by them. All claim to use only "positive" training methods. For more on the companies listed, including the film and television credits of the animals in their employ, see their websites: animalsavvy.net, birdsandanimals.com, hollywoodanimals.com, pawsforeffect.net, and worldwidemovieanimals.com (which claims that the "majority of [its] dogs come from rescues or the pound").

9   In December 2010 *Entertainment Weekly* began complaining about the "dog book
    epidemic" ("Make It Stop!") that followed the "command of the best-seller list"
    by John Grogan's *Marley & Me: Life and Love with the World's Worst Dog* (2005):
    "Bookstores are inundated these days with a steady flow of agonizingly adorable
    books about man's best friend. In fact, the number of dog-related books published
    in the last two months alone easily reaches the double digits. . . . And they are all
    blatantly, painfully the same exaggerated story of hope and triumph-of-the-humane-
    society spirit" (Keith Staskiewicz, "Dog Book Epidemic," *EW*, December 3, 2010).

10 Although, as Katherine Grier details in her book *Pets in America* (2006), celebrity
    dogs like Rin Tin Tin and Lassie have always been used to sell things, especially dog
    food (375–376), as of this writing it is hard not to notice the increase in a related phe-
    nomenon: the possibility that one's own pet might become a star, or at least a product
    "spokesdog" or pet-store advertising model, through classes with names like "Hol-
    lywood 101." In such classes you learn how to train your dog to be useful for photo
    shoots and to perform tricks and behaviors reliably on a motion picture or television
    set. Some also promise to link you up with "animal agents" as well. For examples see
    the websites listed in note 8.

11 China banned a dog-eating festival in 2011 that dated back more than six hundred years;
    see "China Bans Ancient Dog-Eating Festival After Online Uproar," September 11,
    2011, globalpublicsquare.blogs.cnn.com/2011/09/22/china-bans-ancient-dog-eating
    -festival-after-online-uproar/. See also "China Proposes Ban on Dog Meat, Will
    South Korea Follow Suit?" *International Business Times*, June 29, 2011, ibtimes.com/
    china-proposes-ban-dog-meat-will-south-korea-follow-suit-294877.

12 The case of "Pete the Pup" in the *Our Gang* film series (1922–1938) is interesting as a
    record of the change in attitudes toward a given breed, the so-called "pit bull," over
    time and in relation to different mechanisms of representation. As Susan McHugh
    (2004) points out, "pit bulls were such beloved national symbols" for much of the
    twentieth century that the breed was the mascot of the children's films and their
    subsequent reincarnation on television from 1954 on (the series was "syndicated and
    re-run for more than 20 years"). She cites Vicki Hearne's *Bandit: Dossier of a Danger-
    ous Dog* (New York: HarperCollins, 1991) to discuss how "high-profile lawsuits in
    the 1980s led to the pit bull's identification with urban, poor and specifically black
    people, so that members of this breed became the object of subtle (and sometimes
    obvious) forms of racism" (114).

13 J. B. Griswold, "A Dog's Life in Hollywood," *American Magazine* (August 1938),
    offers an interesting snapshot of Hollywood's taxonomy of breeds in the 1930s:
    "Pomeranians and poodles for luxurious boudoir scenes; just plain mutts for kid
    pictures; staghounds and borzois for kings; wires and cockers and Scotties and collies
    for homey touches; pointers and setters for hunters; and shepherd dogs for
    Westerns" (16).

14 In a blog devoted to silent cinema, bioscopic.wordpress.com/2008/11/14/
    first-film-dogs, Luke McKernan suggests that the first cinematic canine possibly
    appeared in Edison's *Athlete with Wand* (1894), although not as a featured player.
    McKernan also discusses the large number of apparently stray dogs in early cinema
    and posits the existence of "canine space" in these films: "What adds to the fascina-
    tion, reinforcing one's belief in the essentially liberated nature of early films, is that
    stray dogs can be found in studio films of the period. The drama is enacted, the
    comedy routine performed, and in the background a dog watches, or wanders past, or
    joins in if it so desires, and this is accepted as part of the total action. 'Canine space' is
    therefore that other space, that world onto which the camera has intruded."

15 Of course, not all audiences find dogs appealing, or seek them out. Michael Schaffer (2009) learned that in his own middle-class neighborhood, his pet Saint Bernard was associated with the "giant teddy bear" character of the "family film" *Beethoven* (1992) and its numerous sequels; in another, poorer area of town, the same dog elicited cries of "Uh-oh, it's Cujo!" (223).

16 At americanhumanefilmtv.org/history-of-the-ratings/, the AHA provides the following account of its history and monitoring processes and criteria:

>   American Humane Association has been protecting animals in films since 1940, and over the years we've developed tried and true methods of ensuring "No Animals Were Harmed"® on movie sets. Our Los Angeles-based Film & TV Unit is the film and television industry's only officially sanctioned animal monitoring program. In 1972, American Humane Association produced its first National Humane Review newsletter, informing members of how animals were treated in recently released movies. A far simpler rating system was used to categorize movies as either Acceptable or Unacceptable. Those ratings were expanded in 1978 to include Believed Acceptable, Questionable, and Inappropriate for Children. The Inappropriate for Children rating was discontinued in 1985 as more parents relied on the Motion Picture Association of America's (MPAA) Ratings Board.

>   Each decade, film and television production increases, and American Humane Association changes its movie reviews to reflect the realities of our coverage capabilities. We had to move passed [sic] the conjecture of Believed Acceptable ratings. A new, simplified rating structure was created and launched during the 2004 integration of our Film & TV Unit website into the umbrella American Humane Association site. Working together, we fine-tuned those ratings to manage the rise in productions and our strict standards.

>   For the first time, movies could surpass our former highest rating of "acceptable" and receive the rating of Monitored: Outstanding and be awarded with the "No Animals Were Harmed"® end credit. When our Certi-fied Animal Safety Representatives™ can monitor significant, but not all, animal action on cooperative productions, those films may receive the rating of Monitored: Acceptable and the modified end credit: "American Humane Association monitored some of the animal action. No animals were harmed in those scenes.™"

While the website gives extensive analysis of how this or that film accomplished the "animal action" in a given film, the organization's resources are limited, and it cannot monitor all of the film and television shows it is expected to cover.

17 Although at americanhumanefilmtv.org/archives/movies/mr.php?fid=22 the AHA discusses the "humane" way that animals were treated in the production of *Amores perros*, it offers the following qualifications: "There is no program of humane over-sight for film in Mexico. Therefore, AHA appreciates the voluntary efforts of the Mexican trainers and handlers who have demonstrated a deep concern for the welfare of the animals in their care during the production. However, although the dogs were unharmed, tranquilization is not allowed under the AHA Guidelines for the Safety of All Animals in Filmed Media. AHA believes that tranquilization of an animal is a risk that we do not recommend for the purposes of filmmaking. Also, AHA's Guidelines are not utilized in Mexico. For these reasons, AHA has rated the film 'Questionable.'"

18 It is surprising that in a recent anthology entitled *Film and Risk* (Hjort 2012), there are essays on stunt doubles and risk, the 2005 film *Grizzly Man*, risks to the

environment posed by making and processing films, and other topics relating to danger and injury to actors and even spectators—but nothing about risks to animals (not even in *Grizzly Man*), or what happens when risk taking is ordered and the risk taker is unaware of the risk and has no agency in regard to it. Eva Novrup Redvall's essay in that volume, "Encouraging Artistic Risk Taking Through Film Policy: The Case of New Danish Screen," discusses a film called *A Soap* (2006), in which a woman character "prefers to keep to herself with her little dog and a romantic soap show on TV" (217), but the risk to, and fate of, the dog "actor" is never mentioned.

19   It is to be hoped that there will be further work done on all the dogs, dog characters, films, and national cinemas we were unable to include here. There appears to be no full history of dogs in any European cinema, for example, although some films have received extended discussion; see the censorship controversies generated by the 1955 British war film *The Dam Busters*, based on a true story that features a black Labrador retriever named Nigger. Two useful encyclopedias of U.S. films and television shows that include dogs are Beck and Clark 2002 and Painter 2008.

Part One

Stars and Featured Players

. . . .

1

Answering a Growl

• •

Roscoe Arbuckle's Talented
Canine Co-star, Luke

JOANNA E. RAPF

In June 1916 the fan magazine *Photoplay* ran a story about actor Jack Pickford's dog, Prince. The article quotes the dog as saying, "Actor dogs have only one growl coming: they don't get enough publicity in the magazines—I mean us stars" (42). Prince is right; dogs had played a significant role in film from its beginnings, but compared to their human co-stars, they had not received much publicity. No dog, for example, had yet been featured on the cover of *Photoplay* or *Motion Picture Magazine*. Several of the dogs that played a significant role in early cinema—even the strays that often wandered into the frame in documentary-style "actualities," as well as early fiction films—can be found listed in books and articles about dogs in the movies. But oddly, Luke, comic actor Roscoe "Fatty" Arbuckle's magnificently trained pit bull terrier (as the American Staffordshire terrier is colloquially known), is rarely mentioned in these treatments of cinematic canine history.[1] This may be because of the 1920s scandal involving the death of a movie starlet that ruined Arbuckle's career, and as his name faded from the pantheon of great silent-era performers, so did Luke's. Or it may be Luke's breed; because of its association with fighting and its presumed viciousness, the pit bull even today receives a bad rap. But it might also be due to Luke's somewhat anomalous status as Arbuckle's family pet, as

Roscoe Arbuckle and Luke. Collection of the author.

well as co-star—ironically, this was likely a significant component of Luke's fame during an era, the 1910s, in which pet ownership was growing across the United States (see Grier 2006). Probably it is a combination of all of these, and while both Arbuckle and Luke deserve more recognition today, this essay focuses on the remarkable accomplishments of "Fatty's" four-legged friend and compares Luke's film work to that of some of his canine contemporaries, especially the better known "Keystone Teddy," a Great Dane mix.

Of the number of dogs that *are* regularly mentioned in histories of animals in film as featured players during the first two decades of the twentieth century, Blair, a border collie owned by Cecil Hepworth, is usually the first. Blair starred as Rover in Hepworth's *Rescued by Rover* (1905), a film Jonathan Burt discusses in some detail in *Animals in Film* (2002), making the useful observation that in the silent era dogs and humans alike had to communicate through gestures and their bodies and without spoken language. A shared understanding between human and animal is therefore expressed visually and takes place "outside the realm of language" (116). The result is a sense of equality between human and animal that does not exist in sound film, where humans have the superior power of words. Conceptually, silent films allowed animals, perhaps especially dogs, to interact with people in ways that made them seem quite human.

Blair's first appearance in a film had actually been in *Alice in Wonderland* (1903), where he was simply a large, unnamed dog; but he went on to play Rover (which, as a result of his popularity, soon became a favorite dog's name) in two more shorts, *Rover Takes a Call* (1905) and *The Dog Outwits the Kidnapper* (1908), in the latter of which Hepworth's daughter, Barbara, played the child. Then there was Jean, known as "the Vitagraph Dog," a border collie owned by Laurence Trimble, an aspiring writer and actor who happened to be on the set of the Vitagraph Studios in Brooklyn in 1908 when the director (who may well have been Edwin S. Porter) was looking for a dog to play in a scene with Florence Turner, known as "the Vitagraph Girl." Both the dog and Trimble stayed on at Vitagraph, and by 1912 Trimble was writing for and acting with John Bunny. Trimble's first directing credit was *Saved by the Flag* (1910), with Ralph Ince (IMDb.com), but what he is best known for are the sixteen to eighteen films he made for Vitagraph with his dog, Jean.

Jean's first starring short seems to have been *Jean and the Calico Doll*, with ten-year-old Helen Hayes, released in August 1910. In an article in the *New York Times* (March 15, 1931, "Miss Hayes and Films: Her First Appearance"), Hayes says she played the juvenile lead "in two pictures in support of Jean, the collie. Jean was the famous dog of the day, and I was very thrilled," but other sources list only one film (see IMDb.com). Often credited as the first canine movie star, Jean died in 1916. Trimble and Vitagraph then tried another dog, Shep, but he was nowhere near as successful as Jean. After World War I Trimble traveled to Germany where he found a military dog, a German Shepherd, who eventually became "Strongheart," a canine star discussed in the next essay in this volume.

The Intelligent Big Barker

Probably the best-known dog star in these early years was Keystone Teddy (also known as "Teddy the Wonder Dog"), sometimes called "the first canine superstar of the American cinema" (Hopwood n.d.). The large brindled dog was featured in at least eighteen shorts at Mack Sennett's studio and was paid an impressive $350 a week during his heyday. Teddy is briefly mentioned in *Photoplay* (November 1914, 93) as having chewed the legs off of a doll owned by child star Clara Horton, but it took a while for his star potential to be recognized. This came about in 1916 with the western short *A Man's Friend*. His next film, *The Nick of Time Baby*, starring Bobby Vernon and Gloria Swanson, was released in December 1916. In it, Teddy rescues a kidnapped baby and reunites him with his parents. The ending, like the ending of Teddy's most famous film, *Teddy at the*

Throttle (1917), shows Gloria, Bobby, and Teddy in a familial embrace. Rob King (2009) has suggested that *The Nick of Time Baby* was illustrative of Keystone's efforts to widen its generic appeal beyond slapstick or "knockabout" comedy and attract a family audience in addition to its established fan base of working-class men. The dog—responsive, welcoming, heroic, an embodiment of unconditional love and loyalty—was a natural vehicle for broadening the audience for Keystone films. King even suggests that Teddy was a "loaded symbol of the films' sentimentalism . . . as a substitute for the child that a grown-up sexual coupling might create, a cipher through which the narratives withhold the sexual meanings of the young lovers' romance" (173). A dog functioning as a child substitute in these early films prefigures the use of dogs in screwball comedy in the 1930s, when, during the era in which the Production Code regulated the content of Hollywood's motion pictures, the visual depiction of sex was verboten and dogs became surrogate children, the most famous, of course, being Asta in the *Thin Man* series (see Ross and Castonguay in this volume). The dog as surrogate child may well apply to Teddy, but it is even more applicable to Luke, both in film and as the Arbuckle family pet in a family that included no children. That Keystone used these dogs to attract women and children moviegoers is obvious in this brief piece about *The Nick of Time Baby* in the *Mack Sennett Weekly* (January 1, 1917, 3): "This comedy will have a strong appeal for the whole family. . . . One of the star performers is a magnificent Great Dane dog—'Teddy'—who is all but human. The women and children as well as 'Pa' will shriek with delight to see 'Teddy' rescuing a baby from a watery grave; taking him home in his great jaws as tenderly as a mother could carry him in her arms."

In a May 1917 *Photoplay* story, Julian Johnson similarly puts the emphasis on Teddy, suggesting that Sennett's standard melodramatic formula isn't very funny until the end, when Teddy comes to the rescue: "Gloria Swanson is the prettiness, but Teddy, a big barker so intelligent that only Shep, 'the dead Thanhouseran we never cease to mourn,' is a fit comparison—Teddy is the temperament and action of this play. So far, Teddy has not organized his own company nor paid himself a $10,000 salary, but we presume these will be the next steps in the annals of this young genius" (86).

Jean's temporary replacement, Shep, is mentioned in passing, but Teddy is clearly the emerging star. His next film for Sennett, *The Road Agent*, was released in February 1917, but it is for *Teddy at the Throttle* that he is remembered today, perhaps just because it, unlike many of Teddy's films that are lost or not available in consumer viewing formats, can easily be seen today.[2] Actually, he only appears at the beginning and then again at the end; in between is a convoluted story of love and greed involving Gloria Swanson and Bobby Vernon (again), and villain Wallace Beery. Teddy is introduced as "Gloria's" pet (stars often played characters with their own names in these films); they dance together, sing together, and are clearly bonded.[3] Then he drops out of the story until Gloria, chained to railroad tracks by villain Beery, has to be rescued in Sennett's favorite melodramatic

Gloria Swanson and Teddy the Wonder Dog in a publicity still for *Teddy at the Throttle* (Clarence G. Badger, Keystone, April 1917). Collection of Adrienne L. McLean.

fashion. She gets out her dog whistle, and Teddy comes to the rescue, jumping out a window, dropping several stories to the ground, running over hills, fording a river, finding Gloria, and then taking a distress message to Bobby.

Besides being a classic last-minute rescue, the final scenes of *Teddy at the Throttle* are in fact very much like rescues Luke had already done in Arbuckle films. For example, at one point on the Sennett cyclorama (a sort of treadmill in front of a moving backdrop), Bobby Vernon, on a bicycle, grabs Teddy's tail in order to be pulled along faster. This seems to be a clear repetition of an earlier scene in *Fatty's Plucky Pup* (1915), in which Arbuckle on a bicycle and Luke on his four legs are racing to save a girl; although Arbuckle doesn't grab Luke's tail (it was shorter than Teddy's), in both cases it is the dogs rather than the men who are the heroes. Teddy saves the day by leaping into the cab of the locomotive and barking enough to warn the engineers of a problem ahead. The dog does not actually pull the throttle, but he gets the engineers to do it just as the train cuts the chains binding Gloria to the tracks. The happy ending, like the ending of *The Nick of Time Baby*—but also *Fatty's Plucky Pup* and *Fatty and Mabel Adrift* (January 1916)—shows three loving heads, a family together: boy, girl, and dog. A slight variation on the familial portrait is that in *Teddy at the Throttle* Teddy is pushed to the side so that Bobby and Gloria can kiss—but his head reappears through the space between their clasping bodies. In some of Arbuckle's films it is actually Luke who receives the kiss.

Teddy at the Throttle was such a hit that Harry C. Carr presumably interviewed Teddy for the July 1917 issue of *Photoplay* ("An Interview in Great Danish: Teddy, the Keystone Dog Graciously Grants an Audience"). Apparently unaware of the lively and talented Luke, Carr wrote that Teddy, among motion picture dogs, was "the only one I ever saw who wasn't a poor, cowering, spiritless, terrorized imitation of an animal." According to Carr, tongue-in-cheek, "motion picture animals fill a sad destiny: most of them are the support of a lot of lazy bums." For the interview Teddy responded to Carr's questions in "Great Danish," and, translated, his answers were as follows:

> I am two years old, and I am from a distinguished family of noble antecedents, although I have a hazy idea that my father and mother were divorced, as I never remember seeing the old man. They began training me when I was a few weeks old. The first thing they taught me was to lie down; the second, to keep out of fights. I was given the latter lesson by having an ammonia gun shot off under my nose while engaged in a rough and tumble scrap. Since then they have taught me about things a dog can learn to do. (26)

Since Teddy chewed Clara Horton's doll in 1914, he was obviously a little older than two at the time of this "interview," but he was now a featured player on the Sennett lot and was lent out to Mary Pickford for *Stella Maris* in 1918 and ended his acting career with Mabel Normand in *The Extra Girl* in 1923, although he has a brief appearance with another canine performer named Cameo (also sometimes called "Cameo the Wonder Dog," who made some dozen films, often uncredited, through the early 1930s) in *The Hollywood Kid* (1924).

A Contract for Life

Coincidentally, 1914, Teddy's first year with Keystone, was also the year Luke entered Roscoe Arbuckle's life. There are conflicting stories about how this happened. A lively but no doubt inaccurate studio publicity story in 1917, connected with that year's release of *The Butcher Boy*, in which Luke has a significant role, relates that the dog, initially named "Lonesome Luke" because "he was so forlorn," appeared in Arbuckle's dressing room as "a wouf-wouf waif"; and after the comedian was unable to locate the owner, the two "adopted each other" (Charles E. Meyer, "Fatty Arbuckle and His Dog Luke Bosom Friends and Fellow Artists, Wherein Is Related the History and Achievements of the World's Greatest Canine Actor," Paramount Publicity Release, April 1917, ACF-BRTD).[4] Luke tells his own story in *Photoplay* (November 1918, 63) in "Speaking for Himself," a tongue-in-cheek parody of the familiar Hollywood success story, arriving in Tinseltown already a full-fledged star after signing a "contract for life" with Roscoe Arbuckle:

> But when I stepped out on the platform of my private baggage car, upon my arrival on the West Coast, and saw assembled to greet me a representative group of the film colony's dog-stars, I knew I'd come home.
>
> A Spitz made a nice little speech and presented a silver-spiked collar as a token of esteem....
>
> On our way to the studio, Fatty put this thing right up to me.
>
> "Luke," he said gravely! "We need you old man. Sign this contract, for $50,000 a week."

A less far-fetched account—and probably the accurate one—is that he was a gift to Minta Durfee, Arbuckle's wife, as a six-week-old puppy, born in December 1913, from D. W. Griffith's assistant director Wilfred Lucas, after whom he was named (Oderman 1994, 70). Andy Edmonds (1991) suggests that Luke was actually a "bribe" to Minta to perform a difficult stunt (82). Regardless of how he joined the Arbuckle family, Luke's first screen appearance may be at the beginning of *The Knockout* (released in June 1914), an early short in which Arbuckle shares screen time with Charlie Chaplin during a boxing match that prefigures Chaplin's own eloquent choreography during a similar match in *City Lights* (1931). Luke does not play a part in the narrative of this film. He appears only briefly at the very beginning, as Arbuckle emerges from a shop, sandwich in one hand and Luke in the other. He shares the sandwich with Luke but then spots Minta and tosses the food aside to go see her. The scene that follows is touching because we see a moment among the three of them onscreen that must reflect the affection they had for each other in real life. As Roscoe holds Luke, both he and Minta lovingly pat the dog's paw but end up in the process patting each other's hands. As his full attention turns to Minta, Roscoe tosses Luke behind him, and he does not reappear in the film. The opening is merely a cameo, introducing a dog who will play bigger and bigger roles as he learns the tricks of the trade.

The evolution of the roles Luke played in early comedy in many ways mirrors the evolution of Roscoe Arbuckle himself, from a talented bit player with Mack Sennett to a star; from knockabout comic routines to a developed character, integral to the plot, whose screen presence often embodied moments of endearing sentimentality, culminating in *Fatty and Mabel Adrift* (1916); and finally ending his career as a bit player again, superfluous to the main comic narrative

A scene from *The Knockout* (Mack Sennett or Charles Avery, Keystone, June 1914) in which Roscoe and Minta lovingly pat Luke's paw. This is Luke's first screen appearance. Digital frame enlargement.

and in the shadow of an up-and-coming star, Buster Keaton. But despite Teddy's fame, along with that of Jean, Shep, and the others, Luke the Biograph Dog has not been remembered as a canine star since. If screen time, narrative agency, and publicity stories are any indication, Luke *was* a star, as big a star at the time as even Teddy was; and the fact that Luke and Arbuckle had "adopted each other" is both an important part of his canine star image and, at the same time, likely to be a reason for Luke's relative obscurity now. Neither Asta, whose real name was Skippy, nor virtually any other canine star besides Luke actually belonged to the actors with whom they worked. And again, perhaps this makes Luke's accomplishments seem less like "acting" than the other dogs who have achieved fame in the movies, especially as Arbuckle's fame, and the films that the pair made together, dimmed or were actively suppressed in the subsequent decade.

Roscoe's Pal

In his study of Keystone, in addition to stressing Keystone's efforts to attract a wider family audience, Rob King (2009) points out that beginning with the studio's merger with Triangle in 1915, Sennett tended to utilize a two-part structure, with one set of writers for the narrative continuity and another group of gag men for the comic business (116–119). Luke was initially used for comic business, but as his training progressed and he became skilled at obeying orders, doing stunts, and sitting still for remarkably long periods of time, he became part of the narrative continuity. Arbuckle began directing his own films with *Barnyard Flirtations* in March 1914, and it was not until he was behind the camera as well as in front that Luke began to be featured. In September 1914 he is seen in the background as Roscoe and Al St. John (Arbuckle's real-life nephew) fight over a girl played by Minta in *Lover's Luck*, but he is obviously not yet ready to take the spotlight. In *Mabel and Fatty's Wash Day* (January 1915), he has moved from background to foreground, but he does little more than sit on a bench as Mabel (Mabel Normand) hangs her wash out. In February Luke at least causes a little action, even if he doesn't do anything himself, in *Fatty's New Role*. Arbuckle, as a bum in a farmyard, sees Luke looking at him, and this causes him to sneak off.

Luke is obviously comfortable in front of the camera in these early efforts and sits beautifully, but from his screen appearances during the winter of 1915 it is likely that it is during this time that much of his trick training was taking place. His first big role, as part of "comic business," is in *Fatty's Faithful Fido* in March. He may have been Minta's dog, but he has become Roscoe's "pal" onscreen. In fact, the first title card says "Pals," and we see Roscoe and Luke together in front of a Chinese laundry. Arbuckle gives Luke a drink from a hose and then takes a drink himself. Most telling of their relationship, and Luke's increased virtuosity, are the little touches. As they go in the door of the building, Arbuckle politely lets Luke enter first. At another point, reiterating the idea of dog as child, Arbuckle tenderly wipes Luke's nose before turning to flirt with Minta. In fact, the memorable parts of this film are not the comic routines between Al St. John and Roscoe Arbuckle as rivals for the girl but the awesome performance of Luke as he now plays a crucial comic role in the narrative by coming to Arbuckle's aid as he fights St. John outside the laundry. It is in this film that the dog first climbs a ladder—as he will later do in several of Arbuckle's films, including *The Cook* (1918) and Luke's last screen vehicle, *The Scarecrow* (1920)—and chases St. John over a rooftop. Luke not only climbs up the ladder once, but as he reaches the top he falls back to the ground (probably not planned), then turns right around and climbs back up. On the roof he navigates a ladder stretched horizontally between two sections of the building and pursues St. John as he tries to hide in a rooftop structure. Luke at first gets him by the coattails, and when the coat comes off, he grabs his tie. This is a famous scene of the two of them as Luke refuses to let go and Al suspends him in the air by the tie. It is reprised in *The Cook* where, after climbing a second ladder, Luke grabs on to St. John's coattails as he clambers up another roof structure. In *Fatty's Faithful Fido* Al is only saved when Luke spots a cat and takes off after it. The film ends as it began—as so many of the Keystones do—in water; only this time, Arbuckle has fallen into a laundry vat, and Luke dives in to be with him. The "pals" are reunited, and Luke has sustained comic sequences of his own. He is clearly an accomplished

A scene from *Fatty's Faithful Fido* (Roscoe Arbuckle, Keystone, March 1915), in which Luke is suspended by Al St. John's tie. Digital frame enlargement.

and skilled performer, participating in both the comic business and the narrative continuity. He is now on the Keystone payroll at $150/week, somewhat less than Teddy was earning at the height of his stardom.

No dog can do quite the number of tricks that a human can—even a dog as smart as Luke—and his gags are often repeated from film to film, like the ladder-climbing mentioned above. Or, in his next film, *Fatty's Plucky Pup* (June 1915), where, like Teddy, he runs on the Sennett cyclorama (a device used again in *Fatty and Mabel Adrift*). *Fatty's Plucky Pup* might almost be seen as two separate films, connected only by the fact that many of the same characters appear in each part. The first is a cute love story, but whether the attraction is more intense between Arbuckle and his girl, played by Josephine Stevens, or Arbuckle and Luke is open to interpretation. As director, Arbuckle does a skillful job of crosscutting between himself at a farmyard fence flirting with the girl on the other side and a pair of dogcatchers (played by Al St. John and Hank Mann) who are after Luke. After an intense chase, Luke is finally caught, but Arbuckle sees the struggle, claims his dog, and in revenge, liberates from the cage on the dog catcher's van all the other dogs that have been caught—a splendid moment for dog lovers! Luke is dirty from the chase, so what follows is a lovely scene of washing, where Arbuckle puts him in his mother's washtub after dumping her laundry on the floor, rubs Luke clean on the washboard, and in a finishing touch, even does his nails. A furious mother kicks them both out, but Arbuckle grabs

The scene at the end *Fatty's Plucky Pup* (Roscoe Arbuckle, Keystone, June 1915), which establishes the family unit: Josephine Stevens, Luke, and Roscoe Arbuckle giving the dog a kiss. Digital frame enlargement.

the tablecloth as he leaves the house and dries Luke with it. Back at the fence, at the conclusion of this part of the film, Luke serves as both child and surrogate lover—a dual function he also has in *Fatty and Mabel Adrift*—as he is put in a high chair like a baby, and then up to the hole in the fence as the girl on the other side puts her mouth up to be kissed. Her mouth meets Luke's instead, and she pulls back in surprise. The section ends with an iris-in, an editing device frequently deployed at the end of films, vignetting Luke who has been the center of this narrative so far before fading to black.

The film could end here, as the editing suggests it might, but it does not; it moves on to part 2 where the dogcatchers kidnap the girl and Luke goes to the rescue. Luke is also responsible for bringing rescuers to Fatty and Mabel in *Fatty and Mabel Adrift*, but in this one, Luke, like Teddy in *Teddy at the Throttle*, actually accomplishes the rescue himself. At one point, Arbuckle, as director, crosscuts between three potential rescuers on the way to save the girl: Luke, Roscoe, and the infamous and inept Keystone Kops. It is during this rescue sequence that we see both Roscoe and Luke on the cyclorama, one overtaking the other. The kidnappers have set up a gun to shoot the girl at three o'clock. It's now a race against time. Luke tries jumping in a window of the shack where the girl is held captive. He can't make it, so he digs under a wall and, once inside, succeeds in untying the ropes of the girl just "in the nick of time." Meanwhile, Roscoe, arriving behind Luke, tries everything the dog did, even digging under the wall of the house. But he's too big. When he finally breaks down the door, the girl collapses in his arms as the three-o'clock gun goes off. Luke, as Teddy will do in the 1917 film, has saved the girl, and this one too ends with a three-shot of the family group. But Luke is in the center—this has been *his* film—and Arbuckle kisses him.

A Star in His Own Right

Luke was now a full-fledged star and stories about him start appearing in fan magazines. A short item in *Photoplay* (September 1915, 129) reads:

> MABEL NORMAND opened the door upon a tragic crime recently in her dressing room. Roscoe Arbuckle's bulldog [*sic*], "Luke" was tearing to pieces one of Mabel's satin slippers, despite its helpless squeaks. Diplomatic relations were all off at once, between Mabel and Luke. The slipper's mate caromed from Luke's head, and he fled arrantly.
>
> Two days later Luke crawled from under a corner of the elevated studio stage with a long-lost bracelet belonging to Mabel. The crime of the slipper was forgotten, and Luke and Mabel joined in an affectionate fade-out.

A story in the *New York Telegraph* (October 31, 1915, n.p., ACF-BRTD) that praises Arbuckle's abilities as a director adds, "Roscoe has but one other hobby—a dog. He is of the bull terrier [page torn here]. He and his master are inseparable companions."

In December 1915 Roscoe, Minta, Mabel Normand, Al St. John, Joe Bordeaux, and Luke—in effect Arbuckle's stock company—all headed to New York to begin making films for Keystone/Triangle in Fort Lee, New Jersey. The last film they shot in Los Angeles before leaving was *Fatty and Mabel Adrift*, which is also the last film in which Luke is utilized from beginning to end for sentimental and narrative purposes. For some reason the credits at the beginning list the dog as "Teddy, the Keystone Dog," but it is clearly a very well trained Luke in his most endearing role, not a Great Dane. Luke is introduced sitting on the lap of Mabel's father, and right away he is involved in the bucolic romance between Roscoe and Mabel. Rob King (2011) has suggested that this idyllic rural setting, along with the sentimental use of the dog, "served Arbuckle's films as a token of refinement, substituting the ideological systems of small town nostalgia for the 'vulgar,' plebian dynamics of knockabout comedy" (208). (One might also argue that pets themselves, of which Luke was one onscreen and off, also represent a sentimental ideal.) Mabel sends Luke to find Roscoe, who is hiding in a haystack. Playfully and affectionately, Roscoe spanks him like a child, and protectively, Mabel takes him back. More than in any of the other Arbuckle films, the dog in this one is clearly a child surrogate, a beloved family member. He accompanies the newly married couple to their ramshackle beach house and goes fishing with Roscoe while Mabel prepares dinner inside and then watches with gentle amusement from the porch as they land a fish and lose it in the surf. This scene is repeated almost identically in *The Cook* (1918), except that two years later Luke sits atop a narrow post rather than the more stable rock in *Fatty and Mabel Adrift*. In *Adrift* Roscoe swings Luke around by the tail of the fish, but in *The Cook* the stunt is even more elaborate. While balanced on top of the post, Luke grabs the end of Arbuckle's fishing pole and then hangs on to it as he is pulled off the post and swung around. Both scenes end with Luke going in the water after the fish.

The most famous sequence in this film has Luke sitting at the table with Mabel and Roscoe for dinner. Roscoe ties a napkin around the dog's neck, and both end up rejecting Mabel's rock-hard biscuits. After Mabel cries, Roscoe gives in and eats them, including Luke in the acceptance of her cooking by tossing him pieces also. The culmination of this sequence is when Mabel happily goes to bed and calls Luke to crawl in with her while Roscoe, also content, sits outside the bedroom door. But before the sequence ends, Roscoe leans over Mabel with Luke snuggled in her arms to give them *both* a shadowy goodnight kiss. In February 1916, Arbuckle's neighbor, Hobart Bosworth, wrote of that kiss, "Many times since I saw 'Adrift' I have said that the business of the shadowy goodnight was the most touchingly poetic thing I have ever seen in a motion

A scene from *Fatty and Mabel Adrift* (Roscoe Arbuckle, Keystone, June 1916) in which both Roscoe and Luke struggle to deal with Mabel Normand's rock-hard biscuits. Digital frame enlargement.

picture" (Oderman 92). Bosworth probably did not remember that this delicate moment also involved kissing the dog.

When the honeymoon cottage is flooded and floats out to sea, thanks to the mischief of rival-in-love played by Al St. John, the last-minute rescue is once again classic Sennett. Luke is sent to Mabel's parents with the distress note. He swims to shore, delivers the note, and the three-way race to the rescue begins, with the inept Keystone Kops falling in the water, Mabel's parents on a bicycle-built-for-two racing Luke on the cyclorama (recall *Teddy at the Throttle* and *Fatty's Plucky Pup*), and everyone getting there in time to save Roscoe and Mabel. The film fittingly ends with the couple kissing in one heart and a final shot of the hero of the film, Luke, in a heart of his own.

Arbuckle's reception in the New York area during 1916 helped to convince him to leave Keystone/Triangle, seeing that there were better opportunities out there. The New York trip also aggravated tensions between him and Minta. An interviewer wrote in April 1916 that Minta was "trying to figure out whether it were better to remain permanently eclipsed by the bulk of his hilarious personality, or to be separated from his company, both person and business" (Yallop 1976, 62–63). By early 1917 they were estranged. She continued to live in New York while he returned to the West Coast at the end of the year. They eventually divorced but remained friendly, which is important because Luke was really Minta's dog. However, she agreed to let Luke continue his film career, although on a less regular basis.

Joseph M. Schenck arranged for Arbuckle to head his own company, Comique Film Corporation, with the films to be distributed through Paramount Pictures. The first film released under this new arrangement was *The Butcher Boy* (April 1917), shot at the Norma Talmadge Film Corporation studios in New York City. This is the film in which Buster Keaton makes his screen debut, and it is the first of fourteen that he and Arbuckle were to do together. Of the fourteen, Luke is in five, but without Mabel Normand the films are not as sentimental and Luke's role is more of the "pal" he was initially rather than a child; he is once again used more for gags than to advance the narrative. In *The Butcher Boy* he is introduced with a title card that says, "Luke tries to be friendly," as he barks and chases after a black cat. Arbuckle works as a butcher, and when a customer asks for ten cents' worth of ground pepper, it is described as a job for Luke. The extended gag that follows is set up in three shots. The first, almost fifteen seconds long, is a medium shot of Luke from the side as he runs on a treadmill that turns a wheel that grinds the pepper. The next shot is a close-up of Luke's face from the front as he doggedly keeps running. The third shot is a ten-second medium close-up again from the side as Luke finishes grinding the pepper. It's a feature moment for Luke and one that shows off his skill as a performer, but it's a stand-alone gag.

He is a little more active in the second part of the film, where Arbuckle, dressed as a girl, enters a girl's boarding school to see his love interest, Almondine

(Josephine Stevens). His familiar rival in love, Al St. John, also enters the school dressed as a girl, which sets up another gag moment as a quizzical reaction shot of Luke is followed by the title card, "A bit confused." During the ensuing chaos in the boarding school, however, Luke does little more than a lot of barking, although he does guard a window to prevent St. John's escape as a title card tells the viewer he is "Loyal to Fatty," and another describes him as "a true friend" as Roscoe and Almondine escape.

But Luke's stardom was built up in the press in connection with this role in *The Butcher Boy*. As David Yallop writes in his 1976 book about Arbuckle, "In that crazy world . . . Luke had become a star himself. . . . What the bull terrier himself made of all this is not recorded, despite the interviews he had" (60). The publicity release from Paramount in April 1917 by Charles E. Meyer, cited earlier, also explains: "Fatty loves dogs with all the devotion capable in a man of his nature. . . . They [meaning Fatty and the dog] speak the same language, have the same thoughts and are such inseparable friends and admirers that they play in each other's support. . . . No less an authority than the comedian-master himself is responsible for the statement that Luke . . . is the greatest dog actor in the world. . . . Luke has learned to play his parts without looking into the face of the camera and without violating other fundamental instructions of the director."

In *Coney Island* (October 1917), shot on location and also with Buster Keaton, Luke unfortunately does not have much of a role. He is little more than a dog on the beach whose digging inspires Arbuckle to do likewise. Imitating Luke, he buries himself in the sand to escape his nagging wife, and the various misadventures of the film follow from there. Here, rather than humanizing the dog, the human becomes a dog, at least briefly. As production ended on *Coney Island*, Arbuckle decided to move the Comique Film Corporation to Los Angeles, and a year went by before Luke appeared in another film, *The Cook* (September 1918).

A review in *Moving Picture World* (September 14, 1918) singled out the dog for special praise, and rightly so, since this is the film cited above in which Luke climbs not one but two ladders in his familiar chase after Al St. John (see Rapf and Green 1995, 155). It is also the film in which Luke sits atop a post during the fishing sequence. Like so many of these comic shorts, it is basically in two parts that are connected only by the people (and dog) involved. The first part, in a restaurant where Arbuckle is a cook and Buster Keaton is a waiter, has a series of marvelous gags, but Luke's only role comes about nine minutes in when he grabs Al St. John by the coattails—St. John is harassing a pretty cashier played by Alice Lake—and begins the chase that will involve the ladder-climbing sequence. At the end of this Luke falls through the roof of the restaurant to land on a table where Arbuckle, Keaton, and one other man have been involved in an elaborate routine of eating spaghetti. Luke is held between Arbuckle and Keaton and licks Arbuckle's face. The men shake his paws, and then inexplicably, we return to the kitchen where Arbuckle puts a bib and a chef's hat on the dog, which is followed by an adorable close-up on Luke's face in an iris-out. This is the end of part 1.

The second part takes place at a Pacific coast Luna Park, where Arbuckle and Luke ride in a goat cart as he heads off fishing. The cashier is still being harassed by Al St. John, so as the film comes to a close, Luke once again takes off after his favorite target, and this chase includes a very impressive long shot of the two of them running up the tracks of a roller coaster. Arbuckle and Keaton try to rescue the girl, and the last we see, they all fall in the water. Unfortunately, *The Cook* is currently incomplete and the conclusion is missing. James L. Neibaur, in his book about Arbuckle and Keaton (2007), quotes from a title card taken from the original press kit: "While the pest waiter is rescuing his girl with the aid of the cook, the courageous Luke dives into the ocean after the tough guy, chasing him so far out into the ocean that he can't swim back to shore. It is fitting that after all this action, everything ends happily" (118).

The dog's antics with Arbuckle and Keaton in *The Cook* were enough to inspire the November 1918 *Photoplay* article *by* "Luke," "Speaking for Himself," mentioned at the beginning of this essay. The caption at the head of the article, next to a picture of Luke, says, "Fatty Arbuckle's dog-star has finally given in to the urge of publicity." The publicity probably helped promote Luke's next film, *The Sheriff* (November 1918), now unfortunately lost. A parody of westerns, and of stars Douglas Fairbanks and William S. Hart in particular, it was made without Keaton (who was in the army). A review of the film in *Moving Picture World* even notes this: "A willing intelligent dog who answers to the name of Luke [does] his best to fill Buster Keaton's place" (quoted in Neibaur 2007, 125). *Motion Picture News* (November 23, 1918) also highlights Luke: "The dog may be justly classed as a star in his own right. His entry into the lonely cabin by digging below the wall in order to save the heroine is a feat that will win sympathy and a good round of applause." This is, of course, quite similar to his "feat" in *Fatty's Plucky Pup*. Hazel Simpson Taylor in *Motion Picture* was not a big fan of the film, but she had praise for one member of the cast: "the dog is easily the star in this play" (Neibaur 2007, 125).

Luke again took a year off until *The Hayseed* (October 1919) in which he does not have any dramatic stunts; he is mainly an observer of action from beginning to end. The film repeats the hide-and-seek in a haystack that Luke and Arbuckle did in *Fatty and Mabel Adrift*, while its most unique gag sequence involves smell, an unusual device for comedy. Arbuckle's pal, Keaton, has given him green onions to eat to help strengthen his voice before he sings as part of the entertainment that takes place in the general store in the evening. The singing is a great success, making everyone cry, but when he is accused by the corrupt constable (played by Jack Coogan Sr.) of stealing money from an insured letter (insured because it has money in it, and something actually done by the constable himself), everyone turns from him as he approaches to plead his innocence. Finally, for support he goes to Luke, who has been watching the whole affair, and even the dog turns away when he smells Roscoe's breath. In the end Keaton reveals the true villain, a fight ensues, and Roscoe sends Luke out and up the road after Coogan this time (Al St. John had left the unit to star in his own series at Fox). A review by Laurence Reid in *Motion Picture News* (December 20, 1919, 4528) again singles out Luke's performance: "And Fatty Arbuckle still has that intelligent dog."

Luke's last film with Arbuckle is *The Garage* (January 1920), an excuse for a series of ingenious gags but with very little plot. Curiously, it was Keaton's favorite of the films he did at Comique, but that may be because he had more creative input in its direction. Luke, described in the credits as a "Mad Dog," doesn't appear until eleven minutes in, and he functions mainly in the familiar role of chasing various characters. At one point he gets Keaton caught in a fence and bites the rear of his pants off, and he is last seen chewing the pants in an alleyway. He is merely an accessory to the slapstick that almost seems a throwback to the early days at Keystone. This return to a gag-based, plotless format disappointed more genteel critics, and it would certainly disappoint fans who may have wanted to see more of Luke. Perhaps Arbuckle was already thinking ahead in terms of his own career, which would move him from the memorable shorts he did with Luke to starring roles in feature films for Paramount. Keaton took over the reins at Comique until Schenck gave him his own studio in the spring of 1920. Arbuckle's genius, however, would be tragically derailed with the scandal that besmirched his name in 1921.

Luke Will Not Forget

By 1920, Luke was probably about seven years old but still in good form. A farcical interview by Delight Evans in *Photoplay* (June 20, 1920, 44) asks about the dog, and Arbuckle replies, "Luke's fine." What follows is some confusion about whose weight is being discussed, so Evans ends the piece, "I never did find out the weight of Luke, the Dog." Arbuckle had now left Comique, but Luke carried on without him in one last short with Buster Keaton. *The Scarecrow* (December 1920) is clearly a Keaton film, and Keaton is a far less sentimental comic than Arbuckle. He is also more mechanically inclined, and the opening of *The Scarecrow* anticipates later familiar Keaton films (such as *The Electric House* [1922]) as he and Joe Roberts (a large Arbuckle replacement), his rival-in-love for farmer's daughter Sybil Seeley, prepare breakfast in a house Rube Goldberg would love. Luke appears somewhat later to eat a pie Seeley has made for her farmer father (played by Keaton's own father, Joe) and placed on a windowsill. Luke's only role in the film is then to be involved in an elaborate chase sequence—his forte—as he takes off, for no obvious reason, after Keaton. He is, once again, called "Mad Dog." But the sequence is a magnificent showcase for Luke, encapsulating much of his artistry from earlier films. He not only climbs up a ladder but climbs down as well, racing after Keaton, jumping in and out of the windows and doors of a wreck of a building and chasing him along the ruined roof ledge. Keaton tries all sorts of ruses to shake the persistent dog, hiding in a bath-tub and finally a haystack. We know from previous films that Luke is a master at finding people in haystacks, but this time it will involve waiting for Keaton to be shot out of a haying machine. When they finally come together, the title card queries "Friends?" and we have what is, in hindsight, a profoundly moving shot of an exhausted and defeated Keaton holding Roscoe Arbuckle's dog. It is as if Luke, the dog that played such an important role in the evolution of Arbuckle's comedy, is the link between Arbuckle and the man who will soon eclipse him in the pantheon of great performers of the silent era.

Then Keaton shakes Luke's paw, and the dog's role in the film is over. In fact, his role in films is over. He and Keaton have become friends, as they should. Keaton was also a dog lover, and his Saint Bernard appeared in several of his films, including *Sherlock Jr.* (1924), on which Arbuckle had a behind-the-scenes role after the scandal that destroyed his public career in 1921. Keaton remained a loyal friend through this, as did Luke, of course. The dog was even mentioned in a *Los Angeles Times* story at the time of the infamous trial in 1921: "Fatty Arbuckle has one sincere mourner whose love and faith no reports can shake. That mourner is Luke, Fatty's old bulldog [*sic*]. . . . This is the longest time that the comedian and Luke have been separated. And out at Fatty's house, Luke sits, disconsolate, at the door, waiting for the familiar step and his well-known voice. He doesn't eat. He waits. Whatever befalls Fatty, Luke will not forget" (quoted in Edmonds 1991, 192–193).

Luke died in 1926; he would have been about thirteen years old. For more than half of his life he performed faithfully, athletically, and artfully in front of the camera. He went from being an affectionate pet to Roscoe and Minta in his first film, *The Knockout*, to achieving his own stardom as Arbuckle began directing. Their stars rose together, with Luke becoming an integral part of the comic narrative by 1915–1916, perhaps most memorably in *Fatty and Mabel Adrift*. It is here that he functions as more than a dog; to Fatty and Mabel, as to Arbuckle himself, he is a child, whose idealized and uncomplicated human characteristics—representative of moral purity in the face of jealousy and corruption—helped to broaden the appeal of the Keystone films to family audiences in a rapidly changing world.

The second decade of the twentieth century was profoundly transitional, with a move from rural-based values to the multifaceted dimensions of urban life, from simplicity to the complexity of a "machine age," and from a time of peace to one of the bloodiest wars the world has ever seen. It was, in different ways, a "turning point for American society, a period that saw many of the key transitions that helped shape the United States into a modern nation" (Keil and Singer 2009, 1). Films reflect their cultural moment, although often uninten-tionally, and this is true of slapstick comedy, with its emphasis on machinelike behavior juxtaposed with the serenity and beauty of natural settings that could sometimes simply be a city park. Anat Pick (2011) has even suggested that the

A scene from *The Scarecrow* (Buster Keaton and Eddie Cline, Joseph M. Schenck, December 1920) in which Buster Keaton and Luke become "friends." This is Luke's last screen appearance. Digital frame enlargement.

complexity of slapstick, with its determinate use of objects and space, may make it the "most philosophical of all cinematic genres" (112). This is not to argue for an overtly existential dimension to Luke's roles; but it is to put forth the idea that his gags, such as running on a treadmill to grind ten cents' worth of pepper, spoof an increasingly mechanistic age, while his unconditional affection and daring rescues in the rural-based comedies remind audiences of the virtues of moral behavior and unselfish actions. That Luke performed all of this in *silent* film, where his bodily language could be the equal of the people with whom he shared the screen, only enhanced his *human* appeal. Recall that in the Paramount publicity piece about Luke (April 1917), Charles Meyer remarked that the dog and Arbuckle "speak the same language, have the same thoughts and are such inseparable friends and admirers that they play in each other's support."

In writing about Strongheart, the dog star that replaced Shep, Jonathan Burt cites J. Allen Boone's "spiritualist" book, published in 1939, entitled *Letters to Strongheart*, in which Boone wrote that the German Shepherd "set an example to humans who needed to return to the values of simplicity, goodness and happiness" (quoted in Burt 2002, 22–23). With Strongheart's acting "there was no barrier between his good inner nature and his outward manifestation of it." The dog gave to audiences an image of a world that was better than the one in which they were living. The same may be said of Luke.

Notes

A special thank you to Steve Massa at the Billy Rose Theatre Division of the New York Public Library of the Performing Arts and Karl Schmidt of the Film and Media Studies Program at the University of Oklahoma for their invaluable help with this essay.

1. Some sources refer to Luke as an "English pit bull dog" (e.g., Oderman 1994, 70). It is not known who actually trained Luke to do the tricks he does in his films or who at least developed the dog's clear natural proclivities for climbing.
2. As of this writing, *Teddy at the Throttle* can be seen online, for example, at wn.com/ Teddy_At_The_Throttle.
3. And yet apparently Swanson, who hated working at Keystone, did her best to forget that she ever co-starred with a popular dog. According to a brief article called "Forgetting Teddy" (*AKC Family Dog Magazine*, September/October 2011, 53), in interviews later in her life Swanson claimed she didn't remember making *Teddy at the Throttle* and recalled "nothing" about her brindled co-star.
4. Arbuckle Clippings File, housed in the Billy Rose Theatre Division of the New York Public Library of the Performing Arts, cited as ACF-BRTD in the text.

Chronological Filmography

Jean and the Calico Doll (Laurence Trimble, August 1910). Jean the Dog.

The Knockout (Mack Sennett or Charles Avery, June 1914). Roscoe Arbuckle [uncredited], Minta Durfee, Edgar Kennedy, Charles Chaplin, Luke [uncredited].

Lover's Luck (Roscoe Arbuckle, September 1914). Roscoe Arbuckle, Minta Durfee, Al St. John, Luke [uncredited].

Fatty and Mabel's Wash Day (Roscoe Arbuckle, January 1915). Roscoe Arbuckle, Mabel Normand, Harry McCoy, Alice Davenport, Luke [uncredited].

Fatty's New Role (Roscoe Arbuckle, February 1915). Roscoe Arbuckle, Joe Bordeaux, Glen Cavender, Edgar Kennedy, Hank Mann, Al St. John, Mack Swain, Luke [uncredited].

Fatty's Faithful Fido (Roscoe Arbuckle, March 1915). Roscoe Arbuckle, Minta Durfee, Al St. John, Glen Cavender, Luke [uncredited].

Fatty's Plucky Pup (Roscoe Arbuckle, June 1915). Roscoe Arbuckle, Josephine Stevens, Joe Bordeaux, Edgar Kennedy, Hank Mann, Al St. John, Luke [uncredited].

Fatty's Tintype Tangle (Roscoe Arbuckle, July 1915). Roscoe Arbuckle, Edgar Kennedy, Norma Nichols [Luke is listed in the cast in Yallop and on IMDb.com, but he does not seem to appear in it.]

Fatty and Mabel Adrift (Roscoe Arbuckle, January 1916). Roscoe Arbuckle, Mabel Normand, Al St. John, Joe Bordeaux, Glen Cavender, Luke the Dog.

The Nick of Time Baby (Clarence G. Badger, December 1916). Bobby Vernon, Gloria Swanson, Teddy the Dog.

The Road Agent (Mack Sennett, February 1917). Teddy the Dog, James Donnelly, Vivian Edwards.

The Butcher Boy (Roscoe Arbuckle, April 1917). Roscoe Arbuckle, Buster Keaton, Al St. John, Josephine Stevens, Joe Bordeaux, Luke the Dog.

Teddy at the Throttle (Clarence G. Badger, April 1917). Gloria Swanson, Bobby Vernon, Wallace Beery, Teddy the Dog.

Coney Island (Roscoe Arbuckle, October 1917). Roscoe Arbuckle, Buster Keaton, Al St. John, Alice Mann, Joe Bordeaux, Luke [uncredited].

Stella Maris (Marshall Neilan, January 1918). Mary Pickford, Ida Waterman, Herbert Standing, Teddy the Dog [uncredited].

The Cook (Roscoe Arbuckle, September 1918). Roscoe Arbuckle, Buster Keaton, Al St. John, Alice Lake, Glen Cavender, Luke the Dog.

The Sheriff (Roscoe Arbuckle, November 1918). Roscoe Arbuckle, Betty Compson, Monty Banks, Luke the Dog. [Lost film.]

The Hayseed (Roscoe Arbuckle, October 1919). Roscoe Arbuckle, Buster Keaton, Jack Coogan Sr., Molly Malone, Luke [uncredited].

The Garage (Roscoe Arbuckle, January 1920). Roscoe Arbuckle, Buster Keaton, Molly Malone, Luke [uncredited].

The Scarecrow (Buster Keaton and Eddie Cline, December 1920). Buster Keaton, Joe Roberts, Sybil Seeley, Joe Keaton, Luke [uncredited].

The Extra Girl (F. Richard Jones, 1923). Mabel Normand, Ralph Graves, George Nichols, Teddy the Dog.

The Hollywood Kid (Roy Del Ruth/Del Lord, 1924). Charles Murray, Louise Carver, Jackie Lucas, Teddy the Dog.

2

The Dogs Who Saved Hollywood

• •

Strongheart and Rin Tin Tin

KATHRYN FULLER-SEELEY AND
JEREMY GROSKOPF

> The Greatest Animal Actor the World
> Has Ever Known! Strongheart [in] *White
> Fang*, Jack London's Mighty Epic of
> Alaska. A Man! A Girl! A Dog!
> —*Niagara Falls Gazette*, July 14, 1925, 11

> Rin Tin Tin, that Fairbanks, Mix and Bar-
> rymore of the canine world, has made his
> best picture.
> —*Variety*, April 7, 1926, 40

"Dog heroes" were top American action-film stars in the 1920s. Strongheart
and Rin Tin Tin, among the early wave of German Shepherds introduced to
the United States at the conclusion of World War I, were beloved by millions
of movie fans as superbly talented canine performers whose abilities, like other
dog stars before them, were uniquely highlighted by silent film. Strongheart was
known as an original "Wonder Dog" and as the most outstandingly skilled actor

of the dozen or more canine cinematic performers of the era (see Rapf in this volume). Rin Tin Tin was sometimes called "The Dog Who Saved Hollywood," as his films supposedly rescued the struggling Warner Bros. studio from bankruptcy. His story is especially steeped in Hollywood mythology, and his trainer, Lee Duncan, constructed fantastical stories about his origins and achievements. "Rinty" (as the dog was nicknamed) was rumored to receive twelve thousand fan letters a week, to earn $6,000 a month, to own solid-gold dog tags and a diamond-studded collar, and to live in luxurious style in his own Hollywood mansion. Susan Orlean, in her hagiographic book about Rin Tin Tin, claims that the dog won the vote for Best Actor for the first Academy Award in 1929 and that this embarrassed officials so much that they gave it to Emil Jannings instead *and* changed the voting rules so that animals could not be nominated for acting awards (Orlean 2011, 88–89). Even Rinty's death was tied to celebrity, as gossip claimed it was in the arms of screen siren Jean Harlow (Basinger 2000, 451). None of this is true, of course, especially Orlean's claim about Rinty and the Oscars (see the introduction to this volume). But that the legends have such resonance is due to the incredible significance of Strongheart and Rinty during the 1920s; the pair romped through many areas of 1920s popular culture—on movie screens across the nation, in film reviews and articles in local newspapers, at personal appearances in scores of theaters, and pictured on commercial products from dog food cans, cereal boxes, and shoe polish tins to Cracker Jack prizes, statuettes, and children's books. Strongheart and Rin Tin Tin were depicted as full-fledged movie stars in the decade's fan magazines, which breathlessly documented their strenuous adventures on set, their publicity appearances, and their everyday life offscreen surrounded by their families of pups sired with their canine spouses.

The enormous success of Rinty and Strongheart as cinematic canines in the 1920s was due to a fortuitous combination of factors—the precedent of earlier nickelodeon-era dog actors, for example the border collies Jean at the Vitagraph studio and Shep at Thanhouser, the Great Dane mix Teddy at Keystone, and Luke, Roscoe "Fatty" Arbuckle's dog, at Biograph; the vogue for the outdoor action film genre in the 1920s; the extraordinary talents of Strongheart and Rin Tin Tin, who moved beyond merely performing tricks to be noted for their athleticism, for their sharp teeth, and dark, fierce visages, and also for their expressive eyes, in which audiences read sorrow and love; and, as a complex cause and result of all of these, the rising status of the dog as pet and companion in U.S. culture. But the celebrity of dog as hero—rather than comic foil or surrogate child, for example—was ultimately engineered by their owners and film publicity agents. Quirky characters Laurence Trimble (who guided Jean and Strongheart) and Lee Duncan (who trained Rinty) devoted their careers to directing, publicizing, and profiting from these gifted animals.

The early years of the twenty-first century have seen a massive growth of interest, in scholarly circles, in the study of human-animal relationships. This scholarly work is particularly interested in our representations of animals. As Nigel Rothfels writes, "the way we talk or write about animals, photograph animals, think about animals, imagine animals—represent animals—is . . . deeply connected to our cultural environment" and our history (Rothfels 2002, xi). Scholarly studies of animal representation have often engaged both with the movies as a form and with dogs as a film subject: the former a result of film's status as one of the foremost narrative mediums of modern life, the latter a result of the ubiquity of dogs as a companion animal in Western culture. It is the rare individual indeed who, in American culture at least, has no "dog-lovers" as friends or who has not watched the heroic adventures of Benji or some other dog on film either as or in the company of a child.

But the importance of the dog in film does more than simply draw attention to a convention in American culture. The various narrative positions we grant to dogs is indicative of the often conflicted ways in which we think about dogs in particular and animality in general. Susan McHugh (2004) cuts to the heart of the complexity of filmic dogs when she poses a question about the remarkable number of animated canines populating the films of Walt Disney over many decades: "If Pluto is Mickey Mouse's dog, then what on earth is Goofy?" (10). Disney weaves together the notion of dog as "companion" and the notion of dog as "protohuman" into cartoon form, side by side, and the general reluctance of any given spectator to give thought to the animality of the characters allows this conflicted representation to slide past unscrutinized.

As such, historical studies of filmic dogs can help us to understand the changing perception of dogs in Western culture, as they move back and forth from a representation of wildness to a representation (much like children) of the embodiment of innocence. Silent-era dog heroes, like Strongheart, Rin Tin Tin, and those who came before, show film's first steps toward humanizing dogs, for better or worse, through stories of heroism, gracing them with both complex intellectual faculties and courage. As many essays in this book explore, dog stars, no less than many of the nineteenth- and twentieth-century literary icons on which their roles are often based, continue to occupy the ground between anthropomorphized and wild, reproducing the visual and narrative templates established from the early years of cinema through the present.

Early Dog Heroes: Jean and Shep

One precedent for filmic depictions of heroic star dogs was set by the career of Jean the Vitagraph Dog. This female black-and-white border collie, appearing in one-reel films from 1910 to 1913, was one of the first American film performers promoted by her real name, while Florence Lawrence was still the anonymous Vitagraph Girl (Slide 1987, 55). Jean came to Vitagraph when her owner, Laurence Trimble, a twenty-five-year-old author of short story fiction from Maine, visited the Brooklyn studio while researching a magazine article on motion picture production. Trimble encountered a film crew having difficulty with a recalcitrant dog performer. Trimble had a natural talent for working with canines, showed the moviemakers how to do it, and then returned to the lot with his own trained and talented dog. Vitagraph hired Jean for $25 per week, and Trimble became a director (Gallo 2000); Jean was subsequently featured in at least twenty films directed by Trimble. She was especially adept in dramatic roles, at various times bringing adult lovers together (in one film, two lovers' rivalry over Jean's ownership drives them apart), being a playful companion to lonely children, or rescuing endangered human infants from fire or kidnapping. She was a full member of the Vitagraph stock company and appeared in numerous films with Florence Turner, John Bunny the comedian, romantic hero Maurice Costello, and Ken Casey the Vitagraph Boy. In the one-reel melodrama *Where the Winds Blow* (1910), shot on location on the Maine coast, Jean helps her poverty-stricken human family stave off starvation by digging for clams along the rocky shoreline to help them earn a living.

"Jean is an inspiration; no one could help making a fine story about her, and no actor could act badly in her support," a 1910 Vitagraph publicity release noted (Slide 1987, 55). While film reviewers found some of her movies to be just minor "program fillers," they praised her performances in sentimental melodramas like *Playmates* (1912), in which a loving stray dog cheers a sick and lonely wealthy child back to health, earning the parents' gratitude. *Moving Picture World* singled out that film, judging it to be "best film of the week" released by an American or European film studio (February 19, 1912, 367; see also the *New York Daily Mirror*, February 21, 1912, 12). Jean's fame with movie audiences spread as Vitagraph featured illustrations of the dog in its advertisements and offered theater managers souvenir postcard portraits of her to give away at its nickelodeons. When she had a litter of puppies, the Vitagraph Company capitalized on it in a half-reel film, *Jean and Her Family* (1913) (*Moving Picture World*, March 28, 1913, 1242). Jean and Trimble departed Vitagraph for a more lucrative opportunity in 1913, joining an independent film production studio in England headed by actress Florence Turner, where the dog appeared in several more films before passing away in 1916.

Meanwhile, in New York, Vitagraph director John Harvey located a replacement collie, Shep, for the studio. However, dog and trainer soon decamped to the Thanhouser film studio, where Harvey directed Shep in a half-dozen one-reel films, most notably the melodrama *A Dog's Love* (1914), whose plot inventively develops Shep's emotions and his active agency. Calling the film "a miniature masterpiece," a *Moving Picture World* reviewer noted that "when Baby Helen [the dog's only companion], stricken down by an automobile, is taken from the tangible world, not only her parents are broken hearted. Shep's grief is consistent and prolonged. He visits the cemetery and mourns over the little flower-strewn mound; from a florist he himself brings flowers; he entices a young woman with a watering pot to come and sprinkle the wilting blossoms, and, like them, he droops at home, refusing to eat anything—even chicken bones." In a remarkable double-exposure shot Shep is shown dreaming of a ghostly Helen, who hugs and beckons him to join her in the afterlife. Despondent upon awakening, he lies down on her grave and dies. "By this time the audience is in the state of rapid-fire winking, and in some quarters there is that furtive movement connected invariably with a covert kerchief search," the review continued. "Then suddenly the situation is saved and the picture ends in a flash of glorious relief with the insert, 'Don't cry, it was only make believe,' preceding a picture of the livest [*sic*], healthiest Baby Helen playing with an equally live and cheerful collie. . . . In its pathos it is quite exquisite, and then it finishes with that little masterpiece of an emotional poultice and sends everyone away with the delightfully mixed up feeling of a streak of sadness sweetly frosted over with relieved happiness" (*Moving Picture World*, October 17, 1914, quoted in Bowers 1997).

A New Generation of Dog Heroes

Despite the momentum these successes gave to produce more dog-themed films, when Shep died unexpectedly early in 1915, and Jean was gone, no other canine actors immediately took similar roles. The economic devastation that World War I dealt to the European film industry sent Trimble back to the United States to look for film work and a new dog to train. In 1920 a New York dog breeder alerted Trimble to the availability of a German Shepherd (at the time also known as Belgian Shepherds, Alsatians, or Red Cross police dogs) named Etzel von Oeringen that had recently been brought to the United States from Germany. Trimble and his screenwriter wife, Jane Murfin, were impressed with Etzel's athletic build, commanding size, and fierce visage, as well as the skills he had acquired through training. German Shepherds, previously little known to Americans, had gained a lot of publicity in newspapers and newsreels during the war, serving both the Allied and Axis armies as canine guards, scouts, messengers, and attackers and helping the Red Cross as rescuers. Shepherds were not cute, cuddly pets but strong, sharply sensed working dogs and snarling, lethal weapons. Etzel had been thoroughly trained as a military dog to jump, chase, and attack; but to become a film performer who could patiently interact with adults and children and perform the kinds of stunts that film plots might call for would require a great deal of retraining. This fierce attack dog did not know how to "play," and (of course) at first only obeyed commands spoken in German. Trimble trained the animal, which they rechristened Strongheart, to take his commands from an arrangement of mirrors "to break him of the habit of looking at his master" (*Los Angeles Times*, May 24, 1931, L12). Strongheart took to his lessons with alacrity and was soon able to perform an astonishing array of athletic stunts and subtle movements, all at his master's cue. Trimble and Murfin formed an independent film production company to create feature-length films starring their dog, whose films they subsequently released through the First National studio.

NOVEMBER   25¢

CLASSIC

COMBINED WITH SHADOWLAND   A BREWSTER PUBLICATION

Strongheart

Strongheart on the cover of *Motion Picture Classic*, November 1923. Collection of Kathryn Fuller-Seeley.

Strongheart's first film, *The Silent Call* (released in November 1921), was enormously popular in both urban and small-town theaters across the United States. Rumored to have cost $100,000 to produce, it supposedly earned $1 million at the box office, playing nearly eight hundred shows at Miller's Theater, a prominent cinema in Los Angeles (*Los Angeles Times*, March 26, 1922, III35; Elwood 2010, 63, 80). Film critics commented excitedly on the novelty of a dog's playing the leading role in a feature film with the aplomb of a Hollywood actor. The *Chicago Tribune* reviewer noted "the remarkable, in fact almost uncanny intelligence and dramatic performance contributed by him. Never for a moment does the beholder feel the director telling this wonderful dog what to do or how to do it, never for a moment do we feel that it is a trick" ("Introducing a Canine Hero Who Can Act," *Chicago Tribune*, April 12, 1922, 24).

Others claimed Strongheart's performance ranked him with Hollywood's current greatest romantic leading men and action stars. "He does all the things that human heroes of melodramas are supposed to do," a review in the *Atlanta Constitution* stated; "He looks handsome—a good deal handsomer than Wallace Reid. He fights bravely—and a good deal more realistically than William S. Hart. He loves family—and decidedly more naturally than Eugene O'Brien. And he hates bitterly—and to a good deal more purpose than any movie actor we've ever seen, because in the end he drowns the object of his hatred after practically chewing him into ribbons." The review concluded, "The greatest actor that the screen has produced is a dog, and he is the greatest actor because he acts just exactly as a dog would act under given circumstances" (*Atlanta Constitution*, February 14, 1922, 7). Strongheart's portrait was even featured on the cover of *Motion Picture Classic*, the most elegant American movie fan magazine, with a profile article, penned by Trimble, detailing the Wonder Dog's daily training and keen emotional and psychological connections with his human handlers (November 1923).

Despite the huge success of Strongheart's first film, his fame was not immediately exploited by featuring him in a constant round of follow-ups, the way that major Hollywood studios were doing with human stars. Trimble and Murfin produced Strongheart's films independently with their own money, rather than with the larger resources or factorylike pressures of a large film studio, so Strongheart appeared in only one full-length film per year. With only five features to his credit, Strongheart's career would be further impeded when Trimble and Murfin divorced in 1926, breaking up their partnership (Elwood 2010, 87). Strongheart's outstanding performances created a new fascination among the public with dog heroes, however, and other Hollywood studios rushed to cash in on the trend and to capitalize on public interest in cinematic canines; they hastily produced their own outdoor adventure films set in the snowy Northwest or on the rugged frontier featuring not cute, huggable pets but big, fierce, wild wolves and athletic, loyal sled dogs.

Such an opportunity was how Rin Tin Tin, another German Shepherd brought over from France by Lee Duncan, a World War I veteran, entered motion pictures in 1922. Every single "fact" about Rin Tin Tin's life is encased in layers of fanciful invention spun by Lee Duncan or the Warner Bros. publicity department, and it has been tempting for authors to fall prey to them. Rin Tin Tin biographer Ann Elwood (2010) cannily describes Duncan as "like the Wizard of Oz . . . a man who hid behind a projection of himself" (3–4). Even the heroic story Duncan spun about rescuing a litter of pups from a bombed out French kennel (Orlean 2011, 11, 29) and discovering the remarkable dog's potential was a significantly embellished tale of actual events. A *Los Angeles Times* article of October 1919 on an upcoming kennel show already falsely elevates the young Rinty's status to "famous war dog" but quotes Lt. Lee Duncan as saying that he and six soldiers had captured a German Shepherd they named Fritz

An ad for Strongheart's *Brawn of the North* (Laurence Trimble and Jane Murfin, Trimble-Murfin Productions, 1922), published in the *Saturday Evening Post*, November 11, 1922.

from a German trench at Thiancourt, France, and mated him with another dog captured in Belgium. In this article Duncan said it was Fritz who was found, sorely wounded, abandoned by fleeing German troops and lying beside the bodies of eleven other dogs that had been killed by an exploding shell; in later stories Duncan claimed it was Rinty whom he found in the bombed-out kennel. Here Duncan states that Fritz was made mascot of a company of U.S. soldiers at Toule, and with the female Shepherd produced a litter of pups. Duncan named the pup Rin Tin Tin after the little good luck dolls made by French women and sold for charity. Duncan then said that he secured a special permit from the French government at Bordeaux to bring the young Rin Tin Tin and a sister back to the United States and that now Duncan was exhibiting Rinty at dog shows (October 13, 1919, II2).

A portrait of Rin Tin Tin taken at Warner Bros. in the 1920s. *Movie Star News.*

No matter what stories Duncan dreamed up, there was no denying that Rinty was intelligent, handsome, and a quick learner, with remarkable athletic abilities to run and to jump to second-story heights. After training Rinty and taking him to perform at dog shows, the Southern Californian Duncan soon connected with filmmakers looking for stunt dogs. Three-year-old Rinty's first major film role apparently came when Duncan convinced a Warner Bros. studio crew that his Shepherd could perform better than the underperforming faux "wolf" they were struggling to use in a low-budget film, *The Man from Hell's River* (1922). Rinty was subsequently featured in the studio's snow country adventure *Where the North Begins* (1923) (with a script written by Duncan), which was a big box-office hit (Elwood 2010, 64). The struggling studio benefited substantially from its new canine star and soon gave him top billing in its trade journal advertisements; Hollywood mythmakers anointed Rin Tin Tin "The Dog Who Saved Warner Bros." Rinty had a longer and fuller career than Strongheart, as he appeared in twenty-four feature films at Warner Bros. in the 1920s compared to a half-dozen Strongheart vehicles. Rinty's fame was also bolstered by Duncan's penchant for embellishing every story about himself and his dog with layers of myth and bravado.

Strongheart's and Rinty's successes led every studio to have its own performing dog or two on the roster; there were more than two dozen dog star wannabes, mostly German Shepherds, that appeared in Hollywood films of the 1920s. But none had the lasting reputation of Strongheart or Rinty—some, like Peter the Great, were talented animals whose careers were prematurely cut short by death, while other canines gave very mixed performances. A reviewer noted of an FBO-released film *The Outlaw Dog* (1927) that FBO's dog hero, Ranger, could actually read signs and knew how to flag down a passing train (*Variety*, June 8, 1927, 19), but in *Breed of Courage*, appearing five months later, the reviewer decided that "Ranger is not a good actor. . . . The heavy practically drags the dog toward him instead of the animal attacking, in several cases the menace falls to the floor, pulling the dog down on top in semblage [*sic*] of a fight" (*Variety*, November 2, 1927, 25).

Movieland's Perfect Stars

Critics reviewing dog hero films regularly singled out the canine stars' intelligence and acting skills for comment. Reviews made the distinction that Strongheart was not merely a "trick dog" that could perform several discrete stunts but an "actor" who could perform a variety of scenes, moods, and actions. They noticed that Strongheart (and subsequently Rinty) seemed to express emotion through his eyes, facial expressions, and body movements. As the *Chicago Tribune*'s review of Strongheart in *The Silent Call* (1922) noted, "The dog is not a trick animal. He doesn't walk on his forefeet or fry pancakes for breakfast. He's just an extraordinarily intelligent creature with a pair of eyes that go to your heart and fangs long and sharp enough to reach it. Who is a picturesque figure against a background of magnificent scenery" (April 12, 1922, 24).

Of Rin Tin Tin's early film *Where the North Begins*, the *Boston Globe* reviewer claimed that although his acting skills were not quite to the level of his canine movie rival,

> He [Rinty] is a remarkable animal, with splendid eyes and ears, and he seems to be wondering what all this acting is about. One minute he is encouraged to tear up the child's clothes, and the next he is made to slink out before the camera. If such a dog is angry, he is really angry, and there's no acting about it. If he wants something, he wants it. When Gabriel Dupre, played by Walter McGrail, is supposed to lash the dog with a whip, it is accomplished without one seeing the dog. It would have been more effective to have him show that he was going to whip the dog and leave the set with the whip, instead of apparently lashing the floor. (December 24, 1928, 2)

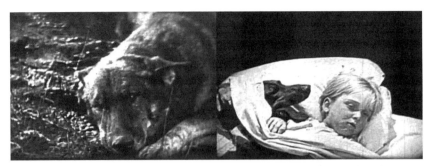

Rin Tin Tin as a domesticated dog in two shots from *Hills of Kentucky* (Howard Bretherton, Warner Bros., 1927). Digital frame enlargements.

The reviewer also claimed that Rinty "enacts so many different moods that it is difficult to believe that one dog could play throughout the film. He can look like a savage wolf one minute. The next he plays with a little Indian child and wears an almost silly smile when he does his antics."

The *Los Angeles Times* noted that "Rin Tin Tin [in *Tracked in the Snow Country* (1925)] is an expressive young actor, and the scene in which he lies at the feet of the man who intends to shoot him is quite without parallel in dog pictures. In fact in the moments when he is standing, or lying still and just looking, the famous dog is far better than in the more active scenes. Perhaps, Rin Tin Tin belongs to that modern school of acting, which expresses everything in the face" (May 4, 1925, 13). But emphasizing that face apparently required a little dash of Hollywood makeup. Lee Duncan claimed that Rinty's dark-colored coat posed a challenge for filming and that the studio prevailed upon Duncan to dust Rinty with talcum powder in order to make him photograph more distinctly and to enable his expressive face and body to contribute further to his performances (ABC publicity sheet for "Adventures of Rin Tin Tin," 1954). An Atlanta reviewer praised Rinty as the consummate silent actor in *Hills of Kentucky* (1927), remarking that "In the action Rin-Tin-Tin does everything but speak and still the eyes and the movements of this dog do speak and speak louder than words" (*Atlanta Constitution*, July 4, 1927, 3).

Praise for the perceived acting talents of Strongheart and Rin Tin Tin illustrates the central importance of facial expression in silent film acting. Screen close-ups of actors' emotion-laden eyes and faces that seemed to communicate their innermost feelings made screen performers such as Lillian Gish, Charlie Chaplin, Rudolph Valentino, and Greta Garbo internationally famous stars of the 1910s and 1920s. "Everything in film depends upon eyes," Gish once noted. "They tell the story better than words" (Leider 2004, 8). Screenwriter June Mathis claimed that eyes were the first thing she noticed about an actor, because they didn't lie: "The soul that looks out of the eyes is the real you" (Leider 2004, 166). As early filmmakers moved away from simply photographing a stage play from the point of view of someone sitting well to the back of a theater, and began to move their cameras in closer to capture close-ups of individual actors' movements and facial expressions, actors, too, had to alter their methods. No longer would broad, sweeping gestures and exaggerated facial reactions of the nineteenth-century stage seem appropriate on film; instead, actors and directors developed more naturalistic and subtle ways to perform before the camera (see Pearson 1992; Staiger 1985). James Naremore (1988) documents the increasing significance to acting across the silent film period of "tiny expressive movements of eyes, face, and hands. The circumstances were just the reverse of conventional theater and everyday discourse, where movement is promoted by utterance, and where gestures either support speech or reveal latent meanings behind it. In silent movies, actors needed to make their few words rise out of their gestures, never forgetting that meaning lay in their eyes and at their fingertips" (48). With silent-film actors developing restrained, understated performances; close-ups magnifying their smallest eye movements, frowns, and gestures into expressive emotional portrayals; and film audiences now sensitized to absorb and interpret this acting style—enlarged on the big screen and surrounded by silent films' accompanying orchestral and organ music scores—it is no wonder that film viewers would impute similar, sensitive acting skills to dog heroes and their large, expressive eyes and handsome faces.

Cultural studies scholars note that the cinematic canines in films like these are characters that possess fully formed personalities, like proper human heroes. As Pete Porter (2006) asserts, there is nothing in the filmic treatment of animals that renders it less likely that we will attribute to them the same "personhood" that we attribute to human characters. Animals, like humans, have discrete and recognizable bodies, self-motivated actions, and imagery that forces us to assume that they are thinking—for example, a close-up on the dog hero's watching eyes. As Jonathan Burt (2002) points out, animal characters often interact with humans in film via a "shared look," which, though it does not necessarily imply similarity of thought (or even understanding), at least links the two species as living and thinking beings (38–40, 69). Burt stresses the possibility of a lack of comprehension between the species and argues that dogs demonstrate to humans "respect without understanding." In dog hero films, however, this fact is always belied by narrative structure and context. The dog-as-hero always displays his comprehension by saving the day. The human then reciprocates with praise—"Good dog."

Film reviewers of the 1920s often noted that Strongheart's and Rinty's films put them into roles analogous to those of the decade's leading male Hollywood stars, especially the strong, athletic, loner heroes of action films, such as swashbuckler Douglas Fairbanks and western star William S. Hart. Hart's steely expressions, honed during his years on Broadway playing Messala the Roman warrior in *Ben Hur* and the title role of the famous western drama *The Virginian*, brought a serious resolve to his many film roles of the 1910s when he played the lone gunfighter of high morals cleaning up evildoing in the Wild West. In films like *Hell's Hinges* (1916) and *Tumbleweeds* (1925) Hart rode alone, was never romantic or emotional, was taciturn and silent in his resolve. "Rin Tin Tin's suffering and adventures are almost analogous to those undergone in countless films by Bill Hart and others of the school of martyred, silent, western heroes," wrote the *Atlanta Constitution* reviewer (February 14, 1922, 7). And as another put it, "Rin Tin Tin shows himself to be as effective a canine actor as ever, shedding real tears when his master dies and portraying most effectively the mental torture of a poor animal pursued and hounded by those who had formerly loved him" (*Variety*, July 22, 1925, 32). Comparing the dog heroes to the swashbuckling Douglas Fairbanks was also high praise from critics, for Fairbanks was the 1920s' greatest embodiment of joyful athleticism, all-American self-confidence, and go-getting personality. Like Strongheart and Rinty, Fairbanks was not primarily a romantic hero, chasing women and pursuing love (actors John Gilbert and Rudolph Valentino had a lock on those roles). The Fairbanks hero saved the damsel in distress as a mere part of saving the day—his greatest joy was to enact Zorro, Robin Hood, or D'Artagnan with energetic jousting against the bad guys and breathtaking physical stunts. Rinty was tagged "The Douglas Fairbanks of Dogdom," with "his most notable stunts being a twelve foot jump, a broad jump clearing ten men crouched in leap frog style, and a twenty foot dive into the water to rescue a human being" ("Silver Sheet Animal Stars in High Life," *Los Angeles Times*, January 1, 1924, E9). Praising Rinty's performance in *Below the Line* (1925), set in southern swamplands, the *Los Angeles Times* reviewer expounded on Rinty's ability to portray suffering, loyalty, and fierceness: "In the earlier sequence where Pat Hartigan, in the role of a villainous deputy sheriff, utterly breaks the brave dog's spirit through brutality, Rin-Tin-Tin gives a remarkable interpretation of a cowardly, fear-stricken animal. He cringes at the approach of a mongrel and runs to shelter when a poodle bites at him. Later on when he senses his kind master, John Harron, and his mother, Edith Yorke, are in trouble, his old fighting spirit is aroused and he brings into action some of his scientifically-trained attributes" (December 7, 1925, A9). The reviewer concluded that the film's climax, in which Rinty singlehandedly fights off a pack of bloodhounds to save his humans, "is probably the most vivid thing of its kind ever seen on the screen—truly a superb piece of acting, it has its human parallel in Richard Barthelmess's fight with the hillbillies in *Tol'able David*," a film famous for the physical and emotional intensity of its violent climax.

Perhaps to offset the tendency to give the dogs too much acting credit, some critics exposed the manufactured/constructed nature of the dog hero's acting skills, such as when an Atlanta reviewer in 1923 wrote, "Acting was harder to learn and harder to teach than other stunts. Rin Tin Tin's greatest difficulty was to learn to take orders without turning his head. His master overcame this by placing him in a room with mirrors for walls so that he could see signals in any position. Gradually he learned to understand the words without the signals. After that it was as easy to direct him as any film actor and often easier"

(*Atlanta Constitution*, October 28, 1923, D1). In the article "Dogs of Screenland Save 'Bad' Pictures," the author noted that "one of the remarkable features of these dogs is that they are often required to show every sign of devotion and love for a character in the picture, who, off stage, they have absolutely no use for, and will not even allow to pet or come near them" (*Los Angeles Times*, September 5, 1923, WF7). Reporters and writers began to talk to trainers about how they manipulated dogs to get the desired expressions and actions, effectively changing a discourse of acting to one of tricks. The "Dogs of Screenland" author goes on to praise and then mock Rinty's athletic abilities as they were sometimes ludicrously employed by far-fetched melodramatic plots: "Besides being a very clever dog actor, Rin Tin Tin is a wonderful all around athlete. He will do a clear high jump over a sixteen hand horse, or a clear broad jump over ten men standing in leap frog position, chew a two inch hemp rope in half in a few seconds. Do a twenty foot dive off a bank or bridge into water and rescue a human body. He will trail a man 700 yards on a trail two hours old and retrieve a postage stamp or other small objects placed at the end of the trail" (*Los Angeles Times*, September 5, 1923, 11).

Nevertheless, the dog hero in the 1920s was often described in the press as "movieland's perfect star" (*Atlanta Constitution*, October 28, 1923, D1). Strongheart was written about as "one motion picture star in Hollywood who has never been divorced, arrested for speeding, mentioned as a co-respondent, hailed as the screen's most perfect lover, or been the object of a prohibition officer's attentions" ("This Screen Actor Leads Quiet Life," *Los Angeles Times*, August 2, 1925, H12). A review of *Clash of the Wolves* (1925) described Rin Tin Tin as "a big handsome actor, with lots of genius, and no conceit. An idol of the ladies who has no idea he's any such thing. A star who's popular with producers, but takes no advantage of the fact and puts his whole soul and all his intelligence into every role he plays, working hard and sincerely every minute, never cheating for the flicker of a Kleig, and who is in addition a family man who loves his wife and is good to his children" (*Chicago Tribune*, December 14, 1925, 23). An Atlanta reviewer noted of Rinty, "It has just occurred to me that Rin Tin Tin is one of the few movie stars about whom I have never heard any scandal. Why is it no one has thought of assuming a knowing look, and say, 'I hear that Mrs. Joe Martin [a movie chimpanzee] and Rin Tin Tin are being seen everywhere together.' Maybe everybody is afraid the know-it-all of the group would promptly come forth with, 'But you're entirely wrong. It's Strongheart she's intrigued with'" (*Atlanta Constitution*, May 9, 1926, F9). Newspaper reporters also found amusement in conducting tongue-in-cheek "interviews" with the canine stars in which the dogs spoke English. Strongheart gave an extended interview to the *Los Angeles Times* expressing sorrow over the unreality of Hollywood moral values. For the same paper, Rinty dished on his human female film co-stars, proclaimed that the movie business is really tough and that actors live "a dog's life" (*Los Angeles Times*, January 20, 1924, F11; March 21, 1926, B14).

The downside of the stardom of dog heroes was experienced not only by the often grueling work and lack of normal activities, especially rest and play, that the canine stars endured (see Elwood 2010). For human actors, writers, and directors there was the mortification of having to play sidekick to a dog. Darryl Zanuck, who got his start in Hollywood writing scenarios for Rinty films, for years expressed how much he had hated doing it (Mosley 1984, 67–71). While Rinty's endeavors brought in needed box-office dollars, they were formulaic adventure films to script. After appearing in three films with Rinty, actor Jason Robards (the dramatic-school-trained father of the later Hollywood star) complained, the tone only partly tongue-in-cheek, to the *Los Angeles Times*:

> It was disheartening. I went to the powers that be. "Mr. Warner and Mr. Warner," I said, "Is that nice? What have I done that I should deserve such treatment? Rinty is as nice a dog as ever barked up a tree; Rinty is a man's pal; Rinty is a great deal more than that. But gentlemen, enough is enough. I have a wife and kiddies to support. I want their faces to light up when I come home o'nights, and when they say to me, Daddy, what are you doing these livelong days? I want to be able to answer, I am not, praise be, acting with Rin Tin Tin." (*Los Angeles Times*, July 31, 1927, C13)

Warner Bros. mercifully tore up Robards's film contract and let him go back to the stage.

Dog Op'ries

Dog hero films of the 1920s (dubbed "dog op'ries" by humorist Will Rogers and other wits) did have pretty standardized plots, primarily following the genres of the western or the north-woods outdoor adventure film (*Los Angeles Times*, February 18, 1924, A7). The dog hero was often introduced in the story as a mixed breed or mixed species—part wolf and part domesticated dog—to frame a story of the dog hero's struggle to decide his path in life, whether to be wild beast or friend and helper of humans. Sometimes he was an orphaned puppy adopted into a wolf pack, or a wolf or wild dog that is transformed through an encounter (or a mythic experience) to gain a close connection to humans. He has to overcome his wild animal urges, but sometimes they emerge to help him be an even fiercer fighter than any regular dog might be.

Cultural studies scholars think of animals like these cinematic dog heroes as "threshold creatures." In her study of dogs in human cultural history, Susan McHugh (2004) asserts that dogs are often narratively used as markers of liminal spaces, being positioned "between nature and culture," between childhood and adulthood, or—as in the classic tale of Cerberus, the multiheaded mythological dog who guards the entrance to the underworld—between life and death (41, 145). Recall, of course, the Thanhouser story *A Dog's Love* for a filmic example of the latter concept, as Shep was placed between the worlds of the living and the dead as he literally lies on a grave. Jonathan Burt (2002) similarly argues that, in modernity, animals in general are often used as the narrative link between "the archaic and the modern" (192). This narrational theory can also be extended into the visual structuring of scenes. For example, dogs often act almost as mirrors—placed directly between linked characters and encouraging the viewer to see the parallels and divergences between the characters on either side. Examples can be found in both the 1914 Thanhouser film *Shep's Race with Death* (in which Shep is constantly positioned between twin girls, one beloved and the other not), and the 1925 protowerewolf film *Wolfblood* (in which a hero and a villain—both suspected of impure blood—are linked). As such a device the dog marks and crosses boundaries—most commonly the boundary between the wild and the domestic.

McHugh's theories also allow us to discuss dogs in their particularity, as she additionally asserts that various breeds go through "cycles of social favor." The breeding of dogs, a practice that is only about three hundred years old, has created a culture in which "breed secures certain meanings for dogs." McHugh's example is the collie (the breed of the later star Lassie), which she says has a recent breed meaning of "loyalty despite class." Lassie chooses the love of her original human family over the wealthy man to whom she has been sold. Additionally, the notion of breed "purity" results in visual stability, as a particular breed evolves an iconic representation that then holds these assumed meanings (McHugh 2004, 58, 66, 90–94, 104–106, 114–115, 128).

The wild dog/wolf scenes in dog hero films of the 1920s allow Strongheart and Rinty to be filmed running across rugged landscapes, jumping over rocks and downed trees, leaping across chasms, majestically posing on the top of rock outcroppings to survey their territory, and leading their packs. Whether he starts as wild or is introduced as a sheepherder or ranch dog, the dog hero is almost always a working dog. No lounging by the fireplace eating dog biscuits and being pampered, or even simply petted, for him. The dog hero has a useful and important place in the ranch or northwestern society, protecting sheep from predators, guiding northwest hunters or tradesmen, serving as companion to a rugged rancher or outdoorsman. The star imagery of both Strongheart and Rin Tin Tin, and several of their film plots, also sometimes involved narratives of wartime trauma during World War I and the strong, fierce characteristics of the breed used in wartime.

The dog hero must also engage in several fierce battles, struggling to defeat villainous men, bad dogs, or even, in one film, an evil condor that has been slaughtering lambs. The dog hero is a lone fighter; no wonder film reviewers compared him to taciturn western star William S. Hart and the athletic loner Douglas Fairbanks. To further milk audiences' anxiety and concern for their dog hero, Rinty's films often featured him having to struggle and make several attempts to achieve his most spectacular physical stunts. In *Find Your Man*

(1924) Rinty plays a dog (Buddy) who a reviewer notes is "the only witness to a cowardly shooting of his master." The villain is afraid the dog will rat him out and orders someone to kill him; instead, the henchman binds and gags Buddy, planning to take him off and sell him, but the dog escapes and rescues his master at the courthouse trial. "Outside one sees the indomitable and faithful Buddy endeavoring to leap over the door and through the transom to the court scene. He tries once and fails. Then a second time without success. After a long run and a terrific leap he gets up and bounds into the crowded room. Horror strikes the real murderer as he sees the four footed hero springing at him with a nasty snarl and bared teeth" (*New York Times*, September 23, 1924, 26).

Sometimes the dog star's heroics surely stretched the viewer's credulity, especially as the "dog op'ry" genre wore on. The reviewer for the *New York Times* termed Rinty's 1924 melodrama *The Lighthouse by the Sea* "lurid" but continues in admiration for the dog if not the plot:

> But the dog's big moment is toward the final chapter when somebody has to light the lighthouse lamp. Dorn is gagged and bound, the heroine has been kidnapped, and the old blind father has been injured by ruffianly bootleggers. Even Rin Tin Tin has been tied up in a strong bag. He gnaws his way free, carries a box of matches over to Dorn who is hung up struggling. The matches can just be touched by the hero's feet and so he manages to ignite some of them, Rin Tin Tin helps his master still further, and then, after Dorn has caused oil-saturated waste to catch fire, the dog scampers up the lighthouse steps with the blazing waste and eventually puts it down the great cylinder, and the streak of light is seen by the revenue cutter. This film is worthwhile seeing for the amazing actions of Rin Tin Tin. (December 29, 1924, 11)

The two dog heroes did have softer sides to display, and here their reported acting skills came to the fore. They nuzzle a human baby or a lamb, they are instantly docile and friendly around sweet frontier heroines, and they show tender love by licking the face of a wounded hero. The dog hero shows love and compassion, worry, and also fear, longing, and guilt, and confusion when they are unjustly accused of doing evil, such as being accused of killing a baby or a lamb. When the northwestern trapper goes to whip Rinty for supposedly killing a baby in *Where the North Begins*, the animal's large dark eyes and face show such sadness, mutely appearing to ask, "Why am I being falsely accused?" (Audiences never seemed to wonder about how such "expressions" were elicited; for more on [often punitive] dog-training methods in this era see Elwood 2010.)

The dog hero film genre, with its thrills and strong emotions, appealed to a wide range of audiences that urban critics sniffed at as "unsophisticated"—children and the small-town audiences who appreciated westerns and action films, but also female audiences who enjoyed feeling sentimental about faithful dogs. Exhibitor trade journals like *Variety* warned theater owners that dog hero

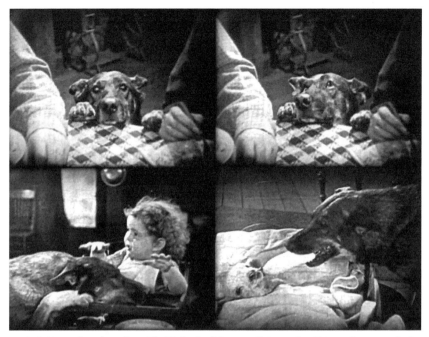

Rin Tin Tin in four shots from *The Night Cry* (Herman C. Raymaker, Warner Bros., 1926), the first two exemplifying his "What did I do?" look. In the fourth image he is feeding a lamb with a baby bottle. Digital frame enlargements.

films did not draw well at big city picture palaces (April 14, 1926, 27). *New York Times* reviewer Mordaunt Hall made especial note of the large numbers of children and mothers in the audience of the Warner Theater for Rinty's *The Night Cry* (1926) and their absorption in the action:

> One little fellow with curly, golden hair clutched the rail, fearing to let go his hold even to clap his little hands. At the same time he wished to let Rin-Tin-Tin know that he appreciated the dog's heroism. So he gleefully yelled his shrill appreciation. There were groans when an eagle swooped down on a child and supposedly carried it away to the rocky heights, and the youngsters thought that neither Rin-Tin-Tin nor the woman would ever get free in time to rescue the little girl. The mother was bolted in a shack, the dog was tethered to a beam, and struggle as he would the rope would not break. It was an awful period to the children, and their delight was boundless when simultaneously the mother managed to slip the bolt on the door and Rin-Tin-Tin broke away from his harness. (April 7, 1926, 26)

Exhibitor trade journal reviewers were also often dismissive of dog hero films and their audiences, except when noting the positive box office returns. Of one Rinty vehicle, *A Race for Life* (1928), the *Variety* reviewer noted that "enjoyment of a picture such as this requires a naïve and sentimental disposition plus a regard for dogs." The reviewer suggested that this film might be suitable for a double bill in an urban theater, but in small towns "the dog opera can and does stand alone, unaided and unapologetic. . . . There is enough heart tug of a sort to have the kids whistling at Saturday matinees" (February 1, 1928, 28). The *Atlanta Constitution* reviewer intimated that Rinty in a romantic setting could inspire women in the audience to swoon as if he were Valentino or John Gilbert: "Paired with a female dog of exceeding beauty, Rinty brings the sighs from the feminine portions of his audiences, and later in the picture, when three puppies are suddenly brought on the scene, the exclamations are decidedly audible" (October 5, 1926, 20). As the *Chicago Tribune* reviewer baldly stated in the headline for its review of Rinty's *The Night Cry*, "Rin Tin Tin will make you weep, but you'll enjoy each sob" (*Chicago Tribune*, May 12, 1926, 39).

Moreover, film reviewers argued over which was the best use of the dog hero: to be the main focus of the film or to have his doings interwoven with a plot about humans. On one hand, some reviewers, like one at the *Los Angeles Times*, criticized the film *White Fang* (1925) for having Strongheart play too minor a role (June 22, 1925, A7). *Variety's* critic, on the other hand, noted that "the most successful pictures featuring Rin Tin Tin, Strongheart and other dog actors have not played up the canine side too strongly, but have introduced it merely as interwoven with a plot of human beings that holds a good deal of interest in itself. *Tracked in the Snow Country* makes the mistake of focusing the spotlight on its animal actors, and its star in particular, to the almost total exclusion of the men and women in the cast. The result seems to be a certain amount of monotony" (July 22, 1925, 32).

Although apparently none of Strongheart's films from his prime years has survived to be restored for viewing today, a half-dozen of Rinty's silent films still exist. For contemporary audiences who can look past the cheaply made sets, sometimes wooden acting of the humans, and often formulaic plots, Rinty is still a vibrant performer. He is portrayed as intelligent—opening doors, cleverly hiding in hollowed logs and under piles of clothes and in children's beds, pointing out a well-stocked fishing hole. He is athletic—climbing trees, boulders, and mountains; racing across fields; swimming in swift rivers. He battles his foes fiercely, tumbling through the air locked in mortal combat with a condor, even when one can see that the pack of wild dogs attacking him might be hand puppets pushed into his face. The viewer is drawn to Rinty's point of view to sympathize with and root for him, such as when he expresses worry and sorrow—he pleads for understanding with his huge sad eyes or looks scared and sad as he grovels on the ground before the master who is about to shoot him. He does cute things to demonstrate his gentleness and sentimentality, nuzzling a human baby in its crib, feeding a lamb from a baby bottle and licking its face, and providing friendship to a lonely crippled child. The dog hero holds up well as a silent film actor.

From Career to Legend

In 1927 critics began to notice that Rinty was getting on in years, and that his stunts weren't quite as astounding as in his earlier days:

> Considering his age, Rin Tin Tin displays wonderful activity in his new film. . . . If this animal was born in the French trenches during the war he is about 9 years old, roughly the equivalent of a man of 63. There are not many men of that age who could go through what Rin-Tin-Tin does in this screen adventure. He is like a d'Artagnan of dogs, and he seems to have many a day in this production. He is cunning enough to keep quiet when the villain is searching for him, and he not only evens up scores with this rogue but saves the heroine from going to her death over a cataract. . . . It is evident that Rin-Tin-Tin is extraordinarily sagacious. He seems to enjoy the work, whether it is diving into the river, hiding in a hollow tree trunk or getting into a barrel of water and ducking every time Ben Harley turns his head in Rin-Tin-Tin's direction. (*New York Times*, March 2, 1927, 29)

For a confluence of reasons, in the late 1920s the dog hero's stardom dimmed. Both Strongheart and Rinty were elder statesmen now, each over seventy in human years, and they could no longer carry out the strenuous action sequences of their prime days. Stunt doubles handled more of the action. Strongheart had been semiretired since Trimble's divorce left the dog in Murfin's hands; he appeared in a relatively small role in one more film, *The Return of Boston Blackie* (1927), and unfortunately this, the sole film available for viewing today, does not show the tired old warrior to advantage. In contrast, Rinty was still a prominent Warner Bros. star, and he made a cameo appearance in the studio's first all-talkie extravaganza *The Show of Shows* (1929), appearing briefly as a master of ceremonies in a color sequence, introducing with his barks a Chinese fantasy musical sequence in which Myrna Loy impersonated an oriental dancer.

The new technology of sound reproduction, added to silent film in 1927, brought waves of upheaval to Hollywood filmmaking. "Talkies" necessitated that actors speak and sing as well as bark; they had to have voices that pleased the microphone and seemed to match their star personalities (Rinty had no reported problems with his voice tests). But they also had to memorize dialogue and emote through long scenes without the constant coaching and intervention of their directors, which was a significant problem for dog actors who needed to take commands from their trainers. Duncan claimed to be able to overcome that difficulty for Rinty by means of silent commands and other tricks. But harder to get around was the public's perceived weariness of westerns, northwestern snow pictures, and lone, silent athletic heroes. William S. Hart had retired, and Douglas Fairbanks was not far behind him. As the Depression deepened in the 1930s, the public seemed to want musicals and fast-paced urban stories of gangsters and cops. The day of the dog hero seemed to be over. In December 1929 Warner Bros. even released the aging Rinty—and therefore Lee Duncan—from his contract (*Variety*, January 8, 1930, 80). The formerly popular western and snow-country action genres were reduced to Saturday afternoon children's show fodder, and Strongheart and Rinty moved over to the Poverty Row studios to make low-budget serials. Strongheart's career ended in 1929 when he reportedly fell against a hot studio light while filming and developed a tumor and died at age thirteen (*Los Angeles Times*, June 25, 1929, A3). Rin Tin Tin's career continued with several more low-budget sound films at the Mascot Studios and a twelve-part serial, *The Lightning Warrior* (1931). Duncan still performed with Rinty in personal appearances at theaters around the country, and explored new media forms; Rinty was featured in a series of popular radio programs geared to children in the early 1930s, a fifteen-minute weekly drama on the NBC Blue Network for which Rinty purportedly barked his own lines in the drama and the commercials (his part was really performed by a sound effects crewman) (*Chicago Tribune*, March 8, 1931, K9). But his career could not last forever, and Rinty died in 1932, at the ostensible age of fourteen (but not in the arms of Jean Harlow). Both dog hero deaths made the front pages of newspapers across the United States.

Fame, however, was not finished with these two talented movie stars. Strongheart and his mate Lady Jule produced a number of puppies whose line continues, although they are not actors. Strongheart has continued to be the face and namesake of Strongheart canned dog food, his face gracing product cans down to the present day. Larry Trimble left film directing in 1926 to spend the rest of his career training seeing-eye dogs; he died in 1954 (*Variety*, February 10, 1954; Gallo 2002). In 1939 J. Allen Boone published a book called *Letters to Strongheart* chronicling his deep emotional connection and communication with the dog during life (he had been a friend of Trimble and Murfin's). After Strongheart's death Boone began writing the dog letters, and these he published as contemplations of the survival of the dog's soul after death and the unconditional love of animals for the humans who are willing to share their lives with them and learn from them. Boone wrote of the enduring qualities of Strongheart's soul that transcended the mere physical body: "goodness, loyalty, understanding, enthusiasm, fidelity, devotion, sincerity, nobility, affection, intelligence, honesty, confidence, strength, gentleness, happiness, gratitude, appreciation, trustworthiness, endurance, integrity, humility, purity, unselfishness, fearlessness, [and] love" (Boone 1939/2007, 4–6). The book and its sequel, *Kinship with All Life* (1954/1976), have been reprinted many times and remain classics of the Spiritualist faith.

Lee Duncan, ever the promoter, continued Rin Tin Tin's exploits, first through the dog hero's son Rin Tin Tin Jr., who continued to "appear" on the radio, in person, and in movie serials throughout the 1930s. Rinty IV (whose coat was a much lighter color than his great grandfather's and so whose direct

Multimedia dog stardom in the 1920s. The covers of the children's books *Strongheart: The Story of a Wonder Dog* (Racine, Wisc.: Whitman, 1926), written by Larry Trimble; and *Little Folks' Story of Rin Tin Tin* (Racine, Wisc.: Whitman, 1927), author unknown. Collection of Kathryn Fuller-Seeley.

relation to the original might be suspect) found television fame in a popular ABC series *The Adventures of Rin Tin Tin* (1954–1959), which featured standard western plots enlivened by the addition of Rin Tin Tin's daring deeds on the frontier with the 101st Cavalry at the side of his boy companion, Rusty (Lee Aaker). Rinty's career was lovingly parodied in Paramount's 1976 comedy *Won Ton Ton: The Dog Who Saved Hollywood*, which features cameo appearances by dozens of old movie stars from the 1920s, 1930s, and 1940s. Seventy years after his death, Rinty remains a subject of fascination; he has been the subject of two recent biographies. Ann Elwood's *Rin-Tin-Tin: The Movie Star* (2010) focuses on meticulous research into the facts rather than the legends about Rinty's film career and examines the details of his training, adding fascinating insights that reconstruct how an intelligent dog could be made to seem to express such a range of emotions and physical abilities in the magical medium of silent film. Susan Orlean's *Rin Tin Tin: The Life and the Legend* (2011) is concerned primarily with Duncan's penchants for storytelling and heroic mythmaking, and her book dwells more on ruminations about the evolution of the place of dogs in human society over the past century and on her own tangential journeys to connect with the quirky characters revolving around Rinty's legacy rather than on unpacking the veracity of the myths and stories themselves.

Strongheart and Rin Tin Tin, the best known of the dog heroes of Hollywood films in the 1920s, left significant legacies in American film and popular culture. They were bona fide movie stars, representing admirable celebrity behavior in press coverage and earning large sums for both their trainers and the production companies for whom they toiled. They won the great loyalty and affection of film audiences in the United States and around the world. They were successful "spokesdogs" and brand symbols for consumer products, pitching shoe polish, children's books, and fresh fruit, as well as dog food. Their highly praised acting and charismatic film personas taught the film industry that nonhuman actors could successfully carry a film narrative, paving the way for future generations of featured performers such as Asta and Lassie, along with Rin Tin Tin IV on television in the 1950s. We can never know how they felt about their work in the movies, no matter how many "letters" we might write to them; but for better or for worse, Strongheart and Rin Tin Tin live on in the dreams of anyone who wants to believe that someday, somewhere, a dog would jump off a cliff to save them or would willingly give its life for a human "master."

Notes

The authors acknowledge the invaluable contributions of Gloria Yoo, who did the bulk of the primary source research and helped enormously in the creation of the illustrations and the writing of the essay. Gloria's passion for scholarship and learning are inspirational.

Chronological Filmography

Where the Winds Blow (Laurence Trimble, December 1910). Jean the Dog.

Playmates (director unknown, February 1912). Julia Swayne Gordon, Hazel Neason, Florence Foley, Alec B. Francis, Edith Halleran, Jean the Dog.

A Dog's Love (Jack Harvey, October 1914). Shep the Dog, Helen Badgley, Arthur Bauer, Ethyle Cooke.

Shep's Race with Death (Jack Harvey, November 1914). Shep the Dog, Mrs. Whitcove, J. S. Murray.

The Silent Call (Laurence Trimble, November 1921). Strongheart the Dog, John Bowers, Kathryn McGuire.

The Man from Hell's River (Irving Cummings, May 1922). Irving Cummings, Eva Novak, Wallace Beery, Frank Whitson, Rin Tin Tin.

Where the North Begins (Chester M. Franklin, July 1923). Clair Adams, Fred Huntley, Walter McGrail, Pat Hartigan, Myrtle Owen, Rin Tin Tin [as Rin-tin-tin].

Find Your Man (September 1924, Malcolm St. Clair). June Marlowe, Rin Tin Tin, Eric St. Clair.

The Lighthouse by the Sea (Malcolm St. Clair, December 1924). William Collier Jr., Rin Tin Tin, Louise Fazenda, Charles Hill Mailes.

White Fang (Laurence Trimble, May 1925). Theodore von Eltz, Ruth Dwyer, Matthew Betz, Walter Perry, Strongheart the Dog.

Tracked in the Snow Country (Herman C. Raymaker, July 1925). Rin Tin Tin, June Marlowe, David Butler, Mitchell Lewis.

Below the Line (Herman C. Raymaker, September 1925). John Harron, Rin Tin Tin, June Marlowe, Pat Hartigan.

Clash of the Wolves (Noel M. Smith, November 1925). Rin Tin Tin, Nanette [dog], Charles Farrell, June Marlowe.

The Night Cry (Herman C. Raymaker, February 1926). Rin Tin Tin, John Harron, June Marlowe, Gayne Whitman.

Hills of Kentucky (Howard Bretherton, February 1927). Rin Tin Tin, Jason Robards Sr., Dorothy Dwan.

The Outlaw Dog (J. P. McGowan, May 1927). Ranger the Dog, Helen Foster, Rex Lease.

Breed of Courage (Howard M. Mitchell, August 1927). Sam Nelson, Jean Fenwick, Stanton Heck, Ogoma [dog].

The Return of Boston Blackie (Harry O. Hoyt, August 1927). Strongheart the Dog, Bob Custer, Corliss Palmer.

A Race for Life (D. Ross Lederman, January 1928). Rin Tin Tin, Virginia Brown Faire, Carroll Nye.

The Show of Shows (John G. Adolfi, December 1929). Frank Fay, William Courtenay, H. B. Warner, Hobart Bosworth, John Barrymore, Mary Astor, Richard Barthelmess, Noah Beery, Sally Blane, Monte Blue, Jack Buchanan [et al.], Rin Tin Tin.

The Lightning Warrior (Benjamin H. Kline / Armand Schaefer, 1931). Rin Tin Tin, Frankie Darro, Georgia Hale, George Brent.

Won Ton Ton: The Dog Who Saved Hollywood (Michael Winner, 1976). Dennis Morgan, Shecky Greene, Phil Leeds, Madeline Kahn, Teri Garr, Bruce Dern [et al.], Augustus von Schumacher [dog].

3

Asta the Screwball Dog

• •

Hollywood's Canine Sidekick

SARA ROSS AND

JAMES CASTONGUAY

In late October 1937, newspaper readers in Gettysburg, Pennsylvania, learned that "a dog's life is not so tough when the dog works in the movies." A syndicated article recounted publicity about the "home" of Skippy, the canine star who played Asta in the popular Thin Man films, along with a number of other iconic screwball roles. Skippy/Asta was said to be the resident of "a full-sized building, with human-sized doors and windows, hot and cold running water, boneburying pits, automatic vacuum flea removers and mechanical cats to chase" (*Gettysburg Times*, October 30, 1937, 8). At the time this article appeared, during the Great Depression, Pennsylvania had received more federal relief than any other state, and "jobless army" protests and labor unrest were widespread (see Coode and Bauman 1981).

The star narrative developed for Skippy/Asta had a great deal in common with those of his human counterparts in Hollywood, right down to the detailed description of the privileged life that he led as a star. Like much that was written about movie stars, of course, Skippy's life of luxury was a fantasy created by studio publicists. In fact, animal stars like Skippy provide the ultimate example of the disconnect between the escapist construct that is the Hollywood star narrative and the actual labor of the film performer. As an animal actor Skippy

Skippy on the set of *After the Thin Man* (W. S. Van Dyke, MGM, 1936). Collection of the authors.

was not in a position to demand better pay or working conditions or to interfere with how studios and filmmakers might choose to represent him, either in publicity or in his performances themselves. His role was purely one of laborer, commodity, and manipulable image.

In fact, unlike his human co-stars, even Skippy's death had little impact on "Asta," the star. In spite of his status as a beloved Hollywood icon and his ongoing popularity, when the hardworking flesh-and-blood dog who first brought the Asta character to life on the screen died in 1944, his passing went unmentioned in the press. With a little bit of makeup to adjust the placement of patches on their coats, new "Astas" were brought in to take his place. If human stars were a replaceable and malleable commodity in Hollywood, how much more so were dog actors, whose star personae could be almost wholly independent of their physical existence? The exaggerated gap between the star "Asta" and the real dogs whose labor brought him to life indicates the relevance to star studies generally of close examination of animal as well as human stars. Animal star biographies and screen performances provide useful insights into the promotional and publicity machinery that Hollywood also employed to construct much of the public's understanding of human stars of the 1930s and 1940s.

In this essay we explore Asta, the canine star, in order to understand his extraordinary and enduring presence within U.S. popular culture. As we will show, the flexibility of Asta's identity onscreen and in various intertexts is key to his cultural meaning, particularly with regard to charged issues that are salient in the screwball comedy, such as class, labor, gender, romance, and marital dynamics. First we examine how Skippy/Asta was constructed as a canine star; then we analyze his roles in individual films. This close look at the making of Asta the dog star not only provides insights into his place in film history but also refreshes our understanding of the constructedness of all star narratives.

The Asta Phenomenon

Commenting on the phenomenal popularity of MGM's *The Thin Man* (1934), William Powell's biographer Roger Bryant (2006) observes that "audiences loved Nick and Nora [played by Powell and Myrna Loy] . . . [but the] moviegoing public also loved Asta, [whose] popularity spawned a national craze for wire-haired fox terriers" (10).[1] According to a Loy biographer, during the 1930s "the threesome [Loy, Powell, and Asta]—elegant, bantering couple plus winsome, mischievous dog—had become emblems of a brand, like Coca-Cola. Their likenesses, on display everywhere, could not be escaped, unless you stayed home day and night with the shades drawn" (Leider 2012, 133).

The popular press reported that the canine actor "receiv[ed] fan letters by the hundreds," and that "movie fans in Chicago almost picked [him] to pieces, getting hairs for souvenirs" (J. B. Griswold, "A Dog's Life in Hollywood," *American Magazine*, August 22, 1938, 16; Alexander Kahn, "Asta, Stand-In Visit Britain," *Calgary Daily Herald*, December 27, 1938, 5). A major star by the end of the 1930s, Skippy/Asta appeared with Loy on the cover of *Modern Screen* (September 1939) and with Powell on the cover of the men's magazine *True Detective* (March 1942). At the peak of his popularity in 1940, newspapers across the United States reported that "not only [does Asta] receive many requests for . . . autographs (paw or nose prints)," but he had earned a "'Boscar' [for being] the best masculine dog performer in the movies" ("'Boscars' Go to Canines," *Los Angeles Times*, February 26, 1940, 8; "Laurels for Animals," *Brookshire [Texas] Times*, November 1, 1940, 7).

Although Asta is conspicuously absent from the initial promotional posters and the opening credits for *The Thin Man*, the first film in the series (he appears for less than two seconds in the trailer), by the time the surprise hit made it to smaller cities and towns, the dog was the star of the show. For the film's run at the Paramount Theater in Ogden, Utah, a large newspaper advertisement

The phenomenal popularity of *The Thin Man* in 1934 created an Asta "craze" along with a black market for wire-haired terrier puppies. Myrna Loy, William Powell, and Skippy in a publicity photo for *The Thin Man* (W. S. Van Dyke, MGM, 1934). Collection of the authors.

featuring an illustration of a terrier (without Powell or Loy) announced, "Asta is the hit of *The Thin Man*. . . and honestly, folks, when a dog can steal a show from two stars like William Powell and Myrna Loy . . . he's some dog!" (*Ogden Standard-Examiner*, July 26, 1934, 3). For the next decade and a half, Asta would remain central to the Thin Man series' marketing and promotion and become an all-encompassing signifier equated with his breed, its representations, and all wire-haired-terrier commodities or products.

Skippy/Asta's popularity and earning potential allowed his co-owner Henry East "to turn down small roles and limit his output to no more than four pictures a year" (*Kingsport [Tenn.] Times*, December 7, 1937, 6). By 1939 Skippy reportedly had a "clause in his contract which [gave] him top screen billing over any

Skippy/Asta became central to the marketing and promotion for the Thin Man series. MGM trade advertisement for *After the Thin Man* (*Motion Picture Herald*, January 2, 1937). Collection of the authors.

other animal actor" (*Burlington [N.C.] Daily Times-News*, July 22, 1939, 4) and was being singled out by critics for his thirty close-ups in *Another Thin Man* ("a record for [an] animal actor") (*Panama City News-Herald*, August 11, 1939, 4). As the above publicity suggests, between the 1934 release of *The Thin Man* and the appearance of Pal in MGM's *Lassie Come Home* in 1943, Skippy/ Asta was routinely described as "the screen's most famous canine star" and "the most beloved dog in motion pictures" ("Asta Most Popular Dog on Screen Now," *Zanesville [Ohio] Sunday Time-Signal*, November 4, 1934, sec. 2, 6; "Skippy Puts on the Dog," *Carroll [Iowa] Daily Herald*, March 11, 1938, 4; "Noted Canine Actor Can't Read but Studies Script," *Los Angeles Times*, November 6, 1938, C3; see also Katharine Roberts, "These Animals Pay Income Taxes," *Los Angeles Times*, November 26, 1939, I12; Orr 1936; Weatherwax and

Rothwell 1950; Edelson 1980; Rothel 1980; Beck and Clark 2002; Allred 2004; Muszynski 2007).

In addition to Skippy/Asta's place in the Hollywood star system of the 1930s and 1940s, film critics and scholars have also acknowledged his significant historical role within the genre of screwball comedy. According to James Harvey (1987), "*The Thin Man* sets the pattern by which screwball couples always have an animal of some kind instead of a child" (123), and Ed Sikov (1989) goes so far as to suggest "that [Asta the] screwball animal . . . [is] perhaps the most prolific actor in the genre" (201). Indeed, Skippy/Asta appeared in three historically significant films from the 1930s screwball cycle: *The Thin Man* (considered to be one of three or four films from 1934 that started the genre [see Balio 1996; Harvey 1987]), *The Awful Truth* (considered by many to be the "purest" screwball film [see Harvey 1987]), and *Bringing Up Baby* (1939), which has not only been described as a "definitive" (Laham 2009), "archetypal" (Gehring 2002), and "extreme" (Wood 2003) screwball comedy but was viewed contemporaneously by movie critics as marking the beginning of the end (or exhausting) the screwball cycle (see Frank S. Nugent, "The Cliché Expert Encounters *Bringing Up Baby* at the Music Hall," *New York Times*, March 4, 1938, 17; Laham 2009, 29).

But it is unlikely that Skippy would have become a canine star, never mind a screwball icon, had MGM not turned Asta from the female Schnauzer of the Dashiell Hammett novel that serves as the series' loose source material into the male wire-haired fox terrier of the films. In addition to launching Skippy's career, this modification changed the character's potential connotations and meanings in important ways, especially as the rise of fascism in Germany and the eventual outbreak of war dominated U.S. headlines. In addition to gendering Asta as Nick's loyal male sidekick, the change in breed avoided the kind of anti-German sentiment later documented by a 1955 *Sports Illustrated* cover story that noted that a "week after World War II was declared . . . dachshunds were being stoned in the streets and kicked and . . . many were having tin cans tied to their tails" (Wells 1955, 39).

Published a year before the release of *The Thin Man*, Leonard E. Naylor's *The Modern Wire Haired Fox Terrier: Its History, Points & Training* (1932) provides a historical understanding of the breed that uncannily anticipates and complements *The Thin Man*'s meanings and structure: "The well-to-do and the working-man appreciate equally his sterling worth. . . . He is the best 'mixer' of all; a democrat with the bearing of a patrician; a dog who fills the picture wherever he may be. His popularity, to those who know him, gives little cause for wonderment; the wonder is that so many dog-lovers up to now have denied themselves the pleasure and privilege of his companionship" (226–232). Naylor's description resonates with arguments made by scholars and critics about the cross-class appeal present in the Thin Man films (discussed below) and the multiple avenues of identification available to its audience as a result (see Castonguay 2011). In addition, this anglicized version of Asta also supports Mark

Winokur's argument that the Thin Man films transform Myrna Loy and William Powell from their early roles as ethnic immigrants, threatening exotics, and foreign villains into the WASP couple Nick and Nora Charles. At the same time, one could argue, following Winokur, that Asta's uncultured and baser animal instincts—including his attraction to fire hydrants—exacerbate the ideological ambivalences and contradictions that undermine *The Thin Man*'s "Fantasy of Assimilation" (Winokur 1996, 176) for 1930s moviegoers.

Another significant adaptation from Hammett's novel is the shift from the more serious literary detective genre[2] to the screwball comedy written by husband-and-wife screenwriting team Albert Hackett and Frances Goodrich. Here, too, according to Diana Thorne in *Nature*, wire-haired terriers were perfectly cast for the part because "they have a wonderful sense of humor [and] are the practical jokers of all dogdom. . . . Undoubtedly, for these qualities, the wire-hair was chosen in preference to any dog to be the light comedian in *The Thin Man* and *After the Thin Man*" ("Diana Thorne's Dog Column," *Nature*, April 1937, 254).

A Suave Technique for Scene Stealing

As we move from discussions of the breed to Skippy/Asta's specific canine star "story," articles begin to emphasize his unique characteristics and talents as an animal actor. As Gertrude Orr put it in her 1936 children's book *Dog Stars of Hollywood*, "Dogs are like people. Some are smarter than others. Some are born to be stars and some are just dogs all their lives. . . . By the time he was a year old, Skippy had made his way through dog college and won his diploma" (chap. 2). According to a *Los Angeles Times* article, kennel owner Henry East "observed that [Skippy's] eyes were not merely expressive, but had definite black rims around them that would lessen the amount of make-up usually necessary to make animal's eyes photograph well" ("These Animals Pay Income Taxes," *Los Angeles Times*, November 26, 1939, I12). In addition to this physical advantage, other stories used anthropomorphic tropes to describe Skippy's remarkable intelligence and unique personal qualities. We learn that "Skippy . . . wants to be a photographer and doesn't care who knows it" (*Gettysburg Times*, November 20, 1937), and that he "studies his scripts" with a strong work ethic and commitment to his craft ("Noted Canine Actor Can't Read but Studies Script," *Los Angeles Times*, November 6, 1938, C3). "Skippy [is] not only one of the most photogenic pups in Hollywood," notes Katharine Roberts in the *Los Angeles Times*, "but [has] a highly magnetic personality and a suave technique for scene-stealing" ("These Animals Pay Income Taxes," I12). The anthropomorphization in Skippy/Asta's star narrative extends to descriptions of the perks he enjoys as a canine star and his skills at promoting himself. According to one article, "Asta of The Thin Man tales has his own dressing room, script bag and script, [and] a canvas container for his dog biscuits," and "he poses for portraits with the aplomb of a Boyer" ("Don't Let Your Pet Read This or He'll Go Howlywood," *Oakland Tribune*, April 29, 1945, 63).

Although Asta's publicity would normally (or inescapably) rely on humans speaking for the dog, Mayme Ober Peak attempted to bring fans even closer to Asta's point of view by adopting his subjectivity and speaking *as* the dog:

> One day, when I was about two months old, a nice looking couple stopped by [the pet store]. . . . Some money passed over the counter [and] I was taken home to North Hollywood. . . . Most of the next year and a half was spent training me, with emphasis placed on what they call obedience. Then I became what is known as "Atmosphere." I didn't get any reputation until they put me in *The Thin Man* with that swell fellow William Powell; that made me what they call a star and changed my name from Skippy to Asta. ("Stars in the Making: How a Dog Was Made a Dog Star," *Boston Globe*, January 9, 1939, 10)

The "nice looking couple" was Henry East and former actress Gale Henry East, who owned the kennel that housed Skippy and employed future Pal/Lassie owner Rudd Weatherwax as his trainer.[3] An article about the Easts in the August 1938 issue of *American Magazine* notes that Skippy "tops the list of plain dogs that are fancy actors [and] is [a] leading star in pictures [who] leads a glamorous life—a dog's life de luxe. He is rated as one of the smartest dogs in the world, and when contracts are signed for his appearance in a picture he gets $200 a week for putting his paw print" (J. B. Griswold, "A Dog's Life in Hollywood," *American Magazine*, August 22, 1938, 16). Although the article notes that another East dog, "Corky [*Garden of Allah* (1936) and *Theodora Goes Wild* (1936)], was bought for $3 by Mrs. East, and last year his income was $3,600," the details of Skippy's acquisition are conspicuously absent, most likely owing to the more complicated ownership history described in an article published in 1941:

> Asta, famous Thin Man dog, had a lean period in his career like every other star. Now one of the biggest money-making dogs of all time, Asta was once given away by his owner and trainer, Henry East, because the movies didn't want him. . . . Fortunately, East held a contract giving him the right to work this dog in a picture if he was ever wanted. Along came Metro-Goldwyn-Mayer's *The Thin Man*. Asta got the job with William Powell and Myrna Loy and became a star overnight. His real name is Skippy, MGM owning all rights to the name "Asta." During the making of *Another Thin Man*, the people owning Asta were divorced and East bought him back at a fancy price. ("Asta, Just Like All Stars, Had Lean Days," *Cumberland [Md.] Sunday Times*, September 21, 1941, 7)

While the above account refers to MGM's legal rights to the character and name "Asta," an earlier promotional story for *The Awful Truth* claimed that "[Skippy] has answered to Asta so much that . . . he refused to respond to his new character name. ("Skippy Puts on the Dog as Mr. Smith in Film," *Carroll [Iowa] Daily Herald*, March 1, 1938, 4). The article eventually reveals that the nickname "Smitty" (from "Mr. Smith") was used because it "sounded enough like Skippy to fool the canine." This publicity thus allowed Columbia to exploit both "Skippy" and "Asta" to promote its film and suggests the degree to which Skippy had become conflated economically and culturally with his Asta role. Although Skippy was never under an exclusive MGM contract like Loy and Powell were, the studio nonetheless owned "Asta," which at once defined the canine's career while complicating it whenever he was cast in non-Asta and non-MGM films.[4]

When the film electrician Alvie M. Jeffers and his wife, who acquired Skippy from East during his "lean days," were divorced a year after release of *The Awful Truth* in 1938, it became front-page news across the country. According to the Associated Press, "Mrs. Jeffers [was seeking] a share in the $19,000 annual earnings of her husband's dog, Asta, canine film star," adding that the dispute was "as screwball as the screwball comedy, *The Awful Truth*, in which Asta played the part of the dog, 'Mr. Smith'" (*Long Beach Independent*, November 25, 1938, 1; see also "Couple Battle over Dog Actor: Film Electrician and Wife Seek Earnings of Talented Canine," *Los Angeles Times*, November 22, 1938, 12). It is quite likely that this less-than-ideal ownership arrangement (compared to other East dogs like Corky, whom they bought outright for three dollars) had a negative impact on Skippy's career, since it meant that the Easts were perhaps less motivated financially to advocate for him in starring or leading roles. This may explain why a series of one-reelers starring Skippy, announced in the *New York Times*, never materialized (January 17, 1938) and why Corky—who did not approach Asta's level of stardom or income—was given equal space in the above-mentioned *American Magazine* article, in which we learn that "Mrs. East declares that Corky is a lot smarter than Skippy, a statement which is challenged by trainers in the kennels" (August 22, 1938, 17).

Unlike Strongheart, Rin Tin Tin, and Lassie, then, who received top billing above and more screen time than their human co-stars, Skippy's roles—although integral to the narrative, marketing, and overall popularity of the films in which he appeared—remained limited to a supporting role or at times that of the "scene stealing" co-star. In its review of the original Thin Man film, the *New York Times* film critic remarked "the wire-haired terrier [is] among [those] who serve the film well." The local reviewer for the *Piqua [Ohio] Daily Call* remarked that "Asta, the wire haired terrier, is deserving of as many compliments as other principals" (July 18, 1934, 6). Similarly, although the *Newark Advocate* described Minna Gombell as being only "competent as the divorced wife" [with] all lesser roles [in] capable hands," the review made a special note that "one of the outstanding roles in the story is that of 'Asta' the terrier" and emphasized that "the dog stands right out in front in ability" (June 29, 1934, 15).

Skippy/Asta, shown in a publicity photo (top) for *The Awful Truth* (Leo McCarey, Columbia, 1937) with costars Irene Dunne and Cary Grant, was arguably the most prolific actor in screwball comedy. In the photo below, for *The Thin Man Goes Home* (1945), with costars William Powell and Myrna Loy, Skippy, who died in 1944, has been replaced by Asta Jr. (billed as Asta) in the role of Asta. Collection of the authors.

The *Los Angeles Times* review of *After the Thin Man* observed that "Asta has his troubles [when his] home is invaded by a stranger [which] turns out to be the main triangle part of the plot" (Edwin Schallert, "Sequel to *Thin Man* First-Rate Entertainment," *Los Angeles Times*, December 31, 1936, 10). When *Another Thin Man* was released in 1939—having been delayed while William Powell was being treated for colon cancer—publicity emphasized that Asta's role would take on even more importance with the introduction of a baby, "Nick, Jr.," into the Charles family, who was "selected after a search which brought 872 babies into the studios for interviews and tests. . . . Powell and Miss Loy still have their pet dog Asta. In *After the Thin Man* Nick and Nora's pet had a mate and a family, [but it] is a bigger part than ever for Asta [in *Another Thin Man*]. The dog has some 30 close-ups" (*Milwaukee Journal*, December 10, 1939, 8).[5]

Although critics never saw Skippy/Asta as overshadowing Loy's or Powell's performances in the Thin Man films, Benjamin Cisler's otherwise unenthusiastic review of *The Awful Truth* in the *New York Times* singles out Asta's stunt gag as the comedic high point: "Its funniest scene [is] that of the dog, Mr. Smith (Asta of *The Thin Man*) playing hide-and-seek, and repeatedly dragging out the incriminating derby hat from where Irene Dunne has hidden it" (November 5, 1937). Similarly, in its review of the 1938 crime drama *I Am the Law*, starring Edward G. Robinson, the *New York Times* claimed that it was "Asta, the incomparable wire-haired terrier of *The Thin Man*, who does the best bit of acting in the film, when a gunman enters through a window to rub Mr. Robinson out" (August 26, 1938).[6]

Before one credits Skippy's increasing number of close-ups entirely to his popularity, however, it is important to note that they resulted in part from Skippy/Asta's advancing age, which led to increased reliance on doubles for stunts, tricks, and any other physically demanding scenes. According to an article written from the set of *Shadow of the Thin Man* in 1944, "They're having a

Skippy the "scene stealer," with Irene Dunne and Cary Grant in a publicity photo for *The Awful Truth* (1937). Photofest.

little trouble with Asta, the wire-haired terrier. After 10 years of stardom in these 'Thin Man' pictures he's getting a little old for the part. Doesn't get around like he did when the first one was filmed back in 1934. But they can't write Asta out of the script as easily as they did the baby, so he has a couple of doubles who do the leaping and running. The real Asta comes in just for the close-ups" (*Frederick [Md.] Post*, June 10, 1944, 4). A special "Magazine Pictorial" in 1945 assured fans that Skippy was keeping Asta in the family by noting that "in between takes he works at training his son, Asta, jr., in the tricks of the trade. Asta, jr., will probably move into pa's place soon, as Asta, sr. is now about due to retire and clip coupons" ("Don't Let Your Pet Read This or He'll Go Howlywood," *Oakland Tribune*, April 29, 1945, 63).

It is significant for our purposes that the primary focus of the 1945 article quoted above is Lassie, who had replaced Asta as the biggest canine star in Hollywood. In addition to preparing the public and fans for a post-Skippy era, MGM's publicity department attempted to manufacture a relationship between the two canine stars in order to capitalize on the success of the studio's popular Thin Man and Lassie serials. For example, when Skippy fathered a litter in 1945 (serving as a "real life" complement to the earlier *After the Thin Man* in which Skippy finds a mate and has a family), a syndicated article announced: "No one appreciates a good father like another proud father! On the set of MGM's *The Thin Man Goes Home*, . . . a large box wrapped in baby pink and blue was delivered to Asta, famous canine actor. Inside were five miniature fire hydrants, also painted in pink and blue, and one larger, a fiery red. They were addressed 'To Asta and the Quints,' meaning the five puppies just presented to him by Mrs. Asta. The accompanying card was signed, 'Congratulations from Lassie and his Sextuplets, another dog-goned good family'" (*Laurens [Iowa] Sun*, February 23, 1945, 8).[7] And when a serviceman flying home for his father's funeral was displaced by Elliot Roosevelt and his wife Faye Emerson's mastiff Blaze, the Associated Press seized the opportunity to exploit the resulting media scandal through "no comments" from Asta and Lassie:

> This is to report that Hollywood's dogs, rich and famous and ordinarily very voluble in matters of public concern, are maintaining discreet silence during the present crises. Usually well informed on current affairs, the Hollywood set is acting like it doesn't know that the most publicized canine in the world today is now in their midst, having arrived in unprecedented fashion—on a big Army cargo plane. The name, as if they didn't know, is Blaze. Obviously, the native dogs have adopted a policy of studied reticence in discussing Blaze. Spokesmen for Asta, the wire-hair interest in the "Thin Man" series, and Lassie, the friendly collie, both of whom work for Metro-Goldwyn-Mayer, said: "Asta, and Lassie have no comment." The spokesman denied that their silence has any political implications. ("Lassie, Asta Remain Reticent in Discussing New Hollywoodite," *Paris [Texas] News*, January 19, 1945, 7)

No doubt intended to provide a brief escape from the realities of war, this article—which ran alongside the casualty lists for local residents "killed in action in the Mediterranean area" or "wounded in action in the European theatre of operations"—shows the prominent position (alongside Lassie) that Asta still occupied in 1940s wartime culture.[8]

When the final installment in the Thin Man series was released in 1947, Erskine Johnson reported that "the original Asta has been dead three years, and the Asta you saw in the last Thin Man picture, and which you will see again in this one, is Zip, son of Asta." The aura surrounding Skippy is magnified as we learn that it now takes four copies to sustain the illusion of the original Asta: "You'll see four Astas in [*The Song of the Thin Man*]—but not, naturally, all at the same time. . . . Dog-trainer Henry East has four wire-haired terriers playing the one role of Asta. One of Henry's Astas is pure white, so Henry gives the dog a makeup dye job every morning to make him match the others. Henry yearns for the good old days of the original Asta. 'He did everything. When he was alive I didn't have to bring a whole kennel to the studio every morning'" (*Blytheville [Ark.] Courier News*, February 4, 1947, 8).

Skippy, like all dogs, had a relatively short life expectancy and even shorter career (roughly the same length as the average career of a romantic leading lady during the studio era). Unlike human actors, however, Skippy's nonhuman status afforded the studio and journalists the opportunity to treat him like an animated character and conflate his identity with the Asta character or brand beginning as early as 1937, when we are told that he could no longer distinguish between his onscreen (Asta) and offscreen (Skippy) identities. By 1947, the breeding and training of additional "Astas," along with inventive stylistic techniques deployed in Skippy's later films, made the death of the "real" Asta an inconsequential throwaway line in a newspaper three years after the fact.

One could argue that Myrna Loy's observation that "I daren't take any chances with Myrna Loy, for she isn't my property" (quoted in Levin 1970, 214), applies equally—if not more—to Skippy and the political economy of the canine star system in the 1930s. As sociologist Bob Torres (2007) has argued, "Neither exactly like human slaves or exactly like human wage laborers, animals occupy a different position within capitalism: they are superexploited living commodities" (39). Torres's additional observation that "animals *never* see a separation between 'home' and 'work,' and find themselves within the grasp of productive capital at all times" (39) is also inordinately relevant to Skippy, whose "home" away from the set was a kennel training facility that supplied dogs to the studios. Consequently, unless we are able to avoid the ethical issue altogether by simply denying animals any subjectivity whatsoever, we must acknowledge that Skippy was exploited as a "living commodity" by his owners and the studios for profit and by film audiences for entertainment.

Performing Asta: Film Style

As with his star persona, Skippy/Asta's status as a nonhuman performer gave the narrative uses to which he was put considerable structural and ideological flexibility. At different points in any given film, he can fulfill roles from clever coconspirator to cowardly comic-relief buddy to judgmental superego. His most significant narrative functions, however, fall into two general categories, both of which are connected to the idea that Asta is not bound by social rules. First, one of Asta's most important narrative functions is enhancing the flexibility of the class status of his human companions. Asta is both highly privileged and utterly unpretentious, qualities that can quite effectively be shared with his human companions. Second, Asta is able to introduce varying degrees of chaos into otherwise formal social situations. Once again, the identification of human characters with Asta can serve to underscore their freedom from social rigidity. At its extreme, the chaos that Asta embodies threatens to overwhelm social order. But those who reject or attempt to ignore Asta may prove themselves to be stuffy and, therefore, undesirable. Somewhere between rigid and utterly anarchic lies the irreverent balance that is at the heart of the screwball comedy. Before looking at how Asta is put to use creating meaning in his film appearances, it is useful to sketch the stylistic strategies used to construct his performances.

Asta's performances are composed of simple strategies that impute various motivations, intentions, and reactions to him. Of course, Asta knew an impressive array of tricks, such as doing back flips, retrieving a hidden object, hiding his eyes, and barking on cue. Foleying (creating sound effects), editing, dialogue, and the occasional use of slow or fast motion cinematography to alter his movements fill in most of the blanks left by the actions that he was trained to perform. A characteristic example in which a trained behavior is augmented by sound effects occurs in *Another Thin Man*, in which Asta "takes care of" the sleeping baby Nicky by pulling up his blanket with his mouth, while the inserted sound of soft whimpering suggests his concern.[9] Similarly, after Asta laps the puddle from a broken bottle of whiskey in *Song of the Thin Man*, a Foleyed burp as he tilts his muzzle suggests drunkenness.

Montage, or juxtaposing otherwise unrelated shots to create meaning, further allows Asta's face (like the actor employed in Lev Kuleshov's famous experiments with editing in the 1920s) to express a variety of emotions. For example, in *Another Thin Man* a shot of a mastiff barking cuts to a shot of Asta running under a stairwell and then to a shot of him peeking around the corner, suggesting fear. The context of a wild party scene in *The Thin Man* would cause a viewer to ascribe very different emotions to Asta in a similar shot of him peeking around the corner of the kitchen door at the revelry before turning to go the other way in apparent disgust. Later in *The Thin Man*, Asta is shown running under a couch when an intruder begins shooting in Nick and Nora's bedroom.

When the intruder is subdued and Nick calls Asta to come out, a shot of Asta creeping with his belly low to the floor is cut with Nick and Nora's disapproving looks to suggest that he is ashamed of his cowardice.

In addition to sound effects and editing, fast- and slow-motion cinematography are occasionally used to suggest hard-to-stage action, as well as some of Asta's more extreme subjective states. For example, in *Shadow of the Thin Man*, slow motion is used to turn Asta's walk into a stalk as he and Nick track down a suspicious noise in a dark locker room, and again later to show Asta's queasiness as he staggers down off of a merry-go-round on which he has ridden with Nick and Nick Jr. When a cat hisses at him in *Another Thin Man*, an undercranked shot of Asta spinning around on the spot, nose to tail, gives his reaction a frantic look, while in *Shadow of the Thin Man* another undercranked shot exaggerates Asta's troubles when he gets caught in a revolving door during a chase.

Although Asta's performance must convey meaning without the assistance of dialogue, one of the most important and distinctive aspects of his screen presence is nevertheless his voice. Asta's high-pitched yapping is used to perform simple narrative functions such as announcing the arrival of characters who are in the dog's company. His barking serves as a sound bridge that announces the arrival of Aunt Elizabeth in *Bringing Up Baby* and of Nick and Nora in *The Thin Man*. It is also heard both on- and offscreen to warn of trouble or announce a discovery, such as when he uses his bark to warn Nick that someone is coming, and later shows him a bracelet hidden in a radiator, in *Shadow of the Thin Man*.

A more distinctive function of Asta's voice is how it raises the level of noise in what we might call the "cacophonous screwball scene." In fact, much of his reputation as the quintessential screwball dog might be traced to this use of his bark. The noise in such scenes is typically a weapon of chaos wielded against conventional behavior. While overlapping dialogue and noise caused by various physical high jinks contribute to the general din in such scenes, Asta's bark puts it all over the top. As further examination will demonstrate, Asta's yapping bark is a primary means by which he is associated with unruly forces in the screwball comedy.

Asta's performances are thus composed of essentially the same elements as other cinematic performances (with the exception of the words in spoken dialogue), although the meaning of his performances is more wholly constructed by devices such as continuity editing, sound mixing, cinematographic tricks, and the work of his coperformers. In fact, it is in large part because of this that the meaning of his acting is so flexible. Interestingly, a scene in *The Awful Truth* momentarily undercuts the idea that there are anthropomorphic motivations underlying Skippy/Asta's cued behaviors. During the divorce proceedings for Jerry and Lucy Warriner, the judge decides to allow Mr. Smith to choose who will have custody of him, implying that the dog will be aware of the choice he is making in going to one or the other of his companions. Both Warriners call to Mr. Smith, but Lucy can be seen to lure him to her with a toy hidden in her muff, and her trick makes her appear to be Smitty's choice. Despite this somewhat self-reflexive hint at the way that trainers construct Skippy/Asta's performance, as with the dog's wider star persona Mr. Smith is subsequently portrayed as engaging in still more abstract thinking than would be involved in choosing his custodian. In a later scene he growls and barks at the back of a newspaper that Lucy is reading. When Lucy asks him what the matter is, he jumps up and indicates a photo of Jerry and his new heiress companion with his paw. "Oh, I see what you mean!" Lucy exclaims, noticing the photo for the first time. In other films it is suggested that Skippy/Asta has the ability to read and spell, identify suspects by their perfume, and tell a good hand of cards from a bad one.

Asta and Class Flexibility

Film style thus has the power to generate nearly any meaning from Asta's actions, and, as a consequence, he can perform a wide variety of narrative roles in his films. He frequently serves the function of the helpful sidekick, as when he repeatedly helps Nick Charles find clues in the Thin Man films, but he can also be an antagonist or obstacle, notably when he steals the fossilized intercostal clavicle so important to paleontologist David (Cary Grant) in *Bringing Up Baby*. He can perform heroically, as when he fights with a leopard in *Bringing Up Baby*, or, as in the running gag in the Thin Man films, he can display comical cowardice. He can be a hedonistic free spirit or a cuckolded "husband," as he is in *After the Thin Man*, which introduces Mrs. Asta and a diverse litter of pups. He reveals a prudish side at the end of *The Thin Man*, as the sleuthing couple gets ready for bed on a train back to California. Nora asks Nick to put Asta in the bottom bunk with her. "Oh, yeah?" Nick asks, tossing Asta perfunctorily into the top bunk while he leans in toward Nora. A pair of close-ups of Asta on the top bunk show him pacing about and then lying down and putting his paws over his eyes, suggesting the amorous activity in the bunk below.

Asta's flexibility as a character is perhaps most marked when it comes to issues of class, a feature of his screen persona that is quite useful given the complex negotiation of class issues that goes on in the screwball comedy. For the screwball romance to succeed, the loving playfulness of the couple must be shown not only to sustain the companionate marriage but also to overcome the boundaries of class. The plausibility of the screwball romance gains considerable support from the identification of the members of the couple with Asta's freedom to transgress the usual social boundaries. A connection to Asta can be a sign of a lack of pretention and a willingness to have fun and to treat anyone as an equal.

Given the privileged lifestyle of most of Asta's screen characters (and his off-screen persona), this might seem counterintuitive. Indeed, one might think that Asta would come across as the spoiled brat of the dog world. This comes closest to being true in *Bringing Up Baby*. Asta, as George, arrives at his opulent suburban Connecticut house on the arm of the wealthy Aunt Elizabeth and proceeds to have his way with everyone and everything in her home. When Susan claims that David is obsessed with George because he thinks he's such a nice dog, Aunt Elizabeth replies, "George is a perfect little fiend and you know it." Skippy and those who indulge him are far more likely to be portrayed as sympathetic—as is even, eventually, the fiendish George himself. At the start of *Another Thin Man* the Charles family arrives at a hotel, and room service immediately brings up a tray with cocktails for Nick and Nora and a bone for Asta, and in *Shadow of the Thin Man* the family maid serves Asta's dinner in a monogrammed bowl on a silver tray, alongside the cocktails. Rather than coming across as evidence of the Charleses' decadent lifestyle, their indulgence of Asta seems to underscore their general democratic attitude, just as the article with which we opened this chapter suggests that Hollywood is a golden land of opportunity for everyone, even dogs.

Key to this acceptance of Asta's excesses is his placement in opposition to stuffiness, a fault that may be ascribed to upper-class and bourgeois characters alike and is perhaps the least forgivable character trait in screwball comedy. One can easily be forgiven for being very rich, it seems, as long as one does not cling to outmoded social constraints and class-based pomposity, and a character's willingness to accept Asta is an excellent test for revealing the absence of arrogance that is so important in the screwball universe.

Asta's ability to cross social boundaries is often quite literal, in that he makes himself at home in locations, from nightclubs to dinner tables to crime scenes to museums, that are usually barred to "his kind." In *The Awful Truth* Mr. Smith is initially ejected from the courtroom in which Lucy and Jerry are contesting their divorce. He is readmitted, however, when the question of his custody comes up, and the judge turns the decision (and, in effect, the courtroom) over to him. A running motif of the Thin Man series is the fact that the couple takes Asta into all manner of high-toned joints where dogs are not typically allowed.[10] This is in fact how Asta is first introduced in *The Thin Man*, as he drags Nora into a nightclub to find Nick. A shot of Asta from behind shows him straining forward on his leash and barking as they rush past the protesting doormen. One of them exclaims, "You can't take that dog in there!" "I'm not taking him," Nora corrects him; "He's taking me!" When Asta finally comes to a stop in front of Nick, the maitre d' insists that he will have to go out, but Nick reassures him that "It's all right—it's my dog."

While introducing Asta as a dog who doesn't observe the rules, this scene also provides a telling preview of Nick's mode of interacting with the world. A former working detective who has retired and "become a gentleman" because of his wife's fortune, Nick retains his numerous connections to the working class and the criminal underworld. A frequently reiterated motif of the films is the fact that every lowlife the couple encounters considers Nick a friend and is ready to do him favors, even those whom he has "sent up the river." In this scene his glib assumption that the rules do not apply to his dog is based as much or more on his almost mystical status as the pal of every working guy as it is on the privilege that comes with freely spending his wife's money.

Much like Asta, Nick thus shares a connection to average Joes even while he hobnobs with the smart set. He is fully prepared to live the good life, and makes frequent jokes about how he married Nora for her money, but he has no desire to ingratiate himself with Nora's high-society relations, and, in *After the Thin Man* and other films in the series, he tweaks their stuffy judgmentalism. This characterization of Nick is consistent with William Powell's complex star persona, which encompassed both the suave and sophisticated gentleman and the regular guy. In his role as Nick Charles, as well as in roles such as a forgotten-man-cum-Boston-socialite in *My Man Godfrey* (1936), he successfully straddles class boundaries. Nora, too, in her role as the perfect, accepting wife, is generally shown to have the ability to look beyond her upper-class background by keeping up with Nick and being a good sport when it comes to his less savory connections. Her occasional qualms and her wisecracks about the "nice people" that Nick knows serve only to reinforce that the couple overcomes their class differences through humor (see Castonguay 2011). Again, as with Nick, her unquestioning acceptance of Asta's right to sleep in her lingerie drawer or dine with the family is emblematic of her general open-mindedness.

After William Powell, Cary Grant is the actor most closely associated with Asta, having appeared with him in both *Bringing Up Baby* and *The Awful Truth*. Like Powell, Grant's star persona had considerable flexibility when it came to a variety of factors, including class status. These two films alone demonstrate his versatility. In *Bringing Up Baby* he is an initially stuffy, hidebound paleontologist, while in *The Awful Truth* he is a glib man-about-town. In both cases, however, his ability to play with Asta (which he only acquires over time in *Bringing Up Baby*) is indicative of his capacity to overcome the boundaries of social rigidity.

As Steve Neale and Frank Krutnik (1990) have noted, the screwball couple must demonstrate their "rightness" for one another through their willingness to engage in play, in contrast with other characters who cling to social conventionality. While playing with one another may be the most direct way to demonstrate their screwball bona fides, playing with Asta can be a useful intermediary. Thus, in *The Awful Truth*, when Lucy and Jerry are estranged, they are still connected by their love for Mr. Smith and their willingness to horse around with him. Jerry is prepared to ignore the social niceties to greet Mr. Smith, and repeatedly gets down on his knees to play with him when in company. In contrast, "wrong man" Dan Leeson (Ralph Bellamy), although he is on the surface more of a man of the people, ignores Mr. Smith, doggedly carrying on with trite conversation in the face of "Smitty's" antics. His rigidity with regard to the dog presages his parochial inability to see past Lucy's apparent sexual transgressions, making him the wrong partner in the film's love triangle.

Similarly, in *Bringing Up Baby*, learning to play with Asta's character, George, is a sign that David is letting go of his inhibitions and is prepared to be a suitable partner for the free-spirited Susan. David is initially antagonistic to the "nasty cur" and is only coerced into interacting with him when the dog steals the intercostal clavicle that he needs to complete his dinosaur skeleton. Nevertheless, he eventually enters into the spirit of things as he and Susan chase George around the Connecticut countryside. A key moment in David's conversion is the scene in which Susan attempts to lure Baby, the leopard, off of a roof by singing "I Can't Give You Anything But Love, Baby." Now holding George in his arms, David not only joins in with the song but also adds the harmony part.

Asta, Chaos, and Unruliness

Asta, consistent with the reputation of his breed as the favorite of the "well-to-do and the working-man" (Naylor 1932, 226), is thus the perfect "everydog," both privileged and unpretentious. He is the antithesis to the stuffiness that serves as an obstacle to modern romance in the screwball comedy and that can be found in both upper-class and bourgeois characters. Transgression of class boundaries is only one component of the unruliness that can quickly progress into chaos. As noted above in the discussion of style, Asta's bark is often a key element of this screwball chaos, serving to amplify the noise of cacophonous scenes in which all attempts to engage in conventional social behaviors are drowned out. Examples include two scenes in *The Awful Truth*, in which chaotic noise disrupts the efforts of Oklahoman Dan Leeson and his "Maw" to carry on conversations with Lucy Warriner; the scene at the end of *Bringing Up Baby* in which pandemonium erupts when Susan, David, and their entourage descend on a small-town jail; and the baby party that a bunch of mugs throws for little Nicky that interrupts the solution to the case in *Another Thin Man*.

A quick but effective "cacophonous scene" occurs in *The Awful Truth* when Jerry uses Mr. Smith to disrupt Dan's attempts to court Lucy. Jerry enforces his right to visit Mr. Smith just as Lucy and Dan are attempting to get to know one another. He plays loudly on the piano and encourages Mr. Smith to yap along with him, while interjecting questions and quips that interrupt Lucy and Dan's conversation. As he does at several other points in the film, he also gets down on the floor to play with Mr. Smith, getting him nicely riled up. Finally, Lucy and Dan are forced to leave to escape the noise.

Their reaction is one of three possible responses when Asta's bark disrupts a situation, which serve as a kind of index of a character's ability to run with the screwballs. The truly clueless, like Dan and his mother, attempt to plow through with their conventional behavior in spite of the noise. At the other end of the spectrum, those who embrace the screwball chaos are just as loud as Asta, contributing to the general ruckus. Somewhere in the middle are those who give up trying to behave conventionally when chaos takes over but are perhaps not yet quite ready to leap into the fun themselves.

Skippy/Asta at the center of the chaos in a publicity photo from *Bringing Up Baby* (Howard Hawks, RKO-Radio, 1938). Photofest.

An example of the latter occurs in *Bringing Up Baby*, in the notorious scene in which Susan's machinations have trapped David in her aunt's house in a negligee, pushing him over the edge so that he exclaims to the startled matron that he has gone "gay all of a sudden!" Arriving with Aunt Elizabeth, George helps complete the process of breaking David down. As the two women carry on a Hawksian overlapping conversation, George adds his loud yapping in David's face at a similar pitch. After making a few attempts to enter the conversation, David is reduced to defeated silence as he sits on the stairs draped in marabou.

In this scene Asta's "voice" is linked with that of the women, particularly Susan, through its aural similarity. This linkage of Asta's unruliness to that of female characters is a repeated element in the films in which he appears. Although socially disruptive behavior is certainly not limited to women in the screwball comedy, as the above example of Jerry playing with Mr. Smith shows, female characters often have the most to gain by a subversion of constraints. The best extended example of this aspect of Asta's narrative functioning comes from the way that he is paralleled with Nora in the Thin Man movies. Nora and Asta often serve similar narrative functions as challenges to Nick's tenuous control of his family life and sidekicks/intruders into his investigation of the murder cases that inevitably present themselves to the "retired" detective. Stylistic devices occasionally underscore the parallels between them, as in *After the Thin Man*, when Nora and Asta both bend over a suitcase with their rear ends in the air, creating a comical comparison of the two.

When considering the parallels between Asta and Nora, it is useful to return to the scene that introduces the pair in *The Thin Man*, as they barge into the nightclub where Nick has been holding forth on how to make cocktails and has assured the maitre d' that Asta is his dog. He then adds, "Uh, and my wife." Nora complains, "Well, you might have mentioned me first on the billing." Nick quips, "The *dog's* well trained. *He'll* behave himself," while Nora gives him a look. Nick proceeds with an attempt to demonstrate some of Asta's tricks, but Asta does the opposite of what he is asked to do each time. As the scene demonstrates, Asta may be Nick's dog and Nora his wife, but neither of them "behaves," instead presenting challenges to Nick's authority, particularly by trying to cross the boundaries between domestic life and the masculine (human) professional world that he inhabits. As Nick and Nora negotiate what it means to have a companionate marriage, the power dynamic between them is always open to contestation.

Though Nora (and, by extension, Loy) gained a reputation as the "perfect," accommodating wife, Nora frequently challenges the limits that Nick attempts to set on her behavior.[11] One of the key points of Nick and Nora's good-natured marital power struggle is the question of the degree of her involvement in the murder cases that Nick reluctantly pursues. Nick frequently includes either Nora or Asta in some aspect of his investigations, bringing Asta along to sniff around crime scenes and discussing clues with Nora. It is Nora who encourages Nick to take on each new murder case, in spite of his intention to remain retired, and he even refers to her at one point in *The Thin Man* as "Dr. Watson." At other points, however, both Nora and Asta are portrayed as hindrances. Asta occasionally steals clues (*After the Thin Man*) and murder weapons (*Another Thin Man*) while Nora causes false alarms (*Shadow of the Thin Man*) and is tricked by false leads (*Song of the Thin Man*). Nick also often attempts to forbid Nora to take an active role in his investigations, particularly when he believes that the action is getting dangerous. In *After the Thin Man*, in particular, he repeatedly shuts out or locks up both Nora and Asta. He has the police lock Nora in a cell and refuses to bail her out until she promises there will be "no more detecting." She promises, but nevertheless continues to get involved, and he later locks her in a room when he doesn't want her to come investigate with him.

Nick's attempts to control Asta meet with similarly mixed success. In *After the Thin Man* he shuts the dog out of his room when he doesn't want him disturbing his night's sleep, but between them, Nora and Asta soon have him up making scrambled eggs and playing ball. When someone throws a rock through the window with a clue tied to it soon after, Asta grabs it and leads both Nick and Nora on a chase to try to retrieve it from him. At one point Nick pushes Nora aside and says masterfully, "Darling, let me discipline him!" Asta, however, completely ignores his stern commands, racing off with the note and the rock. Nick is ultimately able to trick Asta into dropping the note when he recovers the rock and throws it for him but only after Asta has eaten a portion of the clue. His methods for trying to control Asta and Nora, as well as their mixed results, are thus analogous.

As the series goes along, this connection between Asta and Nora and their common refusal to "stay in their place" is diluted somewhat as an additional parallel is developed between Asta and the child Nick Jr. *The Shadow of the Thin Man* opens on an unusual setting for the series: a tranquil park in which children play ball and women stroll with their baby buggies. A medium shot reveals Nick, apparently reading from a book of fairytales. The leash that he holds in his hand tugs him to the right, toward offscreen space. Viewers familiar with the Thin Man films will readily assume that it is the unruly Asta pulling on his leash, as we have seen him do many times before in the series. The camera pans right and tilts down to reveal that Nick is in fact holding little Nick Jr. (Nicky) on a leash. Nicky is also holding a leash and is, in turn, tugged to the right by Asta, who emerges from behind a bush and unsuccessfully tries to pull Nicky toward a fire hydrant. The comedic visual parallel made between Asta and little Nicky suggests the problems that Nick has with the newest unruly member of his burgeoning domestic menagerie. The dialogue confirms it. Nicky suggests, "How about taking the chain off?" "Oh ho, yes," Nick replies, "and have you disappear like you did yesterday? What's your mother going to think?" As the scene progresses, Nick manages to enjoy the pleasures of reading his racing form and having a few cocktails back at his apartment but only through ongoing negotiations for control over his actions with Nicky; Nora, who lures him home from a block away simply by shaking a cocktail shaker; and even Asta, from whom Nicky seeks approval before he will consent to sit down on a park bench. Though it could be argued that Asta's unruliness loses something of its subversive edge when the parallel with Nora is weakened, his association with Nicky's boyish antics opens a new front in the assault on adult male mastery of domestic life.

Asta's Legacy

For nearly eighty years Asta has remained a significant cultural presence as a result of a Thin Man phenomenon that includes films, radio and television programs, popular books, a Broadway musical, online memorabilia, fan websites, and social media. In addition to the post-Skippy films *The Song of the Thin Man* and *The Thin Man Goes Home* with Loy and Powell, a radio series called "The Adventures of the Thin Man" aired on NBC Blue from 1941 to 1943 and on CBS from 1943 to 1949.[12] When MGM Television revived the Thin Man franchise for NBC in 1957, it was the familiar signifier of Asta on his leash that viewers first saw in the opening credits before being introduced to Peter Lawford and Phyliss Kirk as the new Nick and Nora (followed by the official introduction of "Asta as Asta").

As a television celebrity Asta endorsed animal life insurance and was reportedly the first dog to get a policy ("Television Show Terrier First to Get

Insurance," *Kittaning [Pa.] Leader-Times*, September 18, 1957, 17). Several syndicated features about the new Asta (in real life named Native Dancer) and his trainer appeared in newspapers across the country ("A Day in the Life of a Canine Star," *Long Beach Independent Press-Telegram*, September 7, 1958), and Aline Mosby predicted that "Lassie will have to keep a firm grip on her rating bones [because] Asta is making a comeback this fall" (and quoted Asta's trainer claiming that he "is much more clever than Lassie") ("Asta to Challenge Lassie's Bone," *Miami [Okla.] Daily News-Record*, August 7, 1957, 2). As the series struggled to find an audience (due in part to viewers' unwillingness to fully embrace Lawford and Kirk as the new Nick and Nora), Faye Emerson reported that Asta's role would be given more prominence, including moving his bed into Nick and Nora's bedroom; but it was not enough to save the program, which was cancelled after only two seasons ("White-Haired Terrier on Way Up TV Ladder," *El Paso Herald-Post*, January 4, 1958, 8; "To Run or Rerun?" *Daily Variety*, January 9, 1959, 1). In 1975 ABC shot the made-for-TV movie *Nick and Nora* with Craig Stevens and Jo Ann Pflug as a pilot episode for a new series that did not get picked up—and in 1991 the Broadway musical *Nick and Nora* starring Barry Bostwick and Joanna Gleason closed after only nine shows (Army Archerd, "Just for Variety," *Daily Variety*, January 13, 1975, 3; "*Nick and Nora* to Fold After 9 Performances," *Philadelphia Inquirer*, December 11, 1991, E09).

The spate of media appearances by Uggie, the Jack Russell terrier from *The Artist*, the winner of the 2012 Best Picture Oscar, suggests that the canine "sidekick" is still a marketable commodity in twenty-first-century media culture. And although the film's director and writer downplayed any homage to *The Thin Man*, the connection with Asta was a significant part of the film's meaning for many critics and audience members (as reviews and online discussions attest). *Variety* also reported in 2011 that Johnny Depp had committed to co-star as Nick Charles in a remake of *The Thin Man*, emphasizing that the director would "be keen to lock down a top name animal actor to play Asta, the Charles's beloved wire-haired fox terrier" (Justin Kroll, "Rob Marshall to Direct *Thin Man*," *Variety*, May 9, 2011; Ben Child, "Johnny Depp Solves Thin Man Remake," *Guardian*, May 10, 2011).[13] The great flexibility of meaning afforded by this enduring canine sidekick character, both onscreen and in various intertexts, would no doubt facilitate yet another reincarnation of "Asta."

Notes

This project was supported by a grant from the College of Arts and Sciences at Sacred Heart University.

1. In the 1940s, Skippy's owner, Henry East, lamented the persistent "black market" of thousands of wire-haired fox terrier puppies falsely advertised as Asta's offspring (*Ironwood [Mich.] Daily Globe*, May 1, 1944, 4). One example of these Skippy/Asta forgeries appears in a November 16, 1940, classified ad in a local New York paper for wire-haired fox terrier puppies in which the seller claimed that the "father is [the]

brother of Asta of moving picture fame" (*Kingston [N.Y.] Daily Freeman*, 13). Similar to stories about women and girls asking cosmetic surgeons for "Myrna Loy's nose," wire-haired terriers became another way to emulate and imitate the fashionable Thin Man stars and characters.

2. Although *The Thin Man*—which first appeared in serial form in the women's magazine *Redbook*—is less "hard-boiled" than Hammett's *The Maltese Falcon* or *The Glass Key*, the film adaptation makes the lighter or comedic elements even more prominent than the novel, especially by adding Skippy/Asta's sight gags.

3. Rudd Weatherwax was Skippy's lead trainer in the early to mid 1930s while working for the Easts, although his younger brother Frank is sometimes identified as Asta's trainer in later publicity after Rudd had left the East kennel (Robert Weatherwax, personal communication, June 30, 2012). According to fellow trainer Frank Inn (most famous for training the first incarnations of Benji in the 1970s and early 1980s), Rudd Weatherwax was also hired by Rennie Renfroe to train Daisy for the first Blondie film (Beck and Clark 2002, 33). The Weatherwaxes would launch their own successful dog-training business and kennel in 1940 that included Lassie in several incarnations, as well as many other canine actors, though none attained Lassie's tremendous stature (see Weatherwax and Rothwell 1950; Beck and Clark 2002; and Wolf in this volume).

4. Skippy's character name, "Mr. Atlas," in *Topper Takes a Trip* (1938) may have been chosen for its similarity to Asta, although whether this was for practical reasons on the set or marketing reasons (or both) is unclear. Promotional ads for the film included images of Skippy described as "Mr. Atlas (*The Thin Man* Dog)" (*San Antonio Light*, March 9, 1939, 8A).

5. This promotional theme is also reflected the first time the public meets Nick Jr. in the trailer for *Another Thin Man*, as we see the baby being showered with licks of affection from a delighted Asta.

6. The uncredited appearance by a wire-haired terrier in *I Am the Law* is not Skippy (the dog has large black patches on his right side and a white tail). Nevertheless, the dog does provide comic relief in this gangster film when he confuses a hit man who has broken into his owners' home for a potential playmate. This trick or stunt function within the narrative defines Skippy/Asta's brief appearance in *The Big Broadcast of 1936* (1937), in which he plays dead after eating table scraps and unwittingly tricks the film's protagonist, Spud (Joe Oakie), into thinking he's been poisoned. In *Topper Takes a Trip*, although Skippy (as the ghost dog Mr. Atlas) has one scene in which he digs frenetically on the beach, during the most physically demanding scenes for the human actors an invisible Mr. Atlas can be heard barking and growling as he tugs on a pants leg or a bone. The extensive use of dubbed sound along with other special effects for these sight gags (including a scene in which only half of Mr. Atlas's body is visible) may explain why reviewers did not comment on Skippy's performance despite his significant narrative role.

7. Skippy/Asta fans would have recognized this as an example of life imitating art, since—as a promotional article for *The Awful Truth* noted several years earlier— "[Skippy] surpassed Papa Dionne in *After The Thin Man*" (*Gettysburg Times*, November 20, 1937, 8), referring to the fact that Asta fathered five puppies in the film and comparing it to the widely publicized birth of the Dionne quintuplets (or "miracle babies") in 1934, who by 1937 had become a tourist attraction with their own doll set.

8. Another good indication of which dogs were the most culturally significant or famous dogs in 1945 can be found in the article "Canine Horoscopes," which features a discussion of Lassie, Asta, and President Roosevelt's Scottish Terrier Fala ("Canine Horoscopes," *Burlington [N.C.] Daily-Times News*, March 13, 1945, 9).

9. In fact, a similar strategy works for a still harder-to-train category of performer: the baby. Later in the same scene, the sound of a baby's laugh is inserted when Asta licks Baby Nicky, and crying sounds are used to suggest that Nicky has been startled by a gunshot offscreen.

10. In a notable departure from their usual habit of taking Asta with them in their first-class train compartments, in *The Thin Man Goes Home* (1945) Nick and Nora buy tickets in the overcrowded day coach and are forced to ride in the baggage car because Asta is with them. Given the very different context of 1940s wartime culture and its themes of sacrificing and rationing on the home front, the 1930s escapist fantasies of upper-class opulence and excessive drinking are replaced by frugality, moderation, and temperance (as Nick is now drinking apple cider). And given the controversy over the privileges accorded President Roosevelt's real life mastiff, Blaze (discussed above), Asta's newly humble mode of travel seems in line with the prevailing cultural climate.

11. Nora's characterization here also resonates with Myrna Loy's wider star persona, in particular her widely publicized fight to better her contract with MGM (see Caston-guay 2011).

12. Although there was no attempt made to pretend that Powell and Loy were the voices of the radio version of the Thin Man series, when NBC launched the programs, initial publicity pretended that an—or *the*—actual "Asta, the wire-haired pup . . . appears in the 'Adventures of the Thin Man' series" ("Microphone Makes Asta the Happiest of Puppies," *Pittsburgh Post-Gazette*, July 11, 1941, 26). In reality, radio actor Gilbert Mack voiced Asta and demonstrated his technique on the June 8, 1941, episode of NBC Blue's "Behind the Mike" (see radiogoldindex.com/cgi-local/p2.cgi ?ProgramName=Behind+The+Mike for a description and vintageradioshows.com /display_shows.php?sid=429 for audio of this episode).

13. *Entertainment Weekly* lobbied for Uggie to come out of retirement to play Asta, and the film's initial screenwriter, Jerry Stahl, was previously a writer for the Thin Man–inspired television series *Moonlighting* (ABC, 1985–1989) (Chris Nashawaty, "Johnny Depp: Who Will Be His Leading Lady?" *Entertainment Weekly*, April 6, 2012).

Chronological Filmography

The Thin Man (W. S. Van Dyke, 1934). William Powell, Myrna Loy, Maureen O'Sullivan, Skippy/Asta [uncredited].

Big Broadcast of 1936 (Norman Taurog, 1935). Jack Oakie, George Burns, Gracie Allen, Skippy/ Asta [uncredited].

After the Thin Man (W. S. Van Dyke, 1936). William Powell, Myrna Loy, James Stewart, Elissa Landi, Skippy/Asta [uncredited].

The Garden of Allah (Richard Boleslawski, 1936). Marlene Dietrich, Charles Boyer, Basil Rathbone, Corky [uncredited].

Theodora Goes Wild (Richard Boleslawski, 1936). Irene Dunne, Melvyn Douglas, Thomas Mitchell, Corky [uncredited].

The Awful Truth (Leo McCarey, 1937). Irene Dunne, Cary Grant, Ralph Bellamy, Skippy/Asta [uncredited].

Bringing Up Baby (Howard Hawks, 1938). Cary Grant, Katharine Hepburn, May Robson, Virginia Walker, Skippy/Asta [uncredited].

Topper Takes a Trip (Norman Z. McLeod, 1938). Constance Bennett, Roland Young, Billie Burke, Skippy [Asta].

Another Thin Man (W. S. Van Dyke, 1939). William Powell, Myrna Loy, Virginia Grey, Patric Knowles, Asta.

Shadow of the Thin Man (W. S. Van Dyke, 1941). William Powell, Myrna Loy, Barry Nelson. Asta [uncredited].

The Thin Man Goes Home (Richard Thorpe, 1945). William Powell, Myrna Loy, Lucile Watson, Asta.

Song of the Thin Man (Edward Buzzell, 1947). William Powell, Myrna Loy, Keenan Wynn, Dean Stockwell, Asta Jr. [uncredited].

The Artist (Michel Hazanavicius, 2011). Jean Dujardin, Bérénice Bejo, John Goodman, Uggie.

4

Promoting Lassie

● ● ● ● ● ● ● ● ● ● ● ● ● ● ● ● ● ● ● ●

The Animal Star and Constructions of "Ideal" American Heroism

KELLY WOLF

Press materials related to canine stars as dog heroes in the United States from the 1930s through the 1950s often mythologized their subjects through a rhetoric of nationalism, partially owing to the connotative value of the dog—especially large dogs—as loyal, strong, and protective. Although they were continually balanced on the edge of domestication and wildness, dog heroes were always represented ultimately as "ideal" members of society. Despite the fame of the silent-era dog hero, especially Rin Tin Tin, the most recognizable animal performer in the United States probably was, and remains, Lassie, the tan and white rough collie that starred in films and television shows in the 1940s and 1950s and became the exemplar of the dog both as loyal companion and family member but also as a thinking, feeling, communicating entity who lived in perfect harmony and under-standing with the humans lucky enough to own her. This essay focuses on the ways that Lassie's star text was positioned discursively by the studios for which "she" worked[1] and how this positioning came to define dogs both as canine performers and as actual domestic pets in relation to human codes of morality and behavior.

The relationship that emerges between animal stars in Hollywood and their manufactured images necessitates an investigation into the work, both

A glamour portrait of Lassie during the 1940s. *Movie Star News.*

ideological and physical, that these canine actors were invariably enlisted to do. The deployment of the canine star image was instrumental in constructing appropriate standards of obedient behavior and American heroism. The intense physical conditioning and training involved in the labor of achieving this ideal was effaced through the fetishistic practices employed by studio press agents. Animal stars are put through a system of routinized labor, labor that precisely becomes invisible once the animal star in question becomes commoditized through the system of studio publicity. As was true with Strongheart and Rin Tin Tin, the audience was encouraged to subsume its conceptions of the common domestic canine under the idealized rubric of the dog hero provided by the films and their promotional and publicity materials. Both star and common canines can become fetishized commodities as a result, because of the disavowal of the labor involved on the part of both the star dog and trainer.

First, I contextualize Lassie's emergence as a canine film star within larger shifts in societal attitudes toward domestic pets and the industry's desire to capitalize on the popularity and malleability of canine performers. A discussion of the early films in the Lassie franchise reveals MGM's investment in promoting wartime idealism, as well as the studio's initial crafting of the Lassie image. Lassie was marketed as an exemplary figuration of "American" heroism, a construction encouraged by the rhetoric of the press materials related to the films. These publicity tactics attempted to foster a nationalistic identity, through the audience's identification with the star, that was based on gendered and racialized hierarchies. I conclude with an analysis of the manner in which the promotional displays and dog-giveaway contests that were used as part of the *Lassie* campaign reveal some insidious gender anxieties and problematic investments in racial purity within studio constructions of the "ideal" pet. The promotional contests that marketed the idea of Lassie to the public ultimately exploited the childhood fantasy of owning a dog that was as perfect as Lassie appeared to be, making both the star canine and common household pets into forms of merchandise.

American cultural institutions utilize animal imagery and labor to promote a discourse about "viable" conceptions of humanness, and these ideas invariably have an impact on the lives of actual canines. Animal stars cannot speak about their own significance in the ways that human performers are traditionally able to assert themselves. Therefore it is important to analyze the means by which the discourse about animal stars of the past reveals the patterns of thought that placed the canine at the center of definitions of human identity.

How Lassie "Came Home" to MGM

Pal was a disheveled mass of undisciplined willfulness. The eight-month-old collie was proving too much of a burden for his owner; he chased cars obsessively and barked incessantly. Enlisting the help of a well-established Hollywood dog trainer, Rudd Weatherwax, Pal's owner handed off the wayward puppy to the care of the professional who would hopefully rid him of his bad behavior. According to legend, after a few training sessions Weatherwax noticed Pal's ability to respond instantly and consistently to standardized commands and his unwavering intelligence and alertness. When Weatherwax had completed Pal's basic training, he contacted the owner, attempting to schedule the dog's retrieval. Weatherwax discovered that the owner no longer wanted the collie— Pal still chased cars—and the trainer arranged to keep the dog in lieu of the seventy-dollar training fee owed him (Rothel 1980, 91).[2] Pal was by no means the first canine to prove useful for Weatherwax; the trainer was already highly experienced at manipulating the behavior of numerous star animals. From Asta, the intrepid canine detective of the Thin Man film series (see Ross and Castonguay in this volume), to Daisy, the delightfully adorable mixed breed of the prolific *Blondie* film series (1938–1950, plus twenty-six television episodes in 1957), Weatherwax maintained a panoply of trained actors at his Studio Dog Training Center, which he and his brother Frank established in 1940 (Collins 1993).[3]

The production of what would eventually become a series of seven *Lassie* films (with Pal playing the title role) at MGM from 1943 through 1951 (this does not include recent reincarnations or television shows) necessitated that the studio purchase the rights to an extremely popular novella by Eric Knight entitled *Lassie Come-Home*, published in 1940 after having been serialized in the *Saturday Evening Post*. For the grand total of $8,000, the studio gained the entirety of the theatrical rights in perpetuity, ensuring that any of the future profits from the *Lassie* brand would remain in their holdings (Collins 1993).[4] Apart from the financial acquisition of copyrights, the studio's ideological investment in the fictional canine's symbolic worth rested both on the popularity and lucrativeness of previous film dogs and also the changing status of the dog within society that had occurred since the late nineteenth century, one that saw the dog transformed from objectified worker to domestic pet. Kathleen Kete (1994) explains that the increased presence of companion animals in the nineteenth century was not only a defining characteristic of middle-class life but also a means through which the bourgeois communicated ideas about themselves. The middle class increasingly moved away from a utilitarian definition of pets and began to think of them in relation to affect, companionship, and even class distinction (55). Popular media of the late 1800s promoted a sentimentalized view of pets through literature and handbooks that linked the dog with domestic and familial happiness; dogs were also thought of as instrumental in the moral education of children (46). Henry Jenkins (2007) explains that *Lassie Come-Home* is precisely indicative of this shift in the valuation of the canine as the novella seeks to render its protagonist, Lassie, as the embodiment of a nostalgic longing for the traditional values of loyalty and working-class pride lost in the onset of modernity and industrialization (221–222). In the universe that Knight envisioned, the relationship between humans and their dogs was akin to a "moral contract," with Lassie acting as an agent of social reform (219–222). Jenkins also points out that the "linkage of those two sentimental icons—the boy and the dog—was no accident" and utilizes Viviana Zelizer's work on the "sacralization" of the child to explain the coincidental emotional value ascribed to both children and dogs between 1870 and 1930 (222). Children's literature, like *Lassie Come-Home*, became a rhetorical space that mobilized particular conceptions of the ideal pet and invited readers to project their own ideas about morality and loyalty.

Lassie Come Home (1943, the missing hyphen turning the title into a plea rather than describing the dog herself) inaugurated the highly lucrative film franchise throughout which Weatherwax and Pal were under contract. The narrative is an adaptation of Knight's original novella and follows the classic "boy and his dog" thematic as a young Yorkshire boy, Joe, is forced to sell his dog, Lassie, because of the harsh economic climate in England. The scarcity of employment had rendered Joe's father jobless and the family financially destitute. After her new owners take her to Scotland, Lassie ultimately does everything within her power to return home to her master, even crossing the rugged terrain of Scotland and northern

England, swimming rivers, braving storms, and fighting off bandits. The film's success prompted MGM to pursue a sequel entitled *Son of Lassie* (1945), in which the characters from the original have become adults and Lassie has produced a male heir, Laddie. Pal's actual son was used to facilitate the role of the infant Laddie; however, because the filming required a fully adult collie for the remainder of the shooting schedule, Pal also played the role of the mature Laddie. In the sequel Joe and Laddie are engaged in combat during World War II when their air force plane is shot down over Nazi-occupied Norway. Hollywood's attempt to capitalize on the *Lassie* franchise was at this point exploiting America's emotional investment in images of national pride and military success overseas.

The next installment of the series was the only other Lassie film to blatantly utilize wartime imagery, and it also addressed the traumatic aftermath of battle. *Courage of Lassie* (1946) concerns a male collie owned by a young girl, Kathie (Elizabeth Taylor); because of a mistake, the dog is enlisted in the K-9 Corps of the military and trained to kill Japanese soldiers. After returning home, he suffers from a form of post-traumatic stress disorder through which he reverts to an untamed state, killing small woodland creatures and shunning human contact. Lassie is reunited with and eventually rehabilitated by Kathie to his former self; thus, the film serves as a not-too-subtle allegory about returning soldiers and the need for women to take care of them rather than working in the public sphere as they had done during the war.

The remaining four films of the series, released during the postwar period of revitalization, abandoned any narrative references to World War II in favor of further reformulating Lassie as a symbol of community and familial protection. *The Hills of Home* (1948) and *Challenge to Lassie* (1949) feature Scottish locales and highlight Lassie's ability to reconcile problems within the community despite the threats posed by both nature and municipal bureaucracy. The American locations and sensibilities of *The Sun Comes Up* (1949) and *The Painted Hills* (a.k.a. *Lassie's Adventures in the Goldrush*) (1951) promote the potential of Lassie to restore the U.S. nuclear family after traumatic loss or threats.

Because the narrative settings within the Lassie series oscillate between various locations in the United States and the United Kingdom, it is crucial to focus on the actual material conditions behind the production of the series. *Lassie Come Home* and all of the other films in the MGM series were produced within the Hollywood studio system and thus serve as representative examples of how domestic publicity departments customized their marketing strategies for American audiences. It is of primary import to address the extracinematic operations, namely publicity and promotions, that constructed particular images of canine stardom as a form of ideal heroism, an approach that privileges an examination of actual industrial practices over an exclusive focus on the films as texts. Erica Fudge (2002) discusses how "animals are present in most Western cultures for practical use, and it is in use—the material relation to the animal—that representations of the animal must be grounded" (7). Film theory needs to support

Publicity photos like this were used by MGM to anthropomorphize their animal stars by placing them in situations that mirrored human activities. Pal and Elizabeth Taylor appear to be "shaking hands" after a contract signing related to the release of *Courage of Lassie* (Fred M. Wilcox, MGM, 1946). Collection of the author.

any analysis of animal imagery with an investigation into the material conditions that structure the lived experiences of animals. Fudge also points out that an analysis of the rhetorical strategies utilized to characterize animals within historical documents reveals not only the ways in which animal being was conceptualized but also how that society positioned itself in relation to animal life. By learning from the problematic assumptions that fueled the rhetorics of the past, we can craft new methods of speaking about animals and thus change the conditions of contemporary interspecies relations (10–11).

Capitalizing on Lassie

The phenomenon of classical Hollywood stardom has historically relied on a discursive system regulated by studio publicity departments and the popular press. Richard deCordova (1991) recognizes how press-generated discourse encouraged the social transformation of the public's interest in cinema and the subsequent creation of the star as an individual commodity. The star "emerges as an economic reality" around 1909, as picture personalities were beginning to be recognized by either their own names or the names that audiences ascribed to them, but the discourse still primarily centered on the film text (24). After the elevation of particular performers to star status, "the question of the player's existence outside his/her work entered discourse" and thus the regulation of information by the studios was fundamentally altered (26). As the fascination with the extratextual personal lives of the stars grew, the studios had to relinquish complete control over the crafting of the personality's image. The "burden" of disseminating information regarding the stars was shifted in part to the popular press, with the studios still exercising a certain level of influence over the more commercial aspects of image distribution (Musser 2004). Richard Dyer (2000) has explained that the film star's image consists of multiple media texts that are all publicly available, everything from film performances and advertisements to personal appearances and press coverage of their private lives (604). Promotional and publicity materials can be closely intertwined if discursive outlets (fan magazines, newspapers, and gossip columns) primarily disseminate studio material, a tactic used by the studios to maintain some covert control over the images of their stars from the early years of the twentieth century through the decline of the studio system in the late 1950s and beyond (606). Thus the classical film star's identity was always the result of the complex negotiation between public fascination and studio manipulation. In working through a historical genealogy of the film star and the ways in which it has been constructed, P. David Marshall (1997) discusses the "dialectic of knowledge and mystery" that operates as the basis for a screen actor's aura. The less an audience knows about a particular star, the more the publicity department can present a unified image to the public (81).

In attempting to create a star out of an unknown canine actor (Pal), one that would have the strength and longevity to sell the Lassie series films, MGM's publicity crew decided from the beginning that the star's identity had to be synonymous with the title character. MGM utilized its official in-house magazine *The Lion's Roar* to promote the release of *Lassie Come Home* in 1943, and one of the highlights is an article entitled "Canine Cinderella." This feature would be the studio's first major introduction of its new performer, Lassie, and this initial information would trickle down into popular newspaper columns after the film's release and affect all future press stories about the as-yet-unknown player. In detailing Lassie's backstory, the secrets behind her beauty, and the reassuring information that she has injury insurance, MGM crafted a careful image of its new "ingénue," complete with references to "queenly dignity" (*Lion's Roar*, September 1943). It was well established that as part of the process of building a new star's image, a studio would conduct an extensive publicity campaign that included concocting a "discovery" story, shooting glamour photos, and crafting rumors about a possible romance with another star (Harris 1991, 41). *The Lion's Roar* provides everything short of including a love interest in Lassie's discovery narrative and of course provides glamour photos. Other volumes of *The Lion's Roar* detail the "almost human" personality of MGM's "wonder dog" and boast of her huge volume of fan mail (ten thousand letters per week) and luxurious travel accommodations (May 1946).

The immense popularity of *Lassie Come Home*, accompanied by MGM's initial promotion of it, encouraged the studio to continue officially selling the film series on the strength of the Lassie image rather than an unknown performer named Pal. An examination of the studio publicity materials related to the release of the subsequent Lassie films yields strong evidence that the MGM press books elided the existence of Pal in favor of a fusion of star and role.[5] The poster design for the initial release of *Son of Lassie* operates as a complex manifestation of the ways in which the *Lassie* brand contributed to the erasure of Pal's identity. The utilization of both "Lassie" and "Laddie" casting credits, coupled with the prominent display of the film's title, encourages the spectator to misidentify the young collie on the poster as Lassie, the star, rather than the fictional character of Laddie. If an individual was to correctly assume that the collie depicted on the poster was in fact playing the role of "Laddie," even that assumption would inadvertently participate in concealing the existence of the actor "Pal."

This erasure of Pal's identity would also manifest itself through characters he played in the later films. Although the titles of *Courage of Lassie* and *The Painted Hills/Lassie's Adventures in the Goldrush* include the name *Lassie*, the names of the canine characters are, in fact, *Bill* and *Shep*, respectively. These are exemplary instances of the melding of star image and performer into a singular product. Pal had become synonymous with his character, "Lassie," to the point that the series functioned through the branded star image regardless of what role Pal was playing. Pal had become Lassie, and the studios would then use the star image of "Lassie" to market all of the films in which he performed. The Hollywood studio system often typecast its human stars; however, these performers were still able to maintain some semblance of identity distinct from that of their screen roles. Despite the uniqueness commonly attributed to Pal's abilities as an actor, his canine image could not be separated from the representation of Lassie. To illustrate the difference using a human example, Pal's predicament would be akin to a marketing department using the image of Johnny Depp as the character "Edward Scissorhands" from the 1990 film of the same name to advertise Depp's appearance in a 2013 release. No matter how strongly he might be identified with any individual role, Depp is a star whose existence in the world operates independently from the characters he plays, and his name still corresponds to an identifiable star text and marketable identity.

In the case of animal performers, because they cannot possibly control or even materially influence the terms of their own publicity and promotional materials,

Poster for *Son of Lassie* (S. Sylvan Simon, MGM, 1945). Collection of the author.

the audience is denied knowledge of the extratextual identity of animals like Pal on their own terms. As had been the case with previous dog stars, ranging from Teddy the Wonder Dog to Rin Tin Tin to Asta, canine identity was created for them from their looks and breeds (larger dogs were more likely to be cast as dog heroes), the narratives in which they performed, and the words of their trainers and owners, as well as the anthropomorphizing that audiences were encouraged to accept as part of these various discourses. For Pal, audiences were easily able to assume that the actual nature of the canine actor was identical to the idealized images presented. This perception should not be considered a form of audience gullibility but is, rather, something that indicates a belief that a film star's roles and performances tend to be revelatory of a star's personality; they contain clues that if deciphered properly guarantee a greater degree of intimacy with the star (Dyer 1998, 20). The studio's manufacturing of an individual's star text would often appeal to this desire for closeness by producing biographical information that further guaranteed access to a star's "real" private life (Dyer 2000, 611). In Pal's case, when dispersed to the entertainment columns of the major newspapers, some of the "biographical" data was reproduced fairly faithfully, especially information about Lassie's discovery and pampered lifestyle.

At first the fact that Lassie's true name was *Pal* was treated by the press as a "blemish" on her stardom (see, for example, the *New York Times*, February 28, 1943), but over time, newspapers would deviate from the prepared script and delve more deeply into the specificities of Lassie's "real" identity and her "actual" training regime (see the *New York Times*, February 27, 1949). Explicit references to Pal in the press were more prevalent in material that was published closer to the end of the Lassie film series and seemed to operate as appeals to authenticity.[6] An article from the *Washington Post* revealed Pal's past fondness for chasing motorized vehicles and provided amusing warnings about the appropriate gendered pronoun to use while on the studio lot (never *it* or *she*) (Howard C. Heyn, "Lassie's King—Not Queen—of All," July 18, 1948). Dyer argues that as part of the public/private divide that characterizes the star's engagement with the social world, it is precisely this use of sincerity in characterizing the star's private life that persuades fans to accept all of the mass-mediated hype surrounding a particular performer (Dyer 2000, 615). Paradoxically, in alluding to Pal, the press was further fueling public perception of Lassie as a real star, one whose complicated life warranted exclusive coverage.

The anthropomorphization of Lassie became a necessary component of her promotion as the embodiment of perfect American heroism. The marketing of Lassie as an "all-too-human" star was bolstered by the dangerous stunts performed in the films, as well as by the articles written for the film's press books. Many scenes from the Lassie films reinforce the reading of Lassie as an action star performing numerous heroic stunts. We see her swimming the flooded San Joaquin River and scaling high fences in *Lassie Come Home*, jumping off of large bridges into rushing river rapids in *Son of Lassie*, and evading explosive devices that were used to simulate gunfire and bombs in *Courage of Lassie*. Even Pal's trainer, Weatherwax, conceded the potential danger embedded in these stunts: "Lassie was swimming in the river and we had a speedboat and I was supposed to pick her up at a certain point. The throttle stuck and this boat kept going down the San Joaquin River—and Lassie was swimming in the swift current and by the time we could get back to her it was almost too late—but it wasn't planned that way—it was an accident" (Rudd Weatherwax, interview by Hedda

Hopper, Hedda Hopper Collection, Margaret Herrick Library, Academy of Motion Picture Arts and Sciences).

The posters for *Challenge to Lassie* show Lassie engaging in numerous activities with the accompanying headlines "narrow escapes," "standing guard," and "fighting thugs." MGM's marketing of Lassie as its "all-too-human" canine star necessitates this kind of illustration of the performer's impressive abilities. The provocative phrasing of the headline excites spectators, attempting to convince them of the "Daring! Dangerous! Death-Defying!" nature of Lassie's heroism. She consumes almost the entirety of the poster and is centrally located, with supporting images flanking her action pose. The advertising for this film attempts to capitalize on the audience's anthropomorphization of Lassie, a nascent fascination with the canine star's seeming ability to enact human behavioral codes of courage and bravery. In attributing human traits to the canine star, spectators facilitate the schemes of studio publicity and become heavily invested in the perpetuation of this anthropocentric construction.

Generally written by teams of writers working in the publicity departments of the major studios, press book materials were carefully controlled. It is not always clear which of the many articles they contained were printed in newspapers across the country; however, their very existence, as well as the nature of their prose and visual composition, illuminate the tendencies of the studios to market Lassie in a particular manner. Features from *The Sun Comes Up* press book highlight the heroic stunt work that Lassie was engaging in for the scenes in which she had to rescue Claude Jarman's character from a burning orphanage. One feature, entitled "Lassie Hero of Fire Spectacle," combined a discussion of the heroic ability of the canine star with a necessary reassurance that she was humanely treated by the production crew (press book, *Sun Comes Up*, 1949). This method of commentary provides both publicity for the star and the film itself, utilizing the connotative values of "hero" and "spectacle" to reinforce conceptions of Lassie's perfection.

Publicity materials generally took great pains to assure the public that Lassie was being well taken care of during the filming of each of the seven films in the series. When traveling to and from the location shoots during the production of *The Painted Hills*, Lassie supposedly had his own compartment on the train that the production crew utilized and his own station wagon to transport him up to the mountain sets. Throughout all this traveling, he was said to have been accompanied by both Weatherwax and an ASPCA officer, ensuring his well-being. Concurrent with these assertions of fair treatment are prewritten articles testifying to Lassie's "tough" nature as exemplified by his ability to withstand freezing temperatures while filming on location in the High Sierras (press book, *The Painted Hills*, 1951). These articles, alongside others promoting Lassie's "perfection," feed into the canine's star text as an idealized pet, as well as dog hero. Finally, articles within press books for *The Painted Hills* detail Lassie's "real-life" courage and intelligence. In one piece entitled "Lassie's Bark

Poster for *Challenge to Lassie* (Richard Thorpe, MGM, 1949) from press book, *Challenge to Lassie*, University of Southern California Cinematic Arts Library Archive.

Cues Ocean Rescue of 3," the author recounts how, when en route to Catalina Island for filming, Lassie's incessant barking alerted the crew to the presence of a stranded boat, imperceptibly adrift nearby. The Coast Guard awarded the canine hero a certificate of honor for his help in rescuing the passengers (press book, *The Painted Hills*, 1951). The veracity of this piece of news is debatable at best; however, the more pertinent issue here is its employment by the studio publicity department to promote Lassie as a "naturally" intuitive subject whose dynamic personal life and offscreen behavior should be of interest to fans. To a degree arguably not matched by any previous dog heroes or canine sidekicks, Lassie had truly become an entity that incited the kind of traditional fandom reserved for human stars and their private lives.

In addition to utilizing information about Pal's exploits on and off the set to craft public perception of him, studio publicists also created and promoted publicity stunts that both reinforced Lassie's public image as a dog hero and paradoxically complicated it. For example, as Lassie was marketed as the quintessential American hero, studio promotional tactics used the collie for the reinforcement of appropriate standards of civic duty through public displays. For the exhibition of *Challenge to Lassie*, the "Variety Promotional Stunts" portion of the film's press book encourages theater owners to employ collies to act as "Lassie doubles" and to utilize them to "shake hands" with children outside the entrance to the lobby. But at the same time, in contradiction of Lassie's image as a near-human exemplar, exhibitors are warned to securely muzzle the collie being used to ensure protection from liability. Other stunts projected heteronormative gender politics through the figure of Lassie; theaters were encouraged to implore children to bring in their favorite canine stories and pictures for lobby contests, often enacting a gendered hierarchy because only boys were considered for the competition in order to perpetuate the "boy and his dog" theme (press book, *Challenge to Lassie*, 1949). During the release of *Son of Lassie*, exhibitors could use collie doubles that were dressed in signs identifying them as the "son of Lassie" to solicit war bonds and Red Cross funds (press book, *Son of Lassie*, 1944). The exploitation of animal labor simply to facilitate promotional stunts is ethically questionable, and here "ideal" American heroism is achieved through support for both institutional forms of capitalism and gendered hierarchies, and through the use of beings whose agency within the stunts was never taken into account.

Official publicity materials related to Lassie's films are also revelatory in their anxieties over the canine star's potentially transgressive "cross-dressing" performances. Articles contained in the press book for *Son of Lassie* convey an even more virulent form of gender policing than the "boy and his dog" theme required. The publicity department's agenda sneaks its way onto the pages with headlines like "Lassie Resumes 'Her' Rightful Sex. 'She' Is Actually a Male Collie." These statements are often accompanied by a "Did you know?" precedent, structuring them as public service announcements for the edification of the reader (press book, *Son of Lassie*, 1944). In promoting Lassie as an embodiment of ideal American heroism, it became crucial to reinforce heteronormative codes of sexuality that would be instructive to audiences. During the war, the "truth" of Lassie's "real" identity needed to be revealed in order to promote a connection between "natural" heroics, "masculine" behavior, and "male" biological sex. The publicity and promotional material sends the message that using a "feminine" subject (if Lassie actually were a "female" dog) to enact ideal American codes of individualism and bravery might somehow undermine the patriarchal order. An article "written" by Lassie him-/herself, entitled "I'm a Lucky Lassie," states, "I am grateful for a chance to be myself again (a *he-dog*) after the female impersonation in *Lassie Come Home*. After all, I have my *pride*" (press book, *Son of Lassie*, 1944 [emphasis added]). This anxious machination to equate sex and gender was channeled through Lassie by the human members of the publicity crew in order to encourage their version of ideal behavior. The article would also seem to suggest that, if given the choice, Lassie would exercise her/his agency and innately decide to play "male" roles. Thus Lassie becomes the unlikely site of a fervent battle over the proper representation of masculinity in film, whether human or not. A male actor impersonating a female character, without the underlying impulse toward comedic relief, is constructed here as a degradation of morality and pride. As the Lassie films were considered a children's series, it became crucial to promote the "right" ideas about gender roles to America's youth.

Pet Promotions: Breed Frenzy and Racial Purity

While MGM's publicity department was asserting a heteronormative agenda via constructions of Lassie's persona as the perfect "human," the studio was simultaneously encouraging another form of "responsibility," pet ownership, and exerted a visible influence over not only the popularization of the collie breed but also the promotion of its associative relationship to Lassie imagery. In addition to disseminating imagery that would cultivate Lassie's stardom, the studio engaged in irresponsible promotional schemes that negligently encouraged dog ownership, especially of dogs with documented pedigree. There is a disturbing connection between the fetishization of Lassie's star image as the ideal pet and the documented burgeoning of the demand for collies following the release of the films in the franchise. The success of the Lassie series is said to have inaugurated the frenzy by prompting the sale of thousands of collies, often in conjunction with intense theater campaigns that idealized the breed and its biological "perfection." The years directly following the 1943 premiere of *Lassie Come Home* saw a meteoric increase in collie ownership as purebred registrations for the breed went from 3,000 to 18,400 by 1949 (Brown 1993, 4). According to statistics, the collie rose from the twelfth to the third most popular dog breed by 1949 (Helen Colton, "Top Dog in Hollywood," *New York Times*, February 27, 1949). The rise in popularity was most likely due to a multitude of factors, each exercising pressure over the development of the breed. The postwar rise in consumerism and suburban growth as well as the promotion of the breed by studio publicity teams and theater exhibitioners all proved to be forceful influences (Beauregard 2006). Urban flight to the suburbs, in particular, would result in an increased amount of space in which to house and provide for a pet, especially dogs. As pet-keeping assumed more importance in middle-class life, the American postwar economic boom enabled an even greater investment in the dog as an indicator of prosperity. There was a popularization of specialized canine breeds, like the toy poodle and the Pekinese, and exotic species of tropical fish and birds, the ownership of which was thought to convey luxuriousness (Franklin 1999, 88). The "family dog" stood as a sign of middle-class affluence as families were encouraged to spend time on leisure activities and on luxuries like pets.

Particular contests, supported by the studios, fostered a problematic investment in genetic purity by appealing to the entrepreneurial spirit of America's youth. An advertisement in the press book for *Son of Lassie* encourages local theater owners to contact their newspapers so that they could cooperatively engage in a pedigreed dog "giveaway." Citing the success that the *Des Moines Register and Tribune* had in orchestrating a contest in which boys, age twelve to sixteen, would be offered the chance to own a purebred canine as a prize, the MGM publicity department encouraged the development of similar schemes elsewhere (press book, *Son of Lassie*, 1944). The particular contest held by the Des Moines newspaper awarded approximately one hundred dogs to the best carriers of their paper and promoted the competition through a myriad of media, including radio, advertising, mailed letters, and daily news stories. Each method employed the use of production stills from the Lassie films and pictures of Lassie with Laddie by her side, playing into the fantasy of owning a dog as "perfect" as Lassie herself. The grand prize winner of the contest was promised a genuine "son of Lassie," a guarantee grotesque in its privileging of both the passing on of patriarchal lineage and investment in the "purity" of the bloodline. The studio irresponsibly condoned the release of particular dogs to homes that may have possibly been ill-equipped to handle the idiosyncratic behaviors of some of the more temperamental breeds. By promoting tactics like these, the studio reinforced a biological imperative that constructed a racialized hierarchy.

The perpetuation of breed standards within the canine world constitutes one of the world's largest ongoing eugenics experiments, projecting an insidious racial politics that favors "pure" blood over the miscegenation of genetic lines found in the mixed-breed dog. Donna Haraway (2008) has argued that institutionalized forms of breeding systematically privilege the purity of male lineage and utilize sophisticated methods of data-keeping to catalogue various breeds. It is this system of regulating reproductive viability via genetic manipulation that Haraway connects to the histories of eugenics (53). Even Weatherwax contributed to this privileging of the pedigree by imposing the rule that only direct-line descendants of Pal could play Lassie in any film or television program. Pal became an inadvertent and odd index of compulsory heterosexuality, one whose purpose was to reproduce both the bloodline of his breed (read race) and the particular "inherent" traits of Lassie that everyone had come to associate with visions of ideal heroics. Conceptualizing the function of star lineage from a human perspective is far less problematic; even the harshest critiques of nepotism in the film industry do not focus on "pure" breeding as such. While famous Hollywood dynasties like the Fondas, Barrymores, and Coppolas consist of multiple generations of performers, the younger individual stars are marketed as unique personalities and would never be expected to relinquish their identities and act as proxies for their ancestors.

In conjunction with the 1949 release of *Challenge to Lassie*, the studios yet again helped theater owners promote canine ownership through promotional schemes. They suggested that a "Missing Dog Bureau" be constructed in the lobbies of theaters in order to facilitate the adoption of shelter dogs (press book, *Challenge to Lassie*, 1949). Perhaps on a superficial level this would appear a noble attempt to raise awareness of homeless pets, a conception encouraged by the theater's cooperation with the local Humane Society. The inappropriate placement of the "bureau" inside the theater lobby, however, invited audiences to conflate the ideal dogs seen on screen with the desperate pictures of homeless pets that needed to be rescued, just like Lassie. The promotion was structured as a wall of photos that had been contributed by the local Humane Society under which descriptions were written, corresponding to each photo. Promoting the impulsive adoption of a pet without prior knowledge of the dog's physical needs or disposition invites the perpetuation of the shelter cycle. The studios played a role in constructing environments, inside and outside the films, through which canine ownership was promoted. This fed directly into the idealization of particular breeds like the collie and reveals the direct impact that Hollywood could exercise over the lived experiences of actual canines, beyond those who appeared in its films.

Promotional and publicity materials helped to construct the image of Lassie as the "ideal" American action hero through posters, articles, contests, and, of course, the actual films themselves. Problematic promotional stunts that were encouraged by the studios and carried out by theater owners exploited the reception of Lassie as the perfect breed. Her star text was reinforced by the public's disavowal of the labor involved in making Lassie appear to be such a consummate performer. The studio promotional contests negligently popularized breeds like the collie and encouraged an investment in racialized purity. The manner in which animals like Pal were utilized speaks to larger claims about the ethical treatment of animal performers and their work. Industrial constraints during the studio era produced a manifold image of the canine star as the quintessential "American," complicated in part by the studio's own actions and the public itself.

Notes

1. A male collie named Pal played the role of Lassie. When I discuss the star text or constructed images and ideas associated with Lassie, I will refer to Lassie as a "she" because that is how MGM promoted her. When I am discussing Lassie or Pal as an actual material animal I will refer to Pal/Lassie as "he."
2. Weatherwax promulgated the story that he knew immediately that Pal was "extraordinary" (see Weatherwax and Rothwell 1950, 12–14; Edelson 1980, 17), but in fact the trainer did not initially keep the dog but gave him away to an actor friend with a large ranch; indeed, Weatherwax "assumed he would never see Pal again" (Collins 1993, 22;

see also Beck and Clark 2002, 158). Only when he heard that MGM was casting a collie in the leading role of what would become *Lassie Come Home* did Weatherwax buy the now-unkempt dog back, for ten dollars. Pal did not pass any of the auditions but was hired as a stunt dog for the female "show-winning" dog hired to star as Lassie. When the female hire refused to jump into a flooded river, Pal took over and was so impressive that the female dog was "immediately fired" and "a star was born" (Collins 1993, 26).

3. At the time of Pal's casting as Lassie there were only a few dogs at the brothers' school. Two years after the film's release the number had grown to more than seventy, and "those seventy worked so consistently that the brothers had almost twenty assistants just to train the animals and get them to their shoots," with most of them hired as "background players" (Collins 1993, 51).

4. This action would enable the studio to in turn sell all of the rights to Weatherwax in 1950, in lieu of giving him back pay in relation to the production of the last film. Four years later, Weatherwax and Pal were approached to do a television program, entitled *Lassie*, a show that would air successfully on CBS for seventeen seasons and garner awards and profits from merchandise and advertising.

5. A mainstay of classical Hollywood promotion, press books were created for most individual feature films and provided prewritten articles and photos, as well as posters to be used by local newspapers and other exhibition venues. Spaces were left in articles for a theater to insert its own name, and depending on the genre, "tie-ins" and publicity stunts were often suggested—holding "look-alike" contests, stationing nurses in the auditorium during a horror film, and things of that ilk.

6. They also indicated changes in the studio's control over publicity and promotional material as tabloids and other independent modes of star discourse became more prominent.

Chronological Filmography

Lassie Come Home (Fred M. Wilcox, 1943). Roddy McDowall, Donald Crisp, Dame May Whitty, Edmund Gwenn, Elsa Lanchester, Nigel Bruce, Elizabeth Taylor, Pal [as Lassie].

Son of Lassie (S. Sylvan Simon, 1945). Peter Lawford, Donald Crisp, June Lockhart, Pal.

Courage of Lassie (Fred M. Wilcox, 1946). Elizabeth Taylor, Frank Morgan, Tom Drake, Pal [as Lassie].

Hills of Home (Fred M. Wilcox, 1948). Edmund Gwenn, Donald Crisp, Tom Drake, Janet Leigh, Pal [as Lassie].

Challenge to Lassie (Richard Thorpe, 1949). Edmund Gwenn, Donald Crisp, Geraldine Brooks, Pal [as Lassie].

The Sun Comes Up (Richard Thorpe, 1949). Jeanette MacDonald, Lloyd Nolan, Claude Jarman Jr., Lassie.

The Painted Hills (Harold F. Kress, 1951). Pal [as Lassie], Paul Kelly, Bruce Cowling, Gary Gray.

Part Two

Character and Supporting Actors

●●●●●●●●●●●●●●●●●●●●●●

5

Dogs at War

● ● ● ● ● ● ● ● ● ● ● ● ● ● ● ● ● ● ● ●

Military Dogs in Film

AARON SKABELUND

The practical and symbolic deployment of dogs during World War II was unprecedented and has not been replicated since. Although the conflict was heavily mechanized, armies on all sides used canines in numbers and in ways as never before; one analyst estimates that the Allied and Axis militaries employed more than 250,000 canines for a variety of tasks, including as messengers, sentries, draft animals, trackers, and patrol auxiliaries (Kelch 1982, 2). As I have detailed elsewhere, dogs—both real and imagined—were rhetorically deployed through a variety of media forms to mobilize people for war (Skabelund 2011). Armies first used dogs extensively during World War I, but that conflict inspired little figurative mobilization of canines and almost no films featuring military dogs.[1] Ironically, one of the most famous canine actors of the twentieth century, Rin Tin Tin, who was according to publicity stories found as a newborn German Shepherd in the ruins of a bombed-out military dog kennel in 1918, never played a military dog in any of the numerous films in which he—and later Rin Tin Tins—starred. Instead, he and his progeny played police dogs on interwar movie screens and the reliable ally of white settlers fighting off "savage" American Indians and low-class bandits on television in the 1950s. Total mobilization of canines for practical and symbolic ends did not take place until the next global conflagration that occurred after "the war to end all wars."

During World War II, militaries in all combatant nations relied on their civilian populations to supply them with dogs, and this process became a subtle but powerful tool to mobilize people, and especially children, for war. Throughout the first half of the twentieth century dogs were by far the most widespread household pet, increasingly regarded as "members of the family" and assumed to have an intimate connection to children. Dogs therefore linked, in both real and figurative ways, the home front to the battlefront, families with military organizations, and children with soldiers. The donation of the "family dog" to the military produced a sense of one's personally participating in the war effort. Official and private voices sought through national education and media to rally people for war by using dogs as symbols, and, as a result, the metaphorical mobilization of canines surpassed that of any other nonhuman animal.

Canine actors playing military dogs have frequently appeared in narrative films about World War II. Focusing on Japanese and American films made both during and after the conflict, this essay analyzes such movies and the ways that cinematic military canines shaped and reflected their respective country's wartime mobilization and memories of the war. Studios in Japan and the United States produced most of the movies about military dogs, in part simply because their film industries made more films during the war than did their counterparts in Europe and China. The major European countries at war—Britain, France, Germany, and the Soviet Union—had less leeway to devote to making movies, and in the ones they did make they paid little attention to military dogs. Additional factors were at play. Almost immediately after the Nazis came to power in 1933, the German parliament passed a series of progressive animal protection laws that included a ban on the use of animals in film (Arluke and Sanders 1996). Soviet and Chinese communist leaders, in accordance with Marxist criticisms of bourgeois practices, were generally dismissive of pet-keeping. And France, which had a vibrant prewar film industry and pet-keeping culture, was quickly occupied. In contrast, Japan and the United States, especially, were far from the front and had the resources to make many films, including a number about military dogs. For Japan World War II began with the Manchurian Incident in 1931, but until the early 1940s the country's movie studios were insulated from the fighting. This, too, was of course true for the American film industry once the United States joined the conflict in December 1941. Films about military dogs became a distinctive though small subgenre in both countries during the war.

Given the metaphorical mobilization of military dogs in film during the war, it should not be surprising that a number of postwar films also used them to deal with and remember certain aspects of the conflict. Few films that feature military dogs have been set in earlier military conflicts or in other wars since 1945. After World War II, military dogs lost much of their figurative power to mobilize people for war, though not their practical value for military purposes. This decline in symbolic clout has been directly linked to changes in actual practices. While militaries around the world have continued to use dogs, they have established discreet contracts with large private kennels to ensure a steady and reliable supply. This shift effectively eliminated the need to rely on average citizens for dogs. Moreover, an increasing number of people have become generally more suspicious of nationalism, jingoism, and anthropomorphism. Since 1945, probably no films have sought to mobilize people for war in the obvious ways that many films tried to do during the conflict, much less attempt to use stories of military dogs to do so. In addition, commercial reasons have likely been a factor. Hollywood and Japanese studios have made many more films featuring dogs by adopting dog themes into other genre films in the last several decades. As a result of all of these factors, there have been fewer postwar films that feature military dogs, and among those few almost all have been set during World War II.

Wartime Canine—and Human—Mobilization

During World War II, movie studios cast canine actors in roles that contributed to their wider metaphorical mobilization of rallying people for total war. Film historians have detailed how the film industry in both Japan and the United States contributed to wartime mass mobilization, but they have paid little attention to the use of military animals in film (see Koppes and Black 1987; Doherty 1993; Roeder 1995; High 2003). Many military-dog films encouraged people to donate dogs to the military, frequently celebrating the supposed exploits of army dogs and figuratively connecting moviegoers to the military and the war. Other such films conveyed the message that all members of society—whether human or canine, regardless of their gender, age, or fitness—could contribute to the war.

Even as military-dog films encouraged civilians to donate their dogs to the military, canines were not the only ones being mobilized for war. Perhaps the earliest example of this subgenre was *Sensen ni hoeyu* [*Barks at the Battlefront*]. Independently produced by the Tōyō movie studio in 1936, the film was one of many creative works inspired by the story of Kongō and Nachi, two German Shepherds that achieved national fame in the wake of the Manchurian Incident of September 1931, when the Japanese army used a staged explosion on a railway in northeastern China as a pretext to launch an attack on the troops of a local warlord. In the midst of the fighting, the two dogs, it was said, joined in a skirmish and died after killing many enemy soldiers. Their greatly exaggerated exploits were celebrated in newspaper and magazine accounts, a textbook story that was read by fifth-year students across the entire country, and a statue dedicated with great fanfare. As a result, military dogs became a frequent motif in juvenile literature, picture-story shows, board games, songs, children's kimono fabrics, and paintings, as well as *Barks at the Battlefront*, during the 1930s.

Although no copies of *Barks at the Battlefront* appear to have survived, its basic plot can be surmised from contemporary reviews. One critic praised its producers for the movie's realistic use of dogs, which included "moving, tear-jerking scenes" of dogs being hit by gunfire ("Sensen ni hoeyu," *Kinema junpō*, September 21, 1936, 107). The film told of a teenage girl (Fujita Yōko) of a well-to-do family and her dog, Esu (Ace), played by Shitō-gō, a dog owned by a top general and former minister of war. At the beginning of the picture the family's Shepherd dog delivers a new litter, and the girl declares that she will present "our Emperor's Army" with the best dogs as soon as they have been weaned. "Ah," her friend exclaims, "a dog soldier? Oh, how handsome! Our baby brother is going to be a hero on the battlefield." Ace is sent to Manchuria, where he teams with a female Shepherd dog, Doru (Doll), played by Karumen-gō (Carmen), to form a two-gender pair. Together, they apprehend an enemy spy, with no human intervention until after the capture. According to the end of the most detailed review, Ace and Doll depart for the front, presumably to become heroic martyrs— like Kongō and Nachi—in a blaze of gunfire (*Gun'yōken* 5 no. 7, April 1, 1936, 246–247).

We cannot know how the film was received, but as life seemed to imitate art a few years later, it clearly had an audience and some influence. In 1939, three years after the motion picture's release, the *Tōkyō shinbun* daily newspaper featured the "beautiful story of a silent partisan and a young lady," the young lady being Teshima Tamie, a student at a higher girls' school and a member of a wealthy family residing in an upscale neighborhood of the city, and the "silent partisan" Aren, her German Shepherd dog ("Gunken Aren no shi," 1939, Teshima Tamie Album, Yūshūkan War Memorial Museum, Yasukuni Shrine, Tokyo). Aren, as Teshima wrote in an enthusiast newsletter, "left my small loving hand for the large loving hand of the military," specifically the Fourteenth Division based in Manchuria ("Komogomo no kokoro," *Teikoku gun'yōken kyōkai Tōkyō shibu hō*, September 1938, Teshima Tamie Album).

Unlike the fictional Esu in *Barks at the Battlefront*, Aren's demise at the front was due to the disease filariasis, but according to the *Tōkyō shinbun* her death was still heroic. The article quoted Teshima as stating, "As a woman, I cannot stand on the frontline, so I asked Aren to go fight for me." In this manner Teshima echoed the rhetoric of her prescribed gender role: it was her duty to send family members, whether a dog or a male relative, to war in her place. Teshima pasted newspaper advertisements for the movie *Barks at the Battlefront* in an album, so the film likely contributed in some way to her determination to give the dog to the military. The film and other materials, such as another textbook story and accompanying song introduced in 1940 that told of a girl who tenderly raised a German Shepherd puppy and donated him to the military, encouraged audiences to emulate those actions, which were clearly analogous to and in preparation for sending human males off to war.

Several wartime movies conveyed similar lessons to Americans. The first such film was *War Dogs*, released in late 1942. The *Los Angeles Times* recommended that "every youngster . . . should see" the movie, which "shows, in fascinating

Staged publicity photo from *Sensen ni hoeyu* [*Barks at the Battlefront*] (Mikito Yamane, Tōyō, 1936), showing, right to left, Doru [Doll] (Karumen-gō [Carmen]) and Esu [Ace] (Shitō-gō) on each side of their handler. *Gun'yōken* 5, no. 7 (April 1, 1936), cover. Collection of the author.

and dramatic manner, how these canines are trained" ("'War Dogs' Appealing," November 26, 1942, 43). The film begins with a message that slowly flows up the screen: "*This picture is dedicated to you loyal citizens who unselfishly are enlisting your 'Dogs for Defense.' Thanks to the Dogs for Defense organization especially Carl Spitz, who has trained hundreds of dogs. The war dogs you will see in this picture were delivered to the Army immediately after the scenes were photographed. They are doing their part—with you—in our Country's . . . MARCH TO VICTORY!*" (italics in original). The film, which was released at the same time that the federal program "Dogs for Defense" was calling for people to donate their dogs to the military (through newsreels, for example), tells of a boy, Billy Freeman (Billy Lee), who is arrested for stealing two dollars. After the juvenile court judge, Roger (Bradley Page), and his social worker girlfriend, Joan (Kay Linaker), discover that Billy took the money to free his German Shepherd dog, Pal,[2] from the pound, they take an interest in the boy. They pay for Pal to be released; suggest to Billy and his father, William (Addison Richards), that they donate Pal to Dogs for Defense; and arrange for William, a decorated World War I veteran who has fallen on hard times, to be hired at a defense plant and for Pal to be employed as a sentry there. One night German saboteurs attempt to blow up the plant. William dies after he bravely carries the bomb away from the factory, and Pal captures the intruders. In the final scenes Joan finally agrees to marry Roger (on his thirtieth proposal), and they then adopt Billy; and Pal, who is on temporary leave, joins the family before he and Roger, who has joined the marines, report for duty. All ends happily ever after as new wife/mother and son, Joan and Billy, are eager to have husband/father and dog, Roger and Pal, serve their country. As the opening message admonishes, each member of the family is "doing their part," and audience members, too, should do theirs by enlisting their family members—both canine and human—in the military.

Several films made during the next few years—*Sergeant Mike* (1944), *My Pal, Wolf* (1944), and *A Boy, a Girl, and a Dog* (1946)—communicated much the same message. *Sergeant Mike* depicts a cute eight-year-old boy (Larry Joe Olsen) telling a soldier (Larry Parks) who is not happy in the canine corps where he is assigned to train the boy's German Shepherd dog, Mike (the dog's real name), that when he heard his father had been killed in the Pacific theater, he decided to donate his dog. "I wanted to fight," he declares; "Mike and I went down there [to the recruitment office]. But they would not take kids. He joined up and we both felt better." That conversation (and the allure of the boy's widowed mother) lead to an abrupt epiphany for the soldier, who, embracing his assignment, departs with Mike for the Pacific to fight "Jap rats." There Mike is paired with an Airedale, Pearl (also the dog's real name), whom the handlers refer to as "his girlfriend," creating another heterosexual romantic pair that serves heroically. The didactic nature of the film makes its opening dedicatory message nearly unnecessary: "To the war dog who serves in war the same as his human master does, who gets through where machines and men might fail, who gives a life to save a life, we respectfully dedicate this motion picture." Contemporary movie critics took notice of "Hollywood's preoccupation with bringing the war into the home." Of *My Pal, Wolf,* which reached a climax when it required "no less a personage than the Secretary of War" to convince a tearful little girl to send off her beloved German Shepherd dog, Wolf, to serve his country, a *New York Times* reviewer observed the "drama not only brings the war into the home but it drags it right into the nursery" ("'My Pal, Wolf,' Which Drags the War into the Nursery," October 9, 1944, 17). Whether set in America or Japan, films about military dogs were aimed primarily at children and sought to mobilize both dogs and youngsters for war.

Other films suggested that all dogs—and by extension, all people—could contribute to the conflict. Not all dogs were German Shepherds or Airedales, two of the breeds that were the most preferred by militaries. Some, like Laddie, featured in *Son of Lassie* (1945), were not regarded as qualified to become military dogs. In addition to being a collie, Laddie's intelligence, maturity, and courage were severely lacking compared to his mother, Lassie. As highlighted by Kelly Wolf in her essay in this volume, the brains and pluck of Lassie as performed by the canine actor Pal in *Lassie Come Home* (1943) were not an easy act to follow. The film was set in Depression-era Yorkshire, England. A working-class couple, the Carracloughs, are forced by financial hardship to sell their

Movie poster for *War Dogs* (S. Roy Luby, Monogram, 1942), which was distributed in Australia by British Empire Films. Note the emphasis on William and Billy's last name, Freeman. Collection of the author.

son Joe's beloved dog, Lassie, to the wealthy Duke of Rudling (Nigel Bruce), who, assisted by his granddaughter Priscilla (played by preteen Elizabeth Taylor), owns a large kennel nearby. Loyal Lassie, however, repeatedly escapes and returns to Joe (Roddy McDowall), the last time traveling hundreds of miles from the duke's Scottish estate, outsmarting dog catchers and braving a violent storm, to joyfully reunite with the boy who loves her.[3]

In 1945 the sequel *Son of Lassie* set the story in wartime Yorkshire. The duke has converted his Yorkshire estate into a Recruiting School for War Dogs, Mr. Carraclough is serving as the school's head trainer, Joe and Priscilla are in their late teens (played of course by different actors), and the champion collie Lassie has given birth to Laddie. A socially—and romantically—unconfident Joe (Peter Lawford) decides to join the Royal Air Force and to enroll Laddie in the army dog school, but the dog does not perform with smarts or bravery; during training exercises, unlike the German Shepherds, Laddie goes around barriers instead of hurdling them, and rather than attacking he flees from gunfire. "You get bigger," sighs Joe to Laddie, "but you never grow up." Joe might as well be talking about himself; indeed, he seems to be projecting his own insecurities onto the dog. Soon, however, both begin to rise to the occasion. After Joe leaves to begin his training, Laddie, as if imitating the epic journey of his mother, walks forty miles to find him at the military base. Then Laddie sneaks into Joe's airplane just before it departs on a dangerous mission over Nazi-occupied Norway. Forced to parachute when hit by German flak, Joe and Laddie repeatedly avoid capture and ultimately escape back to England, where they are reunited with Priscilla (June Lockhart) and Lassie. "Ah yes," Joe's father exclaims, "our lads have come home." This is one message of the film: war forges "lads" into competent and valiant mature males, whether they are human or canine. Confronted by military service and war, however timid and inexperienced they may be, Joe and Laddie as young males step up to serve and defend those who are too old, too young, or too female to do so. In turn, females such as Priscilla and Lassie (like the Japanese girl Teshima dispatching her Aren to fight) are expected to willingly send Joe and Laddie to war in their stead.

Another type of wartime military-dog film was cartoons. Although cartoons often satirized army life, they inevitably reinforced the idea that war was an appealing and harmless adventure. They imagined military dogs that were completely fictional, but such canines were not that much more divorced from reality than "actual" live-action war dogs such as Ace and Laddie. A Japanese cartoon based on the comic series *Norakuro* was one such example. Norakuro, which is an abbreviation of *norainu* (stray dog) and Kurokichi (the dog's name, which literally means "Black Lucky"), is both the name of a comic series (manga) and several animated cartoon shorts (anime), as well as their main character. The manga appeared from January 1931 to October 1941 in the monthly boy's magazine *Shōnen kurabu* [*Boy's Club*], issued by the publishing giant Kōdansha, and was the longest running and probably the most widely read comic in the 1930s.

Several animated versions, which were loosely based on the manga, appeared in theaters before the main feature film during the same decade. Norakuro's popularity reflected the nationalism, war fever, and enthusiasm for war dogs of the era, particularly after the Manchurian Incident and the heroics of Kongō and Nachi captured the attention of the nation.

Norakuro, though, was a bit more complicated. Unlike Kongō and Nachi and the filmic heroes Ace and Doll they inspired, Norakuro did not explicitly promote bravery or loyalty. His creator, Tagawa (given name, Takamizawa Nakatarō, 1889–1989), was a young avant-garde artist who was influenced by jazz music, socialism, and foreign cartoons and characters, including Felix the Cat (1919–) and Mickey Mouse (1928–). The manga series was proletarian in its instincts: Norakuro, a stray, orphaned mongrel, joins the army as a lowly second-class private and experiences numerous and humorous blunders as he progresses upward in rank until finally retiring as a colonel. In many ways the cartoon provided an irreverent look at the Imperial army, and Norakuro and his fellow dogs' bloopers contested the myth of the Imperial military as immune to surrender, tears, or humor (Yamaguchi 1976, 97–100).

Even as Tagawa demythologized the mystique of the Imperial army, he created an idealized picture of military life that was perhaps even further from reality. Norakuro and his fellow dogs, despite various gaffes, always triumphed, and, as in most cartoons, conflict was a harmless and entertaining affair, at least for Norakuro's Regiment of Fierce Dogs, who never seemed to die. Indeed, the medium of animation helped to infuse them with such immortality. The plasticity and elasticity of animated characters, as media studies critic Ōtsuka Eiji has noted, gives them a sense of invulnerability (2008). No matter what happens to the bodies of cartoon characters, they rarely die and simply bounce right back after normally life-ending incidents. In *Norakuro nitōhei* (1933), for example, Norakuro drives a military truck off an enormous cliff but comes away unscathed. This imaginary world was a favorite of a cohort of youngsters who followed Norakuro's escapades on the page and screen. He introduced soldiering to millions of children, many of whom later entered the armed forces and may have gone off to war with images of Norakuro and his military adventures in their heads.

The influence of American cartoons about military dogs on U.S. audiences paled in comparison to Norakuro's effect in Japan, but they, too, presented a romanticized picture of military life, even as they made light of it. Directed by William Hanna and Joseph Barbera (the creators of the cat-and-mouse team Tom and Jerry, as well as many other well-known cartoon characters), MGM's *War Dogs* (not to be confused with the live-action 1942 film of the same name) was one of a "string of fighting canine cartoons" that nearly every studio made in 1943 (Shull and Witt 2004, 62).[4] As in the other cartoons, its dogs obviously represent human soldiers. *War Dogs* pokes fun at both actual human military training and the short propaganda newsreels—showing dogs being trained and

A scene from *Norakuro nitōhei* (Yasuji Murata, studio unknown, 1933), showing Norakuro marching at the head of the Regiment of Fierce Dogs. Digital frame enlargement.

calling on people to donate their dogs—that were routinely shown before the main feature. The cartoon begins by slowly panning across a number of dogs asleep in their "pup tents." One dreams of chasing a caricatured Japanese soldier who screams gibberish until the dog bites his rear end and flings him out of view. The dog wakes up briefly to record another kill with another tally mark in the dirt. "A portion of each day is devoted to classwork," the narrator later explains; "Here our dogs learn to distinguish between military and nonmilitary objects." The same dog is shown a series of objects, including a machine gun, the sound of which he imitates, and a pinup girl, whom he begins to howl and pant at. Some of the training the dogs do is what military dogs would do, such as running messages, but most of it is what human soldiers do, such as pitching a tent, skiing, and parachuting. As with *Norakuro*, army life and implicitly war are depicted as an adventure of sorts, where no one gets hurt, even after being run over by a tank, as happens to one dog. Portraying soldiers as dogs serves to humanize the dogs and to trivialize military conflict.

The use of an actual "military" dog in another American film seemed to have the similar intent of humanizing the soldiers who adopted him. *Air Force* (1943) tells the story of a single B-17 Flying Fortress, the *Mary Ann*, and its crew as they proceed through time and across the Pacific from the attack on Pearl Harbor, to Wake Island, Clark Field in the Philippines, the Battle of the Coral Sea, and finally to Australia. Before they leave Wake, which is about to be attacked by the

Japanese navy, the crew adopt a small retriever named Tripoli (uncredited) from marines stationed there who have kept him as a pet. As film historians Robert L. McLaughlin and Sally E. Parry (2006) have observed, the dog's presence thereafter "serves as an emotional reminder of the marines' sacrifice" (76). Moreover, the airmen's interaction with the dog serves to depict them as caring and compassionate. In the United States, as well as Japan, photographs of soldiers and their dogs—either actual military dogs or more often unit pet or mascot dogs—often appeared in newspapers. Such photos, like the scenes in *Air Force*, heightened the feeling among people at home that the soldiers who took care of these cherished childhood "buddies" were "our boys," and the sense, as McLaughlin and Parry put it, that they were all part of an imagined "extended family" (76).

Small dogs like Tripoli—and everyone else, human or canine—could contribute to the war on the home front too. This was the moral of another film about a boy and his dog, which had the telling title *The Underdog*. Released in 1943, the plot of *The Underdog* was similar to *War Dogs*, but its focus on a Dust Bowl migrant family in California, who own a midsize, mixed-breed terrier, seemed to make *The Underdog* a *War Dogs* for the working class. As in *War Dogs*, the dog becomes a hero when he captures a pair of saboteurs; the main adult character also enlists in the military in the end. Although each member of the family—of both species—is an "underdog" of sorts, the film's message is that all of them can do their part, whether at home or in the military and regardless of each one's circumstances, to contribute to victory.

Dogged Memories

All of the wartime military-dog films, then, whether American or Japanese, sought to mobilize audiences for war. Several early films encouraged people to donate their dogs to the military. Later films highlighted dogs, regardless of their breed and size, who contributed to the war. After World War II came to an end, however, military dogs did not disappear from movie screens, although they appeared most often, at least in the United States, in the immediate aftermath of the conflict. Since then, the release of military-dog films has been far more sporadic in both Japan and the United States.

In the years immediately after the war several films dealt with the issue of traumatized soldiers returning home from the conflict by focusing on military dogs. Although the target audience of these movies was primarily youngsters, like immediate postwar films noirs such as *The Killers* (1946) they displayed a much darker view of the conflict than wartime films did (see Bodnar 2004). One such movie was *Courage of Lassie* (1946), which had less in common with the earlier films than the title suggests. The by-then-teenage Elizabeth Taylor returned to play a new character, Kathie. Pal, who played Lassie in the first two films as well as the adult Laddie in the second production, played Bill, though he is credited as Lassie. The film's title, Taylor, and Pal, however, were the only connections with the previous films. Here Bill, raised in the mountains of the Pacific Northwest (not Yorkshire), goes off to war to fight the Japanese in the Aleutians (not the Germans in Norway). And unlike *Son of Lassie*, the third film exhibits a much more ambiguous view of the war. Commenting on its production in 1944, the *Los Angeles Times'* Edwin Schallert stated the obvious: "The tale is symbolic of the returned soldiers' experiences" ("Bette Davis Schedule Increased at Warners," August 11, 1944, 10). After being adopted by Kathie as a puppy, Bill becomes an accomplished sheepdog, but one day an accident separates him from Kathie, and he ends up in a veterinary hospital far away. Not knowing whom the dog belongs to, the veterinarian donates him to the military. In Alaska Bill serves heroically; though severely wounded, he leads reinforcements to rescue a unit that is surrounded by enemy troops. By then he is starting to show signs of combat fatigue and is sent home by train. En route he escapes into the wilderness and begins to attack sheep and chickens. Bill eventually encounters Kathie, whom he does not recognize and attempts to attack before losing consciousness. Thanks to Kathie's love, Bill eventually loses his ferocity. A court order, however, has been issued to destroy him, and a hearing is held to determine his fate. The situation looks grim until his army tattoo is discovered, and he is identified as a missing war hero. Kathie's elderly friend (Frank Morgan) makes an impassioned plea for Bill to be spared by recounting his "conspicuous bravery" and linking him to human soldiers returning from the war:

> This letter I made my notes on is from my boy, Gary. He's in an army hospital in New York, and from what he writes he's going through something like Bill here went through. And it just occurred to me that perhaps a lot of our boys will be coming back not quite ready to take up where they left off. They'll have gone through more than most of us could ever think of, and they're going to need patience and love and understanding from us. And most all, perhaps, they'll need time. You know, they didn't become soldiers in a day, and we can't expect them to become civilians in a day either.

Even Bill's accusers are moved, and the judge returns him to Kathie.

It is not clear whether moviegoers were moved or what they thought of Lassie representing veterans, but at least one critic was not impressed. Philip K. Scheuer of the *Los Angeles Times* ("Lassie Has Courage, Too," November 2, 1946) griped:

> There is a dogged something about Hollywood . . . that won't allow it to let a good movie alone. "Lassie" was a good movie—darn good. So M.G.M. took the idea and worried it into a sequel—"Son of Lassie." That was not so good.
>
> Now comes No. 3, "Courage of Lassie," and it's only fair—lots of pretty scenery in Monopack (Technicolor), but a story that is synthetic from the words

"Roll 'em!" Bill is not only shot to pieces in peacetime as well as war; he winds up as a neuropsychiatric case besides. No wonder he growls at people. He should have taken a bite out of them.

Films with similar themes, such as *Danny Boy* (1946) and *Night Wind* (1948), appeared around the same time. These movies played on anxieties about return-ing military dogs who might be suffering from battle fatigue and connected them to concerns about human soldiers returning home. Such fears were not entirely unfounded. Although the U.S. military made an effort to return all dogs donated to their homes, officials warned that the training and experiences the dogs had received made them dangerous and often discouraged former owners from taking them back. The Marine Corps, for example, in a letter to a Jericho, New York, family, who had enlisted a Doberman named Arko, characterized his temperament as "unstable" and "vicious," and wrote that it "strongly recom-mends that ARKO not be returned to a private home" (letter from H. W. Buse Jr., Lieutenant Colonel, U.S. Marine Corps, to Mrs. Klemens Janson, January 15, 1946; letter from Harold C. Gors, Major, U.S. Marine Corps, to Klemens Jan-son, February 1, 1946). Like the title character in *Danny Boy*, Arko served as a Devil Dog in the Pacific and seems to have been psychologically scarred by training and combat, incurring a canine form of what a returning soldier in the film calls "a sort of fog, like I was [in] when I came home from the South Pacific." In typical Hollywood fashion Danny Boy recovered from the trauma— and saved the life of a toddler while at it—but Arko was apparently ferocious and ill-natured for the rest of his life. Recent discussions about military dogs returning from the wars in Iraq and Afghanistan with signs of post-traumatic stress disorder are reminiscent of these motion pictures (see James Dao, "The Dogs of War, Suffering Like Soldiers," *New York Times*, December 1, 2011). But because the military no longer recruits dogs from average citizens, they are not returned to private hands.

Although military dogs did not appear in postwar Japanese films until decades later, canines served in those films, too, as a vehicle for filmmakers to remember some of the lingering legacies of the war. Perhaps the first postwar film to feature military dogs was *Zoku: Haike tennō heika-sama* [*Dear Mr. Emperor II*], a sequel and comedy released in 1964. As film specialist Jasper Sharp (2011) notes, by the 1960s "the war had receded far enough in history to be treated with a more ironic or reflective sense of detachment, with a new gen-eration of filmmakers creating works for a very different audience demographic without direct experience of the war, only its legacy, and existing in a very dif-ferent political reality" (284). It was in this context that *Dear Mr. Emperor II* appeared as one of three servicemen comedies directed by Nomura Yoshitarō for the Shochiku movie studio. The *Dear Mr. Emperor* films featured Atsumi Kiyoshi, the star of *Otoko wa tsurai yo* [*It's Tough Being a Man*], a film series of forty-nine installments that ran from 1969 to 1997. In the *Dear Mr. Emperor* films Atsumi's character is similar to his later, more famous role; he plays a low-ranking dimwit who experiences a succession of sometimes humorous, often melodramatic mishaps that inevitably involve his falling in love with a beautiful woman who does not share his feelings. Except for the romantic elements, Yamaguchi reminds one of Norakuro. Both are orphans and not particularly bright, and both bumble through a series of adventures that poke fun at some of the absurdities of army life. The humor of *Dear Mr. Emperor II*, though, is darker and informed by the disastrous war and humiliating occupation. It shows dead bodies after skirmishes with Chinese troops, the Japanese military forced to depend on cripples and youngsters, discrimination against and the forced labor of Chinese in Japan, the farcical nature of ceremonies to pay respect to the emperor (both before and after the war), and rampant prostitution for American soldiers during the occupation.

The film begins with Yamaguchi being reassigned to a military dog kennel near Beijing in 1944. He is directed to train Tomoharu (Kinta-gō), a German Shepherd dog that has been donated to the military by a woman in Kyoto. Illiterate, Yamaguchi can neither read the care packages that arrive from the woman for the dog, nor can he write responses as he is ordered to do. Soon after Japan's surrender is announced, the dogs' handlers receive a command to abandon all of their partners. Yamaguchi initially refuses to leave Tomoharu but finally relents and decides to shoot the dog so that he will not suffer. But he misses what is presumably a point-blank shot and leaves him behind. Once Yamaguchi returns to Japan, he makes his way to Kyoto and reports to the woman that the dog died heroically. Like many of the other elements in the film, the military dog Tomoharu illustrates the pathos of the past without leveling any serious criticism or demanding responsibility. Unlike *Norakuro*, *Dear Mr. Emperor II* does not provide an idealized view of military life, but it does not muster much of a serious indictment either.

Thirty years later, another film used military dogs to highlight how the war continued to haunt Japanese national memory or how, to put it another way, the postwar era still had not come to an end. In his film *Yume* [*Dreams*], released in 1990 near the end of his life, the renowned director Kurosawa Akira depicted eight dreams based on his own. In the fourth segment, an eighteen-minute nightmare, an army officer (Terao Akira) is returning home after being held as a prisoner of war. He is shown walking along a deserted road at dusk and comes upon a dark concrete tunnel. Suddenly a vicious, snarling military German Shepherd (uncredited), carrying mortars on its back, rushes out of the tunnel threatening the officer. Clearly frightened, the officer manages to edge away from the dog and passes through what feels like an endless walk in the nearly pitch black passageway into the dim light at the other end. He finds, however, that he has not escaped the past as he is followed out of the tunnel by something even more ominous: the embodied ghost of one of his men, Private Noguchi (Zushi Yoshitaka), his face and hands a radiant pale blue, indicating he is dead.

A scene from *Yume* [*Dreams*] (Kurosawa Akira, Kurosawa Productions, 1990), in which a Japanese army officer (Akira Terao) is confronted by a ferocious military dog who carries mortars on its back, just before he enters a long dark tunnel. Digital frame enlargement.

The soldier appears not to realize, or not to want to admit, that he is dead, but the officer convinces him, telling him how he died in his arms; and reluctantly Noguchi stumbles back into the tunnel. Almost immediately, though, the commander's entire Third Platoon marches out to report that they are "returning to base" with "no casualties." They, too, are dead, their skin a light cobalt. The commander tells them the platoon was "annihilated" and expresses his guilt for sending them to die and that he alone survived. He wishes that he "could place all the responsibility on the stupidity of war" but admits his own "thoughtlessness" and "misconduct." "They may call you 'heroes,'" he continues, "but you died like dogs." He pleads for them to "Go back and rest in peace" and orders them "About face!" and to "Forward march" back into the tunnel. As they do, he salutes them but then collapses to his knees, perhaps both from grief as well as relief, but the latter is short-lived as once again the dog emerges from the tunnel, barking even more fiercely and snapping at him as the scene comes to an end. For some members of Kurosawa's generation, at least, there seems to be no end to the dogged memories of war.

In addition to these few postwar films in which military dogs play a central role, there are many more films set during World War II in which they appear. In these films, especially those made by American studios, the dogs function as icons representing a particular group of people. Most often the dogs are German Shepherds because the breed dominated the ranks of military dogs everywhere. It is most closely associated with the Wehrmacht, the Gestapo, the SS, and National Socialist leaders such as Hitler. Like the swastika and black jackboots, the German Shepherd became an icon readily identified in popular culture with Nazi Germany. As a result, German Shepherds make fleeting appearances in a number of films, especially those about the Holocaust, such as *Schindler's List* (1993). Likewise, because the Japanese military deployed German Shepherds in great numbers, some Chinese films use German Shepherds as symbols of Japanese military aggression. In Maoist China several films during the 1960s, such as *Didaozhan* [*Tunnel Warfare*] (1965), showed Japanese soldiers with massive German Shepherds, whom Chinese asserted the Japanese used to compensate for their own lack of height and manliness. More recent films, such as director Ang Lee's *Lust, Caution* (2007), also consciously associate military and guard dogs, many of which are German Shepherds, with the Japanese and their Chinese collaborators.

In the last few decades there have been almost no narrative films specifically about military dogs in Japan and the United States. The most notable recent productions have been two made-for-television movies. The first, *Chips: The War Dog*, was made by Disney in 1990. Based on the true story of an American army dog that briefly became a decorated hero before the commendation was revoked, the movie transforms the tale in ways that clearly reflected the time in which it was made, as well as its intended audience. Chips (Vilas) is portrayed as the canine representative of the so-called Greatest Generation. He hails from a farming family in the rural Midwest, the symbol of an idyllic, simpler time, rather than from the suburbs of New York City, as the actual Chips did. After watching a "Dogs for Defense" newsreel, the family's two children urge their father to donate Chips. The army that Chips enters is a far cry from the actual one during the war. It is racially and sexually integrated: blacks drill alongside whites, and a female officer oversees (and becomes openly romantically involved with) an enlisted man. And apparently not satisfied with the purported exploits that earned the actual Chips a Silver Star, for "courageous actions in single-handedly eliminating a dangerous machine-gun nest and causing the surrender of its crew" ("War Dogs Awards Doubted," *New York Times*, January 15, 1944, 2), the script has Chips's magnificent drill performance persuade stubborn senators to continue to fund the Dogs for Defense program and has him discover a bomb that has been planted to assassinate a gathering of top Allied leaders. Perhaps one should not expect movies to be true to history, but the result is a film that trumpets a pervasive strain of American popular memory that celebrates World War II as the "Good War" and all its participants—even canines in this case—as members of the "Greatest Generation."

In a similar manner, two movies broadcast on Japanese television in 2010 and 2011 provide a window on Japanese war memory. *Sayonara, Aruma: Akagami o moratta inu* [*Goodbye, Alma: The Dog Who Received a Draft Card*] (2010), shown by the national public television station NHK in 2010, depicts a veterinary university student, Asahina Taiichi (Katsuji Ryō), who forges a tight bond with the German Shepherd he adopts and later is reunited with when he becomes a civilian trainer at a military dog training school in Manchuria.

In August 1945 Soviet troops attack after joining the war against Japan, and predictably Alma (San) performs gallantly by delivering a request for reinforcements for a trapped unit. When Asahina and Alma finally make their way to a train that will carry them to safety, there is not enough room for both of them, so Asahina pleads for just Alma to be put on board. In the climactic scene Alma turns on the young man, biting him, which leads to his being left behind and to Asahina being evacuated. This attack is interpreted as Alma's final sacrifice on behalf of Asahina. The second television film, *Inu no kieta hi* [*The Day the Dogs Disappeared*], which was broadcast by Nippon Television during August 2011 as an anniversary special as part of the annual commemorations marking the end of the war that month, told of a family that gave up two dogs for the war. The military drafted the first, Alf (Bīna-gō), a German Shepherd, for service at the front, and then authorities ordered the second, Tōa (Ichigo-gō), a Japanese Shiba, to report as part of a widespread requisition of pet dogs to be put down so that their fur could be used to make military clothing. Although Alf presumably perishes at the front, Tōa is saved when the family's father decides it is his duty to protect the dog because he, too, "is family." In contrast to Americans' tendency to remember the conflict as the "Good War," the war in Japanese popular memory is often remembered as an event that victimized the population, who were unwillingly conscripted, dispatched far from home, and suffered silently. *Goodbye, Alma* and *The Day the Dogs Disappeared* represent canine variants of this pervasive narrative. Movies about military dogs are fewer and have moved from theaters to television, but they continue to mirror and influence how people remember the war.

A scene from the television film *Inu no kieta hi* [*The Day the Dogs Disappeared*] (Kyōji Ōtsuka, Nippon Television, 2011), showing a dog, played by Bīna-gō, looking back toward his mistress, a young girl who is dressed in her school uniform, as he is led away to military service by a soldier and others celebrating his conscription. Digital frame enlargement.

Thus, however they might be imagined on the screen, the cinematic military canines of World War II reflected and shaped the various national inflections of wartime experience and postwar memory, especially those of Japan and the United States. During the conflict film studios in both countries used military dogs to mobilize people for war. Although U.S. army dogs continue today to be deployed for military uses such as tracking, guarding, and finding improvised explosive devices, war films will surely not attempt to metaphorically employ dogs in the way they did in World War II–era films. Just as fighting is increasingly being outsourced to private companies and shouldered by a smaller percentage of American families, the U.S. military has for an even longer period acquired canines for military use from private kennels and not from the public at large. An interest in the work of military dogs remains high, but the intimate connection they once created between home and war no longer exists, and, as a result, army dogs no longer possess the same sort of cultural capital.

The latest military dog to hit the screens reflects these altered realities. Although not a lot is known about the dog—including its gender—a Belgian Shepherd (Malinois) sniffer dog named Cairo attracted a lot of attention for its participation in the raid by Navy Seals that killed Osama bin Laden on May 2, 2011. President Barack Obama even asked to meet him, though when he did so during a visit to Fort Campbell, Kentucky, Cairo was muzzled at the insistence of the Secret Service (Nicholas Schmidle, "Getting Bin Laden," *New Yorker*, August 8, 2011). In the wake of the raid, the *New York Times* speculated that Cairo might be the "nation's most courageous dog" (Gardiner Harris, "To Serve and Protect, and Sniff Out Trouble, an International Dog of Mystery," *New York Times*, May 5, 2010, A16). Yet *Zero Dark Thirty* (2011), director Kathryn Bigelow's cinematic depiction of the hunt for bin Laden, does not exploit the figure of the military dog to the extent seen in films about World War II. The dog, which goes uncredited, makes five brief appearances in the final minutes of the film as the special operation team departs, flies, and executes the raid. Cairo is shown heading toward the tarmac, being the last, with its handler, to board the second Black Hawk helicopter, in a close-up shot during the flight into Pakistan, and then twice on the ground during the operation. Cairo's repeated appearances—including showing it as the last member to board the second helicopter, and especially the close-up with its tongue hanging out of its mouth—acknowledges its participation and paradoxically humanizes the human members of the force. Yet that is the extent of the film's deployment of Cairo. As if to indicate that the dog did not play a decisive role in the raid—it was to be used to sniff out bin Laden if the team was unable to locate him—the film does not show Cairo again after the killings, on the flight back to Afghanistan, or on the ground as the group celebrates its success. This is but one example, but given the changed dynamics of the relationship between societies and war, military dogs in film will probably never be mobilized as they were for World War II, nor will they be remembered in the same way afterward.

Notes

I am grateful to the David M. Kennedy Center for International Studies at Brigham Young University for helping to fund this research and to college staff for technical help with the images. The research assistance of Katherine White and Neil L. York is appreciated, and thanks to Andrew Jenkins for sharing family documents related to Arko. I am especially thankful to Tyran Grillo and Hiroshi Kitamura for their thorough and thoughtful critiques. Throughout this chapter (including the filmography and figure captions), Japanese names appear surname (family name) first followed by personal name.

1. One possible exception is *His Master's Voice* (1925), starring Thunder as Thunder, who tells his son Flash about his adventures as a Red Cross dog during the war. It is telling, though, that he is a Red Cross dog rather than a military dog (Taylor 2009, 9–10).

2. Pal was played by Ace the Wonder Dog; it is interesting that Pal was the real name of the dog who played Lassie in the film series that began the following year (see Wolf in this volume).

3. Because the story was set in the Depression, the filmmakers make only a few allusions to the war. Near the beginning, the narrator refers to the "people of Yorkshire in peace and war" and says, "Lassie is Sam's only saleable possession in these dark, prewar days of depression." In addition, the film's opening message highlights the alliance between Britain and the United States, as highlighted by the life and death of the story's author, Eric Knight. He "was a man of two countries," reads the message. "Born in England, he survived the First World War as a British soldier, only to die in the Second World War, killed in the line of duty in the uniform of the country he had adopted . . . America. With reverence and pride, we dedicate this picturization of his best-loved story to the late Major Eric Knight." Knight, who had lived in the United States for many years, worked with Frank Capra on the "Why We Fight" series and was killed in a plane crash while on assignment for Armed Forces Radio in January 1943.

4. Other cartoons included Universal's *Canine Commandos*, Twentieth Century–Fox's *Patriotic Pooches*, and Walt Disney's *Private Pluto*.

Chronological Filmography

His Master's Voice (Renaud Hoffman, 1925). Thunder the Dog, George Hackathorne, Marjorie Daw.

Norakuro nitōhei: Enshū no maki (Murata Yasuji, 1933). Animated.

Sensen ni hoeyu [*Barks at the Battlefront*] (Yamane Mikito, 1936). Fujita Yōko, Shitō-gō [dog] and Karumen-gō (Carmen) [dog]. [Lost film.]

War Dogs (S. Roy Luby, 1942). Billy Lee, Bradley Page, Kay Linaker, Addison Richards, Ace the Wonder Dog.

Air Force (Howard Hawks, 1943). John Garfield, John Ridgely, Gig Young, Arthur Kennedy, Charles Drake, Tripoli [dog, uncredited].

War Dogs (Joseph Barbera, William Hanna, 1943). Animated.

The Underdog (William Nigh, 1943). Barton MacLane, Bobby Larson, Jan Wiley, Charlotte Wynters.

Lassie Come Home (Fred M. Wilcox, 1943). Roddy McDowall, Donald Crisp, Dame May Whitty, Edmund Gwenn, Elsa Lanchester, Nigel Bruce, Elizabeth Taylor, Pal [as Lassie].

Sergeant Mike (Harry Levin, 1944). Larry Parks, Jeanne Bates, Loren Tindall, Jim Bannon, Larry Joe Olsen, Mike and Pearl [dogs].

My Pal, Wolf (Alfred L. Werker, 1944). Sharyn Moffett, Jill Esmond, Una O'Connor, George Cleveland, Grey Shadow.

Son of Lassie (S. Sylvan Simon, 1945). Peter Lawford, Donald Crisp, June Lockhart, Pal.

A Boy, a Girl, and a Dog (Herbert Kline, 1946). Jerry Hunter, Sharyn Moffett, Lionel Stander, Harry Davenport.

Courage of Lassie (Fred M. Wilcox, 1946). Elizabeth Taylor, Frank Morgan, Tom Drake, Pal [as Lassie].

Danny Boy (Terry O. Morse, 1946). Robert "Buzz" Henry, Ralph Lewis, Sybil Merritt, Ace the Wonder Dog.

Night Wind (James Tinling, 1948). Charles Russell, Virginia Christine, Gary Gray, Flame.

Zoku: Haike tennō heika-sama [*Dear Mr. Emperor II*] (Nomura Yoshitarō, 1964). Atsumi Kiyoshi, Kinta-gō [dog, as Tomoharu].

Didaozhan [*Tunnel Warfare*] (Xudong Ren, 1965). Guodong Han, Jiang Liu, Xiujie Liu.

Chips: The War Dog (Ed Kaplan, 1990; television). Brandon Douglas, Ned Vaughn, Paxton Whitehead, Vilas [dog, as Chips].

Yume [*Dreams*] (Kurosawa Akira, 1990). Akira Terao, Zushi Yoshitaka, Negishi Toshie.

Lust, Caution (Ang Lee, 2007). Tony Leung Chiu Wai, Wei Tang, Joan Chen.

Sayonara, Aruma: Akagami o moratta inu [*Goodbye, Alma: The Dog Who Received a Draft Card*] (Ichiki Masae, 2010; television). Abe Mari, Katsuji Ryō, Ryōhei Abe, Azuma Terumi, San [dog, as Alma].

Inu no kieta hi [*The Day the Dogs Disappeared*] (Kyōji Ohtsuka, 2011; television). Arakawa Chika, Dan Rei, Hirata Mitsuru, Bīna-gō and Ichigo-gō [dogs, as Alf and Tōa].

Zero Dark Thirty (Kathryn Bigelow, 2012). Jessica Chastain, Joel Edgerton, Chris Pratt, Kyle Chandler, Reda Kateb, Jeremy Strong, Jennifer Ehle.

6

Loaded Dogs

• •

Dogs, Domesticity, and "the Wild" in Australian Cinema

JANE O'SULLIVAN

One might expect that dogs figure prominently in Australian cinema. Perhaps this expectation is a result of the centrality of dogs in some well-known and oft-cited Australian prose fictions (such as the turn-of-the-twentieth-century short stories of Henry Lawson and Barbara Baynton). There is also a pervasive notion of dogs as taking their place beside many a farmhand, or as herding in response to the commands of sheep farmers, or as strategically nipping at the heels of wayward bullocks driven along the stock routes of outback Australia. Indeed, the perception that "in the outback the dog is both mate and essential worker" (Marcus 1989/2005, 209) is quite widely held. While such culturally familiar images usually reference the land and lifestyles beyond the reaches of the more densely populated coastal areas of Australia, this somewhat mytholo-gized notion of "a man and his dog" is also replicated in the Kelpies, Australian cattle dogs (Blue Heelers), border collies, and the like that adorn the many and immaculate four-wheel-drives and tradesmen's flat-topped trucks that increas-ingly negotiate the clog and flow of traffic in the coastal cities and urban sprawl.

    An inspection of records of the appearance of dogs in Australian feature films (see Pike and Cooper 1998) reveals that in most cases they are glimpsed only occa-sionally against a vast and largely unpopulated landscape or positioned as minor elements furnishing the domestic mise-en-scène rather than as central participants in the narratives. This is also true of the films discussed in this chapter, all of which are set in "the bush" or "the outback," miles from anywhere or, as is the case with *Babe*, on a farm that could be anywhere. The films that actually afford dogs sufficient focus to qualify for extended treatment in this discussion include *Dusty* (1983), *Evil Angels* (1988, released in the United States as *A Cry in the Dark*), *Napoleon* (1995), *Babe* (1995), *Through My Eyes* (2004), and *Red Dog* (2011). Even in these films, however, in which the canine characters are of great significance, only one acknowledges the individual canine performers in the film credits. In most cases credit is given to various named dog "trainers," "handlers," or "wranglers." In *Babe* only the human actors providing the animal "character voices" are named, and in *Napoleon* the "kennels" of the some fifty puppies that played the title character across the shoot (IMDb.com) are acknowledged for "Breeding and Consultancy." The single exception is *Red Dog*, in which the credits devote a full screen to the words "And introducing Koko as 'Red Dog.'" Whether this acknowledgment—and the substantial coverage given to Koko in online and television documentaries/interviews—is because he occupies more screen time than any other character in the film, or because of a greater appreciation of the contributions and entitlements of nonhuman animals, remains a matter of speculation.

In addition to a common rural or "remote" setting, all of these films define their canine characters as either "good dogs" or "bad dogs" in terms of the manner in which they negotiate the tricky balance between their species' history of wildness as carnivorous predators and their cultural history of domestication—into trained working dogs and human companions, or "pets." The narratives selected for discussion here explore this uneasy divide of nature and culture and, at the same time, examine associated human binaries of masculinity and femininity as they are broadly stereotyped in the Australian cultural mores that inform them. In essence, in the representation of their canine and human male protagonists, the films both condemn and condone wildness as a kind of exuberance and willfulness that exceeds the confines of culture. Rugged individualism and the heroic engagement in risk and adventure are celebrated in the dogs and the men with whom these behaviors are associated, and in relation to whom they stand metaphorically.

At the same time, such an eschewing of culture is potentially dangerous or detrimental to these renegades, as it embodies a disconcerting critique of culture and the order and stability it offers to those who comply with its rules. In these respects the canines in these films resemble the lone male protagonists of the Hollywood western or, indeed, the modern-day drifters of the road movie, a genre that Tara Brabazon refers to in her discussion of *Mad Max* (1979) as an "American genre . . . placed over . . . the Australian landscape" (Brabazon 2001, 153). In resisting or rejecting the domestic—the communal—they are free, unfettered—"wild." Indeed, it has been argued more broadly that "canine nature is understood to be, by definition, itinerant" and that this itinerancy, which evokes "an experience outside the realm of fixed locales and firm rules, is a canine premise" (Brown 2010, 114). These canines can also be likened to the western hero who, "rather than being recuperated into the social order . . . remains caught between two worlds as he looks—perhaps with longing—into the domestic realm to which he clearly does not belong" (Stadler and McWilliam 2009, 308). But that cultural realm, with its assurances and secure respite from isolation, entails relationships and dependencies that produce a perhaps greater risk: that of emotional vulnerability.

In the main, the films selected for discussion here show their dogs, like their human counterparts, teetering on the boundary between civilization and wilderness. This is a precarious position to occupy, but it also offers the possibility of a dog-human relationship beyond that of dominance or submission, one framed as what Wendy Woodward (2008) calls "a threshold space" (116), suggestive of a meeting place neither exclusively "wild" nor exclusively tame. Woodward likens this "threshold" to the "kind of liminality" (116) explored by Donna Haraway (1992). In considering a means by which animals more generally can shed the "object status that has reduced them to *things* in so much Western philosophy and practice," Haraway conceives of them as "inhabit[ing] neither nature (as object) nor culture (as surrogate human), but instead inhabit[ing] a place called elsewhere" (332 [emphasis added]).

Although this discussion of dogs in Australian cinema explores parallels between the human and canine players, the focus it places on films in which a dog's actions and sensibilities are central allows for a discussion that does not "reduce the animal to a blank screen for the projection of human meaning" (Armstrong 2008, 3). Rather, the discussion is underpinned by the understanding that animal-focused narratives, even those within which the animals are "loaded" with cultural significance, can "influence the ways humans conceptualise and respond to 'real' embodied nonhuman animals" (Woodward 2008, 8). The cinematic representations of dogs selected for close attention in this chapter facilitate a positive appreciation of the burden they carry in maintaining an approved balance of canine instinct and cultural restraint.

Dogs in Early Australian Literature and Film

Dogs in various Australian cultural texts have largely been represented as hybrid creatures in that they display obedience, loyalty, and humor while, at the same time, having an unpredictable capacity for rebellion and aggression. Late nineteenth-century and early twentieth-century examples of these canine encounters include two short stories by Henry Lawson ("The Drover's Wife" [1892/1973] and "The Loaded Dog" [1901/1973]) and one by Barbara Baynton ("The Squeaker's Mate" [1902/1976]), in which the dogs are variously portrayed as playful and fiercely loyal. One of the most famous short stories from the Australian literary canon, "The Loaded Dog" tells of three mates, gold miners, who throw the equivalent of a stick of dynamite only to have it retrieved by Tommy, "an overgrown pup" (Lawson 1901/1973, 10) that "seemed to take life, the world, his two-legged mates, and his own instinct as a huge joke" (11). Much of the humor in the story is evoked by the protracted chase and the men's frantic efforts to evade this "loaded" dog as he runs from one to the other, in order to return the "stick." The "happy ending" of the tale sees the "pup" alive and chained in his owner's home, the only casualties being "nearly a dozen other dogs [that] came from round all the corners and under the buildings—spidery, thievish, cold-blooded kangaroo-dogs, mongrel sheep- and cattle-dogs, vicious black and yellow dogs—that slip after you in the dark, nip your heels, and vanish without explaining" (14). Clearly, despite his larrikin antics, Tommy may yet grow into a "good dog," whereas the others, largely untamed, are "bad." The dogs central to Lawson's "The Drover's Wife" and Barbara Baynton's "The Squeaker's Mate" are celebrated for channeling such aggression into the pro- tection of their owners or their owners' "property."

Australian Film, 1900–1977: A Guide to Feature Film Production (Pike and Cooper 1998) reveals only a handful of Australian films that focus on canine characters. The earliest two recorded are, of course, silent films: *Call of the Bush* (1912), with a cast that includes "Bosun, the Dog Hero"; and *How McDougall Topped the Score* (1924), described as "a one-joke story, already familiar to Aus- tralians as a bush ballad" (123). Somewhat reminiscent of "The Loaded Dog," the "joke" in *How McDougall Topped the Score* concerns a sheepdog that runs away with a cricket ball and is pursued by the opposing team, while his mas- ter makes enough runs to win the match. There are only three other films men- tioned, all considerably later: two greyhound stories—*Gone to the Dogs* (1939) and *Queensland* (1976)—and *The Fourth Wish* (1976), which recounts the story of an incurably ill child's wish to own a dog. A common theme in these few films seems to be that of dogs as "man's best friend," be that in the form of willing accomplice or loyal companion.

Beyond the cinema, these valued canine qualities have also been celebrated in statues erected to commemorate famous dogs in Australian folklore, includ- ing that of "The Loaded Dog" in the South Australian mining port of Whyalla and another, "The Dog on the Tuckerbox," in Gundagai country in New South Wales, depicting the loyal dog who refused to abandon his post, guarding his master's possessions long after the man had died. A similar act of canine loyalty and devotion is marked in the statue of "Red Dog," which, like the dog in the 2011 film, is situated within the mining camps and inhospitable landscapes of western Australia, far from the more densely populated and domesticated urban and coastal regions.

The Great Divide

The Great Dividing Range, colloquially referred to as "the great divide," denotes an Australian geological formation, but it also connotes a cultural division of patterns of settlement and types of engagement with the Australian environment. The Great Dividing Range is a mountainous landform that separates much of the east coast of Australia from what is commonly referred to as "the outback." Early European colonists struggled to cross this range in an effort to access and "farm" the land that lay beyond, and although some of this former "bushland" has been settled, the vast majority of the population is still located along the coastal strip, with much of the land west of "the Divide" characterized as uninhabitable, as "the back of beyond" or "the outback." In Australian cinematic narratives those human and canine characters who survive within what Ross Gibson (1994) calls this "preternaturally unmanageable or uncultural" (49) and "unsubdued" (32) landscape are cast as made of wilder, tougher stuff than their coastal counterparts. In many ways, like the prevalent image of the American "Wild West," the Australian "bush" and "outback" are constructed as domains of hegemonic masculinity. Indeed, in addition to the setting, role of landscape, and gender assumptions, these Australian and American films project some similar tensions within their protagonists.

It has been acknowledged that Australian filmmakers, like many from other national cinemas, "indigenize genres, artistic movements and influences," as Tom O'Regan (1996, 1) puts it, and this process is reflected in some of the terms he applies to such outback films, including *The Man from Snowy River* (1982), referred to as a "kangaroo western" (17), and *The Story of the Kelly Gang* (1906), a "bushranger film" (168). *The Overlanders* (1946) and *The Sundowners* (1960) are also characterized as "drover" films and equated with the 1940s "cattle drive western" (169). The main, male protagonists in such Australian films have been seen as "cast from a mould fashioned by American Westerns" and as "strong, silent types, men who prefer decisive action to words, stoics who rarely reveal their emotions, if ever" (Enker 1994, 218). Also, consistent with notions of the American western hero as enjoying a freedom that comes at a price, those who choose an outback life are often depicted as physically and emotionally "lone figures, lost in a landscape" (Dermody and Jacka 1998, 21). In some more recent films, such as *Mad Max 2: The Road Warrior* (1981), this lone figure is depicted as "an archetypal loner, a cowboy of the future" (Murray 1994, 218), who, with his faithful, and selectively savage, Blue Heeler, moves through a land that is "beyond the sedate culture of a compassionate and nurturing civilization, replaced by the parched mental and emotional landscape of outlaw gangs" (Moran and Nieth 2000, 14). This ambivalence about the price of a notional freedom from the domestic comforts and constraints of culture is also registered in depictions of Australian canines, as they negotiate an uneasy relationship on the boundaries of this "great divide." A film that specifically explores this risky negotiation of nature and culture is *Dusty* (1983), in its representation of the literal hybridity of its central canine, a cross-breed of dingo and domestic dog.

Dusty: Across the Divide

The dingo, as Australia's only native canine, has been variously depicted as an efficient hunter, an admirable survivor in an unforgiving natural environment, and a dangerous threat to the human enterprise of claiming and taming the land for domestic livestock production, particularly sheep farming. Julie Marcus (1989/2005) notes that throughout Australian literary depictions of the outback, the dingo is "iconic" and "appears as a wild and predatory, hunting creature, free of all constraint . . . one of the markers of the outback, the wild, of the outside of civilization, and at the same time, the marker of Australian authenticity" (206). Yet one aspect of human-dingo relations that has been commonly represented as a dangerous mistake is that of attempting to domesticate the dingo or the offspring of dingo and domestic dog interbreeding. This mistake is made manifest in the contesting instincts and behaviors of the young dingo-Kelpie cross Dusty.

This film depicts the misrepresentation of Dusty as a male, purebred Kelpie and his sale to an ageing farmhand, Tom Lynch (Bill Kerr), who gives the pup to the son of his employer, a sheep farmer Harry Morrison (Noel Trevarthen). Subsequently, the pup is taken through a process of domestication and training as a working dog, initially under the guidance of the son and then that of Tom Lynch. In what is presented as inevitable, Dusty still retains the hunting instincts of his dingo heritage and takes to killing sheep (Zable 1983, 157; Mayer 1999, 123). When Dusty's night kills are uncovered and the farmer contracts a professional dog trapper, the varying sympathies and allegiances evoked with respect to the fate of Dusty allow insight into "the spiritual intimations that lie just beneath the surface of human beings" (Zable 1983, 158). Yet despite this potential for the dog to serve as a metaphor for the contested desires and duties of the human characters, the film does not "raise the level of human drama in the narrative [to such an extent that it] would deflect attention from the narrative's actual centre, Dusty" (Rattigan 1991, 117). This focus on Dusty is the result of "John Richardson's direction [which] avoids the obvious clichés and . . . manages, like Frank Dalby Davison's novel of the same name, to include the dog's point of view whenever possible" (Mayer 1999, 123). Yet this point of view does not construct a film that privileges the benefits or entitlements of either nature or culture. Rather, its "observational style, its disinclination to heighten its drama or overemphasize character, and its somewhat disjointed, elliptical editing style serve to avoid oversimplification" (Rattigan 1991, 118) of this nature-culture divide.

Consistent with the view of bush and outback films as in many respects constituting Australian "westerns," it has been observed that Tom (and, I would add, the dog trapper) is "reminiscent of John Ford" (Rattigan 1991, 118), whose socially displaced cowboys drift though the small communities scattered across the barren landscapes of Hollywood westerns. In the case of the dog trapper, that cultural displacement is in part conveyed through a gruff and knowing cynicism that, coupled with his physical embodiment of a wayward and nomadic masculinity, makes him disturbingly attractive to the sheep farmer's wife. Her teetering resistance to this implicit "call of the wild" is also apparent in her ambivalent attitude to the partly untamed dog, Dusty, who refuses to "sit and stay."

In its portrayal of the failure of domestication to completely eradicate the lust for freedom given expression in the wild behavior of this hybrid canine, *Dusty* also reinstates a notional "wildness" in the masculinities enacted in the film. The human and nonhuman animals, like the "barely populated continent" they inhabit, are each "figured as a paradox—half-tamed yet essentially untameable [*sic*], conceding social subsistence yet never allowing human dominance" (Gibson 1994, 49).

Napoleon: Lost in the Bush

Napoleon (1985) is a film for young viewers featuring animals as the main characters, all of whom "speak" with human voices (there is no attempt to synchronize facial movement and dialogue, however, for example through process work or manual manipulation or the use of animatronics). The primary character is a male golden retriever puppy, "Napoleon." It is this pup's view of his surroundings, and his fears, aspirations, and heroic fantasies, that carry the narrative. In essence, this is a canine "coming-of-age" story, in which the young protagonist leaves behind home, family, and the familiar and embarks on a quest to find his "true" place as a wild dog. His journey takes him far beyond his suburban backyard in Sydney, across the Great Dividing Range, and into the outback, where he encounters a number of the natural inhabitants, including a wombat, a kangaroo, a frill-necked lizard, a frog-mouth owl, a flock of galahs, one wise old cockatoo, and, most significantly, a dingo and her pups (like Napoleon's, the voices of the dingo pups sound like those of small children; the galah's words are inflected by the "squawk" of this Australian grey and pink cockatoo; and the voice and song of the kangaroo are provided by the actor Barry Humphries, in a voice familiar to many as that of one of his most famous comic characters, "Dame Edna Everage").

Napoleon is lost in the bush, in a manner evocative of many familiar narratives and motifs in Australian literature, painting, and film. He wanders further and further into the bush in search of "the wild dogs" he has first heard howling beyond the high-walled garden of his suburban home. As day is overtaken by night, the puppy vocalizes his fears and thoughts of home, yet he repeatedly shores up his courage by reassuring himself of his own bravery and physical prowess. This is very much the story of a male puppy, the little son who rebels against the protective mother who, to his chagrin, persists in calling him "Muffin." In refusing to heed her cautionary advice, Napoleon clambers into a basket to which are tied masses of balloons. As the wind catches the balloons and lifts

The wild and the domesticated: Napoleon and his surrogate mother keep watch over her dingo puppies in *Napoleon* (Mario Andreacchio, Adelaide Motion Picture Company/Australian Film Finance Corporation/Film Australia, 1995). Digital frame enlargement.

Napoleon into the first, airborne, stage of his quest, his mother, tethered to her kennel, is literally and figuratively constrained by her role as "family pet" and can only bark her concern but is powerless to rescue him.

Despite his fluffy golden locks and bright red neck-ribbon, an encounter with the "wild dogs" allows Napoleon to display a degree of bravery and (short) heroic stature appropriate to his namesake. During a sudden thunderstorm and drenching rain, Napoleon rescues two tiny dingo pups from a rushing torrent that sweeps them from the safety of their lair. As a golden retriever, Napoleon belongs to a breed that has been genetically manipulated into water dogs, designed to retrieve wild ducks and other human prey. As such, Napoleon shows himself to be "naturally" better equipped for this situation than are the dingo pups, and once he has carried each one to the safety of a rock shelf, he is rewarded with their adoration and gratitude. When the female dingo returns to find her pups have been saved from the floodwaters, she takes on the role of Napoleon's surrogate mother, assuring him that "this can be your home until you sort yourself out." Clearly, this "sorting out" concerns Napoleon's quest to become "a wild dog," and the dingo assures him that "in your heart you've been a wild dog all along." His feelings of inadequacy are assuaged by this testament to a residual wildness in the domesticated canine, and Napoleon admits that he misses home and, on the advice of his surrogate mother, realizes that he does not really belong in the wild and that he should return to his rightful place in the domesticated realm of culture—to his home.

Napoleon is a "bad puppy" when he ignores the prescriptions and proscriptions of culture, and the consequences could have been dire. But he survives (this is a children's film, after all), and there is a strong sense that he is a better dog for it all. He has "sown his wild oats," and, assured of his ability to be a dog (if not exactly "wild") rather than just a "Muffin" or a pet, he is able to settle into his life in an urban setting. In the wider context of Australian cinematic narratives in which canine characters are heavily loaded signifiers of the great divide between the human and nonhuman occupants of the coast-as-culture and the outback-as-nature, the fact that the definition and degree of Napoleon's "wildness" is judged in comparison to, and through his interactions with, dingoes is significant.

Babe: Another Babe in the Woods

Babe (1995) concerns an orphaned piglet, "Babe," who is won by a sheep farmer in a guessing competition. Babe finds himself the resident of a farm populated by a variety of farm animals such as ducks, chickens, sheep, dairy cows, and carthorses but no pigs. In this respect the narrative resembles the basic scenario traced in *Napoleon*, that of a very young male animal faced with the difficult and frightening prospect of making his own way in an alien world. In *Babe* the piglet selectively adopts and adapts some of the skills and modes of operation of the border collies on the farm and this, along with what he learns from some of the noncarnivorous animals, such as an appreciation of the importance of trust and cooperation and cross-species consideration, allows him to achieve the higher status and associated longevity enjoyed by the sheepdogs on the farm.

Within the "storybook world" of *Babe*, where "exaggeration . . . seep[s] through everything, including the sets and the cinematography" (Noonan 1999, 226), the dogs are rendered as beautiful. Their glossy, black-and-white coats flash across the impossibly green fields of the farm or ripple in the sunlight, and their eyes glint with intelligence and psychological complexity in numerous lingering close-ups. And they talk, of course, and the mix of computer-generated imagery, animatronics, and "animal cosmetics" (Noonan 1999, 228) creates a family of canine characters capable of conveying nuances of emotion and of articulating a subject position that underpins their privileged place in the hierarchy of animals on the farm, or, as it is expressed in the film, "the way things are."

While Babe is not a dog, this piglet enacts many of the familiar functions, attitudes, and antics commonly associated with domesticated canines. In addition, he and viewers of the film are given insight into the lives of a "family" of domesticated dogs, Rex, Fly, and their litter of puppies. As is the case in *Napoleon*, the young orphan is adopted by the female dog and takes his place along with her own young offspring and, rather than this being a temporary arrangement, Babe remains as a kind of surrogate "child" when Fly's puppies are weaned and sold to neighboring farmers. This is the beginning of Babe's cultural transition from pig to a kind of species hybrid—a "sheepdog-pig."

In this discussion of cinematic representations of canines, of most interest is the always already existing state of same-species cultural hybridity embodied in, and enacted by, the working sheepdogs on the farm. These working dogs, border collies, are indeed situated on the border of domestication and wildness. Bred to bring together their natural chase instinct and their culturally instilled obedience, they respond to human commands to round up but not bring down the sheep that skitter in fright ahead of these predators—these barking, nipping "wolves." This breed is celebrated for walking this fine line between genetic predisposition and studied restraint, and this allows it to take its place alongside other working dogs, as "images of the authentic outback identity" such as is evident in the Blue Heeler and its "devotion to a man, its meticulous obedience and its role in helping impose man's control over the wild, [which] give it a central place in Australian folklore, literature, art, humor and daily life" (Marcus 1989/2005, 209).

Consistent with this gendering of wildness and domesticity, in *Babe* it is the female dog, Fly, whose actions toward Babe replicate the stereotypical nurturing characteristics associated with human, domesticated femininity. In contrast to this, and reinstalling equally stereotypical markers of hegemonic masculinity, the breeding male dog, Rex, is constructed as the emotionally inarticulate, competitive "hard man." Rex's pride, evident in his reluctance to admit to his poor hearing, something he sees as a weakness, functions as a recognizably masculine response, especially in comparison with some of the sentiments more freely expressed by Fly. "As the Alpha-male of the preferred non-human, human companion, Rex is 'top dog'" (McHugh 2002, 160), and he asserts his will through physical domination, always anticipating a challenge to his authority. As Rex growls and bares his teeth, it is clearly a strain for him to contain his all-too-evident distrust of Babe as the unwelcome intruder and competitor for the farmer's favor and for the attentions of Fly. McHugh characterizes Babe's status as Fly's surrogate child as eliciting a kind of oedipal jealousy in her mate, Rex (McHugh 2002, 172), and given the contesting domesticated and wild drivers behind Rex's role within the familial culture of the farm, it is not surprising that violence is unleashed in the form of a savage dogfight, as a result of which Rex must be further tamed. This eruption of savagery stems from his fear of being superseded in his role as potent stud-dog and this, combined with the tensions of being both obedient servant to his master and sufficiently wolverine to effectively control his master's sheep, leads to a diagnosis of a condition requiring either castration or medication. In terms of "wildness," Rex has fallen foul of the fine delineation between a "good dog" and a "bad dog."

Rex is muzzled in a bid to curb his residual "wildness" in *Babe* (Chris Noonan, Kennedy Miller Productions/Universal, 1995). Digital frame enlargement.

Evil Angels and *Through My Eyes*: "Bad Dogs"

The experience of losing a child in, or to, the bush has been a preoccupation in various Australian cultural narratives, and the connection between this anxiety and the fate of baby Azaria Chamberlain has been noted (Pierce 1999). This preoccupation is also evident in numerous Australian films, including *Walkabout* (1971), *Picnic at Hanging Rock* (1975), and *One Night the Moon* (2001). Of most interest here in the narrative of the lost child in *Evil Angels* (1988), released in the United States as *A Cry in the Dark*, and the more recent TV movie, *Through My Eyes* (2004), is the manner in which the conflict between "nature" and culture is revealed as a factor underpinning the perceptions of the Australian "native wild dog," the dingo.

In essence, the narrative of each of these films covers events that began in August 1980, when it was reported that at a campground near Uluru (Ayers Rock), Azaria Chamberlain, baby daughter of Seventh Day Adventists Lindy and Michael Chamberlain, had been attacked and carried off by a dingo. The mother was the only one who claimed to have seen the dingo snatch the child from the tent and disappear into the night. Both films depict the failure of an extensive search to recover the baby, and both films trace the events leading to Lindy Chamberlain's being found guilty of murder, given a life prison sentence with hard labor, and remaining in custody until pardoned in February 1986, and pronounced innocent in June 1987. It was not until June 2012 that the coroner at the Darwin Magistrate's Court finally ruled that it was a dingo that had taken baby Azaria.

Much has been written (Goldsworthy 1986/1997; Pierce 1999; Howe 2005; Marcus 1989/2005) about the range of Australian cultural attitudes (for example, sexism and religious prejudice) and vested interests (of individual police officers, politicians, park rangers, media reporters, and forensic scientists) that informed the course and outcomes of the "Azaria Chamberlain Case" and that are made evident in the two films under discussion. The focus here is the dingo and the manner in which this canine, and its perception by the human characters, is depicted in the films.

As noted in relation to the film *Dusty*, dingoes are wild dogs, native to Australia. While they are regularly baited, trapped, or shot, and thousands of miles of fences throughout the Australian outback have been erected in a bid to keep them from preying on valuable grazing stock, the "innocence" of the dingo in relation to the disappearance of the Chamberlains' baby was asserted with a passion. In one of the many sequences depicting public debate in *Evil Angels*, someone angrily accuses Lindy Chamberlain by asserting that dingoes "are a native creature of Australia—a beautiful animal . . . and if you tell me that bitch is innocent and a dingo is guilty, I'll punch your . . . head in!" Clearly, director Fred Schepisi's representation of the dingo's place in Australian consciousness is in line with Marcus's observation that the dingo "is one of the markers of the outback . . . [and] of the outside of civilization" and a "marker of Australian authenticity" (Marcus 1989/2005, 206). In *Evil Angels* and in *Through My Eyes* the discourses surrounding the trial are revealed as affording the dingo all the positive attributes of a sort of larrikin Australian masculinity, characterized as a free-spirited, rough-and-ready, lovable mutt. Yet it is evident in both films that it was a dingo that had taken the baby.

In *Evil Angels* the sequence depicting the disappearance of baby Azaria reproduces the poor visibility and resulting confusion experienced by everyone in the darkness of the desert at night. Even so, numerous shots are from the point of view of Lindy (Meryl Streep), and from over her shoulder, as she rushes toward the tent. The silhouette of the dog within the tent is clear, as is a glimpse of its golden fur as it shakes something, then exits the tent, a small bundle clearly visible in its mouth, as it runs off into the night. In *Through My Eyes* the focus is very much on the dingo and, in particular, the kinds of interactions between the dingo and various tourists, police officers, and park rangers in the Uluru National Park. This version of events points an accusing finger not only at an Australian ambivalence about dingoes but also at the ill-advised practice of engaging with them in a quasi-domestic relationship.

Through My Eyes more explicitly depicts the police turning a blind eye to such a relationship between one of the park rangers and a troublesome, tourist-tormenting dingo that is affectionately referred to by a number of them as "Ding" and is subsequently viewed as the one most likely to have killed Azaria. The film also includes footage suggestive of the dingo's point of view, motivation, and relationship with various human characters. The dingo's surveillance of the camping ground, including the distance between the adults and the tent, and the subsequent attack on the baby, is filmed using a mix of handheld and tracking shots, positioned low to the ground, simulating the dingo's point of view and, by implication, its careful targeting of the lone infant. In addition, the soundtrack includes the panting and snuffling of the dingo as it carries off its prey and, most interestingly, the film offers two possible destinations. Still using the tracking shots, the film simulates the dingo's path to the house of the ranger who has been feeding it. This cuts to a graphic matching of the progress of the dingo to its "natural" lair, somewhere in the surrounding desert, where it is greeted by a litter of pups.

In presenting these two parallel scenarios, *Through My Eyes* implies, at one level, that the dingo responsible may have been "Ding," the ranger's partially domesticated dog, or the culprit may have been a wild dingo, possibly a breeding female. At another level of interpretation, this second scenario implies a parallel between the human mother's bid to protect her baby and the dingo's instinct to nurture her pups.

Red Dog: "Good Dog," "Bad Dog"

Red Dog (2011) is a film adapted from Louis de Bernières's novel of the same name, which was, in turn, based on a true story of a largely nomadic red Kelpie (played here by a dog named Koko) who traveled the roads of outback western Australia. In this film there are at least three stories: a "man and his dog" story, a larger story of the continually renegotiated relationship between a community of men and the dog they seek to own, and a story of a dog who is his own "man." From the beginning, the dog refuses to obey various miners' encouragements to "stay" or to accept any one of them as his "owner." Later, once ensconced in the seat on the bus nearest to John, his chosen "true master," Red Dog refuses to share the seat with Nancy, the young woman who is later to become John's partner. The miners see Red Dog's willful disobedience as both frustrating and impressive, and for this he is widely celebrated as a good "bad dog."

From the beginning of the film it is apparent that many of the men from the vast open-cut mines of the west are a hardworking, heavy-drinking, gambling, brawling mix of white Australian and European "blokes" who experience loneliness in the isolated mining camps they inhabit. In a sense the life and eventual death of Red Dog helps these men to become more emotionally articulate and to acknowledge an otherwise masked need for an element of domesticity in their lives. In this respect Red Dog saves those who are at risk of emotional atrophy and an excess of "wildness." Ironically, it seems that Red Dog himself is also in need of saving and that an element of his apparent wanderlust has been a kind of quest to find *the* man equipped to be his "one true master." Yet to shed the veneer of independence and indifference in order to entrust his physical and emotional well-being to someone entails the risk of disappointment or loss.

When Red Dog identifies John as "the one," he follows him everywhere, trying to become "John's dog." Significantly, it is only when the miners, in a drunken
gambling spree, decide to bet on how quickly Red Dog can devour a live chicken,
that John steps in and calls "his dog" to heel. In effect, he has saved Red Dog from
a daunting performance of "wildness" and given him a home, and a relationship of
codependency underpinned by the promise of routine, proximity, and permanence.

The paralleling of the lives of man and dog is made evident when John himself is revealed as an erstwhile commitment-phobic drifter, "scared of finding
something worth staying in one place for." After accepting Red Dog into his life,
and as if following the dog's example, John opens himself to a relationship with
a young woman, Nancy, and embraces the prospect of marriage and permanent
residence within the mining community. After John is killed in a motorbike
accident, Red Dog spends weeks waiting for him to come home and then years
traveling the length and breadth of Australia's northern and western regions. The
narrative voice-over interprets this as "searching for John," and, given the intensity of the loyalty and love the dog expresses for John, it is quite conceivable that
Red Dog is actively seeking to reinvoke the numbing anonymity and invulnerability of his previous nomadic life. The complexity of Red Dog's thoughts and
feelings are rendered convincingly through the use of many extreme close-ups
capturing the dog's wide range of facial expressions and the many tracking shots
simulating his point of view.

When Red Dog refuses to be owned by any of the people he meets on his
travels through the desolate coastal and inland reaches of western Australia, pre-
ferring a nomadic movement between various would-be "owners" and a life "on
the road," he, too, manifests the contesting attractions of the tamed and the wild
that compromise Australian cinematic canines.

Red Dog returns to a nomadic life after the death of his much-loved "master" in *Red Dog* (Kriv
Stenders, Woss Group/Screen Australia/Endymion Films, 2011). Digital frame enlargement.

Myths of Belonging

In resisting and responding to the "call of the wild," Red Dog and his cinematic predecessors enact a domestic unease similar to that of the men they resemble. As such they are all "loaded dogs," bearing the burden of signifying a human story and cultural mythology. Yet these dogs are also, and in the first place, living their own lives and "telling" their own tales. When these tales are received on a literal, rather than exclusively allegorical, level, the dogs can function as more than fabled beasts (Harel 2009, 10) through a practice of looking at them, not just seeing through them. Accepting that there is a limit to the extent to which we can actually see into other animals and, in so doing, fully understand or empathize with their lives, we can "imagine non-human experience and sympathetically engage with it by comparing it with our own" (Simons 2002, 86). The centrality and careful consideration given to the concerns of the dogs in these Australian films go some way toward this sympathetic imagining.

As for the geographical and cultural landscape within which these Australian dogs are represented, it has been perceived and subsequently depicted as "so tantalizing and so essentially unknowable-yet-lovable . . . [as to] become the structural centre of the nation's myths of belonging" (Gibson 1994, 49). This is a mise-en-scène fit for such a motley pack of cinematic canines.

Chronological Filmography

Gone to the Dogs (Ken G. Hall, 1939). George Wallace, Lois Green, John Dobbie.

Queensland (John Ruane, 1976). John Flaus, Robert Karl, Alison Bird.

The Fourth Wish (Don Chaffey, 1976). John Meillon, Robert Bettles, Michael Craig, Anne Haddy.

Mad Max 2: The Road Warrior (George Miller, 1981). Mel Gibson, Bruce Spence, Michael Preston.

Dusty (John Richardson, 1983). Bill Kerry, Noel Trevarthen, Carol Burns.

Evil Angels/A Cry in the Dark (Fred Schepisi, 1988). Meryl Streep, Sam Neill, Dale Reeves.

Napoleon (Mario Andreacchio, 1995). [Animals with human voices.]

Babe (Chris Noonan, 1995). James Cromwell, Magda Szubanski, Christine Cavanaugh [plus animals with human voices].

Through My Eyes (Di Drew, 2004; television). Miranda Otto, Craig McLachlan, Peter O'Brien.

Red Dog (Kriv Stenders, 2011). Josh Lucas, Rachael Taylor, Rohan Nichol, Koko [Red Dog].

7

Bullies and Curs

• •

Overlords and Underdogs in South African Cinema

GIULIANA LUND

> I would like us to reaffirm our common
> commitment to a new and better society.
> A resolution can be taken that the dog, so
> long denigrated, so long a symbol of abuse,
> should become a national symbol for the
> humanity of South Africans.
> —Ndebele 2007, 4

In his 2006 proclamation "The Year of the Dog," prominent intellectual Njabulo Ndebele challenged South Africans to reevaluate their treatment of dogs and, by extension, each other. Canines have been subjected to exploitation and violence throughout the turbulent history of the region, from centuries of colonization and decades of apartheid to the long-awaited democracy that arrived in 1994. Furthermore, this pervasive mistreatment of canines has been used to legitimize violence against human underdogs. As Ndebele attests, "the word 'dog' is never far away in the imagining of violence and abuse in our society. You can see how often we have treated people and things as if they were 'just a dog.' . . . 'Dog' is a pervasive metaphor regularly used to justify righteous brutality" (2).

Under the colonial and apartheid regimes, Africans were frequently exploited, abused, excluded, neglected, and left homeless "like dogs" (2). During the state of emergency brought on by the popular revolt against apartheid, both African nationalists and state collaborators were slain "like dogs" in the street (2). Even today, in post-apartheid South Africa, political opponents have been publicly denounced as "dogs to be beaten" (1). A functional democracy, Ndebele asserts, requires a more humane attitude toward others, be they two-legged or four-legged. Though animal protection movements in South Africa have long been a niche concern of the privileged classes, Ndebele recognizes that animal welfare and human welfare are intimately interconnected and need to be tackled together. Moreover, he is not alone in linking the treatment of actual and figurative dogs in his country. This pattern of abuse has become a significant focus of post-apartheid South African cinema, which increasingly features canines as a vehicle for social commentary to address the nation's persistent struggle with violence and the prospects for reconciliation and rehabilitation.

Before exploring the real and metaphoric use of canines in South African cinema, it is important to consider the roles dogs have played in the cultural, economic, and political development of the nation. As Lance Van Sittert and Sandra Swart (2003) recount in their history of dogs in South Africa, the archaeological record reveals that canines have lived alongside humans in the region for thousands of years (140–143). European colonists who arrived at the Cape of Good Hope from the seventeenth century onward dubbed the indigenous canines "kaffir dogs" and considered them inferior to European dogs and a health threat (McKenzie 2003). In their stead the settlers imported guard and hunting dogs whose feats were celebrated, even as their competitors, the African dogs, were denigrated and at times outlawed so as to protect colonial livestock and preserve big game hunting for Europeans (Tropp 2002). The preference for imported dogs was solidified in the nineteenth century as imperial obsessions with race and eugenics led to the invention and promotion of the "pure bred dog" (Swart 2003). Consequently, the South African Kennel Club was founded in 1883 to protect European bloodlines. During the twentieth century the rise of settler nationalism led to the endorsement and popularization of new southern African breeds such as the Rhodesian Ridgeback and the Boerboel (the "dog of the Boers"). While these hardy, powerful breeds were created from a mixture of mastiff, hound, and indigenous ancestors, their white proponents emphasized their proud classical origins (Van Sittert and Swart 2003, 150–152). Throughout the colonial period, these and other bully breeds were employed to protect white settlers and their property from the African wildlife and peoples.

The employment of bullies in support of colonial domination of local populations became increasingly official over the course of the twentieth century. From 1909 the Natal police used dogs for rural patrols, for tracking, and for identifying criminals (Van Sittert and Swart 2003, 163). Beginning in 1962, a year after South African independence, canines were utilized in urban settings to control rebellion (163). The quantity of canines involved in policing increased dramatically through the 1980s, "in direct relation to the escalation of black rebellion against the apartheid state" (163–164). Additionally, canine units assisted the military in locating nationalist insurgents throughout war-torn southern Africa (164). The use of dogs as instruments of surveillance and discipline likewise expanded in the private sector:

> Dogs were also widely employed in defence of private property, many of them trained or even manufactured by the state security apparatus. By the 1970s the police dog school was graduating 300 animals per annum, which, together with a proliferation in private obedience training schools produced a large pool of dogs for corporate and private security. De Beers pioneered the corporate practice . . . and their use was generalized to the rest of the mining industry thereafter. The canine defence of white privilege and property was miniaturised to the private farm and home where breeds renowned for their fierceness were kept or created—such as the *boerboel* and colossus—as deterrent to the real and imagined threat of black revolt and redistribution. (Van Sittert and Swart 2003, 165)

As far as black Africans were concerned, the bully was resented as "an icon of authority, the proxy of state power" (165–166).

Dogs in South Africa, like their human counterparts, were thus divided historically into several distinct groups that met with radically different treatment from those in power. Kaffir dogs, whether rural African hunting dogs or urban curs, were typically treated like pests by Europeans and were consequently abused and at times exterminated. Bullies, in contrast, were valuable working dogs used to protect white property and privilege and so were often treated better than the black servants charged with their care. Meanwhile, purebred pets were pampered by the urban elite who followed in the footsteps of their metropolitan compatriots back in England. The fates of these diverse canine populations continue today to vary according to their divergent social status and value as possessions. Attitudes toward these categories of canines also differ substantially among classes and races.

Modern animal-protection movements in South Africa originated in the nineteenth century among wealthy city dwellers of English ancestry. As Van Sittert and Swart explain, "Urban civilisation defined itself not only in opposition to the animal countryside, but also to backveld sensibilities towards animals, deemed backward and brutish. The urban middle class thus championed a new sensibility embodied by the notions of 'humanitarianism' and 'sportsmanship'" (144). It was this class that gradually enacted legislation for the protection of domestic animals and the conservation of wild animals beginning in 1856 and opened a branch of the Society for the Prevention of Cruelty to Animals in 1872. Yet it was also this class that promoted strict breed standards and rejected as "anathema" the "underclass mongrel pack" (145). Furthermore, the English elite often blamed Africans and Afrikaners (of Dutch ancestry) for poor treatment of domestic animals and for depleting the land's big game. Consequently, the elevation of purebred dogs and other prized animals, seemingly at the expense of the lower classes of humans, created the popular perception that animal protection was merely a self-interested concern of the privileged and that it conflicted with the needs of the laborers who actually cared for, worked with, farmed, or hunted animals for a living. In short, animal-protection movements in South Africa tended to oppose the welfare of dogs to that of human underdogs. Given the association of animal protection with the same elite who protected their privileges with aggressive bullies, it is not surprising that little sympathy developed for dogs in general, and bullies in particular, in the majority of the impoverished population. As a result, it has been an uphill battle for South African writers and filmmakers to convince their compatriots that animal and human interests are compatible.

Like the dogs themselves, literary representations of canines tend to fall into a few historical categories, as Wendy Woodward illustrates (2008, 91–141). Colonial and pro-apartheid literature typically depicts bullies as loyal servants and kaffir dogs as vermin. Anti-apartheid literature challenges the relative privilege accorded the white man's dog over black servants, while acknowledging that both are exploited. Post-apartheid literature goes much further in reconceptualizing all canines as underdogs and exploring the possibility of rehabilitating bullies and curs and integrating them into the national community. Cinematic representations of canines in the last few decades exhibit a similar progression from colonial collaborator or cur to oppressed victim.

In cinematic as in literary works, parallels are drawn between canines and Africans. In colonial narratives heroic dogs represent loyal, civilized Africans, whereas wild and "kaffir" dogs represent rebellious native populations to be subdued. In anti-apartheid narratives the white man's dogs are depicted as collaborators and informants. In post-apartheid narratives the call for humane treatment of canines is based in part on the premise that abuse of dogs promotes aggression toward humans denigrated as metaphoric "dogs"—lackeys or lowlifes. Current attempts to affirm the value of canines and to bridge artificial divisions between bullies, curs, and pets support the project of national reconciliation, promoting understanding and empathy in place of hatred and retaliation. In this spirit Ndebele suggests that if the South African people "stop brutalising the dog, if we stop brutalising ourselves whenever we invoke the cruel image of the dog we have created, we may recover our own humanity, which we lost along the way of our history" (2007, 3). A closer look at the representation of canines in South African cinema promises to shed light not only on the treatment of actual dogs but also on their symbolic value in the nation's evolving sociopolitical conflicts.

The Exemplary Colonial Bully in the Memoir *Jock of the Bushveld*

The South African children's classic *Jock of the Bushveld*, by Sir Percy FitzPatrick (1907), has inspired three film versions, all produced or directed by Duncan

MacNeillie: *Jock of the Bushveld* (1986), *Jock: A True Tale of Friendship* (1992), and *Jock the Hero Dog* (2011). As FitzPatrick's Jock is the original model of the bully from which later cinematic versions evolved, he requires some preliminary consideration. FitzPatrick's memoir, set in the 1880s, recounts his adventures on the colonial frontier of the southern African bush with his hunting dog, Jock. The offspring of a "respected" local bull terrier named Jess and an imported dog with a "great reputation," Jock combines the virtues of the hardy South African settler stock and the refined English purebred (50, 54). Born the runt of the litter, Jock is saved from drowning and then adopted by Fitz. Thereafter, he becomes a supremely brave and loyal companion during their many sojourns in the wilderness. Fitz aims to make his fortune as a transport driver, carrying goods overland by wagon train to the new mining towns of the interior. During these travels the pair hunts for food. After Fitz shoots and wounds the prey, it is Jock's job to track, chase, dispatch, and guard it from scavengers. Jock's tremendous hunting prowess and his perseverance in the face of adversity are abundantly displayed in the many accounts given of his exploits, which include encounters with lions, elephants, kudus, crocodiles, and porcupines.

Jock is presented by FitzPatrick as the ideal colonial dog, and as such is clearly distinguished from both wild dogs and "kaffir dogs" (Gray 1987). Among the many predators and scavengers Jock defeats are the hyenas and wild dogs that roam the bush. Neither FitzPatrick nor Jock recognize any kinship between the domesticated canine and his wild cousins. FitzPatrick recounts with disgust that when wild dogs are forced by hunger to hunt large, hardy prey, they gang up on them and wear them down over a period of hours: "There is something so hateful in the calculated pitiless method that one feels it a duty to kill the cruel brutes whenever a chance occurs" (298). This attitude stands in stark contrast to his open admiration for Jock's dogged persistence in chasing down wounded prey. When an impala ewe, usually "fair game" for hunters, stumbles into camp hounded by wild dogs, the white men decide to spare her, leaving the Africans confused: "a kaffir jumped up with assegai aloft [to kill the ewe]; but Teddy, with the spring of a tiger and a yell of rage, swung his rifle round and down on assegai arm and head and dropped the boy in his tracks" (299). The white men show much greater concern here for the impala than they do for the servant "boy," who cannot understand their charitable intention. Africans are implicitly aligned with wild dogs in having no conception of fair play and no compassion for the suffering of the weak. After saving the ewe, the white men proceed to join Jock in mercilessly picking off as many of the wild dogs as they can.

What distinguishes Jock definitively from his wild cousins is that, for all his ferocious strength, he is extremely compliant. The necessity of Jock's education is emphasized in the text by Rocky, a hardened frontiersman, who explains to the young Fitz that "Men ha' got ter larn: dawgs too! Men ain't born equal: no more's dawgs! One's born better 'n another—more brains, more heart; but I ain't yet hear o' the man born with knowledge or experience: that's what they got ter learn—men an' dawgs!" (37). Both Fitz and Jock learn how to hunt, but in addition Jock learns to obey Fitz and to accept that meat belongs to man. Jock's submission is demonstrated by refusing food from anyone else and refraining from eating pieces of meat placed on his nose until given permission. Dogs who "steal" food from men in this environment are shot.

The cur's lack of respect for the property of the white man seemingly explains the hostility expressed by European colonists and their dogs in this memoir. Kaffir dogs are associated with thieving, as are their cohort, the indigenous Africans. Whereas Fitz's hunting practices are depicted as legitimate and humane, the hunting of the kaffir dogs, like that of the wild dogs, is presented as uncivilized, cruel, and punishable by death. Like Fitz, Jock seems convinced of the inferiority of the native canines, for he has a "hatred of kaffir dogs" and attacks them (and their people) at every opportunity—a practice FitzPatrick finds amusing (329–330). In one scene where Jock routes a group of kaffir dogs that innocently find themselves in the neighborhood, the narrator maintains that "even the kaffir owners . . . broke into appreciative laughter and shouts of admiration for the white man's dog" (330).

The exploits of the bully are consistently presented as highly amusing, both when he launches unprovoked attacks on kaffir dogs and when he does the same to the "kaffirs" themselves. Jock bites one African severely enough that the wound needs to be cauterized. Fitz's main concern on this occasion is that the kaffirs may decamp without finishing their work. He claims that such assaults on Africans are the only situations in which Jock disobeys him, although he admits that Jock does not take his objections seriously—"a dog is just as quick as a child to find out when he can take liberties; he knows that laughter and serious disapproval do not go together" (210). It is simply too much bother for Fitz to stop Jock's persecutions of the Africans and their dogs. First, "it was very important that he should have nothing to do with them, and should treat them with suspicion as possible enemies and keep them off the premises" (209). Second, from Fitz's perspective the harassment of innocent Africans is all in good fun, such that he "preferred to look another way when Jock sallied out" (214).

Jock's belligerence toward "strange kaffirs" is encouraged by a Zulu named Jim Makokel: "Jock disliked kaffirs: so did Jim. To Jim there were three big divisions of the human race—white men, Zulus, and niggers" (209).[1] Although Fitz refers to Makokel, too, as a kaffir, he does express some admiration for the fighting qualities of Makokel's people, the Zulu, only recently defeated by the British, and for Jim himself, the most accomplished oxen driver in the region (192, 195–196). Jock similarly appreciates Jim's "unvanquished spirit," for he is the sole "kaffir whom Jock would take any notice of or would allow to touch him" (203, 163). Indeed, Jim possesses the same virtues as Jock: tremendous strength, fidelity, and readiness for a fight. Unfortunately, as far as Fitz is concerned, Jim is not as obedient as Jock, particularly when desirous of or under the influence of alcohol. At such times Jim wanders off and returns in the middle of the night to beg for meat. Like dogs, African servants are only given meat when their masters choose, and Fitz recounts a case in which a "wagon boy" is brutally whipped for demanding meat (199). Although Fitz does not beat Jim for his drunkenness, in part because the many scars on his back indicate the inefficacy of this tactic, he does resort to shackling Jim like a disobedient dog. Fitz recalls, "I threatened that if he did it again I would tie him up, since he was like a dog that could not be trusted; and I did it" (208). Jim must be taught, like Jock, to respect his master, to stay by his master's side, to eat only what he is given, and to be grateful for all he receives. Fitz adopts a similarly paternalistic attitude toward both his creatures: he acts in what he perceives to be their best interests and is generous and kindly when he can afford to be.

The good "white man's dog," like the good African, is a highly trained, domesticated servant doing the bidding of his master. In contrast, the kaffir dog, like the unruly and uncooperative African, must be beaten into shape or eliminated. This task typically falls to the colonial collaborator, motivated by his disdain and hatred of his untamed cousin. Ultimately, the conflict between the "white man's dog" and the "kaffir dog" becomes a life-and-death struggle. After being relegated to a friend's care as a result of deafness resulting from a kudu kick, Jock meets his demise protecting the man's poultry from marauding kaffir dogs. While out performing his duties in the dark one night, he is mistaken for a thief and accidentally shot. For FitzPatrick, Jock's passing "in the very prime of life" is more fitting than tragic, for he cannot "picture him in a life of ease and idleness . . . with old age, deafness, and infirmities growing year by year" (464). He wishes for him, instead, a glorious death in battle, "hanging on with his indomitable pluck and tenacity, tackling something with all the odds against him, doing his duty" (464). When Jock is dead, FitzPatrick laments that he had not been killed by a lion or buck, and asks, "Would it not have been better for him—happier for me?" (464). Nonetheless, he portrays Jock's shooting by his caretaker as a suitable finish by closing the memoir thus: "inside the fowl-house lay the kaffir dog—dead. Jock had done his duty" (464). Killing the kaffir dog salvages Jock's heroic end in this colonial memoir.

The Liberal Bully in the Film *Jock of the Bushveld*

The movie *Jock of the Bushveld*, an adaptation of FitzPatrick's memoir directed by Gray Hofmeyr, was the first South African film to feature a dog in a starring role (the Staffordshire bull terrier Umfubu). The film came out in 1986 at the height of apartheid atrocities and the resulting international cultural boycott. It expressed a striking nostalgia for the heroic adventures of a seemingly innocent colonial past. The film sticks closely to the spirit of the memoir, while moderating its overtly racist elements. It takes a liberal political stance that criticizes the excesses of colonial brutality without challenging the underlying premises of imperialism or its associated values of martial bravery, perseverance, fidelity, and obedience. The paternalistic dominance of Fitz over Jock, Jim, the Africans, and the wilderness is taken for granted. As Fitz (Jonathan Rands) and Jock travel through the bush, their deep connection to each other and the wild terrain provides the imaginative groundwork for a claim of belonging to and ownership of the seemingly empty land.

This film version of *Jock of the Bushveld* is notable for including explicit violence against animals. The film does not contain any reassurances that no animals were harmed in the making of the movie, so it is unclear whether the violence is real or simulated.[2] Significantly, all Fitz's killing is presented as righteous: the practice of hunting wildlife for food is defended; predators like crocodiles are killed because they represent a direct threat to humans; sick oxen are euthanized with a gunshot to the head. In contrast, the violence of rude frontiersmen such as Seedling is condemned. Seedling (Michael Brunner) is conspicuous for his ill treatment both of Africans and of dogs. He keeps a baboon on a chain and sets it upon outmatched dogs just for entertainment. Ultimately, the heroic Jock vanquishes the powerful baboon. Fitz distinguishes himself from men like Seedling by taking a stand against brutality. In the first instance, he resorts to his fists to save Jock from being drowned. Similarly, he defends Africans who are being unfairly treated by their white masters. His interventions on their behalf go well beyond any described in FitzPatrick's memoir. Moreover, the enlightened Fitz does not allow Jock to persecute passing Africans. He is portrayed as a good master, one who has the best interests of the underdogs at heart, be they actual or metaphorical.

The violence to which dogs are subjected on the frontier remains ever present in this picture. The film depicts Jock's encounter with the kudu that deafens him with a kick to the head. It also portrays the dangers of town life to a deaf dog, thereby justifying Jock's placement at the farm where he eventually gets shot. The film does not shy away from Jock's sad demise, but it does offset it with images of his burial at a site that is now a national monument.[3] The tragedy of the film's ending is also mitigated by the foregrounding of a love story between Fitz and a townswoman named Lilian (Jocelyn Broderick). Despite these innovations, the ending proved too traumatic for international audiences and although the film was popular in South Africa, it did not do well overseas. For this reason, it was decided a few years later to remake the film with a Hollywood ending.[4]

The Canine Conservationist in *Jock: A True Tale of Friendship*

The second adaptation of FitzPatrick's memoir, *Jock: A True Tale of Friendship*, directed by Danie Joubert, with Gitane and Japie playing Jock, incorporates numerous changes intended to make the story more palatable to both an international audience and an increasingly diverse local audience. The film was released in 1992, in the waning years of apartheid, two years after Nelson

Mandela was freed from prison and two years before he was elected president in the nation's first democratic elections. It derives a conservationist message out of the colonial and liberal agendas of the earlier print and film versions. Accordingly, it tones down the violence of the preceding works and gives the bully a makeover. In keeping with this spirit, the producers proclaim, "No animals were injured or mistreated during the making of this film and the Animal Anti-Cruelty League were present during the shooting of certain scenes."

In *Jock: A True Tale of Friendship* Fitz becomes a vocal advocate for conservation. He expresses concerns about overhunting of big game by men who "shoot anything that moves," he frowns upon the ivory trade, and he supports government regulation of hunting. Fitz (Sean Gallagher) draws inspiration from Rocky (Robert Urich), who compares the decimation of big game on the African frontier with the extermination of the American buffalo. The wise old-timer submits that the reason Fitz initially misses when shooting at game is not lack of skill but lack of desire: "You don't believe in killing." Nonetheless, Rocky explains that hunting is "the only way you'll survive out here" and is, moreover, part of the "natural cycle." Rocky plainly distinguishes between hunting for meat and hunting for sport or profit: "We only shoot for the pot; that's all we need, that's all we take." Another conservationist in the film is Jim Makokel (Sello Sebotsane), who halts a charging elephant by reassuring it, "My friend . . . we mean no harm. We are not hunters." Jock follows the example of his master in using violence only for self-preservation. Nearly all killing of animals occurs off camera and is carefully legitimized, as when Fitz shoots a lion to save the lives of Jess and Jock. The story of an adventurer and his hunting dog is thus transformed into the story of a conservationist and his companion. The joy of the kill, so predominant in earlier versions, is carefully excised from this adaptation.

Throughout the second film Fitz is presented as a nurturer rather than a slaughterer of animals. This is exemplified in his compassionate preservation and education of the runt Jock, who is much improved by his attentions. Fitz is shocked by others' callousness toward canines, especially their patronage of dogfights. "Surely, that's not allowed," he exclaims, implying that the government should step in to prevent cruelty to animals. The state, like FitzPatrick, is presented in this liberal conservationist fantasy as a paternalistic force for good, actually or at least potentially protecting the South African land, animals, and peoples. The love Fitz has for his dog testifies to the sincerity of the white man's benevolent intentions in Africa. Jock's gratitude, loyalty, and subservience likewise exemplify an appropriate attitude for the white man's servants, both four-legged and two.

Jock: A True Tale of Friendship offers up a simplistic moral universe meant to appeal to diverse modern audiences. On the one hand, only cruel men mistreat animals and Africans. On the other hand, both Jock and Jim are sanitized—relieved of their shared passion for assaulting indigenous laborers (and, in Jim's case, alcoholism). Good wins out over evil, and the traumas of violence and death

Jock: A True Tale of Friendship (Danie Joubert, Questar Home Video, 1992). In contrast to the original memoir and the first film version of *Jock of the Bushveld*, in which the canine hero dies of an accidental gunshot wound, the second, sanitized version closes as FitzPatrick (Sean Gallagher) swings Jock around joyously on his rifle strap while love-interest Lilian (Faye Masterson) cuddles one of Jock's puppies. Details of video frame enlargements.

are muted. In this update Jess dies, but not Jock, who has puppies at the end with Lilian's terrier bitch to replace his lost dam. The film concludes not with the shooting of Jock and his funeral but instead with Jock swinging playfully from Fitz's rifle strap. This closing image of Jock flying around Fitz, with Lilian (Faye Masterson) in the background holding one of his puppies, whitewashes the violent end met by the original Jock in Fitzpatrick's memoir. What was once a relationship between man and dog centered on the gun—and in which the dog finally dies by the gun at the hands of a man he serves—has become a relationship of innocent play in which the weapon is transformed into a toy.

Rise of the Democratic Underdog in *Jock the Hero Dog*

The latest filmic version of *Jock of the Bushveld* is a 2011 3-D animation, the first film of its kind made in South Africa. *Jock the Hero Dog*, directed by Duncan MacNeillie, further updates and simplifies the moral, while adding musical comedy elements and voicing by popular (mostly American) actors. While the 1992 version contains only a short dream sequence from Jock's point of view, the 2011 animation is largely focalized—and vocalized—through Jock. Fitz, in contrast, is reduced to a kindhearted, bungling naif, peripheral to much of the main action. The promotion of Jock's perspective at the expense of Fitz's enables the film to avoid much of the political baggage of the earlier works. The point of view of the white master is replaced in this post-apartheid work by that of his dog, the other talking animals, and the indigenous Africans.

Jock, the hero, is also reimagined: his bravery no longer epitomizes the colonial battle for mastery over nature; instead, his struggles support the values of environmentalism, social justice, freedom, equality, and reconciliation. The 2011 animation completes the transformation of Jock from bully to underdog, playing up his status as a runt and his persecution by threatening beasts—of the human and nonhuman varieties. Jock is no longer the celebrated hunter, bringing down majestic prey with his jaws; rather, he is the accidental hero, inspired despite his small size to protect the weak and exploited, including Fitz and a panoply of animals enslaved by vicious bosses. Moreover, this latest Jock displays ethical judgment and individual initiative. He explicitly rejects blind obedience, particularly obedience to the wrong men.

MacNeillie's post-apartheid animation Africanizes Jock's origin story. The puppy is given to Fitz by a newly invented character, Baba, a wise and venerable old African voiced by the famous anti-apartheid activist and former archbishop Desmond Tutu. Makokel must actually convince the imprudent Fitz to accept Jock despite his complaints that the puppy does not look like a champion. Though the animated Jock bears some vague resemblance to earlier Jocks, he is not readily identifiable as a Staffordshire bull terrier. Indeed, any implications that Jock is descended from purebred English bully dogs would contradict his presentation as a quintessentially African creature. Snobs view him as a mongrel, not good enough to mate with the French poodle Polly (another innovation), but when he proves his worth, the two are finally accepted as a "good pair." Strength of character wins out over purity of breeding in this post-apartheid morality tale.

The foolish Fitz of 2011 must be guided in all things by his African friends. When an evil white hunter tries to drown the puppy Jock, it is first Jess and Jim who come to his rescue. The animated film displaces Fitz's benevolence and the bush wisdom of the American frontiersman Rocky onto Makokel and Baba. The conservationist perspective of the 1992 film, where animals are preserved for the pleasure and use of humans, is expanded into a full-blown, African-inflected environmentalism. As Baba explains at the top of the film, against a backdrop of ancient cave paintings, "Before our time men lived in harmony with animals. They could communicate and understand one another. But man wanted more. Man wanted control. You animals will pay the price." The film closes with a dedication "to the creatures and environments whose future is in our hands."

Jock the Hero Dog embraces ethical principles adapted to contemporary South Africa and critical of its colonial past. It explicitly condemns the obsession with gold that motivates Fitz's journey into the African interior. The film implies that greed lies behind the evils of colonization and the exploitation of labor, whereas indigenous Africans (both human and nonhuman) appreciate the greater value of spiritual riches. Avaricious frontiersmen neglect and brutalize their servants. Seedling forces animals to race and fight so he can win money. Meanwhile, his dog, Snarly, is plagued by fleas and reduced to eating garbage, and his baboon, George, is kept physically and mentally chained. Jock sets about undermining Seedling's merciless domination and freeing his animal servants. The hero is opposed to violence and does not wish to clash with George. Nonetheless, he "fights for what he believes in," preventing George from harming an innocent. In their climactic fight scene Jock grabs George by the neck, but instead of killing him as in earlier versions, he breaks the iron collar that symbolizes his enslavement. The film suggests that even the nasty bully George and the sniveling informant Snarly are victims. Jock tells George that he has been taking orders from the wrong boss and urges him to flee Seedling. The freeing of Snarly and George and the forgiveness shown them reflects the post-apartheid emphasis on reconciliation epitomized in the proceedings of South Africa's Truth and Reconciliation Commission (1995–2003), in which those who committed politically motivated violence, such as policemen and soldiers following orders, were given immunity from prosecution in exchange for truthful testimony about their crimes. Significantly, while Snarly and George are actually or potentially rehabilitated, Seedling himself, the big boss, is eaten by crocodiles, and no tears are shed for him.

Black Boy and White Dog in *Inja*

Whereas the early Jock narratives celebrate the bully as an instrument of colonial domination over the African bush and its people, and honor him as a brave, loyal, and obedient protector of the white man and his property, post-apartheid cinema challenges this perspective. Although bullies historically were servants of imperialism and instruments of racial oppression and violence, contemporary films such as *Jock the Hero Dog* depict bullies as victims of the manipulations of cruel masters. Whether such bullies are capable of being reformed and reintegrated into a free, egalitarian society remains an open question. The character and fate of the bully is thoughtfully explored in the Oscar-nominated short film *Inja* [*Dog*] (2002), from the South African born writer and director Steve Pasvolsky, who now resides in Australia.

Inja opens during the apartheid period, with a young African boy on a white-owned farm befriending a Boerboel puppy. The boy, Thembile (Anele Vellom), weaves a collar for the puppy, suggesting both affection and desire for ownership. Indeed, the pair seem to share a natural affinity, but their bond is deliberately broken by the Afrikaner farmer, Johannes (Danny Keogh). The farmer forces the boy, at gunpoint, to beat the innocent puppy so that he will grow to distrust blacks and become what is known as a "white dog," a dog purposely trained for racial discrimination and hostility. Forcing Thembile to participate in the "training" of the Boerboel simultaneously teaches the boy to submit to his master's will. Both boy and dog are parallel victims of violence in this scene.

In the second part of *Inja*, set in the post-apartheid period, boy and dog, now grown (the adult Thembile is played by Lizo C. Makambi), still work for the same farmer. Relations between the boss and Thembile, now a farmhand, have mellowed with time and the changing political climate, but the Boerboel remains firm in his terror and hatred of blacks. In the climactic scene Johannes suffers a heart attack, and Thembile is unable to deliver his life-saving medication because the Boerboel stands guard over his fallen master and will not let the black man approach. In the end Johannes orders Thembile to shoot the dog, and the film closes with the sound of a gunshot. Significantly, the boss's final command to his "boy" is as violent as his first, brutalizing both human and canine servants.

Despite the fall of apartheid, *Inja* suggests that not much has changed for the underdogs of South African society, be they human or canine. The divide-and-conquer strategy of imperialism is still at work, setting Africans and dogs against each other when they might otherwise work together in common cause. The true bully here is not the Boerboel, first beaten and then, presumably, killed, but rather the Afrikaner farmer, who continues to maintain a firm grip on the land and its inhabitants. The Boerboel, reminiscent of the title character of the American film *White Dog* (1982), directed by Samuel Fuller, represents the intractable nature of racism. It is difficult to conceive the means to undo the fear and suspicion born of traumatic experience. The question arises whether it is, after all, possible to teach an old dog—or an old man—new tricks.

Disposing of Bullies and Curs in *Disgrace*

Disgrace (2008), directed by the Australian Steve Jacobs, is another post-apartheid picture that features the killing of bullies, as well as curs, as a means to raise doubts about South Africa's progress toward racial reconciliation and peaceful coexistence. The film is based on the award-winning 1999 novel by South African Nobel laureate J. M. Coetzee, who has since emigrated to Australia. The novel is highly controversial in South Africa, as some political leaders argue that it reiterates racist stereotypes of African sexuality, while others maintain that it accepts white guilt and subjugation as the price of peace. Literary and cultural critics, in contrast, tend to emphasize the narrative's sophisticated, self-reflexive structure and anti-authoritarian ethics. The novel, along with Coetzee's *Lives of Animals*, published in the same year, has become a central text for animal studies scholars around the globe.[5] While it is outside the scope of this chapter to survey the vast criticism on Coetzee's oeuvre, it is important to acknowledge the work's powerful impact on public discourse. *Disgrace* takes an unflinching look at humanity's brutality and foregrounds the continuing plight of both animal and human underdogs in democratic South Africa. The film adaptation by Jacobs, with a screenplay written by his wife, Ana Maria Monticelli, and approved by Coetzee, follows the novel closely in plot, dialogue, and symbolism. Dogs—both organic and metaphoric—thus play a central role in this drama of contemporary South Africa, and their tragic deaths epitomize the nation's disgrace.

Like its source, the film *Disgrace* follows the fall from grace of David Lurie (John Malkovich), a literature professor who makes unwelcome sexual advances on one of his "Colored" undergraduates and is brought up before a university disciplinary committee, where he refuses to proffer the desired confession of guilt for his actions. Lurie departs Cape Town to visit his daughter, Lucy (Jessica Haines), who lives on a farm, grows flowers for market, and keeps a small kennel that houses off-duty guard dogs. One day while walking the dogs, David and Lucy encounter a trio of black men from the neighborhood who attack David, rape Lucy, and shoot the dogs. This violence against white homesteaders and their bullies reflects a profound shift in the power dynamics of South Africa. Lurie conjectures that the perpetrators were seeking vengeance for the historical crimes of apartheid. Meanwhile, Lucy seems to accept her altered status and vulnerable position; she decides to keep the (mixed race) child of rape she carries and accepts the protection of the African patriarch Petrus (played by French actor Eriq Ebouaney), her former "dog-man."

Lurie is deeply disturbed by Lucy's submission to Petrus and her utter dependency on him. He protests, "How humiliating to end like this . . . like a dog." It is not a very attractive prospect to end up in the care of Petrus. This enigmatic African expresses concern for Lucy, but it is impossible to discern whether his interest in her is empathetic or instrumental. One scene, in particular, emphasizes Petrus's inhumane treatment of the defenseless. The scene opens in Lucy's home, while she pets her sweet, bandaged Labrador retriever, Milo, the sole survivor of the dog massacre (who substitutes for the taciturn bulldog of the novel). This cozy interior is contrasted with the landscape without, including the intrusive presence of Petrus. The camera cuts repeatedly between Lucy caressing Milo, and Petrus tethering goats for slaughter without access to food or water. Ultimately, Lurie intervenes to provide sustenance to the goats. The juxtaposition of the Luries and Petrus in this scene suggests that the former care more for the welfare of the weak than does the latter. Whites, not blacks, are the protectors of animals in *Disgrace*. Though Petrus is Lucy's dog-man, he seemingly does nothing to prevent and little to rectify the rape of Lucy and the murder of the dogs in his keeping, despite the fact that the perpetrators are familiar to him. That Petrus agrees to look after Lucy and her unborn child thus offers slight consolation.

In contrast to Petrus, Lurie finds himself increasingly impotent and irrelevant in the new nation: he fails to keep his lovers; he fails to influence his students; and he fails to protect his daughter. He finds himself instead gradually taking on a role he initially despises, that of dog-man, volunteering to care for the surplus dogs abandoned at a local clinic. As Lucy notes, the welfare of animals is not a high priority for the new government, and the little funding available is dedicated to "euthanizing" unwanted (but otherwise generally healthy) canines. David accompanies the dogs as they die and ensures that their corpses are disposed of in a dignified manner. In the penultimate scene of the film, Lurie gives up to the needle the lame mongrel with which he has formed a special attachment.

David Lurie becomes a "dog-man" not only because he cares for dogs, but because he is "like a dog" himself. As a white man in post-apartheid South Africa he perceives himself as victimized, subjugated, superfluous, and potentially homeless. He is, at least in his own mind, society's latest underdog. It is thus natural that he comes to empathize with the murdered bullies and callously neglected curs of the Cape. *Disgrace* suggests that democracy has neither rehabilitated the bullies nor rescued the curs. The new overlords continue to tolerate disgraceful retaliations against the weak. Yet the validity of Lurie's observations and the value of his contributions as a dog-man remain open to question. Is the situation really as bleak as he perceives? Could he not reject resignation and actually save the lives of some of the poor mongrels in his care, rather than simply escorting them to their deaths? Jacob's adaptation sows some hope in the final scene, in which the glowing, pregnant Lucy plants seedlings in her garden, joined by Milo and David. By reversing the order of the last two scenes of Coetzee's novel—the reunion with Lucy and the killing of the favorite dog—Jacob's version ends on a slightly more optimistic note, with the promise of new life rather than the triumph of death.

Digital frame enlargements from *Disgrace* (Steve Jacobs, Image Entertainment, 2008). In the first, the family dog, Milo, joins the outraged assault of Lurie (John Malkovich) on a disturbed teenager who has been peeping at his daughter Lucy in the shower, illustrating how dogs are commonly used in South Africa to protect the persons and property of the privileged. In the second, mongrel and man mirror each other, each imprisoned by circumstance; Lurie comes to see himself as an "underdog" in modern South Africa much like the superfluous mutt who is caged for a time before being put down. In the third, Lurie, the "dog-man," lovingly carries his favorite mutt from the pound into the veterinary clinic for euthanasia.

Rescue and Rehabilitation in *Cape of Good Hope*

Whereas the dogs of *Disgrace* mainly end up dead at the hands of humans, canines meet a happier fate in *Cape of Good Hope* (2004), directed by Mark Bamford and cowritten by his wife, Suzanne Kay, American residents in South Africa. The film connects humans and canines in a diverse post-apartheid community of Cape Town. While it deals with weighty subjects such as abandonment, poverty, homelessness, and racial prejudice, its tone is ultimately upbeat, imagining a brighter future for South Africa's human and canine inhabitants.

The Good Hope Animal Shelter sits at the crossroads of the film's intersecting stories. This no-kill shelter is the labor of love of Kate (Debbie Brown), a privileged white woman, who pays for the facility out of her trust fund. Single and middle-aged, she works through her own abandonment issues by saving stray and discarded dogs. Kate contrasts with her mother, who represents a dated version of upper-class feminine vanity and dependency symbolized by her pet pug, Bitsy. Kate is unimpressed by this pedigreed pooch, but her mother is bent on protecting her lap dog's purity by preventing her from venturing into the neighbors' yard. Wealthy Nigerians have moved in next door, and Kate's mother is building a fence to stop Bitsy from fraternizing with their dog. Bitsy, she proclaims, "is not used to such rough company." Her attempt to shore up the failing racial boundaries of democratic South Africa is doomed to failure, however. Dogs are notoriously indiscriminate in their mates, having no conception of breed superiority; they are pawns of racial discourse, not its advocates. The film ends with a humorous shot of the mixed pair happily humping.

Breaking free from the apartheid mores of her mother, Kate strives to tear down social barriers by rescuing curs from Cape Town's African townships. She bemoans the fact that it is usually these mongrels on death row at the city pound. Although she considers them especially intelligent, the white couples who come to her shelter only want to adopt pedigreed dogs. She finds herself wondering, "Why does everyone want purebreds? The mutts are so much smarter." Prejudice against canines of impure blood reflects the continued obsession with race in South African society. The desire for pure blood is not entirely intractable, however, and Kate makes some strides in convincing visitors to her shelter to adopt her lovable mutts.

Kate does rescue one purebred dog, a Rottweiler scheduled to be euthanized because he is supposedly unadoptable—"There's no hope for him. He was trained to attack blacks and there's no untraining them once they're like that." Kate refuses to surrender him to an interested white couple and instead places the bully in the care of Jean Claude, her Congolese dog-man. Jean Claude (Eriq Ebouaney, the same actor who later plays Petrus in *Disgrace*), gradually bonds with the bully and names him Jack, after the children's song "Frère Jacques" (Brother Jack). When Jack growls at a young black boy, Jean Claude explains, "He don't like us blacks. . . . It's not his fault. Someone taught him when he was

Digital frame enlargements from *Cape of Good Hope* (Mark Bamford. New Yorker Films, 2004). The township dog, Tupak, sports a bandage on his forepaw placed there by Thabo (Kamo Masilo). After ignoring other begging children, Kate (Debbie Brown) gives money to Thabo who plays on her sympathies by telling her he needs to pay for an operation for his limping dog.

too young to know any better. But he and I are now good friends." Ultimately, Jack is fully rehabilitated and Jean Claude is able to adopt him, showing that even the "white dog" can be saved. *Cape of Good Hope* thus offers a more optimistic outlook on the potential for racial reconciliation than *Inja* or *Disgrace*.

Concern for the plight of animals in the midst of the human suffering still so prevalent in South Africa may seem trivial or even hypocritical. Indeed, Kate, like many women of her class, initially pays more attention to canine than to human distress. As she drives to her shelter, she passes begging African children on the road without a backward glance. She finally stops when she sees a young boy, Thabo (Kamo Masilo), accompanied by a limping dog with a bandaged foot. She gives him money for an operation only to see his dog prance away, perfectly sound. Thabo later explains that he has more success begging for Tupak than for himself: "When I put the bandage on *my* foot we don't make as much money." Embarrassed by her predictable sympathy for the dog's welfare rather than the boy's, and impressed by Thabo's training skills, she invites him to entertain prospective adopters at the shelter. Thabo's family are initially quite unimpressed by Kate's activities. His grandmother exclaims, with some disgust, "White people. They sure love their dogs," while his mother, Lindiwe (Nthati Moshesh), replies "More than us." The film thereby articulates the problematic association in South Africa of animal protection with white privilege and the mistreatment of Africans.

Ultimately, *Cape of Good Hope* upsets the popular assumption that animal welfare conflicts with human welfare by underscoring the connection between abuse of dogs and abuse of people. The villains of the film are men of power who cruelly betray those who trust them. Stephen (Nick Boraine), Kate's adulterous part-time lover, attempts to rape his maid, Lindiwe, Thabo's widowed mother. When Thabo discovers what has happened, he throws a rock through the boss's window. Before he can escape, Stephen grabs him and Tupak comes to his rescue, growling and biting his pants leg while Stephen beats him with a golf club. Inverting the historic image of the "white dog" protecting the master and his property, the township dog's attack on the Afrikaner rapist represents the underdog's struggle for justice. Significantly, Stephen treats Lindiwe, Thabo, and Tupak with the same careless brutality. When Kate threatens to expose Stephen unless he drops the charges against Thabo, he responds, in Afrikaans, "I knew you loved your stupid dogs, but I had no idea you were a kaffir-lover too." Those who despise and mistreat dogs, the film implies, will likely do the same to people.

Cape of Good Hope posits an analogy between rescue of canines and rescue of humans. Kate is saved from her depressing affair with Stephen by her love for the gentle veterinarian Morne (Morne Visser). Jean Claude not only rescues Jack, but he himself is rescued by his love for Lindiwe. As a Congolese refugee, he is initially rejected by Lindiwe's mother, who calls him a "dirty foreigner" and comments that he "probably has the AIDS." Lindiwe's mother is similarly suspicious of dogs, saying they carry fleas and should not be allowed in bed. In the end, however, the affection, fidelity, and tenacity of the underdog wins out over prejudice, and Jean Claude, Lindiwe, Thabo, Tupak, and Jack form a happy family. This optimistic picture is completed when, in the third narrative thread, an infertile "Colored" couple (a Muslim couple of South Asian descent), decide to adopt an abandoned baby. The husband's first reaction is negative, proclaiming "that's black," and "it's probably got AIDS." In due course, however, his wife convinces him to accept the homeless infant. The film promotes values well suited to the new South African nation: reconciliation, openness, and belonging. It incorporates canines as inspiration to critique racism, cross social barriers, promote empathy, challenge abuse, and fight homelessness. The epigraph to the film quotes Bahá'u'lláh: "He [the True Seeker] should show kindness to animals, how much more unto his fellow-man."

The Year of the Dog

Examination of South African films reveals a striking continuity among cultural, literary, and cinematic representations of dogs. The region's long colonial history and decades of apartheid has marked its public discourse with a number of obsessive concerns, including racial difference, criminal violence, and national reconciliation. The depiction of canines, both historical and fictional, reflects these enduring preoccupations. Apartheid-era films reveal the strong influence of the colonial ethos exemplified in FitzPatrick's *Jock of the Bushveld*, in which the white man's ownership and mastery of the land and its animal and human populations is symbolized through his relationship with his dog. In contrast, post-apartheid films show the more recent but no less profound influence of Coetzee's *Disgrace* (1999), in which both the "white man's dog" and the "township dog" fall victim to society's rage and neglect and testify to the tragic gap between the promise of a new society and the entrenchment of old patterns of prejudice and abuse. Although some of these films aim primarily to entertain rather than edify, nevertheless the canine characters in these works embody fiercely contested national ethics. For this reason they have great contemporary relevance.[6]

A common characteristic of South African films featuring dogs is the analogy between canine and human castes. The films expose, and in later cases undermine, the racial hierarchies that underlie breed distinctions between bullies and curs. In apartheid-era narratives the bully represents the white man's collaborator, the cur his African nemesis. In post-apartheid films the image of the bully evolves to symbolize the fallen white elite, while the cur stands for the victim of abuse, typically a child, woman, or immigrant. Though bullies and curs can still be identified in democratic era cinema, their qualities and fates become deliberately harder to distinguish: in the animated version of Jock, the former bully is fully indigenized and his status as a runt emphasized; in *Inja* the Boerboel has more in common with the African boy who befriends him than with his Afrikaner master; in *Disgrace* both bullies and curs are outcasts in the new society and subject to extermination; in *Cape of Good Hope* bullies and curs alike are rescued and integrated into the same family. Modern South African cinema thereby challenges the ideals of breed purity. Works from *Jock: A True Tale of Friendship* to *Cape of Good Hope* feature prominent scenes of canine interbreeding presented as a positive model for a society in which, not so long ago, segregation was the rule and miscegenation was banned. By challenging distinctions between bullies and curs, post-apartheid cinema strikes a blow against the artificial racial categories that have structured South African society for centuries.

The analogy between canine and human underdogs in South African cinema also enables a reevaluation of the role of violence in society. In apartheid-era works, aggression against animals and humans is justified by threats to person, property, and privilege. Bullies nobly carry out attacks against other creatures, including curs and wild dogs. In post-apartheid cinema, in contrast, violence is only legitimated to protect the vulnerable from assault or exploitation. Bullies and curs thus feature primarily as victims of violence rather than perpetrators and are frequently subjected to abuse and extermination. Shifting portrayals of dogs in South African cinema reflect broader developments in national attitudes toward violence: popular opinion now generally rejects violence as a means of bolstering political and economic power and embraces instead the values of negotiation and reconciliation. The depiction of bullies and curs—stand-ins for collaborators and rebels—as joint victims of violent masters relieves them of responsibility for aggression, promotes the possibility of rehabilitation, and facilitates their incorporation into the new democratic nation.

There is, then, a strong tendency in post-apartheid cinema to present dogs as victims. This tendency reflects, in part, their roles as symbols for other vulnerable social groups. Yet it also indicates a sincere concern for the plight of actual dogs that are neglected and brutalized. Canines can serve both as proxies for people and as subjects in their own right because the interests of both cohorts are conceived as compatible. Recent South African films assert a profound connection between human and canine welfare. To make this affirmation of common ground persuasive, they address the issues that have historically divided the two groups. First, they acknowledge the disturbing history of bullies being used to track, intimidate, and police Africans in the interests of protecting white property and privilege. Second, they make a compelling case that these aggressors are themselves victims of violence and, as such, deserving of forgiveness. Third, they admit the history of hypocrisy in the animal-protection movement in South Africa, conceding that it has traditionally been an upper-class diversion, raising the interests of dogs above those of lower-class people. In addition, some of the democratic era films challenge the prejudicial assumption that Africans are naturally cruel to animals: in *Cape of Good Hope* Jean-Claude, the dog-man, is kind and gentle (contrasting with Petrus in *Disgrace*); similarly, Thabo is nurturing and a good trainer (as Thembile, in *Inja*, might have been if given the opportunity). By confronting the artificial divisions driven by colonial conquest, current cinema advances a new politics of rescue and rehabilitation. This politics asserts that canine and human underdogs share a common fate and must be uplifted together.

Canines in contemporary South African cinema are characterized by suffering and dependency even more than love and loyalty. These dogs are no longer the heroic adventurers of colonial days, nor even the thieving villains; rather, they are casualties of a dysfunctional society. Ironically, current incarnations of canines have less agency, personality, and individuality than their literary and cinematic ancestors. Recent films also make less of an attempt to engage a canine point of view. The most fully developed and independent canine character remains the original Jock, perhaps because he was based on a living dog. While the new animated Jock is the primary focalizer of his own story, there is nothing canine about his perspective: in contrast to the doggy original, the cartoon Jock is merely a mouthpiece for current sociopolitical concerns, and his escapades are confined to the context of fighting animal abuse. Though a few dogs in post-apartheid cinema are given the dignity of names (Milo, Tupak, Jack), they function mainly as objects of affection or pity, not fully formed subjects.

The active role played by canine actors is similarly effaced in recent cinema. Whereas the dogs playing Jock receive prominent billing in the early films of that series, no canines are individually credited in *Disgrace* or *Cape of Good Hope*, only animal trainers and wranglers. Likewise, little attention is paid to actual canines in the critical reception of the films. Concern for the well-being of flesh-and-blood dogs takes a back seat to exploring their metaphorical resonance. Recent movies do proclaim their protection of animal actors with statements in the closing credits to the effect that no creatures were harmed during shooting. However, increased concern for animal welfare has as yet produced neither nuanced images of canines as fully formed subjects nor much appreciation of their actual agency. Such exclusive emphasis on the victimization of dogs in order to promote the cause of animal protection risks inadvertently objectifying them on film and in life.

Overall, the plight of bullies and curs in South African cinema mirrors the plight of their people. Although *Cape of Good Hope* offers reason to be optimistic, the fate of both canine and human underdogs, as of the nation that is their home, remains precarious. The moment is ripe to overcome prejudice and resist aggression. As Njabulo Ndebele suggests, "It is time to step out of our violent history. Let's honour the dog. Let's declare [this year] The Year of the Dog!" (3). In doing so, let us remember always that dogs are more than metaphors. To make strides in promoting their welfare, it is crucial to recognize them as complex agents in their own right, not just helpless victims and proxies for humans.

Notes

1. There seems to be something constitutional in Jock's hatred of kaffirs since his dam, Jess, shares this characteristic (51).
2. In addition to giving top billing to the dog Umfubu, the film credits his owners and trainer, oxen handlers, a veterinarian, and a taxidermist. The inclusion of the taxidermist suggests that some of the animals that appear in the film are dead, though it does not resolve the question of whether they were killed for the purpose of making the film or during shooting.
3. There are statues and plaques dedicated to Jock all along the path of his historic treks,

and even today many pilgrims and tourists follow in Jock's footsteps as they explore the bush.

4. See Kevin Bloom, "The *Jock of the Bushveld* Dilemma," *Daily Maverick*, November 24, 2009, dailymaverick.co.za/article/2009-11-24-analysis-the-jock -of-the-bushveld-dilemma/#.Ud7WrUGTjHQ.

5. For discussion of the representation of canines in Coetzee's novel see Attridge (2000); Donovan (2004); Herron (2005); Dekoven (2009). For an insightful critique of the film version see Du Toit (2009).

6. Treatment of dogs remains highly politicized in South Africa owing to colonial history. Controversy erupted in December 2012 when President Jacob Zuma stated in a speech that "buying and caring for dogs by walking them and taking them to the vet was part of 'white' culture." Furthermore, Zuma claimed that "those who loved dogs more than people lacked humanity." His spokesperson, Mac Maharaj, later asserted that Zuma did not mean that dogs "should not be loved or cared for." According to Maharaj, Zuma was trying to "decolonise the African mind" and used "the well-known example of people who sit with their dogs in front in a van or truck, with a worker at the back in pouring rain or extremely cold weather [or who] do not hesitate to rush their dogs to veterinary surgeons for medical care when they are sick, while they ignore workers or relatives who are also sick" ("Zuma Has South Africa Barking Mad," *The Mercury*, December 28, 2012). In response, many South Africans disputed Zuma's implication that animal welfare and human welfare are incompatible. Several prominent black South Africans took to the Internet to reject the idea that having a dog as a companion is un-African, and to post photographs of themselves and of Nelson Mandela with family pets (see "Dogs Are Not for Africans," *Storify*, December 27, 2012; "Zuma Has South Africa Barking Mad"; Steyn du Toit, "Black South Africans Refute Zuma's 'Dogs Part of White Culture' Claims," *2 Oceans Vibe News*, December 28, 2012). The National SPCA, which enjoys the patronage of Mandela, affirmed that caring for animals benefits people because they live and work together; moreover, "there is no doubt that Black Africans love their dogs," and many serve animals in the veterinary profession and inspectorate ("Proud That Our Beloved Madiba Is Our Patron," *NSPCA*, December 28, 2012). Nonetheless, there is still palpable resentment against dogs and their owners among some Africans who believe canines are treated better than human workers.

Chronological Filmography

White Dog (Samuel Fuller, 1982). Kristy McNichol, Christa Lang, Vernon Weddle, Hans [dog], Folsom [dog], Son [dog], Buster [dog], Duke [dog].

Jock of the Bushveld (Gray Hofmeyr, 1986). Jonathan Rands, Gordon Mulholland, Jocelyn Broderick, Oliver Ngwenya, Mfubu [dog].

Jock: A True Tale of Friendship (Danie Joubert, 1992). Robert Urich, Sean Gallagher, Fay Masterson, Sello Sebotsane.

Inja [*Dog*] (Steve Pasvolsky, 2002). Anele Vellom, Lizo C. Makambi, Danny Keogh.

Cape of Good Hope (Mark Bamford, 2004). Debbie Brown, Farouk Valley-Omar, Parinita Jeaven, Nthati Moshesh, Kamo Masilo.

Disgrace (Steve Jacobs, 2008). John Malkovich, Natalie Becker, Jessica Haines, Eriq Ebouaney.

Jock the Hero Dog (Duncan MacNeillie, 2011). Animated.

8

Things from Another World

• •

Dogs, Aliens, and
Antarctic Cinema

ELIZABETH LEANE AND

GUINEVERE NARRAWAY

All narrative cinema set in Antarctica—the world's only continent with no permanent human population—will to some degree reflect humanity's troubled relationship with nature, understood as both nonhuman animals and the environment. The dog is a key figure through which to explore this relationship. While clearly on the nature side of the traditionally conceived culture/nature binary, the sledge (sled) dog is that (imported) part of nature to which humans have historically most closely related in this environment. With native Antarctic animals scarce during winter, and absent in the continent's interior, personal and working relationships between sledge dogs and humans in Antarctica have (until the very late twentieth century) formed a bridge—if an unstable one—between the human and the natural world. This chapter examines the culture/nature binary through three prominent—and very different—Antarctic films in which dogs are central protagonists: John Carpenter's *The Thing* (1982), Kureyoshi Kurahara's *Nankyoku Monogatari* [*Antarctica*] (1983), and Frank Marshall's *Eight Below* (2006).

Troubling Boundaries in *The Thing*

The eponymous alien of *The Thing* enters the action in the seemingly innocuous form of a dog. Most of the film's long opening sequence focuses on what appears to be a husky, chased across the frozen wastes of Antarctica by a helicopter, a gunman firing at it whenever possible. Arriving at a U.S. base, the dog jumps up and licks the American personnel, while the helicopter lands. The pilot shouts in Norwegian and shoots wildly at the dog, while his passenger, attempting to launch an explosive charge at the animal, accidentally destroys himself and the helicopter. Choosing to side with the dog—a fluffy, seemingly friendly victim of the apparently deranged Norwegians—the U.S. station leader shoots the gunman.

While the Americans deal with the wreckage and organize an expedition to the Norwegian base, the dog is given the run of their station. The animal pads around silently, hiding under the Ping-Pong and card tables, peering at the comings and goings of the men. Ennio Morricone's minimalist heartbeat score, which accompanied the opening helicopter chase, returns with a shot focused on the dog, whose ordinary behavior is rendered strangely sinister by the music and the enigmatic opening sequence. Only when one of the men tells the dog-handler to "put that mutt where it belongs," with other dogs on the station, does the Norwegians' motivation become clear: after partially transforming into a horrific tentacled creature, the dog-Thing attacks and half-absorbs one of the station dogs. Unbeknownst to the expeditioners, it has (the viewer realizes retrospectively) already done the same to at least one of the men. If left to complete the process, it impersonates the man attacked so effectively that his companions do not know whether he is human or alien. With the alien picking off one man after another, eventually only the human protagonist, R. J. MacReady (Kurt Russell) and one of his companions—possibly human, possibly the Thing—are left alone, pictured against the background of the burning station.

Discussing the short story on which *The Thing* was based, John W. Campbell's "Who Goes There?" (1938),[1] Sherryl Vint (2005) argues that "the anxiety about the alien" in the narrative "is largely anxiety about the deconstruction of the species boundary. . . . The thing challenges our idea of the human as something defined through its differences from animals, as the thing becomes either with equal ease" (422–423). As Campbell's tale, like Carpenter's film, is set in the Antarctic interior, there are few specific species via which this deconstruction could take place: no native animals are evident until very late in the tale, and the station (modeled on Richard Byrd's actual Little America) keeps only cows and dogs in addition to its human personnel. A rampaging alien cow might create a sense of bathos—or even comedy,[2] but a dog is a different story. Aaron Skabelund (2011) observes that "canines are boundary crossers and boundary blurrers. Perhaps more than any other animal, dogs pass between domestication and wildness, and within and beyond the control of people. This physical mobility creates symbolic ambiguity, positioning canines between culture and nature. This condition underscores how domesticity/wildness as well as culture/nature are overlapping rather than exclusive categories" (6). As a mediator between culture and nature, a creature that shares intimate physical and emotional spaces with humans, the dog gone bad—turned boundary destroyer rather than boundary crosser—is a convincingly horrific figure. Carpenter allots a larger part to the dog than did Campbell: where the Thing of "Who Goes There?" arrives in obvious alien (frozen) form, and later attacks the dogs, Carpenter's Thing enters as a dog, and this half-innocent, half-ominous figure is pivotal to the first part of the narrative.

The Antarctic sledge dog, because of the unusual character of its environment, brings a series of tensions to the figure of the canine-as-boundary-crosser. Antarctica is a continent where the juxtaposition of culture and nature is especially stark. In his discussion of the aesthetics of deserts and icy places, cultural geographer Yi-Fu Tuan (1993) proposes a theory of home as "a succession of concentric circles": the innermost is "home narrowly defined, or homeplace"— a protected, (semi-)enclosed space; beyond are the rings of "home space," providing decreasing shelter but increasing aesthetic appeal; and at the far edge is "alien space, which is normally perceived as threatening" (139–140). In polar regions these zones "may be compressed to sharply defined and juxtaposed opposites— homeplace is the hut [or station] and immediately beyond is alien space, an expanse of whiteness reaching out in all directions to seemingly nowhere" (154). It is therefore significant that the dog-Thing in Carpenter's film emerges out of the "alien space" and steps directly, and disturbingly without question, into the "homeplace."

This sharp divide between cultural and natural spaces in Antarctica is reinforced by the absence of organic life in much of the continent. Antarctica is mostly bereft of flora,[3] and its animal life is confined to marine mammals and birds inhabiting coastal regions. The interior of the continent is largely empty of nonhuman life, and with the arrival of winter (when Carpenter's film is set), most coastal animals also move north as sea ice surrounds the continent (only Emperor penguins breed there at this time). For people inhabiting Antarctica, or who are at an inland station there, in winter, the only nonhuman sentient life present would consist of animals brought with them for companionship, work, and food.[4] In the early years of Antarctic inhabitation, sledge dogs performed all of these roles. Explorers not only relied on them to complete sledging journeys but, with other companion animals largely unavailable, they formed close emotional bonds with their dogs. Yet on a number of occasions, whether by accident or design, explorers also ate their dogs or, moreover, fed them to each other. Such quasi cannibalism forced onto "man's best friend" sat uncomfortably against a history of polar exploration in which human cannibalism was a recurring theme (Leane and Tiffin 2011).[5]

The sledge dog also signifies a culture/nature hybrid in a more obvious way than most dogs. In relation to Alaskan "sled dogs," Rebecca Onion (2009) notes the power of the "popular myth of the wolf-dog," which emphasizes "the domesticated/wild opposition" (144).[6] Sledge dogs used in the Antarctic—which include Siberian huskies, Greenland dogs, and Alaskan malamutes—are frequently considered to be wolfish, with an associated hardiness and viciousness: Douglas Mawson's meteorologist and sometime dog-handler Cecil Madigan (1913) considered his charges "semi-wolves" that regularly required "a beating which would almost kill the ordinary domestic dog" (146); Richard Byrd (1931) described his teams as "primitive dogs . . . individualists to the last," and referred to their howling as "the wolf in them" (216).

These associations of sledge dogs inform both Campbell's "Who Goes There?" and Carpenter's *The Thing*. The names of two of the Alaskan huskies in Campbell's story—Chinook and Charnauk—allude to a real Antarctic sledge dog, Chinook. The historical Chinook achieved fame in Byrd's first expedition by leaving his devoted owner in favor of the Antarctic wilderness—an action that could be read, as Onion notes, as an indication of "the wild freedom of pure animal instinct" remaining in the domesticated canine (Byrd 1931, 108–109; Onion 2009, 154). Campbell's Charnauk—whose name suggests a mutated version of Chinook—also returns to nature but in a much more disturbing and literal way. Carpenter dispenses with this allusion but creates another association between the dog and the wild. The Norwegians' dog in *The Thing* was played by Jed, a wolf-malamute hybrid who went on to star in *White Fang* (1991).[7] The wolfishness of the intruder to the U.S. camp is a sign that the culture/nature divide has been blurred by a more troubling creature than the ordinary dog. Certainly the cast of the film found Jed unsettling: Richard Masur, who played the dog-handler, recalls in a DVD bonus documentary (*John Carpenter's "The Thing": The Terror Takes Shape*) that he "was a very spooky dog when we started, because he was half-wolf and half-dog, and the wolf half was real dominant in him. He did everything like a wolf. He would never bark. He never growled." Jed was, however, also a "tremendous acting dog," according to Carpenter in his DVD commentary, who notes in particular Jed's ability to look away from rather than toward camera and crew during a shot. This produces an uncanny effect in a key scene: the dog peers into a doorway in what seems a very calculating manner, before choosing to enter another room occupied by a lone man, seen only as a shadow. This animal is both more and less than a dog—more knowing, arguably more "human," than one would expect, yet also more wolf-like, and therefore more wild, than a dog.

The presence of the wolf-dog, then, troubles the culture/nature, domestic/wild binaries of the American camp, where the only other living inhabitants are men and dogs. When the dog/wolf/Thing literally *incorporates* first the dogs and then the human members of the camp, the hierarchy of who-eats-whom and the binaries that sustain it are inverted. The uneasy connection with the eating practices of human explorers has not been lost on critics: Peter Krapp (2008) notes the film's "twist on the companion animal and emergency protein source

Both more and less than a dog; Jed the wolf/malamute hybrid playing the Thing in *The Thing* (John Carpenter, Universal Pictures, 1982). Digital frame enlargement.

for polar explorers" (840).[8] In *The Thing* Carpenter takes the figure of the sledge dog—not simply a boundary crosser, like the domestic canine, but a more disturbing symbol of humanity's contradictory relationship with animals—and makes it the means by which all boundaries between self and other are dissolved.

The film's ambiguous ending suggests a definite defeat for humanity, if not an obvious victory for the alien. If MacReady and his companion are both human, they will inevitably die in a lifeless continent without a "homeplace" to provide shelter. If his companion is the Thing,[9] the alien alone will survive, its next step presumably to colonize whatever native Antarctic animals it reaches (a fear made explicit in Campbell's story). In the end, then, only the truly alien can survive in the Antarctic interior.

Going Wild in *Antarctica*

Only a year after the release of *The Thing*, another film appeared in which dogs in Antarctica form a key part of the narrative: the Japanese production *Nankyoku Monogatari* [*Antarctica*]. Aside from its far-southern setting and canine focus, this film seems to have little in common with Carpenter's. Through the figure of the dog, Carpenter's film evokes Antarctica very specifically as "alien space": inhabitation at this location is tenuous; wilderness here can all too easily overrun and destroy humanity. In the Antarctica of *The Thing* the (un)natural threatens to penetrate the small, discrete, survivable environments that humanity has to fabricate in order even to have a presence on the continent. In contrast, Antarctica's literal threat to humanity is dispelled in the opening sections of *Nankyoku Monogatari*. Symbolically, however, the tenuousness of humanity's control over nature is questioned through the possibility of the domesticated dog going wild.

Nankyoku Monogatari is based on an event that took place in 1958, during the International Geophysical Year.[10] When bad weather and extensive sea ice prevented a replacement wintering team from being airlifted to the Japanese Base Syowa, fifteen Karafuto dogs chained up by the departing team were left to their own devices.[11] This was a time when dogs were increasingly popular as companion animals in Japan. The influence of American culture, produced by the U.S. military presence in Japan along with media texts such as the television series *Lassie* (1954–1974) and the Disney film *Lady and the Tramp* (1955), had "created a vision of middle-class, family-centred consumerism in which the dog was a desirable member" (Skabelund 2011, 178, 182). The abandonment of the dogs in Antarctica caused considerable anger in Japan, with the expedition director receiving a "pile" of mail accusing him of being a "dog killer."[12] It did not help matters that a number of the dogs had been family pets donated to the expedition (Toohill 1985, 5). In a report written shortly after their departure, the expeditioners Toru Kikuchi and Taiichi Kitamura (1960) were at pains to justify the "heart-rending" abandonment of their "canine friends" to the "perturbed" Japanese nation, claiming that "we gave every last ounce of our effort in trying to send off the next wintering party," and praying for "the repose of the souls" of the dogs (89).

Kikuchi and Kitamura's protestations and supplications were to some degree premature, however, as the next expedition, arriving nearly a year later, discovered two dogs, Taro and Jiro, still alive. Their survival made front-page news in Japan and was reported internationally: the front page of the *Milwaukee Journal* (January 15, 1959), for example, featured the story "Japan Going Wild at News of Antarctic Dogs' Survival," while the *Sydney Morning Herald* (February 25, 1959, 3) ran the headline "Dogs Survive Year Alone in Antarctic." The dogs were hailed as "national heroes," monuments were erected to them, and an annual festival was established in their honor (Toohill 1985, 5). They remain two of the three "most famous dogs in Japan today" (Skabelund 2011, 180).[13]

Nankyoku Monogatari, which dramatized the fate of these national heroes, was an appropriately significant production. The film features two of Japan's big-name stars of the time, Ken Takakura and Eiji Okada,[14] and the score was provided by Vangelis, who was much sought-after in the wake of *Chariots of Fire* (1981). The efforts put into location shooting also reflect the quality of the production. While most of the filming took place in northern Canada, the film's budget of 1.1 billion yen (equivalent to approximately US$4.6 million in 1983) included trips to Antarctica by director Koreyoshi Kurahara, lead actor Takakura, and the camera and sound operators, with one voyage undertaken largely to capture penguin footage (Toohill 1985, 10–11).[15] *Nankyoku Monogatari* was a financial and critical success. It grossed 9 billion yen (US$38 million) in theatrical release, and two different English-language versions—one subtitled, one dubbed, and both entitled *Antarctica*—were created by Twentieth Century–Fox for release in the United States and elsewhere (Toohill 1985, 11, 19). The film won a number of Japanese film awards and was nominated for the Golden Bear at the 1984 Berlin Film Festival.

Displacing the Nonhuman Native in *Eight Below*

Over two decades after *Nankyoku Monogatari* appeared, the 2006 Disney remake *Eight Below* imagined dogs, and coextensively humanity, becoming "at home" in a continent that is effectively emptied of its original nonhuman inhabitants.[16] Sandwiched between *March of the Penguins* (2005) and *Happy Feet* (2006), *Eight Below* offered an Antarctic animal adventure in which dogs, rather than penguins, took center stage.

The film tells the story of a group of dogs abandoned over winter at a U.S. Antarctic field base. Although a reasonable box-office success, earning around $120 million worldwide during its cinematic release—almost as much as *March of the Penguins*—*Eight Below* never achieved the high profile of the two penguin films. Among other things, it lacked their claims to Antarctic authenticity. The creators of both *March of the Penguins* and *Happy Feet* went to extreme lengths to achieve their respective forms of accuracy: the documentary-makers endured the hostile conditions of the polar winter to capture the Emperor penguin's breeding cycle for the first time on film, while *Happy Feet*'s animators conducted extensive research in the Antarctic and used sophisticated CGI techniques to create cartoon penguins that look and move like the real thing. *Eight Below* is by contrast marked by a happy obliviousness to the constraints of realism: the dogs frolic in midwinter sunshine at a high latitude and munch on seagulls. The film was shot entirely in the Northern Hemisphere, with establishing Antarctic footage from an earlier documentary spliced in.

There is, however, a brief but telling moment in the Disney film in which the filmmakers acknowledge actual Antarctic history and politics. A close-up of a calendar early in the film establishes the action as taking place in 1993. This decision to set the film back a decade has no explicit diegetic motivation, and few if any concessions are made in terms of set design (apart from the calendar page itself), props, costume, makeup, and hair. The obvious reason behind the early 1990s' setting is the 1991 Protocol on Environmental Protection to the Antarctic Treaty—the "Madrid Protocol"—that precludes the presence of any nonnative species in the continent except humans.[17] The last time dogs overwintered in Antarctica was 1993, the final group being removed from a British station in early 1994. For those who understand the reference, the significance of the date in the film is underscored by one continuous camera movement from the calendar to the dogs sitting below it. Although there is no mention of or other allusion to the Protocol in *Eight Below*, the filmmakers were evidently keen that their narrative stay within its historical and political confines. The result is that, for any viewer aware of the significance of 1993 in the history of canine presence in Antarctica, this drama of the abandonment of a specific group of dogs inevitably evokes a melancholy about the historical removal of the entire species.

At the same time, the setting of *Eight Below* at a point when human concern about the welfare of native Antarctic species became enshrined in international law ironically serves to highlight the film's own displacement of these species in favor of "man's best friend." Antarctic animals are strikingly absent in the film. Admittedly, it would not have been judicious for the canine protagonists to feast on the other hit animal of the season, given that the film was directed at the same "family" market that had so embraced *March of the Penguins*. But no other Antarctic bird—computer-generated or otherwise—makes an appearance. And the other obvious food source, seals, is also absent, except for leopard seals, which the central human protagonist evokes solely as predators. In contrast to the Japanese film version of the same events, *Eight Below* thus presents us with an emptied-out Antarctic landscape: one in which the abandoned dogs can enact an innocent and anthropomorphized inhabitation of the continent.

Two Films, Two Natures

The particular construction of the abandoned dogs' narrative that Disney offers in *Eight Below* is thrown into relief by contrast with the film that it remakes, *Nankyoku Monogatari*. With the original incident still in the living memory of many viewers, the Japanese feature stayed fairly close to the known events: thirteen dogs die, corresponding with the original headcount. In direct contrast, in *Eight Below*, there are fewer dogs overall and the attrition rate is much lower, with six of the eight dogs surviving. Despite the decreased number of canine roles, the Disney film used more dog actors, and they were much more intensively managed. There were multiple canine actors for every dog role—some for close-ups, some for long shots, some dedicated to sledging—and there were two trainers per dog on set, instructing the dogs throughout shooting. Furthermore, the dogs were trained for almost five months before filming started.[18] Kurahara, in contrast, aimed for a more naturalistic effect. The dogs were initially taught "only two basic skills—to pull a sledge and to come when called." They were filmed running free in a fenced-off area to give a sense of their behavior while alone in Antarctica. Kurahara was, he stated presciently, "against the Disney approach of training the animals completely before filming" (quoted in Toohill 1985, 12–13).

While the dogs in the Japanese film were permitted to behave as dogs, Frank Marshall, director of *Eight Below*, highlighted the artifice of his work and the construction of canine behavior. As he notes on a "bonus feature"—"Running with the Dogs: The Making of *Eight Below*"—on the DVD of the film, "it's all about these dogs being incredibly trained to do specific actions to tell the story, and it was our job to capture it on film and make it look very natural." This production of "dogness" is ironically precisely that which comes to transform the dogs into human stand-ins in the course of *Eight Below*. Early on in the film, the dogs are evoked largely as "man's best friend," fulfilling their assigned role as working animals.[19] But there are also in these early stages suggestions of an affinity to humans beyond this role. In the calendar scene, for example, we are shown

An affinity between dogs and humans (and dogs *as* humans) in *Eight Below* (Frank Marshall, Walt Disney Pictures, 2006). Note, at the far right of the frame, the dog that seems to be looking directly at the camera or, more likely, at a trainer adjacent to it. Digital frame enlargement.

the dogs sitting on couches and armchairs much as their human counterparts would do.[20] When the central human protagonists—guide Jerry (Paul Walker), cartographer Charlie (Jason Biggs), and pilot Katie (Moon Bloodgood)—play cards, one of the dogs joins them, as if part of the game. When visiting scientist Davis McLaren (Bruce Greenwood) discusses with Jerry his ill-considered plan to search for a meteorite at a mountain some distance away, Jerry and one of the dogs are always placed in frame together, suggesting that the dog is coextensively an interlocutor in this conversation. If anyone is a breed apart in this scene it is the scientists—McLaren and two others at the base—who are placed on a separate plane of action from the technical staff and dogs.

It is when the humans evacuate during a severe storm, however, that Marshall's making the unnatural natural really comes to the fore. In an ironic role reversal of the Madrid Protocol requirements, dogs are left as the only nonnative species in Antarctica. From this point on they routinely manifest behaviors that are clearly human: "undogly" bodily hexes that are revealed in staging, editing, and cinematography. In one scene for example, Maya, the leader of the group, assumes a position in front of the other dogs as if to address them. She then literally barks orders that her "team" obeys. A conversation ensues between Max and Maya. In this sequence the shot structure conforms to conventions used to demarcate human conversation in cinema. In contrast, in *Nankyoku Monogatari*, the use of a voice-over narration clarifying the dogs' actions in the absence of humans maintains the distance between the two species. Rather than being constructed through cinematic technique as human stand-ins—as in *Eight Below*—the dogs, in being spoken for, are positioned as distinctly not human.

The anthropomorphization of dogs in *Eight Below* takes on a new dimension if it is brought up against the hard reality of survival during a winter in Antarctica. All three "versions" of the story of Taro and Jiro—the original incident (itself reconstructable only through a series of reports and accounts), the

Japanese film, and the Disney remake—provoke the same question: what did they eat? And the same answer offers itself: while the abandoned dogs may have been able to catch Adélie penguins in the warmer months, and Weddell seals and possibly the occasional Emperor penguin in the winter, one obvious food source would have been the dogs who died. In taking advantage of their companions' ill fortune, the surviving dogs would merely have been honoring an Antarctic tradition: explorers Douglas Mawson and Roald Amundsen, among others, had no issue with feeding dog to dog. These dogs had little choice in the matter, but those that Amundsen's Norwegian Antarctic Expedition abandoned in 1912 also "resorted to cannibalism" (Headland 2012, 17). An attempt by the 1961 Japanese wintering party to determine what Taro and Jiro survived on concluded the most likely scenario to be not cannibalism but the only slightly more palatable option of coprophagy—the consumption of excrement, in this case the dung of startled seals (Matsuda 1980). Nonetheless, the question of cannibalism lingers—and the greater the degree of anthropomorphization of the dogs, the more troubling it becomes, recalling early polar exploration narratives that raised the same question.

Needless to say, neither *Nankyoku Monogatari* nor *Eight Below* canvasses this possibility.[21] The Disney film circulates around the dogs' search for food but, although it is implied that food sources are scarce, the dogs nonetheless always seem to be able to find something to eat: on two occasions they consume the aforementioned seagulls, on another they get into supplies at an abandoned hut, and toward the end of their ordeal they feast on a frozen killer whale. *Nankyoku Monogatari* is also explicit about their need for food but is more concerned about ecological authenticity. The seabirds consumed are skuas, not seagulls, and there is also footage of the dog pack savaging a seal on a couple of occasions (scenes that worried the American Humane Association, which classified the film's use of animals as "unacceptable").[22] Penguins, it seems, were off-limits even before their twenty-first-century rise to screen fame: the Japanese film has the dogs lying next to a colony without taking advantage of it. Skuas, shown in *Nankyoku Monogatari* as opportunistic hunters of penguin chicks, are more appropriate fodder for the canine protagonists if the latter are to retain any viewer sympathy.

While both films may have been strategically selective in their representation of the Siberian huskies' consumption of Antarctic species, the earlier film nonetheless embeds the dogs far more firmly into the Antarctic ecosystem than the Disney production. *Nankyoku Monogatari* frames the dogs' story with footage of a variety of different Antarctic animals in the opening and closing credits, and contextualizes the dogs' activities, both before and after their abandonment, with shots of penguin colonies.[23] The film is also at pains to remind viewers that the two survivors, Taro and Jiro, were raised from puppies in Antarctica, which was therefore their only "home." And, when these two dogs encounter humans after their year in the Antarctic, they are initially resistant (as were their

Taro and Jiro react suspiciously to the return of humans in *Nankyoku Monogatari* [*Antarctica*] (Koreyoshi Kurahara, Fuji Television Network/Gakken Co. Ltd./Kurahawa Productions, 1983). Digital frame enlargement.

historical counterparts). The effect is to incorporate the dogs into the Antarctic environment: they are gradually naturalized, depicted as animals who "belong," who have successfully integrated with the continent's native inhabitants, temporarily at least.

Eight Below does feature penguins in long shot early on in the film, and three animatronic or CGI leopard seals appear in the course of the narrative. When the Disney film is viewed against *Nankyoku Monogatari*, however, the emptied-out nature of Antarctica in the later production is starkly apparent. Clearly the producers' decision to do no filming in the Antarctic limited their options, but with animatronics, CGI, and other techniques available, this does not wholly explain the marginalization of Antarctic animals. This marginalization goes beyond near absence: native species are displaced by nonnative ones, as in the seagulls that stand in for skuas, or they are deliberately villainized, as in the leopard seal that attacks Max and savages Maya. After their early appearance in the film, penguins disappear as a life form and function largely as a parodic theme: the film opens with an extreme close-up of a penguin thermometer; McMurdo General Hospital is adorned with a cartoon penguin mural; and inside, on a corridor wall, a poster featuring a penguin warns against frostbite. It is at a bar full of penguin paraphernalia in Christchurch that the lead human protagonists reunite to head south and save the dogs, and a supposedly amusing story about tracking penguins told by Charlie finally enables the team to return to the abandoned base.

Thus, where the dogs of *Nankyoku Monogatari* are never initially humanized and, in the course of the film, are gradually incorporated into the Antarctic ecosystem, those of *Eight Below* are always held apart from this ecosystem. They are constructed both as alien to the continent, and, in their ability to survive a little over 175 days in the ice, as masters over it. Their experience becomes, in this regard, a metaphor for human encounter with the far south: *Eight Below* is the "Heroic Era" of Antarctic exploration done with dogs in the lead, rather than supporting, roles. The film's close reinforces this by declaring that *Eight Below* is "dedicated to the Antarctic explorers and their dogs whose courage and spirit inspired this film." As with the representation of the continent—a representation shot elsewhere and practically emptied of indigenous life—this statement expresses an interest in the conquerors of place rather than the place itself. The dogs' domination of their environment is further underscored by the fact that none of them die directly as a result of the difficulties of their circumstances. While in *Nankyoku Monogatari* dogs fall afoul of ice floes and killer whales, the two who succumb in *Eight Below* do so by virtue of their own natures, not Antarctica's: "Old Jack" cannot summon the energy to escape his collar, and an overly impetuous younger dog accidentally falls over a cliff while "chasing" the aurora australis. The Antarctic winter ultimately has no impact on the dogs' lives, and the lethal potential of their environment is only alluded to in the form of a hostile leopard seal—whom the dogs rout—and the deadly beauty of the southern lights. Moreover, the surviving dogs never become one with their environment. They never "return to nature" as did their real-life counterparts and the heroes of *Nankyoku Monogatari*. Quite the contrary: they are clearly overjoyed at the return of the humans at the end of the film and run into the arms of their "saviors." Implicitly, it is not possible for the dogs to "go native" given that there are so few native species in the film toward whose state the dogs might go. More than this, however, the dogs are simply too human to answer "the call of the wild."

A Disney drama of anthropomorphized dogs is nothing remarkable. The studio is, after all, responsible for dozens of doggy tales, among them classics such as *Old Yeller* (1957) and *The Incredible Journey* (1963). What makes *Eight Below* worthy of comment is the irony introduced by that single calendar shot: the fact that this story of an essentially animal-free Antarctica takes place at the exact moment when the Madrid Protocol was championing the rights of native species. But perhaps, in the end, *Eight Below* is no more ironic than the Protocol itself, which rids Antarctica of all alien species except the one likely to cause it maximum damage.

Despite their generic and stylistic disparities, *The Thing*, *Eight Below*, and *Nankyoku Monogatari* are all part of the same conversation. These films circulate around the culture/nature, civilized/wild binaries, expressing anxieties about the fragility of these binaries in one of earth's wildest environments. In Carpenter's film the tensions that already surround the figure of the sledge dog—companion, working partner and sometime meal, "friend" to humanity in a largely empty continent, and also wolfish, "savage" symbol of the wild—is literalized by the animal's transformation into the alien Thing. The invasion of the base camp by the natural/animal environment becomes an invasion and colonization of the sacrosanct interiority of the human body. *Eight Below* presents the opposite of *The Thing*'s apocalyptic vision. In this family film dogs come to take the place of humans when the latter are temporarily forced out of Antarctica's inhospitable landscape. The film imagines the dogs—and by extension humanity—as impervious to this environment and as masters over it, surviving an Antarctic winter against the odds. Kurahara's film lies somewhere between *The Thing* and *Eight Below*, permitting its canine protagonists to "go wild" but only for a time. Taro and Jiro, raised in Antarctica, are clearly located in the diegesis on the "nature" side of the culture/nature divide. Despite their foray into wilderness, however, they inevitably return to civilization and assume their subordinate place in relation to their human masters—as "man's best friend," the dog cannot be permitted to go too wild. Where *The Thing* is a warning of what might occur if all culture is absorbed into nature, and *Eight Below* is a comforting tale in which nature can be permanently encultured, *Nankyoku Monogatari* attempts to strike something of a balance, accepting the dog's symbolic ability to straddle the culture/nature divide, without locating it permanently on either side.

Notes

1. Carpenter's film pays homage to *The Thing from Another World* (1951), an earlier adaptation of "Who Goes There?" but is closer to Campbell's story than the earlier film, which was set in the Arctic. The 2011 remake of *The Thing*, which keeps Carpenter's title, features a dog—a pet of a minor character—who is destroyed by the alien (offscreen). The alien no longer arrives disguised as a dog, but the 2011 film—hyperaware of its status as remake—ends with a close reproduction of the opening scenes of Carpenter's film in which a "husky"—now identified as the attacked pet dog—is seen bounding across the ice, pursued by a helicopter.
2. In "Who Goes There?" an expeditioner reports the eventual attack on the cows, observing, ironically, "They look funny . . . when they start melting" (Campbell 1938, 86).
3. There are some plants, such as lichens and mosses, in the coastal regions, and grasses grow in the Antarctic Peninsula. We are not referring here to the sub-Antarctic islands, which have their own ecosystems.
4. There has been a surprising range of these over the years. Robert Headland's survey of exotic terrestrial mammals in the Antarctic regions provides the following list introduced to the continent itself since 1821: humans, black rats, mice, cats, dogs, horses, donkeys, swine, cattle, sheep, goats, rabbits, hamsters, hedgehogs, and bats (2012, 3). Many of these, however, are one-off occurrences; dogs have been consistently dominant as companion and working animals at Antarctic bases.
5. Rumors of cannibalism famously surrounded the lost Franklin expedition in the mid-nineteenth century, and they also beset the survivors of the Greely expedition later in the same century. In the Antarctic, Douglas Mawson came under suspicion—probably, in this case, unwarranted—after his surprising feat of survival on the Australasian Antarctic Expedition. During a sledging expedition, Mawson and his companion Xavier Mertz were forced to eat their dogs when the third team member and most of the supplies went down a crevasse. Mertz died on the journey

back to base, and Mawson, who survived the trip on remarkably little food, was later portrayed in the yellow press as a potential cannibal who considered eating his fellow expeditioner. These rumors of cannibalism have persisted to the present day. This incident, and more generally the "contradictory relationships" into which men and dogs were thrown during early Antarctic expeditions, are discussed in "Dogs, Meat, and Douglas Mawson" (Leane and Tiffin 2011).

6. Onion (2009) questions the scientific validity of the myth, noting that analysis "has shown that cross-breeding between husky dogs and wolves was unlikely for a number of biological reasons" (148).

7. A brief biography of Jed is available on the Internet Movie Database at imdb.com/name/nm1058600/. A stand-in dog, colored to resemble Jed, was used for the opening helicopter chase, which was filmed by a second unit in Alaska (Carpenter, feature commentary on DVD release of *The Thing* [2003]).

8. Vint (2005) also notes the threat to identity posed by consumption in Campbell's narrative: to achieve "full humanity . . . one must be the eater and never the eaten: not an animal" (428–429).

9. MacReady's sole remaining companion, the mechanic Childs, is already marked as Other in the context of the narrative by the fact that he is black. Viewers familiar with Carpenter's work, however, would recognize this as a highly self-conscious move on the director's part, signaling the danger of simplistically reading the racial Other as alien. Carpenter has a track record of explicitly engaging with and critiquing ideas of Otherness—*Big Trouble in Little China* (1986) is a hyperbolic case in point.

10. The International Geophysical Year, which ran from 1957 to 1958, was a coordinated international scientific effort, global in scope, with a particular focus on the Antarctic.

11. This was not the first time that a Japanese Antarctic expedition had abandoned a group of Karafuto dogs. The Japanese Antarctic Expedition of 1910–1912, led by Nobu Shirase, left behind twenty dogs when they hurriedly departed from the Bay of Whales in bad weather. In the notes to the English translation of the expedition narrative, the distress this caused the expeditioners is recorded. The two dog-drivers were "subjected to an Ainu investigation on their return to Karafuto/Sakhalin for having abandoned the animals," and Shirase himself "remembered the dogs in his morning and evening prayers" for the rest of his life (Shirase Antarctic Expedition Supporters' Association 2011, 405).

12. Masayoshi Murayama (quoted in Toohill 1985, 2).

13. The third dog, Hachiko, became famous in the 1930s for his loyalty: accustomed to walking his master to the railway station every morning, he continued to visit the station environs for a decade after his master's death (Skabelund 2011, 1).

14. Takakura and Okada also made appearances in Western cinema. Takakura is most notably known for his roles in Sydney Pollack's *The Yakuza* (1975), with Robert Mitchum, and Ridley Scott's *Black Rain* (1989). Okada is best known in the West as the male lead in Alain Resnais's *Hiroshima mon amour* (1959).

15. Natural history documentaries aside, it is unusual for films set in Antarctica to send a crew to the continent. Mainstream films that include action set in the far south, such as *Whiteout* (2009) and *The X-Files* (1998), are most often filmed in Canada, with Norway and Greenland being occasional alternatives.

16. The incident on which *Nankyoku Monogatari* and *Eight Below* are based has also recently been dramatized for television, with the series *Nankyoku Tairiku* premiering in December 2011 on TBS (Tokyo Broadcasting Service).

17. Article IV of Annex II of the Protocol on Environmental Protection to the Antarctic Treaty, which opened for signature in 1991, states, "Dogs shall not be introduced onto land or ice shelves and dogs currently in those areas shall be removed by April 1, 1994."

18. "Running with the Dogs: The Making of *Eight Below*," bonus feature on the DVD release. The list of dog roles and their multiple canine performers can also be found on IMDb.com.

19. In an interview with the *Washington Post*, Sally Jo Sousa, an animal trainer who worked on *Eight Below*, notes that the lead dogs were played by six Siberian huskies and two Alaskan malamutes. See "A True 'Survivor' Story, Dog Version," *Washington Post*, February 16, 2006.

20. There is an interesting contrast here with the dog in *The Thing*, whose periodic positioning under tables or framing by the legs of tables has the effect of characterizing it as sinister and calculating, listening surreptitiously to the men's conversations.

21. For Frank Marshall, who had previously directed *Alive* (1993), survival cannibalism was a familiar topic. *Alive* is based on the true story of a Uruguayan rugby team whose plane crashes in the Andes. The players are consequently forced by circumstance to eat their dead colleagues in order to survive.

22. World News, available at wn.com/nankyoku_monogatari?orderby=relevance& upload_time=this_week.

23. This was facilitated, of course, by the film's production at a time when dog teams remained in the Antarctic and could be filmed there. At the time *Nankyoku Monogatari* was released in 1983, four Antarctic stations—one British, one Australian, one New Zealand, and one Argentinian—maintained working dogs, with their total reaching about one hundred (Toohill 3). The U.S. Antarctic program did not use dogs at this time and had not for many years.

Chronological Filmography

The Thing (John Carpenter, 1982). Kurt Russell, Wilford Brimley, T. K. Carter, David Clennon, Keith David, Richard Dysart, Richard Masur, Jed [dog, uncredited].

Nankyoku Monogatari [*Antarctica*] (Koreyoshi Kurahara, 1983). Ken Takakura, Eiji Okada, Tsunehiko Watase.

Eight Below (Frank Marshall, 2006). Paul Walker, Jason Biggs, Bruce Greenwood, Moon Bloodgood, Wendy Crewson, D. J. [dog], Timba [dog], Koda [dog], Jasmin [dog], Apache [dog], Buck [dog], Noble [dog], Troika [dog], Flapjack [dog], Dino [dog], Sitka [dog], Chase [dog], Floyd [dog], Ryan [dog], Jasper [dog], Lightning [dog].

The Thing (Matthijs van Heijningen Jr., 2011). Mary Elizabeth Winstead, Joel Edgerton, Ulrich Thomsen.

Part Three

Stock, Bits, and Extras

• •

9

Hitchcock's Canine Uncanny

• •

MURRAY POMERANCE

Alfred Hitchcock's mise-en-scène depends intensively on meticulously researched and carefully arrayed social, cultural, and technical details of character, action, and scene. Considerable scholarly attention has been given to Hitchcockian stars as embodiments or exemplifiers of relevant dramaturgical and social detail, but only the scantest attention has been paid to his settings, his use of color and props, what can be read from his costumes, and the work of secondary players who fill in the scenes (see Pomerance 2000–2001). As any afficionado already knows, Hitchcock's films, whether the ones he made at the beginning of his career in England or his later American studio productions, contain a number of secondary players who happen to be dogs, and they are also character players very often signally relevant to the working of a scene. We find, if we look at the considerable and changing presence and action of dogs in Hitchcock's work, an unheralded group of "performances" that lend depth and intrinsic meaning to the Hitchcockian moment. Reviewing Hitchcock's English films, Charles Barr (1999) announces, in fact, that "there is an opening for a scholarly paper on the subject of Hitchcock and dogs" and wonders that dogs and the director's cinematic play with them "seems to constitute one of the minor markers of Hitchcock's authorship" (186, 188). He refers to a number of canine appearances that I do not discuss below, but what follows does carry through with Barr's very insightful suggestion that the Hitchcockian dog is a "kind of moral touchstone" (189), if not, indeed, an outright collaborator.

Hitchcock giving directions to his pup Sarah. Note the Westie's sensitivity to her director's gesture. Margaret Herrick Library, Academy of Motion Picture Arts and Sciences.

As early as Hitchcock's second feature, *The Farmer's Wife* (1928), which takes place in a bucolic English shire (most likely in Sussex), we have a scene that establishes a potent connection with two of our canine friends. They are a pair of Springer spaniels, spotted and frisky, devoted to moving everywhere together. Inhabitants of the shade-dappled Applegarth Farm, and lingering just outside the thatched main house, they share a yard with pigs and cattle but soon leap up and lope inside. We see the intelligence and familiarity with this territory that characterizes their intent, as one by one they move across the stone porch and across the front hallway, then up the wooden stairs. Near the top step they halt, dropping their heads down onto the floor of the landing. But Hitchcock has placed his camera at their level, resting directly on the floor. The two span-iel heads fill the frame, in a portrait entirely obliging to the work of Sir Edwin

Two heads filling the frame, in a portrait reminiscent of Landseer, in *The Farmer's Wife* (Alfred Hitchcock, British International Pictures, 1928). Digital frame enlargement.

Landseer and his colleagues. But more: the widely opened eyes (highlighting this film that is larded with gazes of appreciation and evaluation), the focus just off the lens and in the direction of whatever waits off-camera and yet to come, give a sure indication that these dogs are as interested, as enraptured, by movies as we are. They indicate—they indeed imitate—the viewer swept away, forming a kind of mirror of us as we gaze at them. Hitchcock was always concerned about the sensibilities of his viewer, always interested in addressing his viewer's need of the moment. Here, beginning his long career, we find that he has created a kind of equivalence between the viewer and these dogs—not that Hitchcock meant to demean the viewer but to the contrary: for him, we can surmise, the dog was everything a person ought to be, and these spaniels with their pristine gaze and rapt fascination reflect cinema's promise.

Moreover, prior to the concluding sequence of the film, Hitchcock stages a foxhunt with full regalia. There are some 100 or 120 chipper foxhounds, leaping up to lead the horsemen with cheery bravado, and in a very long shot, as the hunt proceeds across a typical stone bridge that spans a trickling stream all flecked in gay sunshine, we see the wagging elevated tails, like a long parade of tiny waving flags. Only a man who adored dogs, and who was touched by their energy and eagerness to join people in action, could have shot this bridge in such a way as to emphasize that touching line of jiggling tails.

Throughout Hitchcock's career, dogs offered him strategic dramaturgical possibilities for establishing action and relationships that could not be shown otherwise—hence the invocation of the uncanny in my essay's title. Canines and their representations and settings are vital significations of Hitchcock's thought, as well as part of the middle-classness of the public persona that he constructed for himself. Hitchcock, onscreen or off, was never without a dog.

Beneath the Surface Gentility

Hitchcock would have known quite well that a noteworthy and venerable tradition in both English art and English home life was the canine portrait that the shots in *The Farmer's Wife* invoke and was realized with some substantial repetition during the nineteenth and early twentieth centuries by such luminaries as Richard Ansdell (1815–1885), John Emms (1844–1912), Arthur Wardle (1860–1949), Thomas Blinks (1860–1912), Herbert Thomas Dicksee (1862–1942), Maud Alice Earl (1864–1943), Florence Mabel Hollams (1877–1963), and the celebrated (and later insane) Sir Edwin Henry Landseer (1802–1873). Landseer's paintings, in particular, depict not only the grace and beauty of his sitters but their idiosyncratic intelligence and soulful characterization—the tranquility of the snout, the expressiveness of the mouth, the lambent and penetrating openness of the unwavering eyes. With him, as with other painters, but less distinctively so, the image of the dog confronting the artist with its gaze betrays the deep-seated conviction that canines see the human world, understand it, evaluate it, and offer sympathy. It is intriguing that a Hitchcock biographer intuitively saw portraiture, very early in Hitchcock's American career, as a typifier of the filmmaker in his family setting. Describing the Hitchcock suite aboard the *Queen Mary*, Donald Spoto (1984) writes: "Completing [the] almost stereotypical picture of the well-to-do British family were two small dogs—the dark spaniel, Edward IX (so named following the abdication of the previous king), and the white Sealyham, Mr. Jenkins. Indeed, the Hitchcock entourage resembled a Constable grouping, or a curious conglomerate of figures from an early Van Eyck portrait. Yet there was also something faintly fantastic, almost Hogarthian about them, too—something a little raw, untried, and ingenuous beneath the surface gentility" (208–209).

Landseer is himself portrayed in a respectful steel engraving by George Edward Perine (1837–1885), a sketching tablet on his lap, a pen in his hand, a sporty spotted tie loose at his neck. He gazes forward at the viewer with a doggy seriousness, his bewhiskered face lending the appropriate hirsute touch; but behind him a pair of his dogs—a Newfoundland and a mixed breed—peek appreciatively over his shoulders at the picture he is drawing. Often pictures such as the ones Landseer and his contemporaries made would hang in frames in a bourgeois drawing room, but with similar frequency they would be turned into full-colored reproductions, mounted and framed suitably for adorning the walls of middle- and working-class establishments, exactly such spots, perhaps, as the dilapidated London rooming house depicted in a climactic sequence of one of Hitchcock's first American films, *Foreign Correspondent* (1940). Just as the decorative mirror hanging on the wall of the bourgeois *intérieur* could function to draw the outside world in, thus helping to produce for the artful resident an illusion of living in the world (see Gunning 2003), so the dog portrait posed upon the wall could bring the animal world into the human one, even when living dogs were absent. Canine intelligence, canine sensitivity, canine faithfulness, and canine absorption with human goings-on—more generally, the pathetic fallacy of nature attending to and sympathizing with human affairs—could be thus invoked through interior decoration.

The scene in *Foreign Correspondent* is deliciously complex in this regard. During the *Sturm* of the Second World War, an aging diplomat and mentor, Professor Van Meer (Albert Bassermann), has been kidnapped in Holland (through the agency of a fake assassination performed upon an identical double) and hidden away by agents loyal to the Nazi cause. The American hero, Huntley Haverstock (Joel McCrea), has crossed the ocean as a reporter but is now involved emotionally in the international intrigue, because he has fallen for a girl (Laraine Day) who is the daughter of a senior British diplomat (Herbert Marshall) ostensibly connected with the peace movement but in truth secretly allied to the Germans. This man, Fisher, a seductive liar, is in fact responsible for the kidnapping of Van Meer and has now come to the East End of London to meet up with his captive. In a room overwrought with shadows—because the Nazi thugs are keeping the drugged Van Meer under third-degree-style lighting (accompanied by unrelenting big band music)—he finds and approaches his victim, who believes him still to be the peace emissary Fisher, working hard to avoid all-out war. But as Fisher sits with Van Meer, there is a knock on the door and in walks ffolliott (George Sanders), a well-meaning British type who has allied himself with Haverstock in the Nazi hunt. He slides into the room followed by one of Fisher's female aides, who has him at gunpoint. He must sit now and observe the interrogation, as Fisher leans over into intimate social distance with the old man and tries to pry from him the secret of "Clause 27." Van Meer is totally out of it, in every precise way, not being certain of who he is, who Fisher is, where he is, what is going on, or what position Fisher can possibly be taking in asking these intrusive questions. "They think I'm working with them, but really I'm not," Fisher whispers, and we see the lines of the extremely expressive Bassermann's face begin to twitch and spread as his eyes open in acquiescence.

Just as the professor is about to give away what he knows, however, ffolliott's sonorous voice—the principal talent Sanders offers to this part—sounds across space from what might be another planet, saying in effect, "He's one of them. Don't tell him anything." Fisher steps abruptly away. Van Meer is awake to the situation now. "Help me!" he begs, gazing off across his cosmos at the cluster of people gathered on the other side of the room, all watching him (but with different motives). He hisses to Fisher that he is a monster and warns that only when he and his monstrous friends have devoured one another can there be occasion for real peace. Now one of the thugs moves forward to torture Van

Meer, and we hear words coming out of the old man's mouth as the camera fixes its gaze on ffolliott and the woman who has escorted him into the room, both of them cringing at the sight.

In putting this scene before the camera, Hitchcock has positioned upon the wall, just behind ffolliott's back as he makes his entrance, a poster reproduction of a canine portrait, two protective retrievers, something roughly in the style of Landseer. (The normal procedure in Hitchcock's productions was for such effects artwork to be achieved by the designer, in this case Alexander Golitzen; otherwise, the image from which the reproduction was made could have been painted by special effects crew member William Cameron Menzies or could, indeed, have been a real dog portrait reproduction of a work not familiar to me.) The retrievers seem to gaze intently at the room in which they have been positioned as guards, observing both the well-meaning ffolliott and also the abject scholar over on the bed. Hitchcock understood that the reading of a picture is affected, even framed, by the context in which we see it. As throughout this scene we catch glimpses of these two dogs from different points of view in the room, they seem to change in attitude and personality. As ffolliott breezes in, we at first do not see the woman with the gun at his spine; he stands casually, his shadow cast over the dogs behind his back since at this instant he has himself become the trusty watchdog and can literally overshadow them. Afterward, as he resignedly sinks into a chair and sighs, "I'll just sit here," the dogs behind him seem similarly resigned to their postures, one sitting, one curled at his friend's feet. Van Meer begins to awaken, jibes at Fisher about how even though the traitor had feigned hunting for peace, there is "*no* peace, only *war*": we are looking at a concerned ffolliott, shoulders up, with the bespectacled female guardian sternly attentive behind him; behind the two of them are the dogs, reminding us, now in this closer shot, of their aggressive heritage.

A moment later, as Van Meer tells Fisher, "When the beasts like you will devour each other, then the world will belong to the little people," we see Fisher at left watching the bed dispassionately, even apathetically, and in the distance the dogs again, but this time not as beasts. Since Fisher is a beast, these dogs have become dutiful citizens, and we see that the sitting creature is actually staring in a straight line at the reprehensible, now uglified, Fisher. When Van Meer cries out for help, there is a fascinating portrait shot of Fisher with his three male and one female assistants—Nazis all—and ffolliott seated meekly among them. The formality of the standing and sitting postures all neatly arranged into a composition precisely reflects the composition style of the dog painting: no less than these people, the dogs are personalities arranged for a tableau. Then Van Meer whimpers that "there's no help," and with a closer shot of the group, all of them staring off-left at the old man in his bed, we see the dogs in the background, unable to offer help even though their pleasant expressions show that they have transcended this particular bestiality and now glow with the spirit of benevolence. Benevolent, they are nevertheless trapped in two-dimensional rendition just as Van Meer and ffolliott are trapped in this Nazi lair.

In *Foreign Correspondent* (Alfred Hitchcock, Walter Wanger Productions, 1940), Fisher (Herbert Marshall) is second from left, and ffolliott (George Sanders) is seated at the picture's center, as a small audience watches the performance of the torture victim Van Meer off-camera right, in company with a pair of observant retrievers. Digital frame enlargement.

One further observation about dogs in portraiture and these hotel dogs from *Foreign Correspondent*: in typical usage the dog portrait was commissioned by the one who ultimately displayed it, so that the dogs were either his or her own pets in fact or breed types now appropriated for the purpose. The dog in the picture is not "a dog" but "my dog," or "a dog like my dog," and is thus in some way a reflection of "me." But this formula must be twisted when years after its initial display, the dog portrait remains on the wall of a residence now converted to a hotel or rooming house, with a different stranger populating the space night after night. The dogs in this scene are thus nobody's dogs, everybody's dogs, and—here is the Hitchcockian clincher—the pets we desire them to be at the moment in which we see them. They are "our dogs." These free-floating dogs become morphing signifiers, taking up attitude—or offering us readings of their attitude—as the shots and the narrative progress.

If it may seem obvious that dog portraiture built on and intensified a culture of animal love, it was only toward the middle of the nineteenth century that such a state of affairs came into existence, principally through the development of dog ownership from blood sport and hunting to organized kennel competitions (from 1859 onward, and for which strict breed appellations were required) and through the personal devotion and expansive support of Queen Victoria and her consort.

As devoted lovers of dogs, they supported kennel competitions eagerly but also patronized and commissioned work from numerous artists who began to specialize in dog portraiture. Arthur Wardle, for instance, exhibited more than a hundred such paintings at the Royal Academy between 1880 and the end of the 1930s (that is, in the late Victorian and immediate post-Victorian periods). Landseer was a favorite of the queen's, a sort of member of the royal family, who made portraits of many of her animals in domestic (casual) situations. What is interesting from our present point of view is that the paintings of these artists "reached a very wide audience through printed reproductions," as William Secord (2000) suggests. "Very few of Landseer's important paintings of dogs were not reproduced for wide distribution as prints. This was also the case to a lesser extent with John Emms and Maud Earl, but Arthur Wardle took the practice to new levels" (369). In posters, on postcards, and collectible cigarette cards and the like, dogs appeared all over English culture to tease and tickle the sensibilities of their human friends. Thus, we can say with some surety that Hitchcock's own fondness for dogs was, at least in its structure and history, a Victorian pursuit; and in this sequence in *Foreign Correspondent*, the invocation of Landseer-style portraiture in the interrogation scene renders the moral spirit of the action in Victorian terms. Van Meer's invocation of Fisher as an evil beast—standing in for what might later have become a cool analysis of the man's political tactics and sangfroid—is a strident call for morality in international affairs: a Victorian sentiment.

Beasts in Distress

In *Secret Agent* (1936) a British traveler named Caypor (Percy Marmont), presumed by British intelligence to be a German agent in masquerade, is targeted for assassination by the operative Richard Ashenden (John Gielgud), who gives his assistant, the General (Peter Lorre), direction on how and where to commit the fatal act. We are in Switzerland, in the high Alps, and Ashenden is watching Caypor and the General climbing a distant slope through the agency of a long spyglass, this object positioned in a hotel room where Caypor's wife is waiting along with their little dachshund. The dog is in acute distress about something, but no one will attend to it. Hitchcock cuts back and forth from the action on the mountain to the action in the room, finally showing a terminal moment in which Caypor, hardly a dot in Ashenden's field of vision, disappears over the edge of a crevasse. It is the dachshund who reacts, instantly and shrillingly, with a hideous and pathetic wail. More than an indication of the deeply woven bond between a man and his favorite friend, more than an invocation of their virtually telepathic connection, the dog's wailing allows for a shrill, emphatic, sonorous negation of this act of violence, a way of signaling, even as the needs of the secret service are met, that Caypor was the wrong man. By way of extending this signal, and to demonstrate the wife's ineradicable attachment to her husband—otherwise withheld through politesse and decorum—Hitchcock arranges that precisely at the moment of the dog's cry the wife should happen to open her mouth. As the dog is not centrally framed, but the wife is, the illusion is produced that she is the source of the grieving sound, while she cannot possibly be, since she cannot see what has happened to her husband or intuit his death in the way that the dog presumably can. She feels the same uncanny closeness that the dog does, we presume, reading the signal of her "cry."

Through a canine "sensitivity" and "psychic connection" a dramaturgical miracle is here effected: the distant killing, on a mountaintop miles away, is delivered as an act in the most proximate territory, affecting intimate relations and local conversation. Without the dachshund the murder must be imported to the sphere of our present characters through elaborate contrivance now rendered unnecessary. More: lacking a sense of modesty or a fear of judgment, the charming dog can show more apparent feeling for Caypor than even the man's wife can. Faced with this assassination directly, she might gape in horror, perhaps even flood over with tears or collapse, but she would not and could not sing her woe as a dachshund can sing.

A little dog also famously features in *Sabotage* (1936), in the scene that Hitchcock frequently cited as a way of explaining to interviewers the difference between surprise and suspense. A young boy has been sent with a neatly wrapped package to ride a bus and make a delivery on the Lord Mayor's Show Day in London. He does not know—but we do—that inside the package is a bomb, set to go off at 1:45. As he rides with it on his lap, the filmmaker cuts back and forth from views of the boy, views of the package, and views of other riders, to shots of the minute hand ticking down on a large town clock. As I am not working here to produce suspense, I will say outright that the bomb does go off, and the boy, along with all the other riders on the bus, is killed. This moment in the film has as its principal effect precisely what is given before the opening credits, in a huge shot of the dictionary definition of *sabotage*: alarming a group of persons or inspiring public uneasiness. The group of persons, the public, alarmed and made uneasy is the audience, and this disturbance is produced largely thanks to the youth, the innocence, and the general charm of the lad who is victimized. But next to him, cuddled in the arms of its owner (a fur-swaddled matron), is another rider, more innocent and enchanting still and thus even more the object of sabotage, a Jack Russell pup. What, indeed, could be cuter than this little beast, with his one black and one white eye, his little teeth trying to sink into our young hero's shoulder? The pup is quite undecided as to whether it would be better to snuggle back into the woman's protective embrace or to reach forward and nibble on this friendly young stranger—to retreat from, or reach out to, the world. Morally speaking, it's the ultimate question, and the little doggie is giving a flawless and unaffected demonstration of the possibilities. At the instant the hands of the clock move to indicate the designated time, the boy reaches forward to pet the face of the dog. A final gesture, but a gesture of love.

Hitchcock continually guides us to consider again, if the press of our harried lives has caused us to forget or abandon it, the fundamental commandment that directs us to be kind to animals. They inhabit the earth absolutely and in the face of our arrogant dominance, which is to say that our world is also—and was first—theirs. Recall in this light of the Quaker testament *The Peaceable Kingdom*. In the just short of thirty years between 1820 and his death, Edward Hicks painted more than a hundred versions of this definitive proclamation that we must lie down with the animals, share their land and their perspective, create in their presence and within their purview the World to Come (see Andrew Crispo Gallery 1975). All of Hitchcock's films, without exception, point in some way to our imperative need to reconcile our animal selves with the demands of our intelligence, to "lie with the animals." *Young and Innocent* (1937) testifies to a dog's fidelity and trust, as well as to the way a pompous and self-important man learns an important lesson in life, at one particular and swiftly passing moment, through recognition, pause, and response.

Showing compassion for a helpless dog, especially in a circumstance where one's own life is in jeopardy, is a sure sign of intrinsic goodness and thus an important element in any story centering on crime and legal redress, that is, a story where an inner moral state, invisible in the presentation of self and impossible to prove with legally acceptable evidence, rests at the heart. At a beach resort in Devon or Cornwall the writer Robert Tisdall (Derrick De Marney) discovers a film star's body washed up on the beach but is observed by witnesses who believe he strangled her. At the police department, and under interrogation, he meets Erica Burgoyne (Nova Pilbeam), daughter to the chief inspector. Love (and denial) at first sight. He initially escapes the clutches of the law and, hiding in her vehicle, rides out with her into the countryside, where they run out of petrol. Her constant companion is Towser, a brave little Schnauzer that sits in the passenger seat like a proper sidekick. At a critical juncture Erica and Robert are in an abandoned farmhouse when two policemen come to search it. The dog is sitting on the stoop, guarding, and when the two young people have to make a run for it, he is left racing after the car with the policemen behind him. There is no way he'll catch up. Robert wants to race on, but Erica says she'll jump unless he stops, so he pulls up until the dog can hop in, potentially opening himself to capture and a likely conviction for a murder he did not commit. In this way the decency and sweetness of his true temper are revealed to her, and it becomes possible for her to love him.

Without this little piece of business Robert remains an enigma to Erica for a considerable time; indeed, he remains an enigma to us, since we are not present for the murder at the beginning of the film and have only his word that he did not commit it. What is necessary to define him as the innocent he claims to be is a gesture beyond learning, formality, pattern, social stricture, and the law, a gesture made possible, and dramatizable, through the presence of this dog.

Readers of Men (and Women)

The dog's ability to bond with a person—in daily practice one continues to find this uncanny, almost miraculous, and deeply touching—is deployed or exploited in a great many films (see the star careers of Rin Tin Tin and Lassie); but *Rebecca* (1940), the first film Hitchcock made in America, offers evidence of a quite different kind of bond. *Rebecca* depends for its drama on our affiliating intensively with the trepidation and desire felt by a young middle-class British girl (Joan Fontaine) who has met a storied member of the aristocracy more or less accidentally, enchanted him, and been invited by him into a marriage that transports her to one of the great landed estates in England. At Manderley the girl (in the film, as in the source novel by Daphne Du Maurier, she has no name) creeps around like something of a dormouse, rendered abject by the stentorian presence of the housekeeper, Mrs. Danvers (Judith Anderson), and generally trapped in the thrall of wonder produced by the splendidly ancient furnishings, tapestried walls, echoing chambers, and elegant decorations of the place, not to say the omnipresent servants and her husband Maxim's all too perfectly casual sense of *Heimlichkeit* there. The first Mrs. De Winter, Rebecca, is (somewhat recently) deceased, and Maxim (Laurence Olivier) thus appears to his new young wife as a man still caught up in the throes of grief. Our sense of closeness to the new wife must thereby invoke, repeatedly, her discomfort and clumsiness both in terms of architectural topography and social class; and her unbearable consciousness of the ghostly, everlasting, and dominant presence of Rebecca in every nook of this place.

Rebecca had an utterly charming little black spaniel, Jasper, who is—at least for the new Mrs. De Winter—a continual invocation of her memory. As with the innocent girl we climb in wonder up the vast staircase toward the West Wing, then turn to face the gigantic vanilla-cream doorway that leads to Rebecca's private chamber—a chamber we cannot quell the hunger to see with our own eyes—and we find Jasper seated obediently in the corridor outside. He is far too small to be a protector, but perhaps he is Rebecca's harbinger, ready to announce every guest. A bit later, as he is taken on leash by his new mistress for a little stroll down by the beach, Jasper introduces our heroine to Rebecca's stone cottage, a destination Maxim has forbidden to his new wife. And in another scene we also see the two newlyweds bouncing along a cliff pathway with the dog in tow, happy to be together: Jasper is energetic and eager, but also—it is important for us to see—entirely comfortable being at the end of the new Mrs. De Winter's lead. How can we penetrate this comfort, this sense of recognition and ease?

Dogs, after all, sensitive as they are to the personalities, emotional states, and bodily presence of their human friends, do not recognize social, legal, or historical assignations of status or recordings of same. If a man and woman are happy together, a dog may sense and reflect this; if they are merely technically married, the dog will not. The presence of the eager spaniel with Maxim and his new wife offers a pretext for disinterest in legal bonds of all kinds—and this film is full of legalities, with its invocations of the lordly status of Maxim and of his title-holdings, not to mention its presentation of an inquest at which Maxim must testify after the body of Rebecca is dredged up from the sea and her sailboat found to have had a hole in its hull. If the wedding of this girl to Maxim is irrelevant to Jasper, who feels bonded to her anyway, so was the wedding of Rebecca. That Rebecca was Mrs. De Winter, then, is a merely spurious fact. Beyond and above that, she was the personality and spirit of herself; a forbidding spirit, we may now recall, to which Jasper was sufficiently subject that his habit was to wait obediently *outside* her rooms. As the new wife gingerly enters, the dog does *not* accompany her.

I think we must ask a further question of Jasper, however. How are we to interpret that, faithful companion to the vanished Rebecca, he so swiftly and unequivocally switches his faith to this new friend, a stranger to his precinct in every way? The answer, I think, is complex and involves both Jasper and Maxim, Rebecca's two most intimate male friends. (Given the attachment that existed between Rebecca and Danvers, or "Danny," we can presume that male friends were relatively unimportant to the ghost; perhaps the marriage to Maxim was for convenience.) As a lifelong member of the British aristocracy, schooled, we must assume, at a private retreat where emotionalism was suppressed, Maxim is a man to put a polish on every expression of thought and to hold back emotion. His feelings for his dead wife are no one's business but his own, and even his marital joy with the new young woman is denied full overt expression. Yet as the plot weaves on, Maxim's deepest true feelings for Rebecca when she was alive, and his regard for her memory now, are central and critical issues that must be telegraphed to the audience. How to telegraph the deepest feelings of a man who does not express them, except perhaps by invoking a canine doppelgänger, a creature incapable of hiding attitude and feeling and also sufficiently proximate to Maxim that we may associate the two? Maxim, after all, has a dark mustache and dark hair, matching Jasper's.

Let me argue that Jasper's true function in this film, and particularly in his quick befriending of the new Mrs. De Winter, is to signal Maxim's quick readiness at the same. Jasper's behavior is a foretelling—subtle, even coded, yet available to us—of the secret of De Winter and Manderley, a secret opened only at the culmination of this elaborate film. Rebecca was loathed and loathsome, living a sordid life in Manderley at the furthest possible remove from Maxim's affections and trust. Jasper was certainly her dog, but his behavior reveals in the end what being close to Rebecca must have meant even to him.

And in *Suspicion* (1941) a West Highland terrier is used to clinch a depiction of the moral depravity of a man who marries into social class, abuses his wife's inheritance, and alienates her from her family, all the while masquerading as an irremediable roué, gambler, and reprobate. Johnnie Aysgarth (Cary Grant) has by a certain point in the story so mystified, troubled, and irritated Lina McLaidlaw (Joan Fontaine), his new wife—two antique baronial chairs her stern father sent over as wedding presents are glaring boldly from the vitrine of a local shop in town—that, confirmed now in her suspicions that he has not a penny of his own, nor any intent of going to work to earn one, she is brought to the point of eclipsing her normal well-bred reserve and having words with him. She is standing on the rear patio of their new home, with his longtime friend Beaky Thwaite (Nigel Bruce), a pathetically chummy dupe with a heart of gold, just as the sounds of Johnnie's arrival waft out to interrupt her pique.

He comes stumbling into the scene with a pile of packages in his arms, insisting that everybody accept a gift: a fabulously expensive necklace and gown for Lina, a costly walking stick for Beaky. "But wait, I got something for myself," says he, while the other two stand in shocked silence, and a moment later he is back, leading the Westie. This is a perfectly adorable little fellow, who races up to Lina and sits up eagerly at her feet while off-camera Beaky whistles somewhat obnoxiously. But that's it for the dog. He more or less disappears from the scene and does not reappear in the film. Johnnie has no feeling for him, no concern for him, no appreciation for him, no reserve of attention for him. Nor does the pup have any feeling for the essentially abusive Johnnie. Indeed, it is the dog's full and immediate detachment from Johnnie that reveals to us a man who is considerably less than he has been pretending to be.

A far more serious and untrammeled bond of trust and fidelity exists between the philosopher exile Phillip Martin (Vaughn Glaser) and his German Shepherd in *Saboteur* (1942). Man and dog inhabit a forest cabin beside a lake retreat, very much in the spirit of Thoreau at Walden Pond. Indeed, as we discover on meeting Martin, his attitudes have been studied at Thoreau's side: he is a believer in the deep true spirit of man, in pure democracy and liberty, in all of the noblest virtues that America stands on. The Shepherd, a huge protector, is always at his side, standing to peer out the window of the cabin at anyone who presumes to approach, walking gently at his master's side from the kitchen to the fireplace. He has the gift of seeing what Martin does not see, and since Martin is totally blind, the dog is the center of ocularity in this home. The dog does not take part in the action of the film, beyond the perfunctory way in which he recognizes and adopts the wanderer Barry Kane (Robert Cummings), who approaches during a rainstorm. Kane's moral bona fides are in question, since the police believe he has committed sabotage and murder in Los Angeles, and he is now in flight. But the Shepherd takes to him immediately, as does Martin; by living with the dog alone in this place for so many years, the old man has transformed himself into something not only human.

Saboteur is altogether a portrait of a sordid and ugly America, one beleaguered by war production, unremitting surveillance and suspicion, and moral doubt. Phillip Martin is the brightest source of sanity, illumination, and moral guidance. To have him standing alone in his trusting warmth might relegate him to a sort of "blind" optimism, entirely out of key with the diligent war effort against Nazism; indeed, his blindness as he states his views would solidify that casting. But to have him read Barry's character in the trusting presence of a creature we cannot doubt, a creature whose soul we take to be utterly pure and whose interpretation of people we understand to be utterly reliable, gives Martin unshakable ground on which to stand. This not only elevates and strengthens him as a character but in a subtle way, entirely elided in the dialogue, salts his convictions and observations with a grain of undeniable truth.

In *Rebecca, Suspicion*, and *Saboteur*, and perhaps generally in Hitchcock's work, all dogs are guide dogs for the somewhat "blinded" viewer; the dog establishes the terms of our involvement and thus ultimately works as ballast for the narrative. Hitchcock is generally far more concerned to use the animal presence,

A tea break for the German Shepherd Grey Shadow and Robert Cummings, shooting *Saboteur* (Alfred Hitchcock, Frank Lloyd Productions/Universal, 1942). Grey Shadow was a great-grandson of Strongheart. Margaret Herrick Library, Academy of Motion Picture Arts and Sciences.

predominantly its reflection of social attitudes and values already in place, for driving a scene forward. The animal is not in itself the object of his comment, and he presumes upon a kind of Victorian metonymy through which by their presence and poses dogs, always already symbolizing, add crucial nuances of dramatic color to situations that could not be fully and clearly worked through without them (see Burt 2002, 88). Thus, he does not hold with the Lacanian position articulated by Jacques Derrida (1997/2003), that "the animal is a living creature that is only living, as it were an 'immortal' living thing" (131). In its discreet and indissoluble hereness and nowness as posited in Hitchcockian film, the animal is always expressive, thus motive, thus both lingering and evanescing and moving in time, just as the human characters are.

Dogs of Mythology and Modernity

The idea of the dog as implicitly wedded to both cinema and modernity, as well as mythology, is invoked as mortal and fleshly dogs become primary attractions in both *Strangers on a Train* (1951) and *Rear Window* (1954). The dog in *Strangers on a Train*, a Great Dane, is a sweet pet that nevertheless invokes an otherworldly, godly, mythological, and (at least momentarily) terrifying inner surface, whereas the dog in *Rear Window* indexes the brutalizing, monumental, spiritually vacuous superstructure of modernity's skin. In the first case Guy Haines (Farley Granger), a tennis star of international repute and a young beau courting an important U.S. senator's daughter, has endured a chance encounter aboard a train with the spoiled and probably psychopathic aristocrat Bruno Anthony (Robert Walker). The result is a (one-sided) plan for mutual cooperation in a double murder plot, where Bruno dispatches Guy's unfaithful and abusive wife and Guy is put under obligation to kill Bruno's much resented and stridently domineering father. Bruno is warped and dangerous, the film makes patently clear, while Guy, even though a somewhat oily and ambitious bourgeois, is noble and morally clean. He has no intention of committing "Bruno's" murder (Bruno makes the murders possessive: "I did yours; now you must do mine," this structure invoking the specter of a mutual masturbation ceremony among adolescent boys), but to keep the bizarre and impulsive Bruno at bay he pretends that he will. We follow him on his escapade to the Anthony mansion late one night.

The house rests in moonlit silence at the top of a low rise of ground spotted over with ancient pines and perfectly manicured lawns. Guy lets himself in and, following Bruno's hand-drawn map, steps across the foyer and up the long staircase. Only then does he come face-to-face with something Bruno didn't indicate on the map, a force and presence that conjures supreme darkness, impenetrable defense, overwhelming violence, and chilling otherness, and this is the Anthonys' giant black Great Dane, growling with menace and ready to pounce. The dog immediately conjures thoughts of Cerberus, the Underworld,

the wealthy Anthony abode as Hades, Bruno as the devil. In order to exagger-
ate the unearthly and mythically spiritual qualities of the beast, Hitchcock has
several of the close-up frames slowed down so that the animal motion is prolonged, eternalized. Anxious and terrified, Guy feels he will never get past this
dog, never manage to step forward into the bedroom where the father is to be
confronted.

When finally he does find the room, gently open the door, and creep to the
bed, therefore, it is with a double relief: he has escaped the guard, and he can
confront the father with the truth about his deranged son. When he awakens
the sleeping body, however, and begins to blurt out his warning, we see that
it is Bruno himself reposing in his father's bed. He has been testing Guy, not
really aiding him, and Guy must now retreat homeward doubly depressed, having failed at his warning and having fallen even more irrevocably under Bruno's
power, required now to commit the crime at some future moment or face Bruno's wrath. As he leaves the mansion, we see the black form of the Dane watching him quietly from the top of the staircase: the tiny bright eyes far at the top
and rear of the frame seem to say, "I know you. I watch everything you do."

In retrospect, we can reflect in ease that the dog is never unfriendly, only
alert. Guy, after all, is a stranger entering the house. It is the size, the darkness
of the nonhuman form, and the shadow in which it moves, as well as the brief
passage of slow motion, that suggest looming and formidable otherworldliness
and danger. But Guy's terror, his reticence about the whole murder project, his
faltering grip on the social-class ladder all darken any obstructions to his access
to success. Guy's buried hunger is reflected in his projection about this dog, a
projection that Hitchcock caringly adopts and meticulously shares with us.

In substantial thematic contrast, in *Rear Window* the charming, but also
relatively silent, little creature, a Norwich terrier, resides happily with a pair of
bohemians living on the third story of a building opposite our protagonist, Jeff
Jefferies (James Stewart). Inventive (and lazy), the couple has devised a method
of lowering the pup down to the courtyard in a laundry basket affixed to a pul-
ley affair on their balcony. He scampers around, investigating the floral arrange-
ments of a downstairs neighbor, Lars Thorwald (Raymond Burr), finally hop-
ping back into his basket and yipping as a signal that he is ready for the makeshift
elevator to lift him back home. Audiences of the film are typically entertained
by the ascension to human status that this dog appears to have made in mobiliz-
ing the elevation of his own accord, forgetting that he has been trained in this
little routine by a pair of adults who don't like the idea of traipsing up and down
stairs with him. Through this routine, and what turns out in the film's development to be the dog's special intelligence in routing like a detective through
those flowerbeds, he becomes personified, thus seems more than canine. One
night he is found dead in that garden, his neck broken, and the Whistlers (as
his owners are frequently called) come out onto their balcony and call out for
the murderous neighbor to own up: nobody does, except that virtually everyone

comes to have a look. The one exception is Thorwald, who remains unseen by the grieving owners inside his apartment, shrouded in darkness through which the vibrating glow of his cigarette radiates into the night.

The invocation of dogginess in this film is of vital dramatic necessity, since what is required dramaturgically is the discovery of something beneath the flowers, something that for human sensibilities would have remained hidden but that cannot be saved from the well-developed olfactory powers of a dog. The Norwich, as a hereditary ratter, can smell organic material readily, and in this case has apparently responded too vigorously to an olfactory disruption of his surround. Making the dog tiny and adorable serves a secondary function, too: when the neighbors seem unmoved at his death, they become through this cold inattentiveness prototypes of the disconnected modern personality. Affiliated with one another through only the accident of physical proximity—the apartment building is an architectural structure that brings strangers into intimate perceptual distance from one another—these avatars of modernity move in one another's orbit, see without feeling, know only superficially, and recognize through typification and generalization rather than intimate relationship. That as viewers we are led to feel more for this poor doggie than they do positions these bystanding citizens as cool and detached in a way that only disaffected modern city dwellers can be, emphasizes the urbanity and modernity of the story as a whole.

At the end of the film the bohemians have a new puppy and are caught in a tiny pedagogical moment as they teach it how to use the "elevator" they have retained: the device transcends the lives of the creatures who use it, embeds itself mechanically into a superstructure that is beyond human in scale. Hitchcock had given some thought to using a Great Dane for the reprise scene, but "thought better of it" (Krohn 2000, 145).

Dogs and/as Tethers

Perhaps it would serve us to imagine that as Alfred Hitchcock walks his two white West Highland terriers, Geoffrey and Stanley ("in their screen debut" [Spoto 450]), out of Davidson's Pet Shop at the beginning of *The Birds* (1963), he is doing more than merely using his presence onscreen to introduce the locale as one in which important connections are about to be made.

The two handsome, snowy little fellows on two handsome leashes are prefigurations, after all, of the two dotty little lovebirds, green as ripe hazelnuts, that Melanie Daniels ('Tippi' Hedren) is soon to buy inside this place and ultimately chauffeur up to the fated town of Bodega Bay. As Hitchcock walks his dogs, and Melanie approaches the shop, thousands of birds mass distantly over San Francisco; later, too soon later, they move to occupy Bodega Bay. Driving up there, Melanie has her birds in a gilded cage (cage = leash). They sit side by side on a dapper perch, wedged into the front of her sports car, a car she likes

Hitchcock walking Geoffrey and Stanley out of Davidson's Pet Shop on Union Square at the beginning of *The Birds* (Alfred Hitchcock, Universal, 1963). 'Tippi' Hedren is walking in, "unleashed." Margaret Herrick Library, Academy of Motion Picture Arts and Sciences.

to drive with enthusiasm; and the road is curvaceous and liberating. She must swerve left and right, and in a Hitchcockian shot that is somewhat celebrated, the lovebirds lean one way and then the other, in perfect unison. Audiences tend to laugh at this—mostly, I think, because at such a moment the two little birds appear to have will and self-control, just like the humans they are not. Inside the frame of the film, these two birds never leave their cage, nor do the terriers run off their leashes. Why, however, at the moment the engaging birds come into the picture, should we see Hitchcock with his terriers? (There are no other dogs in this film.) Is he invoking, perhaps, the animal world under human control? Tamed and trained, the Highlands connote everything the birds, even with their exceptional intelligence, do not. Except that, of course, the man walking the dogs is only Hitchcock the character. As filmmaker, he has the birds "on a leash," too: every last one of them is his trained pet, his by way of Ray Berwick, his bird handler.

The formula that connects Hitchcock the dog-walker to his dogs, then Hitchcock the filmmaker to his birds, which, under training, behave as though they are untrained, suggests two presences in the film and two kinds of "leash," one that we can see and one that we cannot. Always there is a creator, and always we are on the creator's tether.

In Hitchcock's next and penultimate Hollywood studio film, *Marnie* (1964)—after an interstice of three years, he would make only four more films before his death in 1980—Margaret/Marnie Edgar ('Tippi' Hedren again) has lived all her life with only the *thought* of dogs. It is a child's return home that we see enacted when, early in the film, she visits the narrow little house where her mother lives. Marnie, a young woman perhaps on the cusp of her thirties, is once again the little girl tied to her mother's apron when she is in this place. Near the door, and overlooking the stairway that will have such powerful meaning for her and for viewers of this film, is a portrait of two canines at rest, a tiny Scottish terrier and a sober old Bloodhound, the one, perhaps, playing mother to the other. She never pauses to regard the picture, nor does her mother, so it seems nothing but a decorative fillip covering some empty space. Yet the suggestion is that in this household the patient reposeful attitudes of two loving and friendly dogs constitute together a kind of reverential subject. They overlook the proceedings here—tense, violent, horrifying proceedings—with a benevolence and natural tranquility. During the film Marnie will marry into the Rutland family and experience a foxhunt such as the one we saw in *The Farmer's Wife*, riding bravely among a pack of eager hounds. In *The Farmer's Wife*, however, we don't see the culmination of the hunt, whereas here we do: the dogs are ravenous in their lunging at the prey, and so unequivocally seeing this unexpected wildness raised to a stage where other riders are circling in their provocative pinks, Marnie is thrown into flight mode. Her flight will be fatal in some respects and entirely transforming. So both in the questionable shelter of the mother's nest and in the provocative territory of the husband's home, it is dogs, not people, that signify for her, subtly or explicitly.

In the end, regarding the perambulation of Hitchcock as he moves out of that pet shop in *The Birds* with his dogs, he displays a grace of movement and an erectness of posture that suggest, far from untutored casualness, the discipline inherent in those who feel themselves commanded from above. As much like a puppet, with his two little dogs on their own strings, Hitchcock shows himself to be the pet of still another Force.

Note

A different version of this essay appears as "Hitchcock Goes to the Dogs" in *Film International* 63–64 (2013).

Chronological Filmography

The Farmer's Wife (Alfred Hitchcock, 1928). Jameson Thomas, Lillian Hall-Davis, Gordon Harker.

Secret Agent (Alfred Hitchcock, 1936). John Gielgud, Madeleine Carroll, Robert Young, Peter Lorre.

Sabotage (Alfred Hitchcock, 1936). Sylvia Sidney, Oskar Homolka, Desmond Tester, John Loder.

Young and Innocent (Alfred Hitchcock, 1937). Nova Pilbeam, Derrick De Marney, Percy Marmont.

Rebecca (Alfred Hitchcock, 1940). Laurence Olivier, Joan Fontaine, George Sanders, Judith Anderson.

Foreign Correspondent (Alfred Hitchcock, 1940). Joel McCrea, Laraine Day, Herbert Marshall, George Sanders, Albert Bassermann.

Suspicion (Alfred Hitchcock, 1941). Cary Grant, Joan Fontaine, Cedric Hardwicke, Nigel Bruce.

Saboteur (Alfred Hitchcock, 1942). Priscilla Lane, Robert Cummings, Otto Kruger, Grey Shadow [uncredited].

Strangers on a Train (Alfred Hitchcock, 1951). Farley Granger, Robert Walker, Ruth Roman.

Rear Window (Alfred Hitchcock, 1954). James Stewart, Grace Kelly, Wendell Corey, Thelma Ritter.

The Birds (Alfred Hitchcock, 1963). Rod Taylor, 'Tippi' Hedren, Suzanne Pleshette, Jessica Tandy, Veronica Cartwright, Geoffrey and Stanley [Hitchcock's dogs, uncredited].

Marnie (Alfred Hitchcock, 1964). 'Tippi' Hedren, Sean Connery, Diane Baker.

10

The Dog at the
Side of the Shot

• •

Incongruous Dog (*Canis familiaris*) Behavior in Film

ALEXANDRA HOROWITZ

Familiarity is both a boon and a bane to the domestic dog, *Canis familiaris*. On the one hand, it has allowed dogs to occupy our homes and enjoy a share of the resources, both nutritive and protective, that their humans have secured for themselves. On the other hand, the familiarity afforded by this ubiquity prevents us from seeing dogs for who they are. Generally, humans anthropomorphize: we attribute human characteristics to animals without sound evidence for the existence of those characteristics. In particular, our assessment of the meaning of the dog's behavior, and our extrapolation from that behavior to claims about an individual's or the species' knowledge, cognitive capacity, or emotional experience, is often flawed. That great observer of the natural world, Charles Darwin, was an avowed anthropomorphizer, attributing magnanimity, shame, pride, and a sense of humor to dogs (Darwin 1871/2004). The dog's success at integrating him- or herself into human homes may make it difficult for us to see their true natures: having a shared ancestry with *Canis lupus* tens of millions of years more recent than that with *Homo sapiens*. In this essay I use the science of ethology to explore dogs' roles in films as exemplifying the ways that humans misread the dog. Movies using dogs represent various manifestations of the use of dogs as props, as veritable family members, or even as nonindividuals, instead of as animals.

Bringing Ethology to the Movies

Those people who study animal behavior in natural settings practice *ethology*, the science of animal observation. Ethologists research the biological basis of behavior through field experimentation or through long-term observations of their subjects. These observations can reveal the intricacies of behaviors previously unseen or underappreciated. Behavior that might have seemed unitary is revealed to have many integral component parts. For instance, what may look like simply "play" between two dogs, an enjoyable if uncomplicated engagement, is revealed through frame-by-frame review of video recordings to involve highly coordinated behaviors (Horowitz 2009b). In particular, dyadic rough-and-tumble play includes instances of turn-taking, self-handicapping, role reversal, and metacommunicative play signals sent by the participants (Bekoff 1972; Bekoff and Allen 1998). These behaviors are not just components of play; they are constitutive of it. Long-term observations of dyadic play have revealed that when a stronger dog fails to self-handicap—modifying his actions so as to reduce their severity—with a weaker partner, or when the turn-taking grows asymmetrical, play breaks down. Similarly, observations reveal that if play is attempted prior to sending a "play signal," it is usually unsuccessful. As play bouts involve behaviors used functionally in other contexts, such as reproduction, hunting, and defense, specific signals must be wielded to "frame" the bout; essentially, they indicate "everything that will happen now is untrue" (Bateson 1972). Without a play signal, a bite on another dog's rump is just a bite, worthy of a response of umbrage; preceded by a signal, a subsequent bite is seen as "pretend." This bite can then safely lead to any number of similarly tuned behaviors.

Play serves as an example of a general animal behavior phenomenon: behavior, considered as a category, can be deconstructed, is describable, has relevance, and is context sensitive. While it may appear to a lay observer viewing a moment in an animal's life that the animal is "not doing anything," an animal's behavior is comprehensible if one appreciates the context in which it emerges. That context includes information about the local situation in which the animal finds itself, the animal's age and developmental history, and the perceptual and cognitive abilities of the species.

Standard protocol in animal behavior studies is to compile and use an "ethogram" of behaviors. This ethogram lists the numerable, describable behavioral acts the animal may do. After much research, an ever-expanding catalogue of species-typical behaviors is formed. This catalogue is a perpetually in-progress encyclopedia of behaviors. Characteristic behaviors, poses, expressions, vocalizations, and so on can be named and their contexts described. Ordinarily, this catalogue, and its "entries," would be used to help further delineate a species' behavioral repertoire or to understand a category of behavior previously unexplored. The end state in ethology is never a declaration of a complete understanding of an animal; the desideratum is to view sufficient numbers of behavioral acts in context to allow the observer to reliably describe a species' behavior patterns or to predict an animal's response to various stimuli.

Here I bring this catalogue, and an ethological lens, to assessing dog behavior in an unusual context: in film. With this lens the typicality, realism, and appropriateness of dog behavior in movies can be analyzed.

The Dog in the Lens

Much dog "acting" in movies is a result of explicit training. These days, the training is usually reward-based and derived from a kind of associative learning called *operant conditioning*, first identified and described by the early twentieth-century experimental psychologist Burrhus Frederic Skinner (for more on the history of methods used for training movie dogs see the introduction). This training involves pairing a desired act—sitting, barking, coming on command—with a reward, such as a food treat, verbal praise, or the opportunity to play with a favorite toy. The act does not develop *ab initio*: it is usually "shaped," in the language of operant conditioning, from a simple act into one unusual for the repertoire of the species. For instance, dogs have been trained, through simple associative learning, to water-ski. To so train, one does not wait until the dog spontaneously mounts a ski in the water; instead, one begins by giving the dog an opportunity to, for instance, encounter a ski on dry land. If he steps on it, he is rewarded. Should he then happen to mount the ski and continue to stand on it, he gets rewarded for that. Stay on the ski as it is pulled forward, and the dog gets further rewarded. Through small steps, the dog who came across a ski on land may come to be a skier on water.

The kind of dog acting resulting from operant conditioning is easily recognizable in film. Not only are many of the behaviors atypical of the species; there is also a stable of preferred trained acts that reappear like canid leitmotifs in films: begging on hind legs, "playing dead," and so forth. Most of these behaviors are used for their predesignation as having a fixed meaning and audience effect. For instance, a begging pose is read as an indication of subservience or adorableness. Similarly, a dog covering its eyes with its paws—a behavioral act seeming to convey intention that does not appear to be performed intentionally by dogs without training—is read as a show of modesty or fear. Some acts may be used to represent the sameness of the dog and human experience, such as dancing or vocalizing in a humanlike way. These behaviors are largely conspicuous. In some films the location of the offscreen trainer on set can be deduced from the inclination and attention of the dog. Cueing the animals in real time, the trainer's presence is implied.

I am not concerned in this essay with the transparency of trained dogs' "acting" performances or with that particular (mis)representation of natural dog behavior. Though a listing of so-called dog movies—from *Beethoven* (1992) to the live-action version of *101 Dalmatians* (1996), or the star vehicles of Rin Tin Tin, Lassie, et al.—seems to create a discrete category of films featuring dogs trained to so act, the domestic dog has another, less discussed role in contemporary narrative film. In many films dogs appear at the side of the shot, wandering through a scene. They are used for their simple presence, or they are used as plot devices. These dogs, while they may be trained, are asked to, with their presence, signal an emotion or mood; to, with an action, provide meaning to a scene; to, with their company, reflect something about ourselves. In many cases these dogs are cast as "extras"; in all cases their behavior is not glossed with human voicing but is expected to serve as self-evidently meaningful. In other cases they are mere props instead of individuals.[1] To look at the behavior of these dogs in films is to bring ethology to the movies. The result is the discovery that dogs' cinematic behavior is often jarringly at odds with the meaning that is attributed to it.

We can begin at the beginning of movies, which coincides with the beginning of dogs in movies. With the advent of the new medium of film at the turn of the twentieth century, dogs were immediately implicated. In the various versions of the famous 1895 Lumière actuality *Workers Leaving the Lumière Factory*, dogs move among the factory workers—watching, waiting, running alongside a bicyclist. In *Rescued by Rover* (1905) the collie playing the character Rover rescues an infant stolen by a beggar woman from the child's distracted nanny. The dog appears in the second action scene, staring placidly away from the nanny as she informs her employer of the loss of her child. At a cue from stage left, Rover suddenly exits, and with a jaunty lope in his step runs down the street, allegedly in the direction of the poorer section of town to which the thief has repaired.

Rover not only succeeds in finding the baby; the "everydog" Rover has succeeded in finding his place in film. It was not long after the success of *Rescued by Rover* that scores of films featured animal actors, and many of these films—especially those that, like *Rescued by Rover*, starred dogs—were so popular that the film stock was destroyed from frequent playing. Although only one of Strongheart's films has survived, *The Return of Boston Blackie* (1927), in which he also plays a "character" named Strongheart (see Fuller-Seeley and Groskopf in this volume), it stands as an early example of the kind of behavioral mismatching seen in later films. The story turns on Strongheart's apparent attack on the film's designated villainous character. Said villain reacts as though attacked; Strongheart's master in the film, Boston Blackie (Bob Custer), reacts as though the dog had attacked. What Strongheart the dog actor is doing, though, is ludic: he is *playing*. He jumps onto the man but does not follow through with this "attack" when the man drops to the ground. Instead, the dog pauses—waits for a response—just as dogs do in play, awaiting their play partner's move. When the man finally rises, the "attack" continues with Strongheart pulling the man by his arm. Viewed without presumption of intent, though, the dog's behavior is an apparent engagement in a game of tug-of-war. Strongheart wags his tail loosely, a characteristic sign of play. More evidential is what happens when the villain fails to mind the rules of this "game": when he strikes the dog, the dog does not respond defensively or aggressively. Instead, the dog drops his ears in surprised reply. Of course he does: the dog's expectation has been violated. The man has not play-signaled his benign intent before striking, as one must do in a play session.

Examples of this kind of behavioral dissonance—a dog's actions, viewed ethologically, jarring with the intended meaning of the dog actor's actions—are strewn through the catalogue of films that followed those of Rover and Strongheart. They are especially rife when a dog is not featured in a film but is only a side player. Having a dog in a scene, whether in the background or as part of a family, makes the scene read true, and makes the family seem more familiar. What we will find, though, is that the details of the dog's behavior are often overlooked. Rover, the everydog, stands in for the realness of an actual dog: Rover's appearance and behavior are what the filmmaker imagines, and the audience asserts, that "every" dog looks or acts like. These incidental dogs behave incongruously with their context or assigned roles in discernible ways.

Dissonant Dogness

A sampling of classic and familiar films with dogs appearing in them was chosen for review and analysis. Films featuring dogs both with named roles and with lesser roles were selected. Some films include widely recognized dog roles—*The Thin Man* (1934), *The Wizard of Oz* (1939), *Annie* (1982). In other movies discussed here—*Mary Poppins* (1964), *Oliver!* (1968), *The Royal Tenenbaums* (2001)—the dog is all but uncredited. In these cases dogs seem to have been used to embellish a scene (see also Pomerance in this volume); the presence of a dog in a scene may not even be noted by the audience. Each film-dog's behavior in every scene in which he or she appeared was coded and described in etho-logical language. Not every film had an example of dissonant dog behavior; of those that did, the ways that the dogs' behaviors rang false fall into three distinct categories.

The first category of incongruity relates to communication: a dog vocalizes, and a specific *meaning* of the vocalization is assumed by the human actors. That meaning often diverges from the actual meaning of the vocalization. The sec-ond category concerns the dog's attention in a scene. In particular, dog actors are ostensibly involved in a scene, but their attention, in the form of their gaze, posture, or vector of movement, may indicate otherwise. The final category of incongruous behavior relates to the dog's *non*behavior. In situations that call for a response, or in which a reaction is expected, the attendant dogs fail to acknowledge the exigency. Each of these categories will be discussed in turn.

Incongruous Communication

Dogs, like most social mammals, use numerous methods to communicate to conspecifics. Unlike the social human, much less canid information seems to be vested in vocalizations, and much more is conveyed with other means. The olfactory acuity of dogs, for instance, allows for communication via odor. Odorant messages are worn on one's body or emitted and left for later investigation by another dog. Body language makes use of the position and height of an animal's head, ears, tail, and gaze direction. And, too, dogs vocalize. They bark, of course, but they also growl, yelp, whimper, howl, and snuffle in apparent inter- and intraspecific communication.

For researchers the informative content of these communications is determined by their context. The precise meaning of different kinds of barked vocalizations is still elusive. Indeed, for a long time there was a question whether there *is* meaning in barks. Simply because an animal emits a sound, it does not follow of necessity that the sound is either intended as communicative or even serves as communication to conspecifics at all (Shettleworth 1998). Though Darwin (1871/2004) claimed that dogs make distinguishable barks, expressing eagerness, anger, joy, or demand, the actual sound spectra of barks were not extensively studied until recently. The bark is a classically "noisy" sound with a fluctuating structure and no single identifiable fundamental frequency, the single pitch that defines a heard sound. Currently, most canid researchers agree that there is information in the barks, although some demur that barks are simply attention-getters, the equivalent of a voiced but unmeaningful shout. Research comparing the spectrographs of different barks found some barks to be distinctive (Yin and McCowan 2004) and has identified the different contexts in which distinguishable barks are emitted, such as being left alone ("isolation" bark), asking to go on a walk ("request" bark), at the approach of an unknown person ("stranger" bark), or in play with other dogs or humans ("play" bark). Even naive, non-dog-owning listeners can discriminate and sometimes correctly characterize the context of these barks on the basis of their sound alone (Pongrácz et al. 2005).

In films using dogs, barks are often used to carry meaning: as informative to humans. Indeed, the course of a person's behavior may be changed as a result of the ostensive "information" contained in that bark. Two films demonstrate this well: *Mary Poppins* and *Oliver!* In each a barking dog serves as messenger; in each the bark does not jibe with the message given.

In *Mary Poppins* one scene finds the title character (Julie Andrews) out doing errands with her charges, young Jane (Karen Dotrice) and Michael (Matthew Garber), when they encounter a dog named Andrew (uncredited) on the street. It is a dog known to nanny Poppins, and, consistent with her magical way with the world, she is able to communicate with the dog and understand what he is saying. The notion that there is intelligible, sentence-like language in the dog's barks is not at issue: it is a conceit. But there is also, the script claims, emotional content in the bark: the dog is alerting Poppins to an emergency involving Uncle Albert (Ed Wynn). Uncle Albert has apparently begun laughing so uncontrollably that he is lifted into the air, unable to return to the ground. Poppins responds with alacrity, diverting their outing to go attend to Uncle Albert at once.

Viewed ethologically, however, the dog's behavior is not consistent with an emergency bark. His tail wags loosely and low: a generally relaxed, if uncertain, display. He approaches with an unhurried, jaunty gait, symptomatic of a calm animal. The bark itself, moreover, is more representative of a food request bark. This would be consistent with the role of a dog trained to "speak" on command, with an expected reward of food.

In *Oliver!* a surly character known as Bill Sikes (Oliver Reed) is regularly accompanied by his (uncredited) dog, a bull terrier he calls "Bull's-eye." In a scene near the movie's climax Bull's-eye's vocalizations play a critical role. At a local pub Sikes is conferring with Fagin (Ron Moody) about the fate of Oliver (Mark Lester), whom they have stolen from his new family. Sikes has set the dog to "guard" Oliver by sitting beside him. The benevolent character Nancy (Shani Wallis) has concocted a rousing version of a song and dance, "Oom-pah-pah," as a distraction. Nancy's ploy successfully distracts the men, and as she dances by them, she grabs Oliver. But as she spirits Oliver away, the dog barks. Though the dog remains sitting, and the cacophony in the pub remains, the barking calls Sikes's attention to Oliver's absence.

Bull's-eye's bark is taken as meaningful: it conveys that Oliver has escaped. Unfortunately, if one listens to Bull's-eye's bark, the report he has issued to Sikes is not about the boy's absence. Like Andrew's bark, Bull's-eye's most resembles the cadence and pitch of a "request" bark, used to solicit food or a toy. Bull's-eye may be asking Sikes to interact with him, or for the meal he surely has not yet been given.

In both *Mary Poppins* and *Oliver!* a dog is called into action to change the course of a scene: to bring attention to a character's actions; to alert a character about an urgent situation. The most generous characterization of the directors' use of these dogs' vocalizations is that they are consistent with a theory that barking is predominantly a noise-making activity. Insofar as noisiness will attract attention, these barks serve to do so. But barks have been more carefully studied and characterized than that theory suggests. The kinds of barks these filmic dogs emit do not synch with the meanings they are intended to hold. Furthermore, barks are situated within a greater context: the other behaviors of the barker. In *Mary Poppins* and, to a lesser extent, *Oliver!* the dog's posture and bearing is not consistent with an urgent message. Especially in nonverbal animals, a communication in one modality may be moderated by behavior in other modalities. For instance, a dog's growl with hackles up and tail stiff and erect has a different meaning than a growl emitted from a supine position with tail wagging. These dogs' vocalizations, intended to be the bearer of urgent information, are accompanied by postures that belie that intention.

Incongruous Attention

The second category of filmic dog behaviors involves the *attention* of these incidental dogs. Attention, as represented visually in direction of gaze and bodily stance, and olfactorily in source and length of investigative sniffing, is indicative of the perception, understanding, and interest an animal has in its environment. The domestic dog's use of the attention of others is thought to be a large component of his success at integrating into human society and families. Dogs attend to us: they look at people, especially familiar people, in the eyes, a behavior not typical of any other nonhuman animal. In most species eye contact is used as a threat; prolonged eye contact is not part of expressing familiarity or intimacy, as it is among humans. Dogs do not only hold our gaze; they follow it, as young children learn to do, extending the direction of the eyes to the object or objects that have caught their interest. Young children also learn gaze alteration, in which they look at an object of interest, to the face of an adult, and back again to the object. This kind of gaze pattern serves as a communication: either showing the adult the object, or requesting the object from the adult. Dogs, too, show gaze alteration (Horowitz 2009a).

Thus, one can look at the attention of dogs in films. On this topic two films serve as exemplars of incongruous attention by dogs: *The Wizard of Oz* and *The Royal Tenenbaums*. Many films, including these, also have examples of a specific kind of incongruous attention: a posture that indicates that a dog is not minding *others'* attention.

The Wizard of Oz represents an unusual case study for dog behavior. The movie itself, and the "little dog, too," are highly familiar in contemporary society. Repeated viewings of the film, far from revealing more details, may serve to solidify initial impressions and actually prevent viewers from seeing precisely what is happening. One of the most quoted lines from the film begins a scene that involves a dog. In this scene the heroine, Dorothy (Judy Garland), finds herself in a strange new, colorful world. "I've a feeling we're not in Kansas anymore," she declaims to her dog, Toto (played by a Cairn terrier named Terry), whom she clutches in her arms. Looking around with fascination, Dorothy sets Toto down. He initially seems to follow her interest. Dorothy's attention, and the audience's attention, is suddenly captured by an approaching radiant bubble, quickly growing larger and accompanied by anticipatory music. Out of the bubble Glinda the Good Witch (Billie Burke) will appear. Dorothy is captivated. Just before the bubble reaches the pair, Dorothy's posture is highly anticipatory. Though her back is to the audience, a gawk is implied. At her feet, Toto does a full-body shake, turns in another direction, and casually trots off stage right.

Viewed ethologically, shaking behavior may be used functionally, to remove dirt, dust, or discomfort; it may also be employed when—or to facilitate—changing

A bored or oblivious Toto (Terry) departs while his mistress Dorothy (Judy Garland) is transfixed by the arrival of Glinda, the Good Witch, in *The Wizard of Oz* (Victor Fleming, MGM, 1939). Digital frame enlargement.

activities. In this case Toto shakes before leaving the scene; it appears to be an activity-changing shake. Although the arrival of Glinda in a floating bubble is imminent, with his behavior Toto is expressing his inattention to and lack of awareness of the focal point of the human's attention. On the one hand, Toto is cast in the film as Dorothy's constant companion, who will stay with her through her adventure in Oz. On the other hand, by his behavior Toto reveals himself to be a companion in spirit only: he does not see nor show concern with the object of Dorothy's perception and interest. Indeed, his lack of attention serves as an implicit signal of the fact that Glinda and her floating bubble, a special effect produced by process work after the scene was shot, were not actually present on the set and would have been invisible to Toto/Terry and Dorothy/Garland alike. Garland could pretend to see the bubble; Terry could, or did, not.

The Royal Tenenbaums, in contrast to *The Wizard of Oz*, was produced at a time when much research into dog social cognition had been published and was being publicized. Although dogs are not featured prominently in the movie, they enter periodically as props. In one long sequence a family dog is crushed as a result of reckless driving by one character; moments later, the patriarch of the family, Royal (Gene Hackman), acquires another dog from the firefighters who have responded to the car crash and spontaneously christens the dog "Sparkplug." Royal intends this gift to be a salve to his son and grandchildren,

The Dalmatian Sparkplug in partial attendance at the funeral of Royal (Gene Hackman) in *The Royal Tenenbaums* (Wes Anderson, Touchstone Pictures, 2001). Digital frame enlargement.

whose dog it was that was killed. Sparkplug, a Dalmatian, reappears in another scene near the movie's end, at Royal's funeral. Royal's family and closest associates are gathered in a cemetery, all attendant to the space in the earth into which he has been placed—all, that is, but the dog, who is staring fixedly in the opposite direction. While the dog is ostensibly *with* the family, observing the occasion with them, his attention is elsewhere; he is there figuratively only, doing the film's bidding by his presence alone.

Sparkplug calls to mind an unnamed dog in Gustave Courbet's *A Burial at Ornans*, painted in 1850 (Laqueur 2010). In it, an open grave is encircled by mourners and attendants. The frame is, indeed, filled with people reacting to and attending to the ceremony and each other—but for the dog in the lower right-hand side of the image. The dog is looking—even sniffing, it appears—in another direction entirely. He alone is directed at some other concern. As with Sparkplug, the gravity of death does not move him, nor is he a participant in the

Gustave Courbet's *A Burial at Ornans* (1849–1850, Musée d'Orsay, Paris, France. Available at commons.wikimedia.org/wiki/File:Burial_at_Ornans.jpg).

ceremony. His inclusion can perhaps only be explained as a bit of scenery, not unlike the mesas in the background: they identify a location in space; the presence of the dog identifies a customary habit, dog-keeping, of that time.

In *The Wizard of Oz* and *The Royal Tenenbaums* dogs are inserted for the sake of companionship and as representatives of a family unit. Though a companion would ordinarily be held to certain standards of behavior, as would a family member, in these cases the dog's presence alone is sufficient for membership: neither dog participates in the action of the actor(s) in the scene. Indeed, their bearing, gaze, and, it can be assumed, attention are elsewhere.

Even more common an incongruity is a cinematic dog's lack of eye contact, gaze holding, or facial bearing consistent with listening to someone speaking to it. Examples of this are rife in films. Small dogs are especially well represented here: portable, "toy" dogs can be picked up and placed so as to face a person, allowing the person to apparently communicate—have a dialogue—with the dog. Were another human to behave as dogs in this situation regularly do, failing to fixate on the face of the speaker at all, any pretense of shared understanding would be obliterated.

Incongruous Response

The master deducer Sherlock Holmes, as imagined by Arthur Conan Doyle, is able to draw improbable inferences from the slightest bit of evidence. He is equally skilled at discovering salient information from an *absence* of evidence. In "Silver Blaze" (Doyle 1892/2002), in response to a detective's question about the scene of a crime—"Is there any point to which you would wish to draw my attention?"—Holmes replies:

> "To the curious incident of the dog in the night-time."
> "The dog did nothing in the night-time."
> "That was the curious incident . . ." (272)

The final category of incongruity involves an absence of response where, verily, one is due. While ethological and biological knowledge of dogs has not made their behavior entirely predictable, there are certain responses that can be anticipated. For instance, many dogs' interest or lack of interest in moving objects—from a thrown tennis ball to a fleeing squirrel—can in part be traced to the configuration of photoreceptor cells in the dogs' retinas. Longer-nosed dogs, like Labrador retrievers, tend to have what is called a "visual streak" in their retina: they have a higher density of cells across a horizontal band running the length of the eye. These dogs can see, and thus often respond with enthusiasm to, objects moving on the horizon. By contrast, smaller-nosed dogs, like pugs, tend to have a density of cells at the center of their eyes, called an "area centralis," resembling the fovea in human eyes that allows us to focus well on objects right in front of us. These dogs are less likely to respond to a tossed ball; instead, they are more likely to sit in an owner's lap and gaze into his face (McGreevy, Grassi, and Harman 2004).

Should a retriever not show any reaction to a moving ball, one would think it unusual. Sparkplug, the Dalmatian from *The Royal Tenenbaums*, barely flinches when two rifles are shot at the funeral a mere foot or two from his head. Given dogs' auditory acuity—their hearing is as good as human hearing, and in addition they hear more high-frequency sounds—it defies belief that a dog would not register a response.[2]

In *The Thin Man* (1934) the wire fox terrier Asta regularly accompanies Nick and Nora (William Powell and Myrna Loy) on their adventures and, indeed, occasionally helps extract them from some misadventures (see Ross and Castonguay in this volume). But his actions are often out of keeping with the spirit of a scene. For instance, in one scene Nick and Nora have retired to their beds, when Nora inadvertently lets a stranger into their house, who follows her into the bedroom. Asta is lying on Nora's bed. The stranger produces a gun and threatens them, raising his voice. While the human actors react to the presence of a threatening stranger in the room, Asta, who is facing the door, lies still on the bed and does not react in any way.

This is curious behavior. Dogs not only react strongly to loud noises; they notice changes or novel elements in a known environment, and they are very attentive to new people. One common behavioral complaint owners have about their dogs is that the dogs are said to have an undesired and negative reaction to a category of people: men; people of a different race; people wearing hats. Indeed, the dog's skill at discriminating known people from unknown is sufficiently acute that dogs have for millennia been used as "guards," protecting a domicile by identifying those who do not belong there and deterring or attacking the intruders. While the fox terrier is not a breed trained as a guard, the breed is known to be reactive. The American Kennel Club (AKC) breed standard describes wire fox terriers as "on the tip-toe of expectation at the slightest provocation" (akc.org /breeds/wire_fox_terrier/). In this scene Asta not only does not act like a veritable member of his breed; he is not behaving as any dog would.

Furry Authenticity

In these three categories of dog's filmic behavior, dogs are behaving incongruously with their intended role in the scene in which they appear. The dogs serve as plot devices as much as they do as dogs. Given the use of these dogs, one is left with the impression that they are included to lend an air of authenticity to the scene. Authenticity may be lent by association or by mere presence. In stories revolving around families, a dog may serve as a touchstone, assuming that the family portrayed on film resembles the kind of families that constitute the audience. According to the Humane Society, as of this writing two in five American households include a dog ("U.S. Pet Ownership Statistics," 2012, humanesociety .org); so, too, therefore, might the film family. Relatedly, the domestic dog is considered a kind of interlocutor: a companion not just physically but emotionally. People regularly talk to their dogs and may confidently gloss the dog's seeming response using language. So, too, in film dogs communicate information to humans and sit agreeably listening when the humans want to communicate with them. In the 1982 film musical *Annie*, the long-suffering dog, Sandy, taken in by the lead character endures frequent episodes of the heroine, Annie (Aileen Quinn), singing directly into his face. Sandy's role is not to behave as a dog would and repair to a less noisy environment; it is to apparently listen to Annie as would a comrade or confidant.

In other cases the dog lends an air of authenticity to the background. These dogs may not be involved in the action of a scene at all, or they might appear, as in *Mary Poppins*, for a single purpose and then depart. In the 1987 *Witches of Eastwick*, for instance, dogs are scattered through the movie as typical dogs one might see in a typical town. But ethological examination shows the behavior and appearance of the dogs to be abnormal. Dogs appear in two scenes wandering across streets of the town, unleashed and unaccompanied—and yet clearly cared-for. Their behavior and bearing is quite unlike that of village strays, nor is it typical of owned dogs. Similarly, in the 2010 *Leap Year* a single dog makes a single, odd appearance. A sheepdog, he pops up aside the protagonist waiting at a train station, with no sheep in sight. His vocalizations and behaviors are contextually bizarre: he whines and seems to solicit attention from the girl, then growls and snaps at her unprovoked. As she runs off, he is suddenly quiet. However, the dog makes locational "sense": he is a sheepdog in Ireland, a place of many sheep. Eastwick, a staid town in New England, might, one expects, be home to many well-groomed and nonstray dogs. Both films use dogs as part of the scenery; their behavior and appearance are overlooked.

These uses of dogs—as associates or as merely present—attempt to increase the sense of reality of the scenes in which they appear. However, ethological scrutiny of many dogs' behavior gives the lie to their inclusion. Rather than increasing the realness of the scene, they serve to undercut it.

Guilty Looks

The use of dog characters in the films explored herein is representative of the way that humans misrepresent the dog. Dogs are used for their generic roles—as props, as part of the scenery, as part of the family—but are not considered *as dogs*, as individual animals. Using an ethological approach to consider these filmic dogs' behavior, it is apparent that dogs are regularly acting in ways at odds with their film roles. The examined films, despite their longevity and, in some cases, the acclaim bestowed upon them, have examples of radically incongruent dog vocalizations, attention, and responses (or lack of response).

It appears that the filmmakers are less concerned with the content of the dog—with the dog's posture, with the meaning of a vocalization or gesture—than with introducing an intentionally vague notion that dogs are "about." On the one hand, this is a kind of "reality effect," as Roland Barthes (1986, 141–148) describes it. On the other hand, reality could not truly be the desideratum, nor is it the result. Information about the typical behavior, the sensory and cognitive capacities, and the expected appearance of dogs is widely available. What these dogs "at the side of the shot" demonstrate is the filmmakers' lack of concern with the dog qua dog. The effect is "reality" with an absence of attention to the detail of the real. This use of dogs is a kind of "Rover verisimilitude," the filmic version of "somewhere, a dog was barking" in literature: the dog sets the scene, but the *fact of* the dog is irrelevant.

There is precedent for this disregard of the behavior of dogs. Indeed, it is related to what the zoologist Heini Hediger (1981) called the "assimilation tendency": that is, humans' disposition to see other animate creatures as more or less like ourselves. Humans anthropomorphize: we assume that nonhuman animals have similar subjective experiences to our own. We fail to see the animal's behavior on its own terms, because we have defined the terms: we assume they are humanlike in some way (usually a diminished way). Dogs are treated as furry humans, with simpler emotional and cognitive abilities but essentially the same desires, requirements, and capacity for subjective experience.

Anthropomorphizing of animals has long standing: even Paleolithic art included animals rendered with human features (Mithen 1996). It is not uncommon to hear attributions of jealousy, embarrassment, and shame made to domestic pets. The imagery of Aesop—the happy dog, the persistent tortoise, the industrious ant—persists even when scientific evidence questions these characterizations. But dogs may be the species most often subjected to anthropomorphisms, as they are typically the animals we see when we, with pen in hand, look down at our feet. To some extent we do not see the dog in front of us, because we are blinded by the things that it represents. Dogs serve as the model (human) partner: the ardent listener, the sympathizer, the faithful, and the loving. As such, dogs have long been featured in prose in this fabled form: as reflections of ourselves. Victorian autobiographies ostensibly written "by" the dog, reflecting on the trials and tribulations of their lives as a person would, represent the apex of this trend (Horowitz 2009a).

Anthropomorphisms endure for their utility: in an attempt to understand and manage our environment, we naturally project onto animals motivations and knowledge that may help us to predict other animals' behavior (Horowitz and Bekoff 2007). A contemporary ethological approach makes the veracity of anthropomorphisms an empirical claim. Does a dog's "guilty look" represent its experience of guilt? Is "jealous" behavior when an owner directs her or his attention to another dog an emotional experience or a practical one: go where the attention is being provided? While research suggests that there are better explanations for the "guilty look" than the experience of guilt, and that the personal interest of a desired object or attention is more salient than whether another dog is unfairly receiving it, anthropomorphic language makes up much lay description of animals (Horowitz 2009c; Horowitz 2012). In cognitive ethology the anthropomorphisms made of dogs and other animals have begun to be unpacked. An understanding of dogs born of a sense of familiarity is being replaced by an understanding borne of empirical investigation and scientific confirmation. *Replaced*, not displaced—sometimes the anthropomorphism is well-founded. It is an empirical question, however, in most cases still to be answered.

In films the use of dogs as prop, rather than as dog, continues apace. As punctuation to a scene, to move the plot forward, to set a character's or environment's tone, dogs are used as symbols. But they are animate symbols, and animate symbols that are, training aside, behaving on their own terms. The cinematic disregard for dogs is puzzling, as they are expressive creatures in their own right, perfectly able to convey emotion, transmit information, or show affection. As Susan Orlean (2011) and others have observed, dogs' heyday in films may have been the silent era: as no one could speak, dogs and humans were on more equal footing. "In fact," Orlean suggests, "people look diminished when in silent films"; by contrast, "the purity of a dog's focus was the heroic quality that they brought" to a film (interview with Susan Orlean at the Free Library of Philadelphia, Pennsylvania, December 5, 2011). When talkies began, dogs were diminished, and we stopped looking at them and began imagining them, even when they played "heroes," as silly humans. The result is that, often, the behavior of the dog at the side of the shot reveals how distant dogs, and our view of them, have become.

Notes

Thank you to Adrienne McLean, for conceiving and developing this volume; to Ammon Shea, for his finely tuned linguistic eye; and to Julie Hecht and Emily Cherenack, for cinematic contributions.

1. *Prop* also implies and evokes *property*, another inescapable feature of pets in contemporary culture: their status as equivalent to one's personal effects.
2. Although there was no indication that this was the case with Sparkplug, many Dalmatians are congenitally deaf, so this example may be more complicated.

Chronological Filmography

Rescued by Rover (Lewin Fitzhamon and Cecil M. Hepworth, August 1905). Blair [dog], May Clark, Barbara Hepworth.

The Return of Boston Blackie (Harry O. Hoyt, August 1927). Strongheart the Dog, Bob Custer, Corliss Palmer.

The Thin Man (W. S. Van Dyke, 1934). William Powell, Myrna Loy, Maureen O'Sullivan, Skippy/Asta [uncredited].

The Wizard of Oz (Victor Fleming, 1939). Judy Garland, Frank Morgan, Ray Bolger, Bert Lahr, Jack Haley, Billie Burke, Margaret Hamilton, Terry [dog].

Mary Poppins (Robert Stevenson, 1964). Julie Andrews, Dick Van Dyke, David Tomlinson, Glynis Johns, Karen Dotrice, Matthew Garber, Andrew [dog, uncredited].

Oliver! (Carol Reed, 1968). Mark Lester, Ron Moody, Shani Wallis, Oliver Reed.

Annie (John Huston, 1982). Aileen Quinn, Albert Finney, Carol Burnett, Ann Reinking, Tim Curry, Bernadette Peters.

The Witches of Eastwick (George Miller, 1987). Jack Nicholson, Cher, Susan Sarandon, Michelle Pfeiffer.

The Royal Tenenbaums (Wes Anderson, 2001). Gene Hackman, Gwyneth Paltrow, Anjelica Huston, Ben Stiller, Luke Wilson, Owen Wilson, Bill Murray, Danny Glover.

Leap Year (Anand Tucker, 2010). Amy Adams, Matthew Goode, Adam Scott, John Lithgow.

Afterword

● ●

Dogs at the Digital Divide

ADRIENNE L. McLEAN

> The problem with the puppies is that we
> could only use them for two weeks at a
> time, so you do get a bit attached to them
> and they have to go; they're too big.
> —Alice Evans on DVD extra,
>   *102 Dalmatians* (2000)

> I wish you could talk.
> —Boy to dog in *Marmaduke* (2010)

In the introduction to this book I made reference to MGM's "Dogville Barkies," a series of nine shorts produced between 1929 and 1931. The films were "acted" entirely by trained dogs, in full costume and even makeup, that were "ventriloquized" with the voices of humans (see the photo on page 17). The shorts spoofed feature films of the time: the musical *The Broadway Melody* (1929) became *The Dogway Melody* (1930), the war film *All Quiet on the Western Front* (1930) became *So Quiet on the Canine Front* (1931), the adventure film *Trader Horn* (1931) became *Trader Hound* (1931), the prison film *The Big House* (1930) became (naturally) *The Big Dog House* (1930). And so on. As of this writing, several of the shorts are available on YouTube, and the cable channel Turner Classic Movies also runs them from time to time.

  I first came across the "Barkies," however, in a magazine article entitled "Hol-lywoof Babylon" (Bud Boccone, *AKC Family Dog*, November/December 2010,

48). As the article put it, "Few sights captured on celluloid are as bizarre, some might say grotesque, as the Barkies. An insomniac stumbling upon a Barkie on late-night TV, and seeing a Bulldog and a spaniel in evening dress dancing a rhumba, might get the feeling that someone laced his Ovaltine with LSD." While marveling at the "ingenuity and production values" that went into making the nine shorts—all of the detailed and carefully crafted costumes, sets, and props were scaled to "dog size"; the hand grenades in *So Quiet on the Canine Front* spread "fleas instead of shrapnel"—the writer also notes that the Barkies "veer from appealing to appalling. They were made long before the treatment of animals on movie sets was regulated. The dogs were often manipulated with wires, like marionettes, and the costumes and hot lights must have been terribly uncomfortable. Thanks to the implementation of strict rules concerning the treatment of animals on movie sets, and the advent of computer-generated special effects, today's film dogs needn't suffer such indignities for their art."

In this afterword I want to consider the place of dogs in the digitized mediascape, both in terms of whether CGI (computer-generated imagery) in fact means that dogs truly are no longer "suffering for their art"—it is really, again, our art, not theirs—and in relation to the ongoing proliferation of animated dogs, especially talking dogs, in films that are not, properly speaking, animated. That is, cel animation, in which images are painted or printed on pieces of acetate (originally celluloid) and combined in a camera stand, of the sort used in Disney's *Lady and the Tramp* (1955) or its first *101 Dalmatians* (1961), can very easily make dogs fly, do the rhumba, or speak (cel animation can also be combined with newer digital technologies). And most audiences are aware of how powerfully expressive full-scale digital animation can be; there are few characters more appealing than the talking dog in the 2009 Disney/Pixar film *Up*, for example. Paul Wells, in his book *The Animated Bestiary: Animals, Cartoons, and Culture* (2009), writes that, "At a very simple level, whenever an audience is confronted with an animated film, it recognizes that it is different from live action—its very aesthetic and illusionism enunciates difference and potentially prompts alternative ways of seeing and understanding what is being represented" (5). The sort of films that I explore here, however, do not present themselves as "different from live action" but as potent and sometimes ambiguous mixtures of live action, animatronics, and CGI.[1] Why do we need the "magic to be real" now rather than traditionally animated? What is so powerful about the stories these films tell that they still require the solid presence of "real" dogs, in addition to digitized canine avatars or electronically controlled puppets?

One of the first such films that I watched while researching the subject matter of this book was a 2004 made-for-television movie called *Karate Dog*, which advertised itself as being about "a new breed of action hero!" (the Briard-like dog on the DVD case wears a martial arts headband and holds a police badge) whose voice is provided by comedian Chevy Chase. The uncredited dog, named Cho-Cho in the film, can speak English in addition to being able to do karate, so he and an LAPD "computer expert" (Simon Rex) go after the evil genius (Jon Voight) who has killed the dog's owner (Pat Morita). Cho-Cho also helps the human "hero" with his romantic troubles, and there are several other anthropomorphized dogs in the film who play in a band and dance.

That a film named *Karate Dog* would feature considerable amounts of CGI is not in itself surprising. CGI is now commonly employed in films of all kinds, with the precedent for digitizing animals, especially their "faces," set by the profitable film *Babe* (1995), in which both CGI and animatronics were used to make animals speak and move as realistically as possible. *Babe*'s director, Chris Noonan, has discussed the ways in which the border collies, for example, were trained and handled for the original film (Noonan 1999), and while there were a few techniques that seemed a bit inhumane to me—the instigation of a physical fight between two dogs playing "husband and wife," for example—there is nothing particularly onerous to a dog about being digitized. That is, developments like motion capture (mocap), in which data points are acquired through the use of special markers attached to the performer that are then used to create three-dimensional images in a computer, can be done using live-action footage as well, as was partially the case with *Babe*. Motion control, in which the movements of the camera are precisely regulated by computer, also enables repeated identical passes of the camera and can make a set appear to be peacefully populated by many normally incompatible animals when in reality they were each filmed separately. Animatronics or stop-motion photography can also be used to render "animal action," particularly dangerous stunts, such as when a dog is thrown, shaken, dropped, smashed, and so on (for more on all of these techniques see Finance and Zwerman 2010).[2]

So I was not offended, as others were according to outraged postings to Internet message boards, by the sloppy mismatching of live action and CGI in *Karate Dog* or the poor quality of the CGI in the dog's karate scenes, which mimic the slow-motion "bullet time" of the popular science fiction film *The Matrix* (1999). It is only aesthetically problematic that the clumsily rendered digital avatar of Cho-Cho bears little resemblance to the live dog that "stars" in the rest of the film. Practically, the major issue with CGI as a species of "VFX" (visual effects) is that it is expensive. While the price has dropped precipitously since it was used in *Babe*—when seven seconds of CGI in a shot cost around U.S.$50,000, according to Noonan (1999, 232–233)—it is still extremely expensive to render an entire CGI animal, although once certain elements are created (a talking dog's muzzle, say, or the basic figure of a kung-fu-fighting canine) they can be reused in other shots, and potentially even other films as long as the animals are similar enough.[3] If Cho-Cho suddenly appears to be a weirdly colored puppet with bad rayon hair rather than a real dog, then, it is partly because it was too costly to make him look like anything else.

But I *was* offended by the several scenes in *Karate Dog* that devolved from a subplot involving racing greyhounds, real ones, because I knew from experience the appalling conditions under which so many greyhounds live and die—discarded if

Images from a "making of" extra on the DVD of *Babe* (Chris Noonan, Universal, 1995). The first shows the markers used for mocap (motion capture), the others the real dog's muzzle and his digitized talking one. Digital frame enlargements.

they do not win races or are injured, sold to labs for research if they are not killed first or rescued by one of the many organizations that do their best to rehome retired track racers. What also froze me in my seat was a scene in which Cho-Cho is hanging from the ceiling so that he can insert a compact disk into a booby-trapped computer terminal in order to blow up a bunch of other computers. As the dog swings back and forth in a flimsy harness, he, or rather the voice of Chevy Chase, yells at the Simon Rex character to be careful and chastises him for doing such a bad job at getting him into position to insert the disk. But instead of Cho-Cho, I saw only the real dog, struggling violently in panic as he, or she, was swung back and forth high above the ground. *That* dog, like the greyhounds, could not talk, but it was speaking to me nonetheless (the film was apparently not monitored at all by the American Humane Association). In short, I did not see *enough* difference between the way the dogs were treated, at least part of the time, in *Karate Dog* and the "terribly uncomfortable" situations they must have endured in the Dogville Barkies.

A film's deployment of CGI, then, does not automatically ensure that dogs are always treated as well as they should be, although I am not at all suggesting that dogs, or other animals on the average studio set, are any longer whipped, burned, starved, trussed, wired to windlasses, and the like, as they might have been many decades ago, just to elicit a desired performance in the service of commercial entertainment (see Elwood 2010, 159). Dog training has come a long way since the days of Rin Tin Tin, the Barkies, and even of Lassie; according to the "making of" extras on many of the DVDs I watched, the majority of animal trainers who work in Hollywood employ reward-based shaped-response systems rather than punitive ones. The results of so-called "positive" training are better and faster and create animals that, generally speaking, look (because they usually are) eager to learn rather than cowed or fearful (except, of course, when they are narratively required, and shaped through training with treats or toys, to appear to be cowed or fearful). Humane concerns are certainly more visible now than they were in the classical studio era, and there is obviously a greater fealty paid to the power of regulation as well.

But as we stand here on the digital divide between live action and animation, the question is why we need real dogs at all in these films. As Stephen Prince writes in his book *Digital Visual Effects in Cinema: The Seduction of Reality* (2012), there is a constant tension in animated films between photorealism and exaggeration: "Exaggeration, as the Disney animators knew, provides a pathway not just for emotional expression but for establishing the credibility of a cartoon character. . . . It's the seven dwarfs in *Snow White* [1937] who come to life most vividly, not Snow White or her prince, who are composed more realistically and who were drawn from photostats of live actors who played the roles" (117). Photorealism "poses special challenges that caricature avoids. The caricatures expressed in the dwarfs—Grumpy's scowl and bulbous nose, Dopey's big ears—and their squash-and-stretch moves give them the illusion of life. Snow White, by contrast, moves according to realistic canons of behavior, and the natural contours of her face are less expressive than those of the dwarfs. She can't squash-and-stretch running down a staircase, as do the dwarfs, legs akimbo, noses bumping and thumping the steps" (117).

Moreover, digitally created photorealism runs the risk of sending characters over the cliff into what roboticist Mori Masahiro memorably named, in 1970, "the uncanny valley," which, in Prince's words, describes the point at which a robot (or, now, a digitized character, whether in a film or video game) crosses a "threshold . . . where the imitation becomes so close and exacting that its remaining incompleteness points to its status as a surrogate, as something not real, and this results in a loss of empathy from viewers, a pulling back, as what had seemed so familiar becomes defamiliarized" (Prince 2012, 121–122). Prince links the phenomenon of the uncanny valley to "the realization by Disney and Pixar animators that caricature provides an effective mode for expressing emotion and for eliciting audience participation in the narrative and the lives of the characters. . . . Digital characters whose stylization avoids photorealism are very effective at reaching audiences and have never fallen into the uncanny valley" (122).

Digitized dogs in live-action films, though, are "lifelike," as well as "photorealistic," yet they seem to leap safely across the uncanny valley. This may be because we have already engineered them, through selective breeding, to look somewhat but not precisely like human babies (a characteristic called neoteny, or "juvenilization") and because they assume so many varied shapes that many of them already look like caricatures or stuffed toys—see the Great Dane in *Marmaduke* (2010); the golden retrievers, adult and puppy, in all of the *Air Bud* films; Chihuahuas anywhere; the Dalmatians in all of their films; the Saint Bernards in the *Beethoven* franchise (1992, 1993, 2000, 2008); and so on. A digitized version of my own dog might well fall into the uncanny valley *for me*, but perhaps the strange disjunction of the "impossible" movements and unconvincing appearance of the CGI Cho-Cho, or the pole-climbing whirling-dervish Irish terrier in *Firehouse Dog* (2007), or the pack of almost-but-not-quite-realistic dancing dogs in the musical number at the end of *Marmaduke* (etc.) do not bother most of us because we always already understand dogs as both exaggerated and real, especially given the "family" audience (read children) that most of these films are marketed to.

What really seems to matter to us, what makes these films so popular and profitable (cable channels, "big-box" superstores, Internet sales sites like Amazon .com, rental and streaming outlets like Netflix, and the "family" video section of libraries are loaded with them), is that their dogs—their "real" dogs—understand their humans so perfectly, love them so unconditionally, and help them so profoundly both practically and spiritually, like angels (which indeed they sometimes play) or at least furry family therapists. But arguably the single most significant element in the popularity of these films is that, in many of them, the dogs literally speak. Dogs communicate with us constantly in our ordinary lives, too, but to understand what they are "saying" requires the ethological labor of observation and attention and interpretation, as Alexandra Horowitz points out in the previous essay in this volume. Not so in what has practically become its own subgenre, the "talking dog film" (see listal.com/movies/talking+dog).

Dancing in the dog park that is now for "all dogs"—the Great Dane Marmaduke, center, having realized that it doesn't matter if you're "pedigree or mutt"—in *Marmaduke* (Tom Dey, Twentieth Century–Fox, 2010). As can be seen, the CGI dogs do not look convincingly like the real ones who have performed in the rest of the film. Digital frame enlargement.

As Marjorie Garber writes in the chapter "Talking Dogs" in her book *Dog Love* (1996), even the most "intuitive" live-film dogs before the advent of computer animation rarely spoke; they "barked, whined, nudged, pointed, pushed, pulled, and generally shaped up their human charges, who were often reduced to feats of interpretation ('What, Lassie? What is it, girl? What are you trying to tell us?')" (83). Garber then points to movies like *Homeward Bound* (1993), *Look Who's Talking Now* (1993), and *Fluke* (1995) that feature "the ventriloquized voices of humans playing dogs" (102), with CGI providing muzzle movements to match the words issuing from the dogs themselves. Not all talking-dog films attempt to synchronize animal faces and dialogue; the speaking animals in the Australian film *Napoleon* (1995), discussed in Jane O'Sullivan's essay in this book, are filmed doing various things—in the case of the titular puppy running, playing, being startled by unfamiliar objects, interacting with other animals and so on—but their voices are not synchronized with facial movements of any kind.

A small child might have no difficulty with the mismatch between sound and image in the "unventriloquized" films, but it took a while for this adult, anyway, to get used to what comes across as a kind of telepathic communication not only from animal character to animal character but from animal to film spectator.[4] In fact, what Garber does not mention is that only rarely in talking-dog films can dogs communicate directly with the humans populating the story world. Much like a generic "integrated" Hollywood musical, in which characters sing and dance their emotions to music that does not have a diegetic source but that the film spectator hears clearly as well (and which are similarly utopian), only the audiences of talking-dog films have privileged access to the intraspecies and occasionally interspecies conversations (all of the nonhuman animals can understand one another) in the average feature, whether CGI or not.[5]

Garber proposes that the proliferation of the talking dog in mass media is a logical result of a wider interest in "social relations": "In an age when the conversation between men and women is analyzed in books . . . it is perhaps inevitable that inter-species conversation, between 'man' and his proverbial 'best friend,' has become fantasized and idealized" (85). The talking-dog film, therefore, speaks mainly about our need for dogs as such, and perhaps partly accounts for why we seem to require, with a few notable exceptions, that they be real rather than cartoon dogs. In my introduction I quoted Donna Haraway's strong condemnation of "lots of dangerous and unethical projection in the Western world that makes domestic canines into furry children" (Haraway 2008, 12), and I suggested that however much one agrees with her in principle, the ways that we represent dogs to ourselves, particularly in commercial mass media, are virtually always as a projection of some kind. And at least the drive to anthropomorphization of domestic animals like dogs need not disadvantage them in practical terms; as Haraway also points out, we tend to take better care of our animals once they are felt to be our "companions" as well.

Indeed, one can feel in much of the writing about the growth of "dog culture" in the United States and Europe over the past couple of decades the consternation of critics at just how close many of us have become to our canine "family members" (see Schaffer 2009; Homans 2012). Dogs are not, presumably, embarrassed by the canine birthday parties or graduations or weddings that their owners may host or drag them to; but they may be made physically uncomfortable by the various paraphernalia and settings created by what is obviously a gathering for and by people—perhaps just as uncomfortable as they would feel dangling from a ceiling in a harness. And it does seem clear that many of the films that establish themselves as "live action" still ask dogs to do things that are unpleasant experiences for them, and because dogs want to please us, they will either try to do them or can be "gently" forced to. The American Humane Association website (americanhumanefilmtv.org) provides a lot of detail about how this or that trick is accomplished, film by film: if a Chihuahua is pushed into a mud puddle as in *Beverly Hills Chihuahua* (2008), the mud is "made of filtered water and dye to make it look brown" and the dog "was dried off and rested after each take." If a dog appears to jump or be dropped from a great height as in *102 Dalmatians*, it is a CGI or animatronic "stunt dog" or a stuffed animal, never a real one. If it looks like lots and lots of dogs are running wildly down the street in *Hotel for Dogs* (2009), the dogs were actually filmed running in small batches thanks to motion control. But the website does not explain the hairless Chinese Crested shivering from fear, or cold, in a narrative context in which "she" is supposedly simply "excited!" in *Marmaduke* (2010); and no matter how "gently" a beagle is strapped to a contraption that artificially moves its arms and legs in front of a green screen so that it can be made to appear to fly in *Underdog* (2007), it is still probably a stressful physical situation for any dog.

Another disquieting issue is that, no less than was the case with several other dogs discussed in these pages (see Sara Ross and James Castonguay's essay on Asta), the narrativization of dogs as characters can make real dogs

One of the beagles shown in the contraption by which he or she is made to fly in *Underdog* (Frederik Du Chau, Disney, 2007). Digital frame enlargement from "making of" DVD extra.

interchangeable—the Chihuahuas who play Papi and Chloe in the *Beverly Hills Chihuahua* franchise vary from one film to the other and sometimes from scene to scene; there are several Great Danes playing Marmaduke; and, as one of the epigraphs above breezily points out, puppies do not remain puppies for very long—large-breed puppies, especially, grow very quickly—so if there are juvenile characters in a live-action film, they are only useful for a week or two before the shots no longer match and they have to "go," to be replaced by more puppies whose usefulness is also limited by basic canine biology. In 2007, newspapers reported that several very young puppies had died during the filming of *Snow Buddies* in Vancouver,[6] and awareness has been raised about the sheer numbers of dogs required for the "Buddies" films overall (the five juvenile characters, carefully calibrated by gender, are all played by golden retriever puppies, and there are assorted regular sidekicks played by other breeds) and where they might be coming from.[7] Although the AHA tries to make sure that animals are not obtained from puppy mills, as has been pointed out already the organization is not able to monitor all of the "dog and puppy action" given the sheer number of films that are produced for the direct-to-video "family" market, especially.

No number of appealing digitized canines, or the other fictionalized "real" dogs that this book has considered, can obscure the fact that dogs, in Western culture generally, still occupy an ambiguous place in our lives and entertainment. On the one hand, in Katherine Grier's words, "life with animals seems to offer contact with a particular kind of goodness that cannot be found elsewhere. Like our nineteenth-century predecessors, we still view pets as a force for good" (Grier 2006, 417). Yet, as Aaron Skabelund writes, the "valuation of dogs as essential companions [has also] led to their increased commodification as products that [can] be bought, sold, and thrown out" (Skabelund 2011, 182). In the United

States, he notes, "it is estimated that perhaps a third of dogs are abandoned or given up for adoption before they reach their second birthday, and half of those are euthanized. Indeed, on average, American households keep their pet dogs for only two years, and probably a third of its canine population dies in animal shelters" (186). Karla Armbruster also points to the paradox that "the popularity of fiction, movies, poems, and other stories about dogs in American culture often contrasts with the ways we treat actual dogs.... Analyzing examples of these popular narratives allows us to explore the ways they communicate powerful cultural messages about what it means to be a 'good dog,' along with what these messages suggest that we feel we owe to dogs, both good and bad, and why" (Armbruster 2002, 352; see also Malloy 2011, 10–11).[8] In the films we have discussed throughout this book, clearly good dogs are those who love and assist good, if sometimes entertainingly flawed, human beings, although who counts as human, and indeed who counts as dog, can vary across time and in different social and political contexts. Cultural contestations of the relative values of "cur" and "purebred" continue to wax and wane, connotations that can also accrue to human beings, as the discussions of Australian and South African cinema have shown.

Perhaps the ultimate paradox of the dog at the digital divide, then, is that these films are at once an indication of how profoundly we want and need dogs and how little we actually seem to be striving, in the narratives themselves, to comprehend them as a separate species. I fully understand the appeal of the anthropomorphized or talking dog, and of the stories of these films as well, in which dogs want nothing more than to help us and our children, to make us and our families whole; Michelle Superle calls these anthropomorphized dogs "*transforming substances*—both agents and catalysts that enable families to achieve a fuller humanity" (Superle 2012, 174). (They occasionally also save the universe.) The extraordinary lure of such films and dogs is to suggest that dogs *do*, as we hope and dream is the case, love us unconditionally, and that if they *could* talk, it would never be to criticize or hurt us, although we might well have to endure a lot of poop jokes (many of these films are rated PG for "rude humor"). And although real canines have no interest in monogamy or family life beyond weaning, talking dogs all share "our" family values: "married" parents Papi and Chloe in *Beverly Hills Chihuahua 3* (2012) worry about their children and their education ("I don't like what the pups are learning at school, like polo. These are not good Chihuahua values") and assiduously instruct them in the ways of the world (like how to read "p[ee]-mail"), just like we do with our own children.

But given the fact that we treat dogs like children and also have few qualms about discarding dogs when they fail to act like human beings—James Serpell writes that the "performance of nonanthropomorphic behavior by pets is . . . a frequent excuse to get rid of them," and if "there is a mismatch or incompatibility between an animal's behavior and its owner's anthropomorphic expectations, the animal risks either being punished and abused for its perceived 'misbehavior' or being disposed of" (Serpell 2005, 131)—how do these films encourage

Top, Papi and Chloe's "wedding," which begins *Beverly Hills Chihuahua 2* (Alex Zamm, Disney, 2011). Below, their unhappy "children" in a mud hole at the bottom of a slide. Digital frame enlargements.

children themselves, if not their parents, to see and to think about dogs as they really are; to heed the significance of *both* terms in the label "companion animal"?[9] Marjorie Garber writes,

> If the dog somehow stands for a human fantasy of communication, the nature of that fantasy is far from simple. Opaque and transparent, other and same, talking and mute, the dog stands in for the very complexity of human desire. Like the approval-conveying maternal face beaming at an infant, the dog offers us nonjudgmental recognition. Like the new baby, dogs offer us their needs and their bodies. With them we can innocently regress—we can babble, handle excrement, express affection. But we can also be master, dominate, require submission. The fantasy of the talking dog provides an object lesson in the pleasures and dangers of projection. (Garber 1996, 116–117)

Is it "progress," then, that the DVD version of the 2000 Disney live-action *102 Dalmatians* contains an "extra" called "Dalmatians 101—How to Pick a Dog That Fits Your Personality," presumably meant to prevent the impulsive adoption and subsequent discard of Dalmatian puppies (for which previous Disney films had been held responsible) who bear little more than a visual resemblance to the dogs in the film? On the one hand, the narrator says, "Sure they're cute, but under those spots they're tightly wound springs," "Choose a furry friend carefully," "Get the facts about your favorite dog," and if you must have one, "find an experienced breeder." But on the other hand, the narrator is a partly digitized parrot, "Waddlesworth," a character in the film itself (who thinks he's a dog), and the extra is buried on the second page of the DVD's "bonus material" and is less than two minutes long. (It is far more likely that "Dalmatians 101" was produced to insulate the studio against criticism for having misrepresented the breed as cute and cuddly for so long rather than as a demonstration of humane concern as such.)

In the end the anthropomorphization of the dogs in the "Dogville Barkies" and of all of the digitized dogs that surround us now—in games as well; there is already a website devoted to the "Top 10 Video Game Dogs" (1up.com/features/top-10-video-game-dogs), and one can take care of and train digitized "best friends" too ("Each version of Nintendogs comes with six breeds to choose from, and you can unlock additional breeds by playing with other owners through wireless gameplay!")—is marked more by difference than similarity. Narratively, films like the Barkies have little to do with dogs and their relationship to us, because there are no humans in their world—the shorts are a curiosity, a trick, fascinating and bizarre and clever. The more recent films seem instead to be a chronologically closer point on a line that leads from hero dogs like Rin Tin Tin and Lassie and Benji through sidekicks like Asta and Uggie, in which the dogs grow ever more about us (most of the films end happily, too) even as lip service is paid to some of their nonhuman or at least less appealing canine proclivities (they tear things up, sniff butts, drool, etc.). But the question that remains is whether poop jokes signify an understanding of, and respect for, the dog's essential otherness or are simply film-doggy versions of tropes derived from the conventions of the still-lucrative "gross-out" or aptly named "animal comedy" subgenres.

This book has been about the ways that we use dogs and stories featuring them to think about ourselves and what we value—but again, as Jonathan Safran Foer puts it, "the way animal lives matter is always complicated by how we use animals to shape the landscape of our humanity, both materially and imaginatively" (quoted in Gross and Vallely 2012, ix). The essays have also thus worked to show that if we can never "be" a dog or understand the world as a dog does, we can at least use the photographic record of the many doggy bodies with which we have told our stories to try to understand what those bodies are also "saying," even now—about how they were feeling, how they had been trained, what this or that breed looked like at a moment in time, what it might have been like to serve simultaneously as an agent and as a prop or object. One fact is clear: as long as there are dogs and films, there will always be cinematic canines, and they will continue to interact with our notions about what the dogs we live with are and should be and to affect our ethical responsibilities toward them. The wonderful, soul-squeezing truth is that dogs will always want to be in our company, just as they have for thousands of years, and thus we will always put them in the stories we tell to and about ourselves.

But unless the Academy of Motion Picture Arts and Sciences begins to manufacture its statuettes out of rawhide or liver or to stuff them with squeakers, dogs will never, ever, care about winning Oscars.

The volume editor's "small mix" dog watching Asta in *After the Thin Man* (W. S. Van Dyke, MGM, 1936). High-definition television has made it easy for dogs and cats to respond to animals as such on the television screen, although they usually lose interest once they learn that the representations lack other markers of liveness, such as smell.

Notes

1. A partial list of these films would include *Homeward Bound* (1993), *Look Who's Talking Now* (1993), and *Fluke* (1995); *101 Dalmatians* (1996) and *102 Dalmatians* (2000); *Doctor Dolittle* (1998), *Doctor Dolittle 2* (2001), *Dr. Dolittle 3* (2006), *Dr. Dolittle: Tail to the Chief* (2008), and *Dr. Dolittle: Million Dollar Mutts* (2009); the three *Beverly Hills Chihuahua* films (2008, 2011, 2012); the two *Cats and Dogs* entries (2001, 2010); the five films in the *Air Bud* series (1997, 1998, 2000, 2002, 2003) and its six spin-off "Buddies" films *Air Buddies* (2006), *Snow Buddies* (2008), *Space Buddies* (2009), *Santa Buddies* (2009), *Spooky Buddies* (2011), and *Treasure Buddies* (2012)—with another, *Super Buddies*, scheduled for release in 2013; *Men in Black II* (2002), *Snow Dogs* (2002), *Good Boy!* (2003), *Bailey's Billions* (2005), *Charlotte's Web* (2006), *Underdog* (2007), *Firehouse Dog* (2007), *Hotel for Dogs* (2009), *Marmaduke* (2010), and *Marley & Me: The Puppy Years* (2011). Some of these films feature extensive product placement—*Hotel for Dogs* for Pedigree dog food, *Marmaduke* for Petco, for example.

   However, my focus on live-action and CGI is not to say that all cartoon dogs are cute; see the conventionally animated film *My Dog Tulip* (2009), based on the 1956 book by J. R. Ackerley, which, as Mikita Brottman put it, was probably not nominated for the Palm Dog because its dog was "too real for comfort" rather than being "cheaply sentimental" like those of so many other dog films ("A Dog Film That's Actually About a Dog," *Chronicle of Higher Education*, November 19, 2010, B16). See also the short *Dog* (2001), a stop-motion film in which the old and ill dog of a young boy who has just lost his mother is killed by the boy's father to stop the dog's suffering; the film implies that the mother may have been similarly dispatched by the father as well.

2. Interestingly, dog animatronics do not work well in close-up or to create fully expressive canine characters. In Chris Noonan's words, "Where animatronics didn't work for us [in *Babe*] were with the dogs. . . . I think the reason they didn't work is because we know dogs so well. . . . We are so very attuned to reading dogs' faces that . . . no matter how brilliantly you've made its eyes or mouth to mimic a real dog's, after a certain time on-screen you can pick it as an inanimate object" (Noonan 1999, 240).

3. Actual figures are hard to come by, but according to "Indies Blow Up Filmmaking with CGI" (studio360.org/2012/jun/22/indie-film-cgi/), "As technology drops in price, computer-generated imagery (CGI) is trickling down, and low-budget films now have an opportunity to compete with Hollywood on its own turf." According to Cosmas Demetriou (personal communication), who works in the industry, a digital version of a dog muzzle in something like a "Buddies" film would likely now cost around $15,000, and to animate it $7,000 to $10,000 per shot. But the cost could then be amortized across the film and, potentially, other films as well. This means that the purchase or rental of multitudes of golden retriever puppies for a "Buddies" film might be one of the cheaper items in the budget and thus a factor in the continuing use of live dogs in these films. The website thenumbers.com puts the profits for *Santa Buddies* so far at close to $45 million in DVD sales, with the others ranging from $16 million (for the newest, which has not been out for as long) to $38 million each; production costs are not available, but the fact that new films are still being produced suggests that the franchise remains profitable.

4. In addition to *Napoleon* see *The Dog Who Saved Christmas* (2009), *The Dog Who Saved Christmas Vacation* (2010), *The Dog Who Saved Halloween* (2011), *The Dog Who Saved the Holidays* (2012), or *The Adventures of Bailey: The Lost Puppy* (2011).

5. As of this writing, a couple of interesting variations on the "talking dog" formula have appeared. In the comedy/drama *Beginners* (2010), starring Ewan McGregor

and Christopher Plummer, the Jack Russell terrier Arthur (played by a dog named Cosmo) appears to communicate telepathically through subtitles with the McGregor character. And in the wordless Oscar-nominated animated short *Adam and Dog* (2011), which dramatizes the introduction of man and dog in the Garden of Eden, Adam learns to bark rather than the other way around. There is, confusingly, only one dog in the Garden of Eden; at the end of the film, when Adam and Eve are expelled from it, the dog willingly follows them out into the desert, the implication being that dogs value their relationships with humans over all other things. How that single dog begat a species is left unaddressed.

6. See goldenretrieverforum.com/golden-retrievers-main-discussion/13813-snow-buddies-movie-golden-puppies-die.html. See also "Hollywood Dog Movies: Very Bad for the Dogs," thepoodleanddogblog.typepad.com/the_poodle_and_dog_blog/2006/04/hollywood_dog_m.html ("Expecting a puppy to behave like a dog in the movies is like expecting the birds and squirrels to help you pitch a tent when you go camping in the woods").

7. The puppy characters—Budderball, Rosebud, Buddha, Mudbud, and B-Dawg—all have gender-proper yet politically correct "likes" and "dislikes" that can be found enumerated on the Disney "Buddies" website (see disney.go.com/disneyvideos/liveaction/buddies/#/home) along with links to purchase DVDs and related merchandise. Despite the construction of the characters as distinct from one another, these films do not search for or feature what Susan McHugh calls "dogs as isolated individuals—the canine 'star' or charismatic breed dog" (McHugh 2004, 170), but rather depend upon them as interchangeable canine types. Along the same lines, twenty-two yellow labs all played the same "lovable bad dog" Marley in *Marley & Me* (2008).

8. As Michael Schaffer notes, the attention that is paid to pets is felt by some to be immoral given the continued suffering of people around the world, but he argues that it is ultimately a "consumer choice": "No one starts talking about third-world starvation when someone spends $3,000 on a flat-screen TV. . . . If we're going to start enumerating immoral consumer choices, I'd argue that spending money to care for a pet would rank near the bottom of the list. . . . For whatever reason," he continues, "it is spending on pets—more often than purchases of new televisions or donations to art museums—that prompts soul-searching about affluence and want. I suspect the contrasts will grow in the next few years" (255–257).

9. Karla Armbruster also notes that most dogs "are given up because they become inconvenient due to changes in their human companions' life circumstances or to minor behavior problems that could readily be addressed through obedience training rather than because of major, insoluble issues such as deep-seated aggression" (Armbruster 2002, 352). There is little basic dog training shown ever in commercial films—and when a trainer does appear, he or she is too often a figure of ridicule; see, for example, the one played by Kathleen Turner in *Marley & Me*. The lack of attention to training and behavior occurs in interesting conjunction with popular reality television series that are devoted to "correcting" issues caused for families by "problem dogs"; see the shows starring Cesar Millan (*The Dog Whisperer*, 2004–2012; *Leader of the Pack*, 2013–present) or Victoria Stillwell (*It's Me or the Dog*, 2005–present).

Works Cited

Popular magazines, newspapers, and other primary or archival materials, including websites, are cited in the text or notes of individual essays. All websites were accessible as of June 2013.

Allred, Alexandra Powe. 2004. *Dogs' Most Wanted: The Top 10 Book of Historic Hounds, Professional Pooches, and Canine Oddities.* Dulles, Va.: Brassey's.

Andrew Crispo Gallery. 1975. *Edward Hicks: A Gentle Spirit.* New York: Andrew Crispo Gallery.

Arluke, Arnold, and Clinton R. Sanders. 1996. *Regarding Animals.* Philadelphia: Temple University Press.

Armbruster, Karla. 2002. "'Good Dog': The Stories We Tell About Our Canine Companions and What They Mean for Humans and Other Animals." *Papers on Language and Literature* 38 (4): 351–376.

Armstrong, Philip. 2008. *What Animals Mean in the Fiction of Modernity.* Oxford: Routledge.

Attridge, Derek. 2000. "Age of Bronze, State of Grace: Music and Dogs in Coetzee's *Disgrace.*" *Novel* 34 (1): 98–121.

Baker, Steve. 2001. *Picturing the Beast: Animals, Identity, and Representation.* Urbana: University of Illinois Press.

Balio, Tino. 1996. *Grand Design: Hollywood as a Modern Business Enterprise, 1930–1939.* Berkeley: University of California Press.

Barr, Charles. 1999. *English Hitchcock.* Moffat, U.K.: Cameron and Hollis.

Barthes, Roland. 1986. *The Rustle of Language.* Translated by Richard Howard. Oxford: Blackwell.

Basinger, Jeanine. 2000. *Silent Stars.* New York: Knopf.

Bateson, Gregory A. 1972. *Steps to an Ecology of Mind.* New York: Ballantine.

Baynton, Barbara. (1902) 1976. "The Squeaker's Mate." In *The Penguin Book of Australian Short Stories,* edited by Harry Heseltine, 63–77. Harmondsworth, Middlesex: Penguin.

Beauregard, Robert A. 2006. *When America Became Suburban.* Minneapolis: University of Minnesota Press.

Beck, Ken, and Jim Clark. 2002. *The Encyclopedia of TV Pets: A Complete History of Television's Greatest Animal Stars.* Nashville: Rutledge Hill Press.

Beers, Diane L. 2006. *For the Prevention of Cruelty: The History and Legacy of Animal Rights Activism in the United States*. Athens: Ohio University Press.

Bekoff, Marc. 1972. "The Development of Social Interaction, Play, and Metacommunication in Mammals: An Ethological Perspective." *Quarterly Review of Biology* 47 (4): 412–434.

Bekoff, Marc, and Colin Allen. 1998. "Intentional Communication and Social Play: How and Why Animals Negotiate and Agree to Play." In *Animal Play: Evolutionary, Comparative, and Ecological Perspectives*, edited by Marc Bekoff and John Byers, 97–114. Cambridge: Cambridge University Press.

Bodnar, John. 2004. "*Saving Private Ryan* and Postwar Memory in America." In *The World War Two Reader*, edited by Gordon Martel, 435–448. London: Routledge.

Boone, J. Allen. (1939) 2007. *Letters to Strongheart*. Whitefish, Mont.: Kessinger.

———. (1954) 1976. *Kinship with All Life*. New York: Harper and Row.

Bowers, Q. David. 1997. *Thanhouser Films: An Encyclopedia and History*. Portland, Ore.: Thanhouser Film Associates. CD-ROM.

Brabazon, Tara. 2001. "A Pig in Space? *Babe* and the Problem of Landscape." In *Australian Cinema in the 1990s*, edited by Ian Craven, 149–158. London: Frank Cass.

Brown, Laura. 2010. *Homeless Dogs and Melancholy Apes: Humans and Other Animals in the Modern Literary Imagination*. Ithaca, N.Y.: Cornell University Press.

Brown, Susan M. 1993. "Foreword: A Charismatic Collie and Her Fifty-Year Influence." In *Lassie: A Collie and Her Influence*, edited by Susan M. Brown, 1–5. St. Louis, Mo.: Dog Museum.

Bryant, Roger. 2006. *William Powell: The Life and Films*. Jefferson, N.C.: McFarland.

Burt, Jonathan. 2002. *Animals in Film*. London: Reaktion.

Byrd, Richard E. 1931. *Little America: Aerial Exploration in the Antarctic and the Flight to the South Pole*. London: Putnam.

Campbell, John W. [as Don A. Stuart]. 1938. "Who Goes There?" *Astounding Science-Fiction* (August): 60–97.

Castonguay, James. 2011. "Myrna Loy and William Powell: The Perfect Screen Couple." In *Glamour in a Golden Age: Movie Stars of the 1930s*, edited by Adrienne L. McLean, 220–244. New Brunswick, N.J.: Rutgers University Press.

Coetzee, J. M. 1999. *Disgrace*. New York: Viking.

———. 1999. *Lives of Animals*. Princeton, N.J.: Princeton University Press.

Collins, Ace. 1993. *Lassie: A Dog's Life*. New York: Penguin.

Coode, Thomas H., and John F. Bauman. 1981. *People, Poverty, and Politics: Pennsylvanians During the Great Depression*. East Brunswick, N.J.: Associated University Presses.

Cooper, Jackie, with Dick Kleiner. 1981. *Please Don't Shoot My Dog: The Autobiography of Jackie Cooper*. New York: William Morrow.

Coren, Stanley. 1994. *The Intelligence of Dogs: Canine Consciousness and Capabilities*. New York: Free Press.

———. 2000. *How to Speak Dog: Mastering the Art of Dog-Human Communication*. New York: Simon and Schuster.

———. 2002. *The Pawprints of History: Dogs and the Course of Human Events*. New York: Free Press.

———. 2012. *Do Dogs Dream? Nearly Everything Your Dog Wants to Know*. New York: Norton.

Darwin, Charles. (1871) 2004. *The Descent of Man*. London: Penguin.

deCordova, Richard. 1991. "The Emergence of the Star System in America." In *Stardom: Industry of Desire*, edited by Christine Gledhill, 17–29. New York: Routledge.

Dekoven, Marianne. 2009. "Going to the Dogs in *Disgrace*." *ELH* 76: 847–875.

DeMello, Margo, ed. 2010. *Teaching the Animal: Human-Animal Studies Across the Disciplines*. New York: Lantern.

Dermody, Susan, and Elizabeth Jacka, eds. 1988. *The Screening of Australia: An Anatomy of a National Cinema*. Vol. 2. Paddington, N.S.W., Australia: Currency Press.

Derr, Mark. 1997. *Dog's Best Friend: Annals of the Dog-Human Relationship*. New York: Henry Holt.

———. 2004. *A Dog's History of America: How Our Best Friend Explored, Conquered, and Settled a Continent*. New York: North Point Press, 2004.

Derrida, Jacques. (1997) 2003. "And Say the Animal Responded?" Translated by David Wills. In *Zootologies: The Question of the Animal*, edited by Cary Wolfe, 121–146. Minneapolis: University of Minnesota Press.

Doherty, Thomas. 1993. *Projections of War: Hollywood, American Culture, and World War II*. New York: Columbia University Press.

Donovan, Josephine. 2004. "'Miracles of Creation': Animals in J. M. Coetzee's Work." *Michigan Quarterly Review* 43 (1): 78–93.

Doyle, Arthur Conan. (1892) 2002. "Silver Blaze." In *The Adventures and Memoirs of Sherlock Holmes*. New York: Random House.

Du Toit, Andries. 2009. "Lost in Africa: *Disgrace*, Whiteness, and the Fear of Desire." *A Subtle Knife: Reflections on Myth, Politics, and Desire*. Weblog, September 17, asubtleknife .wordpress.com/2009/09/17/lost-in-africa-disgrace-whiteness-and-the-fear-of-desire.

Dyer, Richard. 1998. *Stars*. London: British Film Institute.

———. 2000. "Heavenly Bodies: Film Stars and Society." In *Film and Theory*, edited by Robert Stam and Toby Miller, 603–617. Oxford: Blackwell.

Edelson, Edward. 1980. *Great Animals of the Movies*. Garden City, N.Y.: Doubleday.

Edmonds, Andy. 1991. *Frame-Up!* New York: William Morrow.

Elwood, Ann. 2010. *Rin-Tin-Tin: The Movie Star*. Lexington, Ky.: CreateSpace.

Enker, Debi. 1994. "Australia and the Australians." In *Australian Cinema*, edited by Scott Murray, 210–225. St. Leonards, N.S.W., Australia: Allen and Unwin.

Finance, Charles, and Susan Zwerman. 2010. *The Visual Effects Producer: Understanding the Art and Business of VFX*. New York: Focal Press.

FitzPatrick, Percy. 1907. *Jock of the Bushveld*. New York: Longmans, Green.

Franklin, Adrian. 1999. *Animals and Modern Cultures: A Sociology of Human-Animal Relations in Modernity*. New York: Sage.

Fudge, Erica. 2002. "A Left-Handed Blow: Writing the History of Animals." In *Representing Animals*, edited by Nigel Rothfels, 3–18. Bloomington: Indiana University Press.

Gallo, Joe. 2000. "Flashback: New England Director Larry Trimble." imaginenews.com/ Archive/2000/MAR_2000/Text/FEAT06.htm.

Garber, Marjorie. 1996. *Dog Love*. New York: Touchstone/Simon and Schuster.

Gehring, Wes D. 2002. *Romantic vs. Screwball Comedy: Charting the Difference*. Metuchen, N.J.: Scarecrow.

Gelman, Rita Golden. 1980. *Joe Camp's Benji at Work: America's Most Huggable Hero*. New York: Scholastic.

Gibson, Ross. 1994. "Formative Landscapes." In *Australian Cinema*, edited by Scott Murray, 44–59. St. Leonards, N.S.W., Australia: Allen and Unwin.

Goldsworthy, Kerryn. (1986) 1997. "Martyr to Her Sex." In *The Oxford Book of Australian Essays*, edited by Imre Salusinszki, 258–262. Melbourne: Oxford University Press.

Gray, Stephen. 1987. "Domesticating the Wilds: J. Percy FitzPatrick's *Jock of the Bushveld* as a Historical Record for Children." *English in Africa* 14 (October): 1–14.

Grier, Katherine C. 2006. *Pets in America: A History*. New York: Harcourt.

Grogan, John. 2005. *Marley & Me: Life and Love with the World's Worst Dog*. New York: HarperCollins.

Gross, Aaron, and Anne Vallely, eds. 2012. *Animals and the Human Imagination: A Companion to Animal Studies*. New York: Columbia University Press.

Gunning, Tom. 2003. "The Exterior as *Intérieur*: Benjamin's Optical Detective." *boundary 2* 30 (1): 105–129.

Haraway, Donna J. 1992. "The Promises of Monsters: A Regenerative Politics for Inappropriate/d Others." In *Cultural Studies*, edited by Lawrence Grossberg, Cary Nelson, and Paula A. Treichler, 295–337. New York: Routledge.

———. 2003. *The Companion Species Manifesto: Dogs, People, and Significant Otherness*. Chicago. Prickly Paradigm.

———. 2008. *When Species Meet*. Minneapolis: University of Minnesota Press.

Hare, Brian, and Vanessa Woods. 2013. *The Genius of Dogs: How Dogs Are Smarter Than You Think*. New York: Dutton.

Harel, Naama. 2009. "The Animal Voice Behind the Fable." *Journal for Critical Animal Studies* 7 (2): 8–20.

Harris, Thomas. 1991. "The Building of Popular Images: Grace Kelly and Marilyn Monroe." In *Stardom: Industry of Desire*, edited by Christine Gledhill, 40–44. New York: Routledge.

Harvey, James. 1987. *Romantic Comedy in Hollywood, from Lubitsch to Sturges*. New York: Knopf.

Headland, Robert K. 2012. "History of Exotic Terrestrial Mammals in Antarctic Regions." *Polar Record* 48 (2): 123–144.

Hediger, Heini K. P. 1981. "The Clever Hans Phenomenon from an Animal Psychologist's Point of View." In *The Clever Hans Phenomenon: Communication with Horses, Whales, Apes, and People*, edited by Thomas A. Sebeok and Robert Rosenthal, 1–17. New York: New York Academy of Sciences.

Herron, Tom. 2005. "The Dog Man: Becoming Animal in Coetzee's *Disgrace*." *Twentieth-Century Literature* 51 (4): 467–490.

High, Peter B. 2003. *The Imperial Screen: Japanese Film Culture in the Fifteen Years' War, 1931–1945*. Madison: University of Wisconsin Press.

Hjort, Mette, ed. 2012. *Film and Risk*. Detroit: Wayne State University Press.

Homans, John. 2012. *What's a Dog For? The Surprising History, Science, Philosophy, and Politics of Man's Best Friend*. New York: Penguin.

Hopwood, Jon C. n.d. "Teddy the Wonder Dog: Pooch Was Silent Film Star at Mack Sennett's Keystone Studio." voices.yahoo.com/teddy-wonder-dog-pooch-was-silent-film-star-at-5901730.html?cat=40.

Horowitz, Alexandra C. 2009a. *Inside of a Dog: What Dogs See, Smell, and Know*. New York: Scribner.

———. 2009b. "Attention to Attention in Domestic Dog (*Canis familiaris*) Dyadic Play." *Animal Cognition* 12: 107–118.

———. 2009c. "Disambiguating the 'Guilty Look': Salient Prompts to a Familiar Dog Behaviour." *Behavioural Processes* 81: 447–452.

———. 2012. "Fair Is Fine, but More Is Better: Limits to Inequity Aversion in the Domestic Dog." *Social Justice Research* 25 (2): 195–212.

Horowitz, Alexandra C., and Marc Bekoff. 2007. "Naturalizing Anthropomorphism: Behavioral Prompts to Our Humanizing of Animals." *Anthrozoös* 20 (1): 23–35.

Howe, Adrian, ed. 2005. *Lindy Chamberlain Revisited: A 25th Anniversary Retrospective*. Sydney: Southwood.

Jenkins, Henry. 2007. "Her Suffering Aristocratic Majesty: The Sentimental Value of Lassie."

In *The Wow Climax: Tracing the Emotional Impact of Popular Culture*, 215–245. New York: New York University Press.

Keil, Charlie, and Ben Singer, eds. 2009. *American Cinema of the 1910s: Themes and Variations*. New Brunswick, N.J.: Rutgers University Press.

Kelch, William J. 1982. "Canine Soldiers." *Military Review* 62 (October): 32–41.

Kete, Kathleen. 1994. *The Beast in the Boudoir: Petkeeping in Nineteenth-Century Paris*. Berkeley: University of California Press.

Kikuchi, Toru, and Taiichi Kitamura. 1960. "Management of Sledge-Dogs and Journeys with Them During the First Wintering (Feb. 1957–Feb. 1958), the Japanese Antarctic Research Expedition." *Antarctic Record* 9: 55–90.

King, Rob. 2009. *The Fun Factory: The Keystone Company and the Emergence of Mass Culture*. Berkeley: University of California Press.

———. 2011. "Roscoe 'Fatty' Arbuckle: Comedy's Starring Scapegoat." In *Flickers of Desire: Movie Stars of the 1910s*, edited by Jennifer M. Bean, 196–217. New Brunswick, N.J.: Rutgers University Press.

Koppes, Clayton R., and Gregory D. Black. 1987. *Hollywood Goes to War: How Politics, Profits, and Propaganda Shaped World War II Movies*. Berkeley: University of California Press.

Krapp, Peter. 2008. "Polar Media." *Information, Communication & Society* 11 (6): 831–845.

Krohn, Bill. 2000. *Hitchcock at Work*. London: Phaidon.

Laham, Nicholas. 2009. *Currents of Comedy on the American Screen: How Film and Television Deliver Different Laughs for Changing Times*. Jefferson, N.C.: McFarland.

Laqueur, Thomas W. 2010. "What Do Dogs Do in Western Art?" Paper presented at the meeting "Dogs, Humans, and Other Animals: A Conversation." Berkeley, California, June 24–26.

Lawson, Henry. (1892) 1973. "The Drover's Wife." In *Henry Lawson's Best Stories*, edited by Cecil Mann, 1–8. Sydney: Angus and Robertson.

———. (1901) 1973. "The Loaded Dog." In *Henry Lawson's Best Stories*, edited by Cecil Mann, 9–15. Sydney: Angus and Robertson.

Leane, Elizabeth, and Helen Tiffin. 2011. "Dogs, Meat and Douglas Mawson." *Australian Humanities Review* 51: australianhumanitiesreview.org/archive/Issue-November-2011/leane&tiffin.html.

Leider, Emily W. 2004. *Dark Lover: The Life and Death of Rudolph Valentino*. New York: Faber and Faber.

———. 2012. *Myrna Loy: The Only Good Girl in Hollywood*. Berkeley: University of California Press.

Levin, Martin, ed. 1970. *Hollywood and the Great Fan Magazines*. New York: Arbor House.

Lippit, Akira Mizuta. 2000. *Electric Animal: Toward a Rhetoric of Wildlife*. Minneapolis: University of Minnesota Press.

Madigan, Cecil. 1913. "Our Dogs." In *The Adelie Blizzard*, edited by Archie McLean, 143–147. Adelaide: Mawson Centre, Australian Polar Collection, South Australian Museum. 184AAE item 4.

Malloy, Claire. 2011. *Popular Media and Animals*. New York: Palgrave Macmillan.

Marcus, Julie. (1989) 2005. "Prisoner of Discourse: The Dingo, the Dog, and the Baby." *Anthropology Today* 5 (3): 15–19. In *Lindy Chamberlain Revisited: A 25th Anniversary Retrospective*, edited by Adrian Howe, 201–219. Sydney: Southwood.

Marshall, P. David. 1997. *Celebrity and Power: Fame in Contemporary Culture*. Minneapolis: University of Minnesota Press.

Matsuda, T. 1980. "Survival of *Sakhalin* Dogs." *Kyokuchi* 31: 49–52.

Mayer, Geoff. 1999. "*Dusty*." In *The Oxford Companion to Australian Film*, edited by Brian

McFarlane, Geoff Mayer, and Ina Bertrand, 122–123. South Melbourne: Oxford University Press.

McGreevy, Paul, T. D. Grassi, and Andrew M. Harman. 2004. "A Strong Correlation Exists Between the Distribution of Retinal Ganglion Cells and Nose Length in the Dog." *Brain, Behavior, and Evolution* 63 (1): 13–22.

McHugh, Susan. 2002. "Bringing Up *Babe*." *Camera Obscura* 17 (1.49): 149–187.

———. 2004. *Dog*. London: Reaktion.

———. 2011. *Animal Stories: Narrating Across Species Lines*. Minneapolis: University of Minnesota Press.

McKenzie, Kirsten. 2003. "Dogs and the Public Sphere: The Ordering of Social Space in Early Nineteenth-Century Cape Town." *South African Historical Journal* 48 (1): 235–251.

McLaughlin, Robert L., and Sally E. Parry. 2006. *We'll Always Have the Movies: American Cinema During World War II*. Lexington: University Press of Kentucky.

McLean, Adrienne L. 2009. "Putting 'Em Down Like a Man: Eleanor Powell and the Spectacle of Competence." In *Hetero: Queering Representations of Straightness*, edited by Sean Griffin, 89–110. Albany: SUNY Press.

Mithen, Steven J. 1996. *The Prehistory of the Mind: The Cognitive Origins of Art, Religion and Science*. London: Thames and Hudson.

Moran, Albert, and Errol Nieth. 2000. *Film in Australia: An Introduction*. Melbourne: Cambridge University Press.

Morell, Virginia. 2013. *Animal Wise: The Thoughts and Emotions of Our Fellow Creatures*. New York: Crown.

Mosley, Leonard. 1984. *Zanuck: The Rise and Fall of Hollywood's Last Tycoon*. Boston: Little, Brown.

Murray, Scott. 1994. "Australian Cinema in the 1970s and 1980s." In *Australian Cinema*, edited by Scott Murray, 70–146. St. Leonards, N.S.W., Australia: Allen and Unwin.

Musser, Charles. 2004. "The Changing Status of the Actor." In *Movie Acting: The Film Reader*, edited by Pamela Robertson Wojcik, 51–58. New York: Routledge.

Muszynski, Julie. 2007. *The Red Book of Dogs: Hounds, Terriers, Toys*. New York: Collins Design.

Naremore, James. 1988. *Acting in the Cinema*. Berkeley: University of California Press.

Naylor, Leonard E. 1932. *The Modern Wire Haired Fox Terrier: Its History, Points & Training*. London: H. F. & G. Witherby [Kindle edition].

Ndebele, Njabulo S. 2007. "The Year of the Dog: A Journey of the Imagination." In *Fine Lines from the Box*. Roggebaai, South Africa: Umuzi. njabulondebele.co.za/images/uploads/The_Year_of_the_Dog_dun.pdf.

Neale, Steve, and Frank Krutnik. 1990. *Popular Film and Television Comedy*. New York: Routledge.

Neibaur, James L. 2007. *Arbuckle and Keaton: Their 14 Film Collaborations*. Jefferson, N.C.: McFarland.

Noonan, Chris. 1999. "Makin' Bacon." In *Second Take: Australian Film-Makers Talk*, edited by Raffaele Caputo and Geoff Burton, 219–250. St. Leonards, N.S.W., Australia: Allen and Unwin.

Oderman, Stuart. 1994. *Roscoe "Fatty" Arbuckle*. Jefferson, N.C.: McFarland.

Onion, Rebecca. 2009. "Sled Dogs of the American North: On Masculinity, Whiteness, and Human Freedom." In *Animals and Agency: An Interdisciplinary Exploration*, edited by Sarah E. McFarland and Ryan Hediger, 129–155. Leiden: Brill.

O'Regan, Tom. 1996. *Australian National Cinema*. London: Routledge.

Orlean, Susan. 2011. *Rin Tin Tin: The Life and the Legend*. New York: Simon and Schuster.

Orr, Gertrude. 1936. *Dog Stars of Hollywood*. New York: Saalfield.

Ōtsuka, Eiji. 2008. "Disarming Atom: Tezuka Osamu's Manga at War and Peace." Translated by Thomas Lamarre. *Mechademia* 3: 111–126.

Painter, Deborah. 2008. *Hollywood's Top Dogs: The Dog Hero in Film*. New York: Midnight Marquee.

Pearson, Roberta. 1992. *Eloquent Gestures: The Transformation of Performance Style in the Griffith Biograph Films*. Berkeley: University of California Press.

Pick, Anat. 2011. *Creaturely Poetics: Animality and Vulnerability in Literature and Film*. New York: Columbia University Press.

Pierce, Peter. 1999. *The Country of Lost Children: An Australian Anxiety*. Cambridge: Cambridge University Press.

Pike, Andrew, and Ross Cooper. 1998. *Australian Film, 1900–1977: A Guide to Feature Film Production*. Rev. ed. Melbourne: Oxford University Press.

Pomerance, Murray. 2000–2001. "Two Bits for Hitch: Small Performances and Gross Structure in *The Man Who Knew Too Much* (1956)." *Hitchcock Annual* 9: 127–145.

———. 2006. "Animal Actors." In *The Schirmer Encyclopedia of Film*. Edited by Barry Keith Grant. Vol. 1, *Academy Awards—Crime Films*, 79–84. Detroit: Thomson Gale.

Pongrácz, Péter, Csaba Molnár, Ádám Miklósi, and Vilmos Csányi. 2005. "Human Listeners Are Able to Classify Dog (*Canis familiaris*) Barks Recorded in Different Situations." *Journal of Comparative Psychology* 119 (2): 136–144.

Porter, Pete. 2006. "Engaging the Animal in the Moving Image." *Society & Animals* 14 (4): 399–416.

———. 2010. "Teaching Animal Movies." In *Teaching the Animal: Human-Animal Studies Across the Disciplines*, edited by Margo DeMello, 18–34. New York: Lantern.

Prince, Stephen. 2012. *Digital Visual Effects in Cinema: The Seduction of Reality*. New Brunswick, N.J.: Rutgers University Press.

Pryor, Karen. (1985) 2002. *Don't Shoot the Dog! The New Art of Teaching and Training*. New York: Bantam.

Rapf, Joanna, and Gary Green. 1995. *Buster Keaton: A Bio-bibliography*. Westport, Conn.: Greenwood Press.

Rattigan, Neil. 1991. *Images of Australia: 100 Films of the New Australian Cinema*. Dallas: Southern Methodist University Press, 1991.

Roeder, George, Jr. 1995. *The Censored War: American Visual Experience During World War Two*. New Haven, Conn.: Yale University Press, 1995.

Rothel, David. 1980. *The Great Show Business Animals*. La Jolla, Calif.: A. S. Barnes.

Rothfels, Nigel, ed. 2002. *Representing Animals*. Bloomington: Indiana University Press.

Schaffer, Michael. 2009. *One Nation Under Dog: Adventures in the New World of Prozac-Popping Puppies, Dog-Park Politics, and Organic Pet Food*. New York: Henry Holt.

Secord, William. 2000. *Dog Painting: The European Breeds*. Woodbridge, Suffolk: Antique Collectors' Club.

Serpell, James. 2005. "People in Disguise: Anthropomorphism and the Human-Pet Relationship." In *Thinking with Animals: New Perspectives on Anthropomorphism*, edited by Lorraine Daston and Gregg Mitman, 121–136. New York: Columbia University Press.

Sharp, Jasper. 2011. *Historical Dictionary of Japanese Cinema*. Plymouth, U.K.: Scarecrow.

Shettleworth, Sara J. 1998. *Cognition, Evolution, and Behavior*. New York: Oxford University Press.

Shirase Antarctic Expedition Supporters' Association, eds. and comps. 2011. *The Japanese South Polar Expedition, 1910–12: A Record of Antarctica*. Translated by Lara Dagnell and Hilary Shibata. Eccles, Norwich, and Bluntisham, Huntingdon: Erskine Press and Bluntisham Books.

Shull, Michael S., and David E. Witt. 2004. *Doing Their Bit: Wartime American Animated Short Films, 1939–1945*. Jefferson, N.C.: McFarland.

Sikov, Ed. 1989. *Screwball: Hollywood's Madcap Romantic Comedies*. New York: Crown.

Silverman, Stephen M., with Coco the Dog. 2001. *Movie Mutts: Hollywood Goes to the Dogs*. New York: Abrams.

Simons, John. 2002. *Animal Rights and the Politics of Literary Representation*. Hampshire, U.K.: Palgrave.

Skabelund, Aaron Herald. 2011. *Empire of Dogs: Canines, Japan, and the Making of the Modern Imperial World*. Ithaca, N.Y.: Cornell University Press.

Slide, Anthony. 1987. *The Big V: A History of the Vitagraph Company*. Rev. ed. Metuchen, N.J.: Scarecrow.

Spitz, Carl, with Bernard Molohon. 1938. *Training Your Dog*. Boston: Marshall Jones.

Spoto, Donald. 1984. *The Dark Side of Genius: The Life of Alfred Hitchcock*. New York: Ballantine.

Stadler, Jane, and Kelly McWilliam. 2009. *Screen Media: Analysing Film and Television*. Crows Nest, N.S.W., Australia: Allen and Unwin.

Staiger, Janet. 1985. "The Eyes Are Really the Focus: Photoplay Acting and Film Form and Style." *Wide Angle* 6 (4): 14–23.

Suarès, J. C. 1993. *Hollywood Dogs*. San Francisco: Collins.

Superle, Michelle. 2012. "Animal Heroes and Transforming Substances: Canine Characters in Contemporary Children's Literature." In *Animals and the Human Imagination: A Companion to Animal Studies*, edited by Aaron Gross and Anne Vallely, 174–202. New York: Columbia University Press.

Swart, Sandra. 2003. "Dogs and Dogma: A Discussion of the Socio-political Construction of Southern African Dog 'Breeds' as a Window on Social History." *South African Historical Journal* 48 (1): 190–206.

Taylor, Jordan. 2009. *Wonder Dogs: 101 German Shepherd Dog Films*. Bainbridge Island, Wash.: Reel Dogs Press.

Toohill, Ian. 1985. *Antarctica: The Most Incredible True Story Ever Told*. Film Study Guide. Melbourne: Peter Collins.

Torres, Bob. 2007. *Making a Killing: The Political Economy of Animal Rights*. Oakland, Calif.: AK Press.

Tropp, Jacob. 2002. "Dogs, Poison, and the Meaning of Colonial Intervention in the Transkei, South Africa." *Journal of African History* 43 (3): 451–472.

Tuan, Yi-Fu. 1993. "Desert and Ice: Ambivalent Aesthetics." In *Landscape, Natural Beauty, and the Arts*, edited by Salim Kemal and Ivan Gaskell, 139–157. Cambridge: Cambridge University Press.

Van Sittert, Lance, and Sandra Swart. 2003. "*Canis Familiaris*: A Dog History of South Africa." *South African Historical Journal* 48 (1): 138–173.

Vint, Sherryl. 2005. "Who Goes There? 'Real' Men Only." *Extrapolation* 46 (4): 421–438.

Weatherwax, Rudd B., and John H. Rothwell. 1950. *The Story of Lassie: His Discovery and Training from Puppyhood to Stardom*. New York: Duell, Sloan and Pearce.

Wells, Paul. 2009. *The Animated Bestiary: Animals, Cartoons, and Culture*. New Brunswick, N.J.: Rutgers University Press.

Wells, Reginald. 1955. "Badgered Dog: Once the Most Disliked of Breeds, Dachshunds Have Outlived Their Wartime Stigma and Now Rank Fifth as Favorite Pets." *Sports Illustrated*, December 12, 36–40, sportsillustrated.cnn.com/vault/article/magazine/MAG1130538/index.htm.

Winokur, Mark. 1996. *American Laughter: Immigrants, Ethnicity, and 1930s Hollywood Film Comedy*. New York: St. Martin's.

Wolfe, Cary, ed. 2003a. *Zoontologies: The Question of the Animal*. Minneapolis: University of Minnesota Press.

Wolfe, Cary. 2003b. *Animal Rites: American Culture, the Discourse of Species, and Posthumanist Theory*. Chicago: University of Chicago Press.

Wood, Robin. 2003. *Hollywood from Vietnam to Reagan . . . and Beyond*. New York: Columbia University Press.

Woodward, Wendy. 2008. *The Animal Gaze: Animal Subjectivities in Southern African Narratives*. Johannesburg: Wits University Press.

Yallop, David A. 1976. *The Day the Laughter Stopped: The True Story of Fatty Arbuckle*. New York: St. Martin's.

Yamaguchi, Masao. 1976. "Norakuro wa warera no dōjidai jin." *Chūō kōron* 91 (3): 84–100.

Yin, Sophia, and Brenda McCowan. 2004. "Barking in Domestic Dogs: Context Specificity and Individual Identification." *Animal Behaviour* 68: 343–355.

Zable, Arnold. 1983. "Dusty." *Cinema Papers*, no. 43 (May-June): 157–158.

Notes on Contributors

James Castonguay is an associate professor of Communication and Media Studies at Sacred Heart University. He has published articles in *American Quarterly*, *Cinema Journal*, *The Velvet Light Trap*, *Discourse*, *The Hitchcock Annual*, *Bad Subjects*, *Global-E*, and several anthologies, including *Glamour in a Golden Age: Movie Stars of the 1930s* (2011).

Kathryn Fuller-Seeley is a professor in the Department of Radio-TV-Film at the University of Texas at Austin; in addition to numerous journal essays and contributions to anthologies, she is the author or editor of several books, including *Hollywood in the Neighborhood: Historical Case Studies in Small Town Moviegoing* (2007); *At the Picture Show: Small Town Audiences and the Creation of Movie Fan Culture* (2001); and *Children and the Movies: Media Influence and the Payne Fund Controversy* (1996, with Garth Jowett and Ian Jarvie).

Jeremy Groskopf is a Ph.D. candidate in the Department of Communication at Georgia State University, where he is specializing in silent film history. His essay on the Atlanta Better Films Committee's children's matinee program of the 1920s will be published in *The History of Moviegoing in Atlanta*, edited by Matthew Bernstein (University of Georgia Press).

Alexandra Horowitz is a professor of psychology at Barnard College, Columbia University. She earned her Ph.D. in cognitive science at the University of California at San Diego; her research addresses a wide range of questions involving animal communication and attention, play behavior, interspecies comparisons, imitative behavior, metacognition, and anthropomorphisms. In addition to many scholarly articles relating to animals and dog behavior, she is the author of *Inside of a Dog: What Dogs See, Smell, and Know* (2009) and *On Looking: Eleven Walks with Expert Eyes* (2013).

Elizabeth Leane is a senior lecturer in English and ARC Future Fellow at the University of Tasmania, where her position is split between the School of Humanities and the Institute for Marine and Antarctic Studies. She is the author of *Antarctica in Fiction: Imaginative Narratives of the Far South* (2012) and *Reading Popular Physics: Disciplinary Skirmishes and Textual Strategies* (2007); she is a coeditor of the collections *Considering Animals: Contemporary Studies in Human-Animal Relations* (2011) and *Imagining Antarctica: Cultural Perspectives on the Southern Continent* (2011). She is the Arts and Literature editor of the *Polar Journal* and has traveled to the far south as an Australian Antarctic Arts Fellow.

Giuliana Lund is an associate professor of English at the University of Houston–Downtown with a doctorate in comparative literature and literary theory from the University of Pennsylvania. She has published several essays on contemporary southern African culture and cinema, including "Black Death, White Writing: André Brink's *The Wall of the Plague* as a Narrative of National Reconciliation" (*Safundi* 2011); "'Healing the Nation': Medicolonial Discourse and the State of Emergency from Apartheid to Truth and Reconciliation" (*Cultural Critique* 2003); and "Harmonizing the Nation: Women's Voices and Development in Zimbabwean Cinema" (*City and Society* 1999). Her current research in postcolonial and posthumanist studies revolves around the ethics of human-canine relations.

Adrienne L. McLean is a professor of film studies at the University of Texas at Dallas. She is the author of *Being Rita Hayworth: Labor, Identity, and Hollywood Stardom* (2004) and *Dying Swans and Madmen: Ballet, the Body, and Narrative Cinema* (2008), as well as numerous journal articles and book chapters. She has edited or coedited several anthologies, and is the coeditor, with Murray Pomerance, of the ten-volume series "Star Decades: American Culture/American Cinema" (Rutgers University Press, 2009–2012).

Guinevere Narraway lectures in the School of English, Journalism, and European Languages at the University of Tasmania and is a visiting fellow in the Department of Media and Communications at Goldsmiths, University of London. She has published ecocritical work on film and photography and is currently coediting a book on the representation of nature in cinema.

Jane O'Sullivan is a senior lecturer in Media and Communication Studies and is a member of the Posthuman Literary and Cultural Studies Research Group at the University of New England, Australia. Her teaching and research areas include film studies, gender studies, and, more recently, critical animal studies. She has published work on the representation of gendered power relations in film, television, theater, and prose, with particular attention to narratives of workplace gender equity in film and television and masculinities in Australian film.

Murray Pomerance is a professor in the Department of Sociology at Ryerson University and the author of *Alfred Hitchcock's America* (2013); *The Eyes Have It: Cinema and the Reality Effect* (2013); *Tomorrow* (2012); *Michelangelo Red Antonioni Blue: Eight Meditations on Cinema* (2011); *Edith Valmaine* (2010); *The Horse Who Drank the Sky: Film Experience Beyond Narrative and Theory* (2008); *Johnny Depp Starts Here*

(2005); *Savage Time* (2005); *An Eye for Hitchcock* (2004); and *Magia D'Amore* (1999). He has edited or coedited numerous anthologies, including *The Last Laugh: Strange Humors of Cinema* (2013); *Hollywood's Chosen People: The Jewish Experience in American Cinema* (2012); *A Little Solitaire: John Frankenheimer and American Film* (2011); and *Cinema and Modernity* (2006). He edits the "Horizons of Cinema" series at SUNY Press, and the "Techniques of the Moving Image" series at Rutgers University Press, where he also coedited the "Screen Decades" and "Star Decades" series with Lester D. Friedman and Adrienne L. McLean, respectively.

Joanna E. Rapf is a professor of English and Film and Video Studies at the University of Oklahoma. In researching an essay on Roscoe Arbuckle entitled "Both Sides of the Camera: Roscoe 'Fatty' Arbuckle's Evolution at Keystone," for *Slapstick Comedy* (2010), edited by Rob King and Tom Paulus, she became interested in Arbuckle's dog, Luke. She also has published books on Buster Keaton, Sidney Lumet, and *On the Waterfront*, and coedited, with Andy Horton, *A Companion to Film Comedy* (2012).

Sara Ross is an associate professor of Communication and Media Studies at Sacred Heart University. She has published articles in *Camera Obscura, Film History, Aura, Modernism/Modernity*, and several anthologies. Her research interests include late silent film, romantic comedy, and the development of female characters in Hollywood.

Aaron Skabelund teaches courses on Japanese history and the Second World War at Brigham Young University. He is the author of *Empire of Dogs: Canines, Japan, and the Making of the Modern Imperial World* (2011); "'By Running . . . / By Fighting . . . / By Dying . . .': Remembering, Glorifying, and Forgetting Japanese Olympian War Dead," in *Sport in Society* (2011); and "Public Service/Public Relations: The Mobilization of the Self-Defense Force for the Tokyo Olympic Games," in *The East Asian Olympiads, 1934–2008: Building Bodies and Nations in Japan, Korea, and China* (2011). He is currently working on a book on the social and cultural history of the post–World War II Japanese military, known as the Self-Defense Force. He is the author of numerous articles on dogs and children in war, fascism and dogs, and imperialism and canine cultures.

Kelly Wolf is a Ph.D. candidate at the University of Southern California in the Department of Critical Studies in the School of Cinematic Arts. Her research interests include animal studies and the intersections of animals with stardom and labor issues within the Hollywood film industry, production studies, media industries, alternative citizenship, and television theory and history. Her work has been published in the *European Journal of Cultural Studies* and *Spectator*.

Index

Page numbers for illustrations are in italics.